Julian Ralph

Our Great West

A Study of the Present Conditions and Future Possibilities of the....

Julian Ralph

Our Great West
A Study of the Present Conditions and Future Possibilities of the....

ISBN/EAN: 9783337187439

Printed in Europe, USA, Canada, Australia, Japan

Cover: Foto ©ninafisch / pixelio.de

More available books at **www.hansebooks.com**

[See page 386

HEADING A STEER ON THE FOOTHILLS

OUR GREAT WEST

*A Study of the Present Conditions
and Future Possibilities of
the New Commonwealths
and Capitals of the
United States*

BY

JULIAN RALPH

AUTHOR OF "HARPER'S CHICAGO AND THE WORLD'S FAIR"
"ON CANADA'S FRONTIER" ETC.

ILLUSTRATED

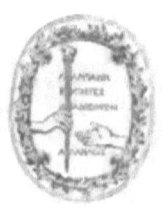

NEW YORK
HARPER & BROTHERS PUBLISHERS
1893

Copyright, 1893, by HARPER & BROTHERS.

All rights reserved.

PREFACE

If the territory described in the following pages was part of any other region than our West, it might be said of this book that it is a description of certain new States at the close of the nineteenth century. That is what it was intended that it should be, **but the** inpouring of population, and the rapid and bewildering changes which accompany the phenomenal progress in that part of our country make it certain that, during the seven years before the actual close of **the** century, present description will gain the character of history or reminiscence.

However, another and dominant characteristic of these studies may fix upon them a value not to be so speedily lost. That feature is the part of each chapter wherein I have tried to point out the **future** possibilities of these imperial reaches of plains and mountain country—and of the cities that distinguish them—between **the Great** Lakes and the Pacific coast. Many of the possibilities **here** pointed out are sure of fulfilment, yet will not be realized **until the** newer part of our country is more populous than the older part.

This is, perhaps, the first comprehensive book upon **these regions** (made most famous in literature by Parkman, Irving, and Lewis and Clarke) that has little to say of the Indians who are now kept apart from the **whites**, on reservations, and cut no important figure anywhere. It is perhaps the first book upon the great West which makes no account of the hunting of wild game, so difficult to indulge in **and of** so little account now, in the experiences and resources of **the** present population. **Furthermore, the** vanishing cowboy—once a great **as** well as **a** picturesque factor in several of these States—gets little notice, yet all that he deserves. In a word, in place of a work upon the once wild West, **the** reader will here find a series of chapters upon **a** noble group of commonwealths under complete government, well administered. It will be found that these States are joined by swift railroads, equipped nearly like our own in New York and Pennsylvania; that they are peopled by practical, sober, nineteenth-century folk, who, where their already numerous cities have sprung up, are supplied with modern hotels, fine churches, extraordinary schools, beautiful theatres, and all the modern conveniences of street travel, electric lighting, elevators, and the rest that goes with what we are not to be blamed for characterizing as "civilization."

Standing between us of the East and these new States are certain midland capitals which are growing as never cities grew before—in population, size, manufactures, commerce, and wealth. Since they are the great trading posts of the people beyond, descriptions of them and explanations of the sources of their greatness belong in such a book as this.

The more important of these chapters have appeared in HARPER'S MAGAZINE. Others have been published in HARPER'S WEEKLY. It has been remarked of them that they betray none of that feeling of superiority to the alleged crudeness and newness of the western people which, with or without reason, it seems to have been expected that an eastern writer would exhibit. I hope that is true. Certainly, in travelling in the West and in writing these chapters, I was conscious of no feeling stronger than one of admiration for the energy and boldness of the people except it was of a sense of pride in the heartiness of that spirit of equality and democracy which dominates them, and the like of which I had not known anywhere else.

As to the statements of fact herein made, it has not surprised me that they have escaped challenge and correction even after such wide and brilliant publicity as HARPER'S MAGAZINE gives to its contents. I say I was not surprised, because the statements are not my own, but are those of the best informed and shrewdest men in the cities and States under discussion. Had I attempted to study every valley, every sample of quartz, every colony of Swedes or Hollanders, every tendency of commerce, every development of cities and the details of every business of which I have written, I would have found myself sentenced for life to the task of writing one article, with a certainty that even that one would contain errors. As an alternative, I chose to become a chronicler for those who were giving or had given their lives to the study of the different branches of knowledge herein treated. If mistakes are yet to be found here they will be, none the less, my own mistakes, for they will betray a failure to verify as many times as possible each bit of information I obtained. This I tried to do, and, with the hope that the result will be found of value as well as of interest, I intrust it and myself to the public.

THE AUTHOR.

ASBURY PARK, N. J., 1893.

CONTENTS

CHAP.		PAGE
I.	THE CITY OF CHICAGO	1
II.	CHICAGO'S GENTLE SIDE	30
III.	"BROTHER TO THE SEA"	64
IV.	CAPITALS OF THE NORTHWEST	107
V.	THE DAKOTAS	139
VI.	MONTANA: THE TREASURE STATE	173
VII.	GLIMPSES OF PAST, PRESENT, AND FUTURE	212
VIII.	WASHINGTON: THE EVERGREEN STATE	276
IX.	COLORADO AND ITS CAPITAL	312
X.	WYOMING—ANOTHER PENNSYLVANIA	345
XI.	A WEEK WITH THE MORMONS	391
XII.	SAN FRANCISCO	417
XIII.	WAYS OF CITY GOVERNMENT OUT WEST	445

ILLUSTRATIONS

	PAGE
HEADING A STEER ON THE **FOOTHILLS**	*Frontispiece*
GRAND ARCH, PICTURED ROCKS, **LAKE SUPERIOR**	65
THUNDER **CAPE, NORTH SHORE**	67
TRAP-**ROCK CLIFFS, NORTH SHORE**	69
THE NORTH SHORE, **LAKE SUPERIOR**	71
NAKED **INDIANS IN MONTREAL**	75
IN THE HARBOR AT **DULUTH**	79
THE MISSIONARY	85
THE LOCK AT "THE SOO"	89
TROUT-FISHING	91
ORE DOCKS AT MARQUETTE, THE **LARGEST IN THE WORLD**	95
LIGHT-HOUSE AT MARQUETTE	98
ELEVATORS AT DULUTH, WEST SUPERIOR **IN THE DISTANCE**	101
LOADING A WHALEBACK BARGE	103
A **WHALEBACK** DESCENDING THE RAPIDS OF THE ST. **LAWRENCE**	105
MAP **OF NORTH AND SOUTH DAKOTA**	155
MAP OF **MONTANA**	181
IN COTTON-WOOD PARK, **GREAT FALLS**	229
LOWER FALLS	233
PART OF LOWER FALLS FROM BOTTOM **OF CAÑON, LOOKING** NORTH	237
CROOKED FALLS	241
PART OF RAINBOW FALLS, **FROM** THE **SOUTH SHORE, LOOKING NORTH**	245
CAÑON OF THE MISSOURI **RIVER, BELOW GREAT FALLS**	249
MANITOBA RAILROAD BRIDGE, GREAT **FALLS**	253

	PAGE
MAP OF WASHINGTON	279
MAP OF COLORADO	317
MAP OF WYOMING	351
OLD-STYLE HOUSE AT LOGAN, UTAH	407
SAN FRANCISCO BAY	419
SEAL ROCKS	423
JEFFERSON SQUARE	427
MARKET STREET	431
UNION SQUARE	435
CLIFF HOUSE	439
CALIFORNIA STREET	443

I

THE CITY OF CHICAGO

With few exceptions, the great expositions of the world have been held in Christendom's great capitals, and the cities that have known them have been scarcely subordinate to the expositions themselves in the attractions they have offered to the masses of sight-seers who have gathered in them. Chicago lacks many of the qualities of the older cities that have been chosen for this purpose, but for every one that is missing she offers others fully as attractive. Those who go clear-minded, expecting to see a great city, will find one different from that which any precedent has led them to look for. Those who go to study the world's progress will not find in the Columbian Exposition, among all its marvels, any other result of human force so wonderful, extravagant, or peculiar as Chicago itself.

While investigating the management and prospects of the Columbian Exposition, I was a resident of Chicago for more than a fortnight. A born New-Yorker, the energy, roar, and bustle of the place were yet sufficient to first astonish and then to fatigue me. I was led to examine the city, and to cross-examine some of its leading men. I came away compelled to acknowledge its possession of certain forceful qualities which I never saw exhibited in the same degree anywhere else. I got a satisfactory explanation of its growth and achievements, as well as proof that it must continue to expand in population and commercial influence. Moreover, without losing a particle of pride or faith in New York—without perceiving that New York was affected by the consideration—I acquired a respect for Chicago such as it is most likely that any American who makes a similar investigation must share with me.

The city has been thought intolerant of criticism. The amount of truth there is in this is found in its supervoluminous civicism. The bravado and bunkum of the Chicago newspapers reflect this quality, but do it clumsily, because it proceeds from a sense of business policy with the editors, who laugh at it themselves. But underlying the behavior of the most able and enterprising men in the city is this motto, which they constantly quoted to me, all using the same words, "We are for Chicago first, last, and all the time." To define that sentence is, in a great measure, to account for Chicago. It explains the possession of a million inhabitants by a city that practically dates its beginning after the war of the rebellion. Its adoption by half a million men as their watchword means the forcing of trade and manufactures and wealth; the getting of the World's Fair, if you please. In order to comprehend Chicago, it is best never to lose sight of the motto of its citizens.

I have spoken of the roar and bustle and energy of Chicago. This is most noticeable in the business part of the town, where the greater number of the men are crowded together. It seems there as if the men would run over the horses if the drivers were not careful. Everybody is in such a hurry and going at such a pace that if a stranger asks his way, he is apt to have to trot along with his neighbor to gain the information, for the average Chicagoan cannot stop to talk. The whole business of life is carried on at high pressure, and the pithy part of Chicago is like three hundred acres of

New York Stock Exchange when trading is active. European visitors have written that there are no such crowds anywhere as gather on Broadway, and this is true most of the time; but there is one hour on every week-day when certain streets in Chicago are so packed with people as to make Broadway look desolate and solitudinous by comparison. That is the hour between half-past five and half-past six o'clock, when the famous tall buildings of the city vomit their inhabitants upon the pavements. Photographs of the principal corners and crossings, taken at the height of the human torrent, suggest the thought that the camera must have been turned on some little-known painting by Doré. Nobody but Doré ever conceived such pictures. To those who are in the crowds, even Chicago seems small and cramped; even her street cars, running in breakneck trains, prove far too few; even her streets that connect horizon with horizon seem each night to roar at the city officials for further annexation in the morning.

We shall see these crowds simply and satisfactorily accounted for presently; but they exhibit only one phase of the high-pressure existence; they form only one feature among the many that distinguish the town. In the tall buildings are the most modern and rapid elevators, machines that fly up through the towers like glass balls from a trap at a shooting contest. The slow-going stranger, who is conscious of having been "kneaded" along the streets, like a lump of dough among a million bakers, feels himself loaded into one of those frail-looking baskets of steel netting, and the next instant the elevator-boy touches the trigger, and up goes the whole load as a feather is caught up by a gale. The descent is more simple. Something lets go, and you fall from ten to twenty stories as it happens. There is sometimes a jolt, which makes the passenger seem to feel his stomach pass into his shoes, but, as a rule, the mechanism and management both work marvellously towards ease and gentleness. These elevators are too slow for Chicago, and the managers of certain tall buildings now arrange them so that some run "express" to the seventh story without stopping, while what may be called accommodation cars halt at the lower floors, pursuing a course that may be likened to the emptying of the chambers of a revolver in the hands of a person who is "quick on the trigger." It is the same everywhere in the business district. Along Clark Street are some gorgeous underground restaurants, all marble and plated metal. Whoever is eating at one of the tables in them will see the ushers standing about like statues until a customer enters the door, when they dart forward as if the building were falling. It is only done in order to seat the visitor promptly. Being of a sympathetic and impressionable nature, I bolted along the street all the time I was there as if some one on the next block had picked my pocket.

In the Auditorium Hotel the guests communicate with the clerk by electricity, and may flash word of their thirst to the bar-tender as lightning dances from the top to the bottom of a steeple. A sort of annunciator is used, and by turning an arrow and pressing a button, a man may in half a minute order a cocktail, towels, ice-water, stationery, dinner, a bootblack, and the evening newspapers. Our horse-cars in New York move at the rate of about six miles an hour. The cable-cars of Chicago make more than nine miles an hour in town, and more than thirteen miles an hour where the population is less dense. They go in trains of two cars each, and with such a racket of gong-ringing and such a grinding and whir of grip-wheels as to make a modern vestibuled train seem a waste of the opportunities for noise. But these street cars distribute the people grandly, and while they occasionally run over a stray citizen, they far more frequently clear their way by lifting wagons and trucks bodily to one side as they whirl along. It is a rapid and a business-like city. The speed with which cattle are killed and pigs are turned into slabs of salt pork has amazed the world, but it is only the ignorant portion thereof that does not know that the celerity at the stock-yards is merely an effort of the butchers to keep up with the rest of the town. The only slow things in Chicago are the steam railway trains. Further on we will discover why they are so.

I do not know how many very tall buildings Chicago contains, but they must number nearly two dozen. Some of them are artistically designed, and hide their height in well-balanced proportions. A few are mere boxes punctured with window-holes, and stand above their neighbors like great hitching-posts. The best of them are very elegantly and completely appointed, and the communities of men inside them might almost live their lives within their walls, so multifarious are the occupations and services of the tenants. The best New York office buildings are not injured by comparison with these towering structures, except that they are not so tall as the Chicago buildings, but there is not in New York any office structure that can be compared with Chicago's so-called Chamber of Commerce office building, so far as are concerned the advantages of light and air and openness and roominess which its tenants enjoy. In these respects there is only one finer building in America, and that is in Minneapolis. It is a great mistake to think that we in New York possess all the elegant, rich, and ornamental outgrowths of taste, or that we know better than the West what are the luxuries and comforts of the age. With their floors of deftly-laid mosaic-work, their walls of marble and onyx, their balustrades of copper worked into arabesquerie, their artistic lanterns, elegant electric fixtures, their costly and luxurious public rooms, these Chicago office buildings force an exclamation of praise, however unwillingly it comes.

They have adopted what they call "the Chicago method" in putting up these steepling hives. This plan is to construct the actual edifice of steel framework, to which are added thin outer walls of brick, or stone masonry, and the necessary partitions of fire-brick, and plaster laid on iron lathing. The buildings are therefore like enclosed bird-cages, and it is said that, like bird-cages, they cannot shake or tumble down. The exterior walls are mere envelopes. They are so treated that the buildings look like heaps of masonry, but that is homage paid to custom more than it is a material element of strength. These walls are to a building what an envelope is to a letter, or a postage-stamp is to that part of an envelope which it covers. The Chicago method is expeditious, economical, and in many ways advantageous. The manner in which the great weight of houses so tall as to include between sixteen and twenty-four stories is distributed upon the ground beneath them is ingenious. Wherever one of the principal upright pillars is to be set up, the builders lay a pad of steel and cement of such extent that the pads for all the pillars cover all the site. These pads are slightly pyramidal in shape, and are made by laying alternate courses of steel beams crosswise, one upon another. Each pair of courses of steel is filled in and solidified with cement, and then the next two courses are added and similarly treated. At last each pad is eighteen inches thick, and perhaps eighteen feet square; but the size is governed by the desire to distribute the weight of the building at about the average of a ton to the square foot.

This peculiar process is necessitated by the character of the land underneath Chicago. Speaking widely, the rule is to find from seven to fourteen feet of sand superimposed upon a layer of clay between ten and forty feet in depth. It has not paid to puncture this clay with piling. The piles sink into a soft and yielding substance, and the clay is not tenacious enough to hold them. Thus the Chicago Post-office was built, and it not only settles continuously, but it settles unevenly. On the other hand, the famous Rookery Building, set up on these steel and cement pads, did not sink quite an inch, though the architect's calculation was that, by squeezing the water out of the clay underneath, it would settle seven inches. Very queer and differing results have followed the construction of Chicago's biggest buildings, and without going too deep into details, it has been noticed that while some have pulled neighboring houses down a few inches, others have lifted adjoining houses, and still others have raised buildings that were at a distance from themselves. The bed of clay underneath Chicago acts when under pressure like a pan of dough, or like a blanket tautened at the edges and held clear of underneath support. Chicago's great office buildings have basements, but no cellars.

I have referred to the number of these stupendous structures. Let it be known next that they are all in a very small district, that narrow area which composes Chicago's office region, which lies between Lake Michigan and all the principal railroad districts, and at the edges of which one-twenty-fifth of all the railroad mileage of the world is said to terminate, though the district is but little more than half a mile square or 300 acres in extent. One of these buildings—and not the largest — has a population of 4000 persons. It was visited and its elevators were used on three days, when a count was kept, by 19,000, 18,000, and 20,000 persons. Last October there were 7000 offices in the tall buildings of Chicago, and 7000 more were under way in buildings then undergoing construction. The reader now understands why in the heart of Chicago every work-day evening the crowds convey the idea that our Broadway is a deserted thoroughfare as compared with, say, the corner of Clark and Jackson streets.

These tall buildings are mainly built on land obtained on 99-year leasehold. Long leases rather than outright purchases of land have long been a favorite preliminary to building in Chicago, where, for one thing, the men who owned the land have not been those with the money for building. Where very great and costly buildings are concerned, the long leases often go to corporations or syndicates, who put up the houses. It seems to many strangers who visit Chicago that it is reasonable to prophesy a speedy end to the feverish impulse to swell the number of these giant piles, either through legislative ordinance or by the fever running its course. Many prophesy that it must soon end. This idea is bred of several reasons. In the first place, the tall buildings darken the streets, and transform the lower stories of opposite houses into so many cellars or damp and dark basements. In the next place, the great number of tall and splendid office houses is depreciating the value of the humbler property in their neighborhoods. Four-story and five-story houses that once were attractive are no longer so, because their owners cannot afford the conveniences which distinguish the greater edifices, wherein light and heat are often provided free, fire-proof safes are at the service of every tenant, janitors officer a host of servants, and there are barber-shops, restaurants, cigar and **news-stands, elevators, and a** half-dozen **other conveniences not found in** smaller houses. It **would seem, also, that since** not all the people **of Chicago** spend their **time in offices, there must soon come an** end **of the** demand for these chambers. **So it** seems, but not **to** a thoroughbred Chicagoan. **One of** the foremost business men in **the** city asserts **that** he can perceive no reason why **the** entire business heart of the town—that square half-mile of **which I** have spoken—should **not soon be all** builded up of cloud-capped **towers. There will be a need for them,** he says, **and the money to defray the cost of them will** accompany **the demand. The only trouble he foresees** will **be in the solution of the** problem **what to do with the people who will then crowd the streets as never streets** were clogged before.

This prophecy relates to a **little block** in the city, but the city itself contains 181½ square miles. It has been **said** of the many annexations **by** which her present size was attained that Chicago reached out **and took to** herself farms, prairie land, and villages, and that of such material the great city now **in part** consists. This is **true.** In suburban trips, **such as those I took to Fort Sheridan and Fernwood, for** instance, **I passed great** cabbage **farms, groves, houseless** but plotted tracts, and long reaches **of the former prairie. Even yet Hyde** Park is a **separated settlement, and a dozen or more** villages stand **out as** distinctly **by** themselves **as ever** they did. **If it were true, as her rivals insist,** that Chicago added all this tract merely to get a high rank **in the** census reports **of** population, the folly of the ac**tion** would be either ludicrous **or** pitiful, according to the **stand**-point from which it was viewed. But the true **reason** for her enormous extension of municipal jurisdiction is quite as peculiar. The enlargement was urged and accomplished in order to anticipate the growth and needs of the city. It was a consequence of extraordinary foresight, which recognized the necessity for a uniform system of boulevards, parks, drainage, and water provision when the city should reach limits that it was even then seen must soon bound a compact aggregation of stores, offices, factories, and dwellings. To us of the East this is surprising It might seem incredible were there not many other evidences of the same spirit and sagacity not only in Chicago, but in the other cities of the West, especially of the Northwest. What Minneapolis, St. Paul, and Duluth are doing towards a future park system reveals the same enterprise and habit of looking far ahead. And Chicago, in her park system, makes evident her intentions. In all these cities and in a hundred ways the observant traveller notes the same forehandedness, and prepares himself to understand the temper in which the greatest of the Western capitals leaned forth and absorbed the prairie. Chicago expects to become the largest city in America—a city which, in fifty years, shall be larger than the consolidated cities that may form New York at that time.

Now on what substance does Chicago feed that she should foresee herself so great? What manner of men are those of Chicago? What are the whys and the wherefores of her growth?

It seems to have ever been, as it is now, a city of young men. One Chicagoan accounts for its low death rate on the ground that not even its leading men are yet old enough to die. The young men who drifted there from the Eastern States after the close of the war all agree that the thing which most astonished them was the youthfulness of the most active business men. Marshall Field, Potter Palmer, and the rest, heading very large **mercantile establishments, were young fellows. Those who** came **to Chicago** from England fancied, **as it is** said that Englishmen **do, that a man may not** be trusted with **affairs until he has lost** half his hair **and** all his teeth. Our own Eastern **men were apt to** place wealth and success at the **middle of the scale of** life. But in Chicago men under thirty were leading in commerce and industry. The sight **was a** spur to all the young men who came, and they also pitched in to swell **the size and successes of the young men's capital. The easy making of money by the loaning of** it **and by handling city realty—sources which** never **failed with shrewd men—not only whetted the** general **appetite for big and quick** money-making, but **they provided the** means for the establishment and **extension of trade in other** ways and **with the West at large.**

It is one of the peculiarities **of** Chicago that one finds not only the capitalists but the storekeepers discussing **the** whole country with a familiarity as strange to a **man** from the Atlantic **coast as** Nebraska is strange to **most** Philadelphians **or New-**Yorkers. But the well-informed and "hustling" Chicagoan **is** familiar with **the** differing districts of the entire West, **North, and South,** with their crops, industries, wants, financial status, **and** means of intercommunication. **As in London** we find men whose business **field is the** world, so in Chicago we find the business **men** talking not of one section or of Europe, as is largely the **case in New** York, but discussing the affairs of the entire country. The figures which garnish their conversation are bewildering, but if **they** are analyzed, or even comprehended, they will reveal **to** the listener how vast and **how** wealthy a region acknowledges Chicago as its market and its financial and **trading** centre.

Without either avowing or contesting any part of the process by which Chicago men account for their city's importance or calculate its future, let me repeat a digest of what several influential men of that city said upon the subject. Chicago, then, is the centre of a circle of 1000 miles diameter. If you draw a line northward 500 miles, you find everywhere arable land and timber. The same is true with respect to a line drawn 500 miles in a northwesterly course. For 650 miles westward there is no change in the rich and alluring prospect, and so all around the circle, except where Lake Michigan interrupts it, the same conditions are found. Moreover, the lake itself is a valuable element in commerce. The rays or spokes in all these directions become materialized in the form of the tracks of 35 railways which enter the city. Twenty-two of these are great companies, and at a short distance sub-radials made by other railroads raise the number to 50 roads. As said above, in Chicago one-twenty-fifth of the railway mileage of the world terminates, and serves 30 millions of persons, who find Chicago the largest city easily accessible to them. Thus is found a vast population connected easily and directly with a common centre, to which everything they produce can be brought, and from which all that contributes to the material progress and comfort of man may be economically distributed.

A financier who is equally well known and respected in New York and Chicago put the case somewhat differently as to what he called Chicago's territory. He considered it as being 1000 miles square, and spoke of it as "the land west of the Alleghanies and south of Mason and Dixon's line." This region, the richest agricultural territory in the world, does its financiering in Chicago. The rapid increase in wealth of both the city and the tributary region is due to the fact that every year both produce more, and **have more to sell and less to buy. Not long ago the rule was that a stream of goods ran eastward over the Alleghanies, and another stream** of supplies came **back, so that the West** had little gain to show. But during the past five years this **back-setting current has** been a stream of money **returned for the products** the West has distributed. The West **is now** selling to the East and to Europe **and getting** money in return, because it is manufacturing **for itself, as** well as tilling the soil and mining **for the** rest **of the** world. It therefore earns **money** and acquires **a** profit instead of continuing **its former** process of toiling merely **to obtain from the** East **the** necessaries of life.

The condition in which Nebraska and Kansas find themselves is the condition **in which a great part of the West was placed not** long ago—a condition of **debt, of being** mortgaged, and of having to **send its** earnings to Eastern capitalists. That is **no longer** the case of the **West** in general. The debtor **States now** are Kansas, Nebraska, the two Dakotas, **and western** Minnesota; **but** Iowa, Illinois, Ohio, Indiana, Missouri, Wisconsin, **and** Michigan (the States **most** closely tributary to Chicago) have paid off their mortgages, and are absorbing money **and investing** it in local improvements. What **they earn is now their own,** and it comes back to them **in the form of money.** This money used **to be** shipped to **the East, to which these** States were **in debt,** but now it **is invested where it is** earned, and the consequence has been **that in the last five or six** years the West has rarely **shipped** any **currency** East, but has been constantly drawing it from **there.**

In this change of **condition is seen an** explanation of **much that** has made **Chicago** peculiar. She has been what she would call "hustling." **For** years, in company with **the entire** Western country, she has been making money only to pay debts with. That, they say, is why men in Chicago have talked only "business;" that is why Chicago has had no leisure class, no reservoir of home capital seeking investment. The former conditions having changed, now that she is producing more and buying less, the rest will change also.

When we understand what are the agricultural resources of the region for which Chicago is the tradingpost, we perceive how certain it was that its debt would be paid, and that great wealth would follow. The corn lands of Illinois return a profit of $15 to the acre, raising 50 to 60 bushels at 42½ cents a bushel last year, and at a cost for cultivation of only $7 an acre. Wheat produces $22 50 an acre, costs a little less than corn, and returns a profit of from $12 to $15. Oats run 55 bushels to the acre, at 27 cents a bushel, and cost the average farmer only, say, $6 an acre, returning $8 or $9 an acre in profit. These figures will vary as to production, cost, and profit, but it is believed that they represent a fair average. This midland country, of which Chicago is the capital, produces two thousand million bushels of corn, seven hundred million bushels of oats, fifty million hogs, twenty-eight million horses, thirty million sheep, and so on, to cease before the reader is wearied; but in no single instance is the region producing within 50 per cent. of what it will be made to yield before the expiration of the next twenty years. Farming there has been haphazard, rude, and wasteful; but as it begins to pay well, the methods begin to improve. Drainage will add new lands, and better methods will swell the crops, so that, for instance, where 60 bushels of corn to the acre are now grown, at least 100 bushels will be harvested. All the corn lands are now settled, but they are not improved. They will yet double in value. It is different with wheat; with that the maximum **production will soon** be attained.

Such is the **wealth** that Chicago counts up as tributary to her. By the railroads that dissect this **opulent** region **she is** riveted to the midland, the southern, and **the western** country between the Rockies and the Alleghanies. She is closely allied to the South, because she **is** manufacturing and distributing much that **the South** needs, and can get most economically from her. Chicago has become the third **manufacturing** city in the Union, and she is drawing **manufactures** away from the East faster than most **persons in the** East imagine. **To-day** it is a **great Troy** stove-making establishment that **has** moved to **Chicago**; the week before it was a **Massachusetts shoe factory that went** there. Many great **establishments have gone** there, but more **must follow, because** Chicago **is** not only the centre **of the** midland **region** in respect of the distribution of made-up wares, but also for the concentration of raw materials. Chicago must lead in the manufacture of all goods of which wood, leather, and iron are the bases. The revolution that **took** place in the meat trade when Chicago took the lead in that industry affected the whole leather **and hide industry.** Cattle are dropping 90,000 skins a week in Chicago, and **the trade is** confined to Chicago, St. Louis, Kansas City, Omaha, and St. Paul. It is idle to suppose that those skins **will** be sent across the **Alleghanies** to be **turned into** goods and sent back again. Wisconsin has **become** the great tanning State, and all over the district close **around Chicago** are factories and factory towns where hides are turned into leather goods. **The** West still gets its finer goods in the East, but it is **making the** coarser grades, and to such an extent as to give **a** touch of New England color to the towns and villages around Chicago.

This is not an unnatural rivalry that has grown up. The former condition of Western dependence was unnatural. The science of profitable business lies in the practice of economy. Chicago has in abundance all the fuels except hard coal. She has coal, oil, stone, brick—everything that is needed for building and for living. Manufactures gravitate to such a place for economical reasons. The population of the north Atlantic division, including Pennsylvania and Massachusetts, and acknowledging New York as its centre, is 17,401,000. The population of the northern central division, trading with Chicago, is 22,362,379. Every one has seen each succeeding census shift the centre of population farther and farther West, but not every one is habituated to putting two and two together.

"Chicago is yet so young and busy," said he who is perhaps the leading banker there, "she has no time for anything beyond each citizen's private affairs. It is hard to get men to serve on a committee. The only thing that saves us from being boors is our civic pride. We are fond, proud, enthusiastic in that respect. But we know that Chicago is not rich, like New York. She has no bulk of capital lying ready for investment and reinvestment; yet she is no longer poor. She has just got over her poverty, and the next stage, bringing accumulated wealth, will quickly follow. Her growth in this respect is more than paralleled by her development into an industrial centre."

So much, then, for Chicago's reasons for existence. The explanation forms not merely the history of an American town, and a town of young men, it points an old moral. It demonstrates anew the active truth that energy is a greater force than money. It commands money. The young founders of Chicago were backed in the East by capitalists who discounted the energy they saw them display. And now Chicago capitalists own the best street railway in St. Louis, the surface railway system of Toledo, a thousand enterprises in hundreds of Western towns.

Chicago has been as crude and rough as any other self-creating entity engaged in a hard struggle for a living. And latterly confidence in and exultation over the inevitable success of the battle have made her boastful, conceited, and noisy. But already one citizen has taken to building houses for rental and not for sale. He has arranged an imitation Astor estate as far ahead as the law will permit, which is to say to one generation unborn. Already, so they boast in Chicago, you may see a few tables in the Chicago Club surrounded by whist-players with gray locks and semispherical waistcoats *in the afternoons during business hours!*—a most surprising thing, and only possible at the Chicago Club, which is the old club of the "old rich." These partially globular old whist-players are still in business, of course, as everybody is, but they let go with one hand, as it were, in the afternoons, and only stroll around to their offices at four or five o'clock to make certain that the young members of the other clubs have not stolen their trade while they were playing cards. The other clubs of Chicago merely look like clubs, as we understand the word in New York. They are patronized as our dining-clubs are, with a rush at luncheon-time, although at both ends of the town, in the residence districts, there are clubs to which men drift on Sundays.

And here one is brought to reflect that Chicago is distinctly American. I know that the Chicagoans boast that theirs is the most mixed population in the country, but the makers and movers of Chicago are Americans. The streets of the city are full of strange faces of a type to which we are not used in the East—a dish-faced, soft-eyed, light-haired people. They are Scandinavians; but they are as malleable as lead, and quickly and easily follow and adopt every Americanism. In return, they ask only to be permitted to attend a host of Lutheran churches in flocks, to work hard, live temperately, save thriftily, and to pronounce every j as if it were a y. But the dominating class is of that pure and broad American type which is not controlled by New England or any other tenets, but is somewhat loosely made up of the overflow of the New England, the Middle, and the Southern States. It is as mixed and comprehensive as the West Point school of cadets. It calls its city "She-caw-ger." It inclines to soft hats, and only once in a great while does a visitor see a Chicagoan who has the leisure or patience to carry a cane. Its signs are eloquent of its habits, especially of its habit of freedom. "Take G——'s candy to the loved ones at home," stares from hundreds of walls. "Gentlemen all chew Fraxy because it sweetens the breath after drinking," one manufacturer declares; then he adds, "Ladies who play tennis chew it because it lubricates the throat." A bottler of spring water advertises it as "God's own liver remedy." On the billboards of a theatre is the threat that "If you miss seeing Peter Peterson, half your life will be gone." In a principal street is a characteristic sign product, "My fifteen-cent meals are world-beaters;" yet there are worse terrors for Chicago diners-out, as is shown by the sign, "Business lunch—quick and cheap."

But the visitor's heart warms to the town when he sees its parks and its homes. In them is ample assurance that not every breath is "business," and not every thought commercial. Once out of the thicket of the business and semi-business district, the dwellings of the people reach mile upon mile away along pleasant boulevards and avenues, or facing noble parks and parkways, or in a succession of villages green and gay with foliage and flowers. They are not cliff dwellings like our flats and tenements; there are no brownstone cañons like our up-town streets; there are only occasional hesitating hints there of those Philadelphian and Baltimorean mills that grind out dwellings all alike, as nature makes pease and man makes pins. There are more miles of detached villas in Chicago than a stranger can easily account for. As they are not only found on Prairie Avenue and the boulevards, but in the populous wards and semi-suburbs, where the middle folk are congregated, it is evident that the prosperous moiety of the population enjoys living better (or better living) than the same fraction in the Atlantic cities.

Land in New York has been too costly to permit of these villa-like dwellings, but that does not alter the fact that existence in a home hemmed in by other houses is at best but a crippled living. There never has been any valid excuse for the building of these compressed houses by New York millionaires. It sounds like a Celtic bull, but, in my opinion, the poorer millionaires of Prairie Avenue are better off. A peculiarity of the buildings of Chicago is in the great variety of building-stones that are employed in their construction. Where we would build two blocks of brownstone, I have counted thirteen varieties of beautiful and differing building material. Moreover, the contrasts in architectural design evidence among Chicago house-owners a complete sway of individual taste. It is in these beautiful homes that the people, who do not know what to do with their club-houses, hold their card-parties; it is to them that they bring their visitors and friends; in short, it is at home that the Chicagoan recreates and loafs.

It is said, and I have no reason to doubt it, that the

clerks and small tradesmen who live in thousands of these pretty little boxes are the owners of their homes; also that the tenements of the rich display evidence of a tasteful and costly garnering of the globe for articles of luxury and *virtu*. A sneering critic, who wounded Chicago deeply, intimated that theirs must be a primitive society where the rich sit on their door-steps of an evening. That really is a habit there, and in the finer districts of all the Western cities. To enjoy themselves the more completely, the people bring out rugs and carpets, always of gay colors, and fling them on the steps —or stoops, as we Dutch legatees should say—that the ladies' dresses may not be soiled. As these step clothings are as bright as the maidens' eyes and as gay as their cheeks, the effect may be imagined. For my part, I think it argues well for any society that indulges in the trick, and proves existence in such a city to be more human and hearty and far less artificial than where there is too much false pride to permit of it. In front of many of the nice hotels the boarders lug out great arm-chairs upon the portal platforms or beside the curbs. There the men sit in rows, just as I can remember seeing them do in front of the New York Hotel and the old St. Nicholas Hotel in happy days of yore, to smoke in the sunless evening air, and to exchange comments on the weather and the passers-by. If the dead do not rise until the Judgment-day, but lie less active than their dust, then old Wouter Van Twiller, Petrus Stuyvesant, and the rest of our original Knickerbockers will be sadly disappointed angels when they come to, and find that we have abandoned these practices in New York, after the good example that our first families all set us.

It is in Chicago that we find a great number of what are called boulevarded streets, at the intersections of which are signs bearing such admonitions as these:

"For pleasure driving. No traffic wagons allowed;" or, "Traffic teams are not allowed on this boulevard." Any street in the residence parts of the city may be boulevarded and turned over to the care of the park commissioners of the district, provided that it does not lie next to any other such street, and provided that a certain proportion of the property-holders along it are minded to follow a simple formula to procure the improvement. Improved road-beds are given to such streets, and they not only become neat and pretty, but enhance the value of all neighboring land. One boulevard in Chicago penetrates to the very heart of its bustling business district. By means of it men and women may drive from the southern suburbs or parks to the centre of trade, perhaps to their office doors, under the most pleasant conditions. By means of the lesser beautified avenues among the dwellings men and women may sleep of nights, and hide from the worst of the city's tumult among green lawns and flower-beds.

Chicago's park system is so truly her crown, or its diadem, that its fame may lead to the thought that enough has been said about it. That is not the case, however, for the parks change and improve so constantly that the average Chicagoan finds some of them outgrowing his knowledge, unless he goes to them as he ought to go to his prayers. It is not in extent that the city's parks are extraordinary, for, all told, they comprise less than two thousand acres. It is the energy that has given rise to them, and the taste and enthusiasm which have been expended upon them, that cause our wonder. Sand and swamp were at the bottom of them, and if their surfaces now roll in gentle undulations, it is because the earth that was dug out for the making of ponds has been subsequently applied to the forming of hills and knolls. The people go to some of them upon the boulevards of which I have spoken, beneath trees and beside lawns and gorgeous flower-beds, having their senses sharpened in anticipation of the pleasure-grounds beyond, as the heralds in some old plays prepare us for the action that is to follow. Once the parks are reached, they are found to be literally for the use of the people who own them. I have a fancy that a people who are so largely American would not suffer them to be otherwise. There are no signs warning the public off the grass, or announcing that they "may look, but mustn't touch" whatever there is to see. The people swarm all over the grass, and yet it continues beautiful day after day and year after year. The floral displays seem unharmed; at any rate, we have none to compare with them in any Atlantic coast parks. The people even picnic on the sward, and those who can appreciate such license find, ready at hand, baskets in which to hide the litter which follows. And, O ye who manage other parks we wot of, know that these Chicago play-grounds seem as free from harm and eyesore as any in the land.

The best parks face the great lake, and get wondrous charms of dignity and beauty from it. At the North Side the Lincoln Park commissioners, at great expense, are building out into the lake, making a handsome paved beach, sea-wall, esplanade, and drive to enclose a long, broad body of the lake-water. Although the great blue lake is at the city's edge, there is little or no sailing or pleasure-boating upon it. It is too rude and treacherous. Therefore these commissioners of the Lincoln Park are enclosing, behind their new-made land, a watercourse for sailing and rowing, for racing, and for more indolent aquatic sport. The Lake Shore Drive, when completed, will be three miles in length, and will connect with yet another notable road to Fort Sheridan twenty-five miles in length. All these beauties **form** part of the main exhibit at **the Columbian** Exposition. Realizing this, the municipality **has not** only voted $5,000,000 **to the** Exposition, **but** has set apart $3,500,000 for beautifying and improving the city in readiness **for the** Exposition **and its** visitors, even as a bride bedecketh herself for her husband. That is well; but it is not **her beauty that will** most interest the visitors to Chicago.

I have an idea **that** all this **is very** American; but what is to be said of the Chicago Sunday, with its drinking shops all wide open, **and its** multitudes swarming out on pleasure bent? And **what** of the theatres **opening** to the **best night's business of the week at the hour** of Sunday **evening service** in **the churches?** I suspect **that this also is American—that** sort **of American that develops under** Southern and **Western influences not dominated** by the New England spirit. And yet the **Puritan** traditions are not without honor and respect in Chicago, witness the fact that the city spent seventeen and a quarter millions **of** dollars during the **past** five years upon her public schools.

Another thing that I suspect is American, though I **am** sorry to say it, is the impudence of the people **who wait on the** public. It is quite certain that **the more intelligent a** man is, the better waiter **he** will make; **but** your free-born **American acknowledges** a quality **which** more than offsets his intelligence. **In** pursuit of knowledge I went to a **restaurant, which** was splendid if **it** was not good, **and the** American who waited **on me** lightened his service with song in this singular manner: "Comrades, com— you said coffee, didn't yer?—ever **since** we were boys; sharing each other's sor—I don't think we've got no Roquefort—sharing each other's joys. Brie, **then**—keerect!" **(I recall this** against my country, not against Chicago restaurants. A city which possesses Harvey's, Kinsley's, or the Wellington need not be tender on that point.) But it is as much as a man's self-respect is worth to hazard a necessary question of a ticket-seller in a theatre or railroad depot. Those *bona fide* Americans, the colored men, are apt to try their skill at repartee with the persons they serve; and while I cannot recall an instance when a hotel clerk was impudent, I several times heard members of that fraternity yield to a sense of humor that would bankrupt a Broadway hotel in three weeks. In only one respect are the servitors of the Chicago public like the French: They boast the same motto—" Liberty, equality, fraternity."

There is another notable thing in Chicago which, I am certain, is a national rather than a merely local peculiarity—I refer to dirty streets. In our worst periods in New York we resort to a Latin trick of tidying up our most conspicuous thoroughfares, and leaving the others to the care of—I think it must be the Federal Weather Bureau to whose care we leave them. However, nearly all American cities are disgracefully alike in this respect, and until some dying patriot bequeathes the money to send every Alderman (back) to Europe to see how streets should and can be kept, it is, perhaps, idle to discuss the subject. But these are all comparative trifles. Certainly they will seem such to whoever shall look into the situation of Chicago closely enough to discover the great problems that lie before the people as a corporation.

She will take up these questions in their turn and as soon as possible, and, stupendous as they are, no one who understands the enterprise and energy of Chicago will doubt for a moment that she will master them shrewdly.

These problems are of national interest, and one is a

subject of study **throughout Christendom.** They **deal with** the disciplining **of the** railroads, which run through the city **at a level with** the streets, **and** with **the establishment of an** efficient system **of drainage or sewage.** A start **has** been made for the handling **of the sewage** question. The little Chicago River flows naturally into **the great** lake; but years ago an attempt **to** alter its course was made by the operation of pumping-works at Bridgeport, within the **city limits,** whereby 40,000 gallons of water per minute **are pumped** out of the **river,** and into a canal **that connects with** the Illinois River, and thence with the Mississippi and the Gulf of Mexico. At most times **this causes** a sluggish flow **of the river** southward away **from** the lake. Water **from the lake is also pumped into the river to** dilute its waters, **but it remains a noisome stream,** a sewer, in fact, **whose waters at** times flow or are driven into Lake Michigan to **pollute** the city's water supply. "Measures have been **taken** to construct a large gravity channel as an outlet **for** the sewage into the Illinois River. The Chicago Sanitary District has been **formed** by act of Legislature; nine trustees have been elected to supervise the construction of the channel, engineers have been set **at work** upon surveys," and perhaps the channel which will result **will serve the** double purpose of disposing of the sewage and establishing a navigable waterway connecting Chicago **and her** commerce with the **Mississippi** River. It is said **that this will cost Chicago** twenty millions of dollars. **Honestly done, it will** certainly be worth whatever it costs.

Chicago's water supply **has been linked** with this sewage problem. It does not join with it. Once the sewage matter were settled, the old two-mile crib in Lake Michigan would bring to town water than which there is none more **pure on** earth. The five-mile tunnel and

25

crib now in course of construction (that is to say, the tunnel and gate pushed five miles out into the lake) certainly will leave nothing to be desired, even as the sewage is now ordered.

The railroad question is more bothersome. Chicago is criss-crossed by a gridiron of railway tracks. Practically all of them enter the city and dissect the streets at grade; that is to say, at the level of the city's arteries. Speaking not too loosely, the locomotives and cars mangle or kill two persons on every week-day in the year, or six hundred persons annually. The railroad officials argue that they invented and developed Chicago, and that her people are ungrateful to protest against a little thing like a slaughter which would depopulate the average village in a year. In so far as it is true that they created the city, they will but repeat the experience of that fabled inventor whose monstrous mechanical offspring claimed him for its victim, for, in a wholesome public-spirited sense, that is what must become their fate. Chicago is ten miles deep and twenty-four miles wide, and the railroads (nearly all using a number of tracks) all terminate within 4000 feet of the Rookery Building. I rely on the accuracy of a noted Chicagoan for that measurement. The Rookery is situated very much as the Bank of England is in London and as the City Hall is in New York, so that it will be seen that Chicago is at the mercy of agencies that should be her servants, and not her masters.

Some railroad men, looking from their stand-point, assert that it will cost Chicago one hundred millions of dollars to overcome this injury to her comfort and her safety. This assertion is often echoed in Chicago by men not in the railroad business. On the other hand, I shall be surprised if the railroads do not have to bear a large share of the cost, whatever it may prove to be, because I take it that Chicago will **not fail to** profit **by the experiences of other** cities **where** this problem **has** already been **dealt with, and where it has not been so** lightly taken **for** granted **that when railroads are in the way of the** people, **it is the people, and** not **the railroads,** who **must** pay to move them out of the way. The sum **of present** human judgment seems to be that the cost is divisible, and that the railroads should look after their tracks, and the people after their **streets.**

The entire nation **will observe with** keen interest the manner in which **Chicago deals with** this problem, not with any anticipation **of an** unjust solution that will trespass **on the** popular **rights,** but to note **the determination of the** lesser question, whether the railroads **shall be compelled to** sink their tracks in trenches or to **raise them on trusses,** or whether, **as has also been suggested,** all **the** roads shall combine **to** build **and** terminate at a common elevated structure curving around the outside of the thick of the city, and capable of transferring passengers from road to road, as well as of distributing them among points easily accessible from every district.

One would think it **would be to the** advantage of the principal railway corporations to try at once to effect an agreement among themselves and with the city for this reform, because, as I have said, the railroads are now **the** slowest of Chicago's institutions. **The reduced speed** at which the municipality obliges them **to** run their trains must be still further modified, and even the present headway is hindered by the frequent delays at the numerous crossings of the tracks. This **is a** nuisance. Every occasional traveller feels **it, and what** must **it be** to the local commuters who live **at** a distance from their business? **They** move by slow stages **a** quarter of an hour or more before the cars in which they ride are able to get under the scheduled headway. But it is more than a local question. It is one of the peculiarities of Chicago that she arrests a great proportion of the travelling public that seeks destinations beyond her limits in either direction. They may not want to go to Chicago at all, but it is the rule of most roads that they must do so. They must stop, transfer baggage, and change railroads. Often a stay at a hotel is part of the requirement. If this is to continue, the public might at least have the performance expedited. Both the local and the general nuisance will, in all likelihood, be remedied together. It is the aim of all progressive railroad managers to shorten time and prevent transfers wherever possible; and delays against which the entire travelling public protests cannot long avoid remedy.

In interviews with Chicago men the newspapers have obtained many estimates of the number of visitors who will attend the Columbian Exposition. One calculation, which is called conservative, is that ten million persons will see the display. It is not easy to judge of such estimates, but we know that there is a wider interest in this Exposition than in any that was ever held. We know also that in the foremost countries of Europe workmen's clubs and popular lotteries have been established or projected for the purpose of sending their most fortunate participants to Chicago—a few of many signs of an uncommon desire to witness the great exhibition.

Whatever these visitors have heard or thought of Chicago, they will find it not only an impressive but a substantial city. It will speak to every understanding of the speed with which it is hastening to a place among the world's capitals. Those strangers who travel farther in our West may find other towns that have builded too much upon the false prospects of districts where the crops have proved uncertain. They may see still other showy cities, where the main activity is in the direction of "swapping" real estate. It is a peculiar industry, accompanied by much bustle and lying. But they will not find in Chicago anything that will disturb its tendency to impress them with a solidity and a degree of enterprise and prosperity that are only excelled by the almost idolatrous faith of the people in their community. The city's broad and regular thoroughfares will astonish many of us who have imbibed the theory that streets are first mapped out by cows; its alley system between streets will win the admiration of those who live where alleys are unknown; its many little homes will speak volumes for the responsibility and self-respect of a great body of its citizens.

The discovery that the city's harbor is made up of forty-one miles of the banks of an internal river will lead to the satisfactory knowledge that it has preserved its beautiful front upon Lake Michigan as an ornament. This has been bordered by parks and parkways in pursuance of a plan that is interrupted to an important extent only where a pioneer railway came without the foreknowledge that it would eventually develop into a nuisance and an eyesore. Its splendid hotels, theatres, schools, churches, galleries, and public works and ornaments will commend the city to many who will not study its commercial side. In short, it will be found that those who visit the Exposition will not afterwards reflect upon its assembled proofs of the triumphs of man and of civilization without recalling Chicago's contribution to the sum.

II

CHICAGO'S GENTLE SIDE

When I wrote my first paper upon Chicago I supposed myself well-equipped for the task. I saw Chicago day after day, lived in its hotels and clubs, met its leading business men and officials, and got a great deal which was novel and striking from what I saw around me and from what I heard of the commercial and other secrets of its marvellous growth and sudden importance. It is customary to ridicule the travellers who found books upon short visits to foreign places, but the ridicule is not always deserved. If the writers are travelled and observant spectators, if they ask the right questions of the right men, and if they set down nothing of which they are not certain, the probability is that what they write will be more valuable in its way than a similar work from the pen of one who is dulled to the place by familiarity. And yet I know now that my notes upon Chicago only went half-way. They took no heed of a moiety of the population—the women, with all that they stand for.

I saw the rushing trains of cable-cars in the streets and heard the clang-clang of their gongs. It seemed to me then (and so it still seems, after many another stay in the city) that the men in the streets leap to the strokes of those bells; there is no escaping their sharp din; it sounds incessantly in the men's ears. It seems to jog them, to keep them rushing along, like a sort of

Western conscience, or as if it were a goad or the perpetual prod of a bayonet. It is as if it might be the voice of the Genius of the West, crying "Clang-clang (hustle) — clang-clang (be lively)," and it needs no wizard sight to note the effect upon the men as they are kept up to their daily scramble and forge along the thoroughfares—more often talking to themselves when you pass them than you have ever noticed that men in other cities are given to doing. I saw all that, but how stupid it was not to notice that the women escaped the relentless influence!

They appear not to hear the bells. The lines of the masculine straining are not furrowed in their faces. They remain composed and unmoved; insulated, inoculated. They might be the very same women we see in Havana or Brooklyn, so perfectly undisturbed and at ease are they—even when they pass the Board of Trade, which I take to be the dynamo that surcharges the air for the men.

I went into the towering office-buildings, nerving myself for the moment's battle at the doors against the outpouring torrent and the missile-like office boys who shoot out as from the mouths of cannon. I saw the flying elevators, and at every landing heard the bankers and architects and lawyers shout "Down!" or "Up, up!" and saw them spring almost out of their clothes, as if each elevator was the only one ever built, and would make only one trip before it vanished like a bubble. The office girls were as badly stricken with this *St. Vitus hustle* as the men, which must account for my not noticing that the main body of women—when they came to these buildings to visit husbands or brothers—were creatures apart from the confusion; reposeful, stylish, carefully toiletted, serene, and unruffled.

I often squeezed into the luncheon crowd at the Union

League Club and got the latest wheat quotation with my roast, and the valuation of North Side lots with my dessert; but I did not then know that there was a ladies' side-entrance to the club-house, leading to parlors and dining-rooms as quiet as any in Philadelphia, where impassive maids in starched caps sat like bits of majolica-ware and the clang-clang of the car-bells sounded faintly, like the antipodean echoes in a Japanese sea-shell. I smoked at the Chicago Club with Mayor Washburne, and the softening influence of women in public affairs happened not to come into our talk; with Mr. Burnham, the leading architect, and heard nothing of the buildings put up for and by women. Far less was there any hint, in the crush at that club, of the Argonauts—those leisurely Chicago Club-men who haunt a separate house where they loaf in flannels and the women add the luxurious, tremulous shiver of silk to the sounds of light laughter and elegant dining.

And every evening, while that first study of the city went on, the diurnal stampede from the tall buildings and the choking of the inadequate streets around them took place. The cable-cars became loaded and incrusted with double burdens in which men clung to one another like caterpillars. Thus the crowded business district was emptied and the homes were filled. Any one could see that, and I wrote that there was more home-going and home-staying there than in any large Eastern city in this country. But who could guess what that meant? Who could know the extent of the rulership of the women at night and in the homes, or how far it went beyond those limitations? Who would dream that—in Chicago, of all places—all talk of business is tabooed in the homes, and that the men sink upon thick upholstering, in the soft, shaded light of silk-crowned lamps, amid lace-work and bric-à-brac, and in the blessed atmosphere of music and **gentle voices—all so soothing and so highly esteemed** that it is there **the custom for the men to gather accredited strangers and guests** around **them at home for the enjoyment of dinner, cigars, and cards,** rather than at **the clubs and in** the hotel **lobbies.** I could not know it, **and so, for one reason and** another, the gentle side of Chicago **was left out of that** article.

"Great as Chicago is, the period **of** her true greatness is yet to come," writes Mr. James Dredge, **the** editor of London *Engineering*, **and one of the** British commissioners to our Columbian Exposition. "Its commencement will **dawn** when her inhabitants give themselves time to realize that the object of life is **not** that **of incessant** struggle; that the race is not **always to the** swift, but rather to those who understand **the luxury and advantage** of repose, as well **as sustained** effort." In whichever of our cities an Englishman stays long enough to venture an opinion **of it** that is what he is sure to say. It is true of all of them, and most true of Chicago. But to discover that there is a well-spring of repose there requires a longer acquaintance than to note the need of it. There **is** such a reservoir in Chicago. **It is** in the souls, the spirit **of the** women, and **it is as notable** a **feature of the Chicago homes as of those of any** American city. But the women contribute **more than** this, for, from the **polish of** travel **and** trained **minds** their leaders reflect those **charms which find expression** in good taste and manners, a love of **art** and literature, and in the ability to discern what is **best, and to distinguish** merit and good-breeding above **mere wealth and** pedigree.

What **the** leaders do **the** others copy, and the result is such **that I** do not believe that in any older American city we **shall** find fashionable women so anxious to be considered patrons of art and of learning, or so forward in works of public improvement and governmental reform as well as of charity. Indeed, this seems to me quite a new character for the woman of fashion, and whether I am right in crediting her with it the reader will discover before he finishes this paper. It is necessary to add that not all the modish women there belong in this category. There is a wholly gay and idle butterfly set in Chicago, but it is small, and the distinctive peculiarity of which I speak lies in the fact that in nearly all the societies and movements of which I am going to write we see the names of rich and stylish women. They entertain elegantly, are accustomed to travel, and rank with any others in the town, yet are associated with those forceful women whose astonishing activity has worked wonders in that city. The Chicago woman whose name is farthest known is Mrs. Potter Palmer. She is the wife of a man who is there not altogether improperly likened, in his relation to that city, to one of our Astors in New York. Yet she is at the head of the Woman's Department or Commission of our Exposition, and is active in perhaps a score of women's organizations of widely differing aims. Her name, therefore, may stand as illustrating what has been here said upon this subject.

There is no gainsaying the fact that, in the main, Chicago society is crude; but I am not describing the body of its people; it is rather that reservoir from which is to spring the refinement and graces of the finished city that is to be here considered. If it is true that hospitality is a relic of barbarism, it still must be said that it flourishes in Chicago, which is almost as open-armed as one of our Southern cities. As far as the men are concerned, the hospitality is Russian; indeed, I was again and again reminded of what I have read of the peculiarities of the Russians in what I saw of the pleasures of the younger generation of wealthy men in Chicago. They attend to business with all their hearts by day, and to fun with all their might after dark. They are mainly college men and fellows of big physique, and if ever there were hearty, kindly, jolly, frank fellows in the world, these are the ones. They eat and drink like Russians, and, from their fondness for surrounding themselves with bright and elegant women, I gather that they love like Russians. In like manner do they spend their money. In New York heavy drinking in the clubs is going out of fashion, and there is less and less high play at cards; but in Chicago, as in St. Petersburg, the wine flows freely, the stakes are high. Though the pressure is thus greater than with us in New York, I saw no such effects of the use of stimulants as would follow Chicago freedom were it indulged in the metropolis. And a lady, who is familiar with the gay set, told me that the Chicago women of that circle join the men with such circumspection, when dining, that the newspaper reports of the flushed faces and noisy behavior of our own rapid set at the opera after heavy dining seem to them both shocking and incredible.

But enough of what is exceptional and unrepresentative. The Chicago men are very proud of the women, and the most extravagant comments which Max O'Rell makes upon the prerogatives of American ladies seem very much less extravagant in Chicago than anywhere else. Their husbands and brothers tell me that there is a keen rivalry among the women who are well-to-do for the possession of nice houses, and for the distinction of giving good and frequent dinner-parties, and of entertaining well. "They spend a great deal of money in this way," I was told, "but they are not mercenary;

they do not worship wealth and nag their husbands to get more and more as do the women of the newer West. Their first question about a new-comer is neither as to his wealth nor his ancestry. Even more than in Washington do the Chicago women respect talent and vie with one another to honor those who have any standing in the World of Intellect." In the last ten years the leading circles of women there have undergone a revolution. Women from the female colleges, and who have lived abroad or in the Eastern cities, have displaced the earlier leaders, have married and become the mistresses of the homes as well as the mothers of daughters for whose future social standing they are solicitous.

The noted men and women who have visited Chicago, professionally or from curiosity, in recent years, have found there the atmosphere of a true capital. They have been welcomed and honored in delightful circles of cultivated persons assembled in houses where are felt the intangible qualities that make charming the dwellings of true citizens of the world. For costliness and beauty the numerous fine residences of Chicago are celebrated. Nowhere is there seen a greater variety in the display of cultivated taste in building. In a great degree fine houses are put up in homage to women, and we shall see, if I mistake not, that these women deserve the palaces in which they rule. But, to return to the interiors of the homes, what I find to praise most highly there is the democracy of the men and women. It is genuine. The people's hearts are nearer their waistcoats and basques out there. They aren't incrusted with the sediment of a century of caste-worship and pride and distrust. They may be more new and crude—and all else that we in the East are in the habit of charging them with being—but they may thank God for some of the attributes of their newness. They are more genuine and natural and frank. **They are more** truly American, **and** if I like **them, and** have let that liking appear in what **I have written of** them, it is because their democracy **is sufficient to overwhelm a** myriad of their faults.

I have seen a thing in Chicago—and have seen it several more times than once—that I never heard of **anywhere** else, and that looked a little awkward at first, **for a** few moments. I refer to a peculiar freedom of **intercourse** between the sexes after a dinner or on a **rout—a** *camaraderie* and **perfect** accord between the men and the women. In **saying this I refer** to very nice matrons and maidens in very nice social circles who have nevertheless stayed after the coffee, and have taken part in **the flow** of fun which such a time begets, quite as if **they** liked it and had **a** right to. In one case the men **had withdrawn to** the library, and a noted entertainer was in the full glory of his career, reciting a poem or giving a dialect imitation of a conversation he had overheard on a street-car. The wife of the **host** trespassed, with **a little show** of timidity, to say that the little girls, her daughters, were about to go to bed, and wanted the Noted Entertainer to "make a face" for them—apparently for them to dream upon.

"**Why, come in,**" said the host.

"**Oh, may we?**" **said** the wife, **very** artlessly, and in came all the **ladies of** the party, who, it seems, had gathered in the hallway. The room was blue with smoke, but **all** the ladies "**loved smoke,**" and so the evening wore on gayly. **The only sign of** recognition **of the** novelty of the situation was **an** occasional covert allusion to the stories **that a certain shy** and notedly modest **man** *might tell* **if the** ladies were not present, but **all** that was said or told was as pure as crystal, and the **whole** evening **was so** enjoyable that if any man missed the customary after-dinner "tang" he was disinclined to mention it.

The next occasion was in a mansion on the lake-side. An artist and a poet, well known in both hemispheres, were the especial guests, and the company generally would have been welcome in the best circles in any of the world's capitals except, possibly, in New York, where it is said that an ultra swell personage told the Lord Chief Justice of England that he had met no explorers, historians, poets, scholars, generals, or naval heroes, "because none of them is in society." Of the ladies one was literary, one was a philanthropist and reformer, and the others were just wives—but wives of the brilliant fellows, and all able to coach the men and to tell queer little bits of their own experiences. When the coffee was brought on, on this occasion, there was no movement on the part of the women towards leaving the table. No suggestion was made that they do so; there was no apology offered for their not doing so; the subject was not mentioned. There were glasses of "green mint" for all and cigars for the men. Then the stories flowed and the laughter bubbled. The queer thing was that there was no apparent strain; all were at perfect ease—the ladies being as much so as most men would have been without them. One of the women told two long stories of a comical character, imitating the dialect and mannerisms of different persons precisely as a man given to after-dinner entertaining would have done. Once there was a pause and a little hesitation, and a story-teller said, "I think I can tell this, here, can't I?" "Why, of course, go on," said his wife. So he told whatever it was, the point being so pretty and sentimental that it was a little difficult to determine why he had hesitated unless it was that it had "a big, big D" in one sentence.

I have been present on at least a dozen occasions when the men smoked and drank and the women kept with them, being—otherwise than in the drinking and smoking—in perfect fellowship with them. Such conditions are Arcadian. They are part and parcel of the kinship that permits the Chicagoans to bring their rugs out and to sit on the stoops in the evenings. It will be a sad day when Chicago gets too big and too proud, and when her inhabitants grow too suspicious of one another to permit of such naturalness.

In the Victoria Hotel barber-shop for men, open to the lobbies of the hotel, I saw a young woman seated in a high-chair and having her tresses brushed, next to a man who was being shaved; but I will not mention that as another sign of the freedom of the women, lest I make the same impression on the reader as I once did, quite without deserving the rebuke I got, upon the interpreter at a hotel in Havana. I there saw a woman very strangely dressed, and, pointing her out to that official, asked him how he accounted for her being on the street in that attire. He threw up both hands. "Oh, great Heavens," he exclaimed; "now you will go back and write in a book that the women of Havana wear the costume like that, while I, who have lived here all my life, never saw nothing like it."

Their stylishness is the first striking characteristic of the women of Chicago. It is a Parisian quality, apparent in New York first and in Chicago next, among all our cities. The number of women who dress well in Chicago is very remarkable, and only there and in New York do the shop-girls and working-women closely follow the prevailing modes. Chicago leads New York in the employment of women in business. It is not easy to find an office or a store in which they are not at work as secretaries, accountants, cashiers, type-writers, saleswomen, or clerks. It has been explained to me that women who want to do for themselves are more favored there than anywhere else. The awful fire of twenty years ago wrecked so many families, and turned so many women from lives of comfort to paths of toil, that the business men have from that day to this shown an inclination to help every woman who wants to help herself. Women are encouraged to support themselves, honored for their efforts to do so, and gallantly assisted by all true Chicago men who have the native spirit. We shall see that great results have sprung from this necessity of one sex and encouragement by the other. But one notices the little results everywhere, every day. Observe, for instance, this sign in the cable-cars:

>   THE LADIES DON'T SPEAK OF IT
>   BUT THEY ARE AGAINST THE
>   SPITTING HABIT IN THE STREET CARS.
>   JUST ASK THEM.

The influence of the homes is felt everywhere. It is even more truly a city of homes than Brooklyn, for its flats and tenements are few. Such makeshifts are not true homes, and do not carry household pride with them in anything like the degree that it is engendered in those who live in separated houses which they own. Such, mainly, are the dwellings of Chicago. In that city there are no blocks of flats, tenements, or apartments (by whatever name those barracks may be called).

One of the famous towering office buildings of Chicago is, in the main, the result of a woman's financiering. I refer to "the Temple" of the Woman's Christian Temperance Union, an enormous and beautiful pile, which is, in a general way, like the great Mills Building in Broad Street, New York. **It is thirteen stories high**, it cost **more than** a million of dollars, and the scheme of **it as well as the execution** thereof, from first to last, **was the work** of women and children. Mrs. Matilda **B.** Carse, who is grandiloquently spoken of in the Chicago newspapers as "the chief business woman **of the** continent," inspired and planned the raising of **the** money. For ten years she advocated the great work, and in the course of that time she formed a corporation called "The Woman's Temple Building **Association**," for carrying forward the project. She **was** elected its first president, in July, 1887, and it was capitalized **at $600,000.** Frances Willard, of the National **organization of the** Union, co-operated towards enlisting **the interest and aid of** the entire Temperance Union sisterhood, which adopted the building as its headquarters or "temple." Four hundred thousand dollars worth of **the** stock was purchased with what is referred to as "the outpouring of 100,000 penny banks," and bonds were issued **for** $600,000. The **building is** expected **to yield** $250,000 a year in rentals. The income is to be divided, one-half to the National organization, and the rest, *pro rata* to the various State organizations, according to the amount each subscribed to the fund. Mrs. Carse's was the mind which planned the financial operation, but the credit of carrying it out rests with **Miss** Willard, the several other leaders of the Union, **and the good women** everywhere who have faith in them.

Mrs. Carse is the woman **to whom the members of the** Chicago Woman's **Club refer all** plans for raising **funds.** The Chicago Woman's Club **is the** mother of **woman's** public work in that city. An explanation of what **that** means seems to me to rank among the most surprising of the chapters which I have had occasion to write as the result of my western studies. I know of no such undertakings or co-operation by women elsewhere in our country. This very remarkable Woman's Club has 500 members and six great divisions called the committees on Reform, Philanthropy, Education, Home, Art and Literature, Science and Philosophy. The club has rooms in the building of the famous Art Institute. It holds literary meetings every two weeks, each committee or division furnishing two topics in a year. The members write the papers and the meetings discuss them. Each committee officers and manages its own meetings; the chairwoman of the committee being in charge, and opening as well as arranging the discussions. The Art and Literature and the Science and Philosophy committees carry on classes, open to all members of the club. They engage lecturers, and perform an educational work. Apart from these class meetings, the club-rooms are in use every day as a headquarters for women. They include a kitchen, a dining-room, and a tea-room—tea, by-the-way, being served at all the committee meetings.

The membership is made up of almost every kind of women, from the ultra-fashionable society leaders to the working women, and includes literary and other professional women, business women, and plain wives and daughters. "And," say the members, "women who never hear anything anywhere else, hear everything that is going on in the world by attending the club meetings." It is impossible to name all the women who are conspicuous in the club. Of the fashionable women, such ones as Mrs. Potter Palmer, Mrs. Dunlap, a brilliant society leader, and Mrs. Charles Henrotin are active members. Frances Willard, the head of the Temperance Union, is a member, and so is Mrs. Carse. She is a wealthy woman also, as well as one of great force of mind. Mrs. Caroline K. Sherman, a writer widely known for her energetic **pursuit of** philosophical studies, is active **in the Science and** Philosophy classes. Mrs. George **E. Adams, wife of the member** of Congress of that **name from** Illinois, is **a social ruler, and yet is** very active in the hard work the club undertakes. She helped **raise** the University Fund, of which I shall speak. **A very** active personage, not of the fashionable class, **is Miss** Ada C. Sweet, who was disbursing officer at **Chi**cago, under four Presidents, for the Pension Bureau, and paid out something more than **a** million of dollars **a** year. She devotes her right hand **to** the defense of **her** sex, and her **left** hand to her **own** support. Of other leaders on the gentle side of that robust city there **will be mention as their** works here are considered. **As far** as any **one can see, the** wealthy and fashionable women are **as active** as any others. Those who are referred to as representative **of** the riches and refinement of the town not only have given of their wealth, but of their sympathy and time in the various movements I am about to describe.

Each woman on entering **the** club designates which **division she** wishes to enter. **Her** name is catalogued accordingly, and she works with that committee. Each committee holds periodic meetings, at which subjects are given out for papers and discussion at **the next ses**sion. The Home Committee, for instance, deals with the education **and rearing** of children, domestic **service,** dress reform, decorative art, and kindred subjects. **That** has always been the method in the club, but a result of that and other influences has been that "Chicago ladies have been papered to death," as one **of** them said to me, and in the last few years the development of a higher purpose and more practical **work** has progressed. It began **when** the Reform Committee undertook earnest work, and **ceased** merely **to** hear essays and discuss prison reform, to go "slumming," and to pursue all the fads that were going. This committee began its earnest work with the County Insane Asylum, where it was found that hundreds of women were herded without proper attention, three in a bed, sometimes; with insufficient food, with only a counterpane between them and the freezing winter air at night, and no flannels by day. The root of the trouble was the old one—the root of all public evil in this country—the appointment of public servants for political reasons and purposes. The first step of the Reform Committee was to ask the county commissioners to appoint a woman physician to the asylum. Dr. Florence Hunt was so appointed, and went there at $25 a month. She found that the nurses made up narcotics by the pailful to give to the patients at night so as to stupefy them, in order that they, the nurses, might be free for a good time. The new doctor stopped that and the giving of all other drugs, except upon her order. Then she insisted upon the employment of fit nurses. She and the women doctors who followed her there suffered much petty persecution, but a complete reform was in time accomplished, and the woman physician became a recognized necessity there. To-day, as a consequence, the asylums at Kankakee, Jackson, and Elgin—all Illinois institutions—have women physicians also. I am assured that no one except a physician can appreciate how great a reform it was to establish the principle that women suffering from mental diseases should be put in charge of women. Mrs. Helen S. Shedd was at the front of the asylum reform work, which is still going on.

She next led the Reform Committee into the Poorhouse, where they went, as they always do, with the plea "There are women there; we want a share in the charge of that place for the sake of our sex." They have adopted the motto, "What are you doing with the women and children?" and they find that the politicians cannot turn aside so natural and proper an inquiry. The politicians try to frighten the women. They say, "You don't want to pry into such things and places; you can't stand it." But the Chicago ladies have proven that they can stand a very great deal, as we shall see, on behalf of humanity; especially feminine humanity. "You are using great sums of money for the care of the poor, the sick, the insane, and the vicious," they say. "One-half of these are women, and we, as women, insist upon knowing how you are performing your task. We do not believe you bring the motherly or the sisterly element to your aid; we know that you do not understand women's requirements." That line of argument has always proved irresistible.

While I was in Chicago in August some of the women were looking over the plans for four new police-stations. It transpired as they talked that they have succeeded in establishing a Woman's Advisory Board of the Police, consisting of ten women appointed by the Chief of Police, and in charge of the quarters of all women and children prisoners, and of the station-house matrons, two of which are appointed to each station where women are taken. Through the work of her women, Chicago led in this reform, which is now extending to the chief cities of the country. Now, all women and juveniles are separated from the men in nine of the Chicago precinct stations, to one of which every such prisoner must be taken, no matter at what time or on what charge such a person is arrested. The chief matron is Mrs. Jane Logan, a woman who came to Chicago from Toronto and became conspicuous in the Woman's Club and in the Household Art Association. Miss Sweet "coaxed her into the police work," and the mayor appointed her chief matron. She has an office in a down-town station, where the worst prisoners are taken as well as the friendless girls and waifs who drift in at the railway stations. The waifs are all taken to her, and she never leaves them until they are on the way back to their homes, or to better guardianship. She maintains an "annex," kept clean and sweet, with homelike beds and pictures, and to this place are taken any first offenders and others, of saving whom she thinks there is a chance. Female witnesses are also kept there instead of in the prisoners' cells, and all who go to the annex are entirely secluded from reporters as well as all others. Two of the best matrons of the force are in charge day and night. All women and girl prisoners are attended at court, even the drunken women being washed and dressed and made to look respectable. Mrs. Logan always goes herself with the young girls to see that they are not approached, and in order that if it is just and advantageous that they should escape punishment she may plead with the court for their release. Formerly, every woman who was arrested was searched by men and thrown in a cell in the same jail-room with the male prisoners. Lost children, homeless girls, and abandoned women were all huddled together. The women of the city "couldn't stand it," they say. They worked eight years, led by Miss Sweet, to bring about the now accomplished reform.

In all cases in which women complain of abuse or mistreatment by the police or others, Mrs. Logan sits on the Police Trial Board "to show the unfortunate woman that she has a friend." The Board is composed of five inspectors and the assistant chief of police, and the president asked her to join its sessions whenever a woman is involved in any case that comes before it.

The police do not oppose the work of the women. Desperate and abandoned females used to make fearful charges against the patrolmen and others on the force under the old regime. Under the new system there is a great change in this respect.

Mrs. Logan is described as beautiful and refined, as gentle and unassuming in the highest degree, as about thirty-five years of age, and as having humanity for her propelling force—almost for her religion. Just now she wants to have the police-patrol wagons covered for the protection of female prisoners, and, to make sure of her arguments, she recently rode across the city in one of those carts. Her work is a prolonged effort of patience, kindness, and justice. Last Christmas-time seventy-five girls were arrested for shoplifting. She found one, eighteen years of age, flat on her face on a cell floor. She took her to the annex, away from the sight of prison bars, and got her story from her. It was that she was of a respectable family, and had come to town to work as a stenographer, but could get no employment. Her brother sent money for her board in a quiet household, but she had little other money, and in time she spent her last cent. She mended her gloves until they were mended all over, and then her stockings gave out. She drifted into a store, saw the profusion of things there, and stole three handkerchiefs, thinking she would sell them. She was caught in the act. As she could not go to trial until morning, Mrs. Logan went to her boarding-house and explained that she was "going to spend the night with friends." Next day, to oblige the chief matron, the court released the girl, and then Mrs. Logan told the police reporters the whole story, and got their promise that they would not publish a word of it. Mrs. Howe, the president of the Advisory Board, sent ten dollars to the girl, and she returned five dollars "for the next girl who needed it." She is nicely situated now, through the efforts of the women. I heard many such stories of Mrs. Logan's work. She is incessantly rushing about, getting passes and money, sending for the ladies of the Advisory Board to go to court or to the station-houses; telegraphing to parents to take back runaway girls and boys; and speaking for those who have no one else to say a kind word for them.

Mrs. R. C. Clowry, wife of the manager of the Western Union Telegraph Office, is a member of the Police Advisory Board; she is also on the Woman's Commission of the World's Fair and is a musical composer of some celebrity. She and Miss Sweet are the representatives of the Woman's Club on the Board. From the Woman's Protective Agency to the Board came Mrs. Fanny Howe, the president of the Board, and Mrs. Flora P. Tobin.

Mrs. Howe is also president of the Protective Agency, one of the most remarkable humanitarian organizations in the city. Its founder, Mrs. J. D. Harvey, is the daughter of Judge Plato, who was distinguished among the early settlers of the town; but one of the greatest workers in it, and the person who has done the most towards developing it, is Mrs. Charlotte Cushing Holt. She is tenderly described by her friends as "a very small, short, pretty, doll-like woman, in a quakerish reform dress;" and it is added that "the amount of work she can do is astounding." She is studying law just now, because she needs that branch of knowledge in order to advise the poor. Her husband, Granville Holt, is well known in the city. They have no children, but very many of these women have families. The majority are very happily married, I am assured. The Protective Agency protects women and children in all their rights of property and person, gives them legal advice, recovers wages for servants, sewing-women, and shop-girls who are being swindled; finds guardians for defenceless children; procures divorces for women who are abused or neglected; protects the mothers' right to their children. It has obtained heavy sentences against men in cases of outrage—so very heavy that this crime is seldom committed. In a matter akin to this, the women of this society perform what seems to me a most extraordinary work. It is a part of the belief of these ladies that all women have rights, no matter how bad or lost to decency some of them may be. Therefore they stand united against the ancient custom, among criminal lawyers, of destroying a woman's testimony by showing her bad character. This these women call "a many-century-old trick to throw a woman out of court and deny her justice."

As an instance of the manner in which they display their zeal on behalf of the principle that no matter how bad a woman is she should have fair play, there was this state of affairs: Five mistresses of disorderly resorts had brought as many young girls to Mrs. Logan, and had said they wanted them saved. The girls were pure, but had been brought to the houses in question by men who had pretended that they were taking them to restaurants or respectable dwellings. The Agency caused the arrest of the men implicated; and when the first case came up for trial, the Agency sent for fourteen or sixteen married women of fine social position to come to court and sit through the trial to see fair play. When the bagnio-keeper, who was the chief witness against the prisoner, took the stand, she testified that the girl had been told that her house was a restaurant where she was to have supper. Undeceived, she was greatly frightened, and the woman took charge of her. Then the counsel for the defence began to draw out the story of the woman's evil life and habits. He was rebuked from the Bench, and was told that the woman's character for chastity could not affect her testimony, and that when counsel asked such questions of women witnesses the Court would insist that similar questions be put to all male witnesses in each case, with the same intent to destroy the force of their depositions. Thus was established a new principle in criminal practice. In the other cases prosecuted by the Agency the same array of matrons in silks, laces, and jewels was conspicuous in the court-rooms. The police and court officials are said—and very naturally, it seems to me—to have been astonished at this proceeding by women of their standing. But the women have not only gained a step towards perfect justice for their sex, they say that their presence in court has put an end to the ribaldry that was always a feature of trials of the kind. Not far removed from this work has been the successful effort of the women to raise what is called "the age of consent" from twelve to sixteen years.

The Philanthropy Committee of the Woman's Club began its active work in the county jail, where it found a shocking state of affairs. There was only one woman official in the jail, and at four o'clock every afternoon she locked up the women and went away. When she had gone the men were free to go in, and they did. The women of the committee demanded the appointment of a night matron, and the sheriff said he required an order from certain judges who were nominally in charge. This they obtained, and then they were told they must secure from the county an appropriation for the proposed matron's salary. The county officials granted the money conditionally upon the nomination for the place being made by the Woman's Club. The matron was appointed, the work of reform was begun, and it was as if a fresh lake breeze had blown through the unwholesome place. The men cannot intrude upon the women now, and little vagrant girls of ten to fourteen years of age are no longer locked up with hardened criminals. The children have a separate department, where toys and books and a kindly matron brighten their lives while they are awaiting trial. Still another department in the jail is a school for the boys, who are sometimes kept there three or four months before being tried. It was after this work in the jail that the Philanthropy Committee took up the police-station reforms. The first matrons who were put in charge of the stations were political appointees, except a few who were nominally recommended by the Woman's Christian Temperance Union. The whole system was a sham; the women had to have political backing; they were not in sympathy with the movement, and were not competent. They were "just poor," and had large families, and merely wanted the money. There are twenty-five satisfactory matrons now. Each appointment was first recommended after investigation by the women of the Police Advisory Board, which endeavors to secure those who have not large families or absorbing cares at home, but who have time to spare, and character, nerve, and tact.

A few years ago there was a movement among Chicago men for the foundation of an Industrial School for Homeless Boys who were not criminals. The idea was to train the boys and put them out for adoption. The plan languished and was about to be abandoned, when the Woman's Club took hold of it. A Mr. George, a farmer, had promised to give three hundred acres of land worth $40,000 if any one would raise $40,000 for the buildings. The Woman's Club rose "as one man," got the money in three months, and turned it over to the men, who then founded the Illinois Manual Training-school at Glenwood, near the city. An advisory board of women in the club attends to the raising of money, the provision of clothing, and the exercise of a general motherly interest in the institution, which is exceptionally successful.

This list of gentle reforms and revolutions is but begun. The Education Committee of this indomitable club discovered, a few years since, that the statute providing for compulsory education was not enforced. The ladies got up a tremendous agitation, and many leading men, as well as women, went to the Capitol at Springfield and secured the passage of a mandatory statute insuring the attendance at school of children of from six to fourteen years during a period of sixteen weeks in each year. Five women were appointed among the truant officers, and the law was strictly carried out. It is found that it works well to employ women in this capacity. They are invited into the houses by the mothers, who tell them, as they would not tell men, the true reasons for keeping their children from school, as, for instance, that they have but one pair of shoes for six children. A beautiful charity resulted from this work. There was established in the club an aid society. Mrs. Murray F. Tuley, the wife of Judge Tuley, a woman long identified with free kindergarten work, became very active in establishing this society. She interested all classes, obtained the use of a room in the City Hall, recruited workers from the Church societies, the Woman's Club, and from almost everywhere else, to sew for the children. She got the merchants to send great rolls of flannels, and shoes and stockings by the hundreds of pairs. These are stored in the room in the City Hall, and when the truant officers discover a case of need they report it, and the Board of Education orders relief granted through the truant agency.

Some members of the Woman's Club are physicians, such as Dr. Sarah Hackett Stevenson, Dr. Julia Holmes Smith, Dr. Mary A. Mixer, Dr. Marie J. Mergler, Dr. Julia Ross Low, Dr. Frances Dickinson, Dr. Elizabeth L. Chapin, Dr. Sarah H. Brayton, Dr. Rose S. Wright Bryan, and Dr. Leila G. Bedell. There are between 200 and 250 women doctors in Chicago, by-the-way, and in the club are two women preachers. While I am pausing to mention these distinctive features I will add another which interested me, and that is the manner in which the members' names are printed in the annual book of the club. This is it:

Signature.	Address.
AGNES POTTER HUTCHINS,	Mrs. JAMES C. HUTCHINS, 231 Forty-seventh St.
ELLEN BULLARD JENNY,	Mrs. H. W. JENNY, 530 Orchard St.
ANNIE W. JOHNSON,	Mrs. FRANCIS A. JOHNSON, 3807 Langley Av.
TRYPHENA Y. JOHNSON,	Mrs. WILLIS F. JOHNSON, 390 Dearborn Av.
SUSAN C. LL-JONES,	Mrs. JENKIN LL-JONES, 3939 Langley Av.

But to return to the physicians, who most blamelessly led me into this excursion: Mrs. Dr. Julia Ross Low came to the club one day with a solemn tale of the need of a hospital for sufferers from contagious diseases. There was none in the city. No hospital would take such cases, and they were kept at home to endanger whole neighborhoods. She told of the fearful results of contagion in places where whole families occupied one room, and where, when disease came, two or three must die. Her words made a great impression. A Mrs. Benedict, who had lost two children by some dread disease, offered to give ten thousand dollars towards founding such a hospital; but it was discovered that under the law the hospital must be a public institution. Therefore, a monster mass-meeting was held last fall. The county and city officials attended, and so did many physicians and a host of influential persons. Franklin Head presided, under the rule the women have adopted of asking men to preside on such occasions so as not to offend ultra-conservative minds. Strong resolutions were adopted, and later the press helped the movement enthusiastically. The women say that the Chicago newspapers always co-operate with them gallantly and ardently. The county commissioners then appropriated thirty thousand dollars and put up a building, the planning of which was supervised by the women.

In this case, as whenever a committee has more than it can do, the whole club took hold. "Now, everybody pull for the contagious hospital," was the signal, and every woman in the club dropped everything else, went home, enlisted the husbands, fathers, and brothers, and so quickly stirred all Chicago.

Last May one of the committees invited President Harper, of the Chicago University, to deliver an address on the Higher Education of Women, and particularly upon the plans of the university in that respect. He made it evident that the university plans were very liberal; that women were to have the same advantages as men, the same examinations, the same classes, the same professors, and that they would be eligible to the same professorships. Considering the great endowment of the institution, this was seen to be the fullest and richest opportunity that American women enjoy for the pursuit of learning; but it also came out that, although there had been five hundred applications from the graduates of other female schools and colleges, there were to be no accommodations whatever for them. The donations to the university had come in such a way that no money could be set apart for the construction of dormitories. The chairman of the Education Committee (all the heads of committees in the club are called "chairmen") proposed that the club pledge itself to raise $150,000 for a Woman's Building for the university. The motion was carried unanimously, a committee was appointed, and in sixty days (on July 10, 1892) it had collected $168,000. Three different women gave $50,000 each, so that when the committee had time to count what it had, there were $18,000 more than were needed. Of course, dollars never go begging for a use to which to be put, and these will be used for interior appointments. Another committee was appointed to insure the planning of a building satisfactory to women, and to furnish the apartments, which are not to be merely bedrooms, but are to include a large assembly-room, dining-rooms and parlors, a gymnasium, library, baths, and whatever; the parlors being common to every two or three bedrooms, and all the appointments being homelike and inviting.

Mrs. Dr. Stevenson was in the chair when this great movement was set on foot, and she has since interested Chicago anew by demanding bath-houses on the lake front for the boys, and afterwards for the poor in general. She began by doing violence to a strong tradition as to the relation between women and naked boys in bathing. She asked Mayor Washburne to suspend the ordinance forbidding boys to bathe in the lake within the city limits. The first that the people knew of it was the sight of swarms of little shavers, and some big boys and men, fringing the water's edge with their shining bodies. She got the mayor to permit them to go in wherever it was not dangerous, and to order the police to patrol the lake shore and mark the unsafe places. During the intense heat of July the promiscuous bathing went on—in no way offensively, it seemed to me—and after that a boat-house was found by the energetic doctor, who had it converted into a bath-house, with dressing-rooms, with a basement full of water for those who could not swim, and a door admitting to the lake those who could. This is but the beginning of what promises great results, for the women are solidly abetting Dr. Stevenson, and she is going to have two more lake baths, and then some large, complete, all-the-year-round bath-houses in the poorer quarters of the town.

A very remarkable member of the Woman's Club is Jane Addams, of whose gentle character it is sufficient to say that her friends are fond of referring to her as "Saint Jane." She is not robust in health, but, after doing more than ten men would want to do, she usually explains that it is something she has found "in which an invalid can engage." She is a native of Illinois, is wealthy, and while on a visit to London, becoming interested in Toynbee Hall, evolved a theory which has brightened her own and very many other lives. It is that "the rich need the poor as much as the poor need the rich;" that there is a vast number of girls coming out of the colleges for whom there is not enough to do to interest them in life, and who grow ennuied when they might be active and happy. It is her idea that when they interest themselves in their poor brothers and sisters they find the pure gold of happiness. She asked the aid of many ladies of leisure, and went to live in one of the worst quarters of Chicago, taking with her Miss Ellen Starr, a teacher, and a niece of Eliza Allen Starr, the writer.

She found an old-time mansion with a wide hall through the middle and large rooms on either side. It had been built for a man named Hull, as a residence, but it had become an auction-house, and the district around it had decayed into a quarter inhabited by poor foreigners. The woman who had fallen heir to it gave it to Miss Addams rent free until 1893. She and Miss Starr lived in it, filled it plainly but with fine taste, with pictures and ornaments as well as suitable furniture and appointments for the purposes to which it was to be put. A piano was put in the large parlor or assembly-room, which is used every morning for a kindergarten. A beautiful young girl, Miss Jennie Dow, gave the money for the kindergarten, and taught it for a year. Miss Fanny Garry, a daughter of Judge Garry, organized a cooking-school, and, with her young friends to assist her, teaches the art of cooking to poor girls.

A great many of the best known young men and ladies in North Side circles contribute what they can to the success of this charity, now known as Hull House, and the subject of general local pride. These young persons teach Latin classes, maintain a boy's club, and instruct the lads of the neighborhood in the methods of boyish games; support a modelling class, a class in wood-carving, and another in American history. Every evening in the week some club meets in Hull House—a political economy club, a German club, or what not. Miss Addams's idea is that the poor have no social life, and few if any of the refinements which gild the intercourse that accompanies it. Therefore, on one night in each week, a girls' club meets in Hull House. The girls invite their beaus and men friends, and play games and talk and dance, refreshing themselves with lemonade and cake. The young persons who devote their spare time to the work go right in with the girls and boys, and help to make the evenings jolly; one who is spoken of as "very swell" bringing his violin to furnish the dance music. The boys' club has one of the best gymnasiums in the city. The boys prepare and read essays and stories, and engage in improving tasks. There is a *crèche* in the Hull House system, and the sick of the district all go there for relief. College extension classes are also in the scheme, and public school-teachers attend the classes with college graduates, who enlist for the purpose of teaching them.

One of the new undertakings of the Chicago women is the task set for itself by the Municipal Reform League. It was organized in March, 1892, by the ladies who were connected with the World's Fair Congresses, a comprehensive work, for the description of which I have no space. A large committee was studying municipal reform when they decided to found an independent society, to endure long after the World's Fair, and to devote itself to local municipal reform, and especially to the promotion of cleanliness in the streets. A mass-meeting was held in Music Hall, and Judge Gresham presided. Many of the city officials and the local judges came and the hall was crammed. Among the speakers were the mayor, the commissioner of public works, and the health commissioners. A clergyman arraigned them as responsible for the sorry state of the streets, and was followed by Miss Ada C. Sweet and Dr. Stevenson. A public meeting was held next day in the Woman's Club to organize the new society. Ada C. Sweet was elected president, and the other offices were filled by women. A constitution was adopted, after one had been framed, to admit everybody to membership who would express a desire to assist in the work and to keep their own premises in order. Six hundred members are on the rolls, and these include one hundred men, among whom are millionaires and working-men. Money has been contributed liberally, but only the secretary receives compensation. The work performed is all in the direction of forcing the public officials **to do their** duty. The Health Department is in charge **of the alleys and** the Street Department of **the** streets. To keep these departments up to their work, all the members of Miss **Sweet's** society are constituted volunteer **inspectors**, pledged to report once a week whatever remissness they discover. Thus the society has the eyes of argus to scan the entire city. Where these eyes are kept wide open the greatest improvement was already apparent (August **1892**). Miss Sweet knows what every contractor is doing as well as who is negligent and who **is** faithful, and she **says** she knows that there is not **a** single contractor whose contract could not be annulled to-morrow. She insists that the plan adopted by her society, if pursued, will transform Chicago into the model city of the world so far as public tidiness is concerned. Already many wealthy ladies drive down the alleys instead of the streets, and even walk through the byways; and so do many influential men, for the purpose of detecting negligence and reporting it. The complaints are forwarded, in the society's formal **manner, to** the responsible commissioners, and they do all they can, Miss Sweet admits, yet are rendered measurably impotent because **they** cannot appoint proper inspectors. The reformers will not stop until they have destroyed the entire contract system, and have made the police do the work of inspection. Already ten policemen are detailed to this work, and eighteen more are to extend the system. An amazing and disheartening discovery attended the beginning of this undertaking. The garbage of the city was supposed to be burned as it accumulated; instead, it was being dumped in a circle of hillocks around the outskirts of the town. A plan for disposing of it by fire had failed, and the officials sat helplessly down and gave up the job. The women took up the task, and now (July, 1892) three methods are undergoing trial, and 180 tons a day are being burned. That mere incident in the history of this movement for clean streets is a grand return for the investment of interest in the project which the public has made.

Miss Sweet is no beginner at these almost superhuman tasks of awakening a great community to a perception of its rights and its requirements. Three years ago she found that the police-patrol wagons were the only vehicles in Chicago for the transporting of the sick and injured. Men and women, falling ill or meeting with disabling accidents, were picked up by the police and carted home or to the hospitals in heavy open patrol wagons built with springs fitted to bear a load of two dozen patrolmen. She first tried to get the officials to buy and equip ambulances and organize an ambulance corps in the Police Department. Failing in this, she raised money among her friends, and had an ambulance made and fitted with necessary appliances for the sick and desperately injured. She presented it to the city, requesting that it be put into immediate use in the Central District. The Police Department at once, in the spring of 1890, began using the ambulance instead of the patrol wagon, and when this was written the vehicle had travelled 18,000 miles and carried 2,000 patients. Slowly the city took up the idea, and now the Police Department has six of these ambulances in use, each one carrying a medical man. It also maintains a corps of men trained to the care of the sick and the injured. More of the wagons are promised, and a perfect ambulance system extending over the whole city is not a far distant consummation. "This," Miss Sweet tells me, "is the only piece of work I have yet done of which I am really proud, but my pride is tempered by keen realization of how far short of my hopes the enterprise still remains." She is no blue-stocking, but a wholesome, genial, robust woman of an old maid's age, if thirty-five be that, but with a young girl's spirits and delights.

Mrs. James M. Flower, a member of the School Board and of a family of great social distinction, should be mentioned here as having, with other noble dames, organized and pushed to success a training-school for nurses. The Art and Literature Committee of the Woman's Club also deserves credit and mention for raising money for a scholarship at the Chicago Art Institute, the prize being given each year to the girl or boy graduate of the public schools who shows the most artistic talent.

These unusual activities and undertakings are but a part of what the women are doing, and are in addition to the kindly and humane efforts which the reader had doubtless expected to hear about, and which but parallel those which interest and occupy American ladies everywhere. There are proportionately as many workers in the hospitals, schools, and asylums, as many noble founders and supporters of refuges and hospitals, as many laborers in Church and mission work in Chicago as in New York or Boston. If the readers understand that those of which I have told are all added, like jewels upon a crown, to all the usual benefactions, the force of this chapter will be appreciated.

There are in Chicago, as elsewhere, Browning and Ibsen and Shakespearian circles and clubs, and if the city boasts few *littérateurs* or artists of celebrity, there is no lack of lovers and students of the work of those who live elsewhere. The Twentieth Century Club, founded, I believe, by the brilliant Mrs. George Rowswell Grant, is the most ambitious literary club, and has a large and distinguished membership. It meets in the houses of wealthy ladies, and is at times addressed by distinguished visitors whom it invites to the city. The Chicago Literary Club is another such organization, and of both these men as well as women are members. The Chicago Folk-lore Society, a new aspirant to such distinction, was organized in December, 1891; the first meeting being called by Mrs. Fletcher S. Bassett at the Chicago Woman's Club rooms. Eugene Field, of whose verse and of whose delightful personality Chicago cannot be too proud; George W. Cable, General and Mrs. Miles, Mr. and Mrs. Potter Palmer, Dr. Sarah Hackett Stevenson, Charles W. Deering, Mr. and Mrs. C. Henrotin, and Mr. and Mrs. Franklin MacVeagh are among the members. The motto of this society illumines its field of work. It is, "Whence these legends and traditions?" It has started a museum of Indian and other relics and curios, and may make an exhibition during the World's Fair. It will certainly distinguish itself during the congress of folk-lore scholars to be held in Chicago in 1893. The president of the society is Dr. S. H. Peabody. The directors are all women: Mrs. S. S. Blackwelder, Mrs. Fletcher S. Bassett, and Mrs. Potter Palmer; and the treasurer is Helen G. Fairbank.

I had a most interesting talk with one of the women active in certain of the public works I have described, and she told me that one reason why the women succeeded so well with the officials and politicians is that they are not voters, are not in politics, and ask favors (or rights) not for themselves but for the public. That, she thought, sounded like an argument against granting the suffrage to women; but she said she would have to let it stand, whatever it sounded like. She said that the Chicago men not only spring to the help of a woman who tries to get along "but they hate to see her fail, and they won't allow her to fail if they can help it." She remarked that the reason that active Chicago women do not show the aggressive, harsh spirit and lack of graceful femininity which is often associated with women who step out of the domestic sphere, is because the Chicago women have not had to fight their way. The men have helped them. She gloried in the strides the women have made towards independence in Chicago. "A fundamental principle with us," she said, "is that a girl may be dependent, but a woman must be independent in order to perform her all functions. She must be independent in order to wisely make a choice of her career—whether she will be a wife and mother, and, if so, whose wife and mother she will be."

III

"BROTHER TO THE SEA"

You see Lake Superior best, as an incident in crossing the continent, when travelling over the Canadian transcontinental railroad, and of all the various "scenic wonders" that the different crosscontinental railroads advertise, not one seems to me more grand or more grandly beautiful than this. For more than half a day the cars glide along the shore, whose irregularities provide a wide diversity of scenery, in woods, among rocks, and every few minutes close beside the closed ends of the great bays which spread out into an ocean-like endlessness of water. Each time that I have made the journey it has been my good-fortune to see the lake clear, smooth, and brilliant, as if it were a vast mirror that Dame Nature might have been holding up to herself. And the lake, like a huge bowl of quicksilver, has each time caught and held the brilliant scene around it—the cloud-littered shining skies, the quiet stately forests, and the towering rocks, which rise in all the forms of turrets, pinnacles, ramparts, castellated heaps, and frowning walls, now green, now red, now purple, and anon dull brown or ashen.

Lake Superior is almost everywhere noble, grand, impressive, majestic. Its surroundings are, for the most part, far more suggestive of what one fancies the ocean should be than are those of the oceans themselves. Old Crowfoot, with his marvellous faculty for aptly nick-

GRAND ARCH, PICTURED ROCKS, LAKE SUPERIOR

naming whatever new thing he saw, was never happier than when he tried to express in a phrase the impression Superior made upon his mind. The Canadian officials were bringing him on a sight-seeing tour to Montreal from the Blackfoot territory on the plains, where he ruled the wildest Indians of Canada; and when he saw the greatest of all lakes, and saw it again and then again, until he comprehended its majesty, he said, "It is the Brother to the Sea."

It is the largest lake in the world, and the largest body of fresh water. It is 380 miles in length and 160 miles across in its widest part. Its watery area of 32,000 square miles proves it to be the size of the State of Indiana, or four times as big as Massachusetts.* It is about 600 feet above the sea-level; but the Government charts show that in its deepest part the water has a depth of 231 fathoms, or 1386 feet, so that there, at least, the lake is more than 700 feet below the surface of the sea as well as 600 feet above it. North of Keweenaw Point, on the south side, there is a depth of 1008 feet, and great depths, above 500 feet, are scattered all about the lake. Its shore line is 1500 miles in length.

One very dignified English authority terms Lake Superior "the head of and chief reservoir for the most magnificent system of inland navigation in the world," a system which, if taken to embrace the water route from the source of the St. Louis, emptying into the head of the lake, to the mouth of the St. Lawrence, is 2100 miles in length. Curiously enough, the same plateau in Minnesota wherein the St. Louis has its beginning is also the starting-point of the Mississippi and the Red River of the North. But Lake Superior owes little to the St. Louis. It receives the waters of 200 rivers, and drains a territory of 53,000 square miles exclusive of its own area.

The lake is practically the property of the United

---

* The United States Geological Survey makes its area 31,200 square miles, its length 412 miles, its maximum breadth 167 miles, its maximum depth 1008 feet, and its height above the sea-level 602 feet.

States. The Canadians own the beautiful north shore, but very little of the lake itself. The main body of the traffic on the lake is ours by a right that cannot be questioned, for it proceeds from our vastly greater population, and from our possession of the coal supply of

THUNDER CAPE, NORTH SHORE

the continent, which gives to American vessels the cargoes with which to return westward after having floated grain and ore eastward.

Lake Superior is a capricious monster, demanding skilled seamanship and the use of powerful and stanch boats, the majority of which are comparable with the vessels in our Atlantic coasting trade. The lake is a veritable womb of storms. They develop quickly there, and even more speedily the water takes on a furious character. It is always cold, and the atmosphere above and far around it is kept cool all summer. I have been told, but cannot verify the statement, that the temperature of the water in the open lake never rises above 46° Fahrenheit. As a rule, the men who sail upon it cannot swim. The lake offers no inducement to learn the art, and, alas! those who are expert swimmers could not keep alive for any great length of time in the icy water. When I was making inquiries upon this point, I found, as one almost always does, some who disputed what the majority agreed upon. I even found an old gentleman, a professional man of beyond seventy years of age, who said that for several years he had visited the lake each summer-time, and that he had made it a practice to bathe in its waters nearly every day. It was chilly, he admitted, and he did not stay in very long. But many sailors, among them some ship and steamship captains, confirmed my belief that few Lake Superior seamen have learned to swim, and that the coldness of the water quickly numbs those who fall into it. I asked one captain how long he supposed a man might battle for life, or cling to a spar in the lake. He answered, very sensibly, it seemed to me, that some men could endure the cold longer than others, and that the more flesh and fat a man possessed, the longer he could keep alive. "But," he added, "the only man I ever saw fall overboard went down like a shot before we could get to him. I always supposed he took a cramp."

The bodies of the drowned are said not to rise to the surface. They are refrigerated, and the decomposition which causes the ascent of human bodies in other waters does not take place. If one interesting contribution to my notes is true, and there be depths to which fishes do not descend, it is possible that many a hapless sailorman and voyager lies as he died, a century back perhaps, and will ever thus remain, lifelike and natural, under the darkening veil of those emerald depths.

The great, fresh, crystal sea never freezes over, and yet its season for navigation is very short. This is due to the ice that makes out from the shores, the points, and the islands, and closes some of the harbors. One captain told me he had seen ice five miles out from the light-house on Thunder Cape, and that is an island in deep water. In 1880 the season opened on April 5th; in 1888 it began on May 21st. In 1880 it closed on December 3d, and in 1883 there was navigation until December 30th. But those are extreme dates. As a rule, navigation opens in the middle of April and closes in the middle of December.

But there are two obstructions for which Lake Superior is notorious, and they rank next to the ice, and still further limit navigation for some lines of ships. These evils are the fogs and the snow-storms, and of

TRAP-ROCK CLIFFS, NORTH SHORE

the two the fogs are the more numerous and the snow is the more dreaded. In the summer Dame Superior wears her fogs almost as a Turkish wife wears her veils. There is a time, in August, when the only fogs are those which follow rain; but the snow begins in September, so that the reader may judge of the sort of navigation the lake affords. The Canadian Pacific steamships (Clyde-built ships that are like our Havana and Savannah boats) are in service only between May and October, and it is the snow which curtails their season. It snows on the great lake just as it does on the plains, in terrible flurries, during the course of which it is impossible to see a foot ahead, or to see at all. Mark Twain did not exaggerate the character of these storms when he described the fate of men who were lost and frozen to death within pistol-shot of their cabins. It has a way of snowing on Superior, by-the-way, as late as June and as early as September; in a light and frolicsome way, to be sure, but it snows, nevertheless. As for the fogs, though they are light and often fleeting after midsummer, they are sufficiently frequent during the rest of the season of navigation to have given the lake a distinguished bad character in the minds of those who sail the warmer lakes, and I have had a captain tell me that he has made seven voyages in succession without seeing any lights on his route from Port Arthur to "the Soo."

But its charms outweigh all its caprices and atone for its worst faults. It is supremely charming, a vast nursery for exquisite effects, and a play-ground of beauty. Out on its broad bosom it imitates the sea exactly. There was no apparent difference in the immensities of the two bodies, and the view within the speeding circle of the horizon was that of the same deep blue field of veined and ruffled water. By day the patent log kept up its angry whistle, and the clumsy gulls, with their broken-looking wings, beat the air and sounded their baby treble in a soft shattered cloud over the vessel's wake. The sky was never to be forgotten—not soft like that over southern Europe, but of the clearest, purest blue imaginable, and yet a blue to which the sunlight lent an active living tone like that of flame diluted or transformed. On no visit did I ever see the sky free of clouds, and I cannot imagine it so, but Lake Superior

THE NORTH SHORE, LAKE SUPERIOR

fair-weather clouds, always cumuli, of course, are the softest, roundest, most feather-like vagrants that ever loafed like lazy swans in heaven's ethereal sea.

One peculiarity of Lake Superior cannot be too strongly dwelt upon or exaggerated. That is its purity, the wonderful cleanness and freshness of it, and of its atmosphere and of its borders. It must become the seat of a hundred summer resorts when the people visit it and succumb to its spell. Think what it is! A volume of crystalline water in which all Scotland's surface could be sunk like a stone—of water so clear and translucent that one may see the entire outlines of the vessels that cleave its surface, so pure that objects may be distinguished on the bottom at a depth of 20 feet; 45 feet they call it who have to do with the lake, but I was unable to see through more of it than 21 feet. Fancy such an expanse of water so clear, and then picture it bordered by 1500 miles of balsamic forests, which extend backward from the lake to distances that overreach States and provinces. Travellers accustomed to frequent transcontinental journeys look longingly forward in the summer to the time when they shall be passing the great lake, either to the northward or southward, certain that the daylight hours will be pleasant and that the night-time will be cool. Cleanliness—perhaps I should say tidiness—is everywhere the characteristic of Superior. Its famed and stately walls of rock delve straight downward into it and rise sheer above it without giving nature the slightest chance to make a litter of rocks or dirt at their feet. While other rocky shores of other waters stand apart or merely wet their toes in the fluid, these monsters wade in neck-deep, and only expose their heads in the sunlight, fathoms—sometimes 200 fathoms—from the bottom. Terrible prison walls these become to shipwrecked drowning mariners, for they extend in reaches sometimes 25 miles long without offering a finger-hold for self-rescue. Tourists who have seen the Pictured Rocks will understand this feature of the lake's boundaries.

Again, Superior's waters lend themselves to the most exquisite effects, to the most opulent coloring, by their surroundings and in themselves. Those extravagant chromatic surprises in nature which cause the Western people to rave over the charms of their most beautiful resort, Mackinac, are at the command of all who visit Lake Superior at any point around the spectacular sea. A thousand lovelier Mackinacs are there. The same charms, the same mysterious colorings, the same gorgeous effects, illuminate the view from the coal-docks of Duluth, the cottages at Marquette, the wharves of Port Arthur, the decks of the steamers that cruise among the Apostle Islands, or the canoes of tourists or half-breeds who fling their fly-lines or haul their nets in the lonesome caves and neglected harbors where nature's is the only other presence. To begin with, the Lake Superior water is always green where it is comparatively shallow. If you are observant, you will notice that it is green in your pitcher, green in your washbowl, and green in your shaving-mug wherever you put up on the shores. It is not a repellent green; it is the green of the pea-vine, of thinned chartreuse— the lively, beautiful green of a thick cake of pure ice.

Everywhere, then, the edge of the water is of this beautiful emerald hue, showing its color against the pink sand, against the brown and red rocks, against the dark green forests. At a distance it insensibly deepens and changes into blue, but by such degrees that the indigo of the greatest depth is approached through slight changes beyond the first sky-color to the turquoise, and from that to the deeper hues. With every change in

NAKED INDIANS IN MONTREAL.

the atmosphere the views change. A strong sun will lave great fields of the water with a flood of salmon-colored light; and a brilliant moon, which at times silvers a wide swath upon the surface, will yet, under other conditions, tinge the water with a blush of pink.

Fit and true it was for Longfellow to fix in Lake Superior the mysterious climax of his legend of Hiawatha. The lake has impressed itself deeply upon whatever of religion is felt by the Indians upon its borders—and those of all the Algonquin family, whose tribes reach from the Rocky Mountains to the coast of Maine. Every here and there, upon the rocks which the Chippewas treat as altars, or in the swift currents that race between them, the red men offer gifts to the spirits which they fancy are domiciled there. As far as I have been able to comprehend their favorite legend of that Minnebajou (or Nana-bejou) who seems to have been the creator and yet subordinate to God, it was in Superior that he sought his yet enduring rest after he had constructed the present earth in the waters that swallowed a former one. There are several of his homes in various parts of the lake. And well may Superior breed mysticism in the minds of savages, for it is given to startling tricks. The mirages that are seen upon it have bestowed upon it a peculiar and distinct fame. They are known to the people of the lake only as "reflections." I have heard many sailors describe the wonderful ones they have witnessed; I would give another journey out there to see one. Men have told me that they have seen Duluth when they were 185 miles away from it—upside down and in the sky, but distinctly Duluth. One sailor said that at one broad noonday he suddenly saw a beautiful pasture, replete with an apple-tree and a five-rail fence, shining green and cool before him, apparently close at hand. The effect the clear air produces by apparently magnifying objects seen upon the lake is most astonishing. To illustrate what I mean, let me tell what happened the very last time I saw the lake. I was on a tug-boat, and upon coming out of the cabin I saw ahead of me a tremendous white passenger steamship. The boats were approaching one another at right angles, and this new-comer loomed up like a leviathan among vessels, bigger than one of our new naval cruisers, high above the water as a house would look. I called attention to it, and a companion, familiar with the lake, replied,

"I wonder what boat it is; she's a whopping big one, isn't she?"

Something distracted my attention, and five minutes afterwards, when I looked at the approaching vessel again, she had passed the mysterious point at which she was most exaggerated in apparent size, and had become an ordinarily large lake steamer. But that was not the end of the trick. She began to dwindle and shrink, growing smaller and smaller in size, until the phenomenon became ridiculous. In time the elastic boat had become a very small passenger propeller, and I found myself wondering whether she would be discernible at all by the time we were abreast of her. But at that the optical frolic ceased. A small screw steamer of the third class was what she proved to be.

Lake Superior was once a great deal deeper lake than it is now. All along the Canadian shore any one may see the former coast levels that now form pebbly terraces hundreds of feet above the present water. At Duluth the beautiful Terrace Drive above the city lies along a former coast line that was 470 feet higher than the present level of the lake. Perhaps the most compact picture of the first dawn of Lake Superior upon

IN THE HARBOR AT DULUTH

the ken of white men, indirectly through their relations with the Indians, is drawn by Washington Irving in his *Astoria*.

"It was the fur trade," he says, "which gave early sustenance and vitality to the great Canadian provinces." As the valuable furs became more and more scarce near the settlements, the capital among which was Montreal, the Indians went farther west upon their hunting expeditions. "Every now and then a large body of Ottawas, Hurons, and other tribes who hunted the countries bordering on the Great Lakes would come down in a squadron of light canoes laden with beaver-skins and other spoils of their year's hunting. . . . Montreal would be alive with naked Indians running from shop to shop, bargaining for arms, kettles, knives, blankets, bright-colored cloths, and other articles of use or fancy, upon all which, says an old French writer, the merchants were sure to clear at least 200 per cent." Thus came into existence a new class, called *coureurs des bois*, or rangers of the woods. They were men who had originally gone abroad with the red men on hunting expeditions, but who saw how a point could be gained upon the merchants at home by going out among the Indians or meeting them in the forests, there to peddle necessaries and ornaments from well-stocked canoes in exchange for peltries. In their track went out the missionaries; for none but an Indian ever went farther than the traders in those days, and eventually the Hudson Bay men—a still later growth—crossed the continent in advance of the solitary and devout clergy. When we have considered these actors upon the scene, and have understood that the *coureurs des bois* came to live with the red men, and created a body of half-breeds who were destined to be both white and red in their affiliations and their neutral influence, we may imagine that we can see the vanguard of the host that in time reached Lake Superior.

The first white men to see the lake were *coureurs des bois*, it is safe to say, but the first recorded visits are mainly those of missionaries of the same stock that are to-day living adventurous and solitary lives in what is left of the wilderness, now shrinking closer and closer to the arctic regions. "The Soo" was first visited by the missionaries in 1641, and they honored the brother of their king by calling the rapids the "*Sault de Gaston*." Nineteen years afterwards Père Mesnard conquered the rapids with his canoe, and found himself out upon the great waters of Superior. That was in 1660, and what they then called the lake I have not learned; but in 1771, in a map published by the Jesuits, it is inscribed "*Lac Tracy, ou Supérieur*." In that map the neighboring lakes are named *Lac des Ilinois* and *Lac des Hurons*. In 1668 there arrived Père Marquette, that saintly man whose name lives anew in that of a progressive lake port, and whose memory is honored by every intelligent man in all that vast region. He was accompanied by Claude Dablou when, having brought his wasted body there to end his days, as he thought, in a brief attempt to spread the gospel, he landed at the place which he renamed *Sault Ste. Marie*, and founded there the first settlement in Michigan. Messrs. Chanart and d'Esprit (sieurs des Radison and des Groselliers) have left a record of their visit to the western end of the lake in 1661, six years before Père Allouez and a company of traders reached there, and eighteen years before Du Lhut arrived with a band of *coureurs des bois* to make the neighborhood of the city that bears his altered name his place of residence for several years. After these, by a great stride over the slow-making pages of history, we come to find the great Hudson Bay

Company, and its rival the Northwest Company of fur-traders, conducting a systematized business on the north shore of the lake; while in time the American Fur Company, under John Jacob Astor's management, copied the methods of those corporations on the south side. Trading-posts grew into fortified places, trails spread into roads, and settlements around mission houses developed into villages. Then, two hundred years after its discovery, Lake Superior stood still for many years —for nearly forty years—so that its present history, solid and certain in its promises as it is, resembles the record of a mushroom.

The date of the last enlargement of the lock of the Sault Ste. Marie Canal is the date upon which to base all computations of the age of the present lake traffic and its consequences. That lock was enlarged and newly opened in 1881. Marquette, "the Queen City of Lake Superior," is an old place of former industry, but it is a mere baby in its present enterprise. Superior dates from 1852 "on paper," but from 1881 in fact, while Duluth is only a few years older. Port Arthur, the principal Canadian port, owes itself to the Canadian Pacific Railway, now about seven or eight years of age, and many of the cities of the future are not yet discovered, while of great resorts that are to be, like Munising and Nepigon, only those two are known, and they are known only to the most enterprising sportsmen.

The men of the Lake Superior region will in time form a new conglomerate, if I may use a geologist's term. The sailors of the great unsalted sea are a very nautical-looking lot of men—as spare of flesh, as bronzed and leather-skinned, as if they were from Maine; but the surprising thing about them, so far as I may trust my observation, is that they all obtained their training on the lakes. I did not find one who had ever seen the ocean, and I thought I detected among them a tone of contempt whenever they spoke of the genuine sea, as if they were of the opinion that the Atlantic is a sort of juvenile campus for playing at sailoring, whereas it requires grown men to battle with the lakes.

Along-shore one meets with a queer hodgepodge of men. On the United States side the Scandinavians are very numerous. They are highly spoken of by the Americans. They are bankers and merchants there, as well as laborers and household servants. They have spread themselves over all parts of the new field with wonderful assimilative capacity. They are a sturdy, shrewd, thrifty, and ambitious people, as a rule. They make the strangest mess of speaking English at first, and we may expect a new touch in dialect literature when writers who understand them begin to treat of them. Yet they are sufficiently important to render a knowledge of their native tongue very advantageous to Americans, and I found the general passenger agent of a great railroad in the lake region assiduously studying Swedish. There are many Welshmen in that country, but I only heard of them in the mining regions. For the rest, the people are American, with all which that implies; that is to say, some have an American tree with roots two centuries old, and some carry naturalization papers.

Over on the half-deserted Canadian side the rulers of Canada—who are the Scotch first and the English second—are conspicuous in the towns, settlements, and heavier industries. But the hunting and fishing are still so good that the red Chippewayan servants of the Hudson Bay Company still patrol the streams in canoes and traverse the winter snow fields with sledges dragged by "huskies," those ill-used Eskimo dogs whose fare is said to be "one part fish and nine parts clubbing." Gaunt

THE MISSIONARY

and tireless prospectors, axe in hand and pack on back, walk northward among the rocks, far ahead of civilization. Hudson Bay factories are yet the stations, as the waterways are yet the only roads, once you get beyond the rails of the transcontinental road skirting the very edge of the lake.

The lake and a vast region around it is a sportsman's paradise, and a treasury of wealth for those who deal in the products of the wilderness—furs, fish, and lumber. At little Port Arthur alone the figures of the fishing industry for the market are astonishing. In 1888 the fishermen there caught 500,000 pounds of white-fish, 360,000 pounds of lake trout, 48,000 pounds of sturgeon, 90,000 pounds of pickerel, and 30,000 pounds of other fish, or more than a million pounds in all. They did this with an investment of $3800 in boats and $10,000 in gill and pound nets. This yield nearly all went to a Chicago packing company, and it is in the main Chicago and Cleveland capital that is controlling the lake's fisheries. The white-fish is, in the opinion of most *gourmets*, the most delicious fish known to Americans. The lake trout are mere food. I am told that they are rather related to the char than to the salmon. They are peculiar to our inland waters. They average five to ten pounds in weight, and yet grow to weigh 120 pounds; but whatever their weight be, it is a mere pressure of hard dry flesh, calculated only to appease hunger.

But I find that on both shores of the lake there is a growing feeling that, in spite of the millions of "fry" the Fish Commission dumps into that and the other lakes, the vast reservoirs of delicious food are being ruined by the same policy and the same methods that make our lumbermen the chief criminals of the continent. Men who have spent years on the lakes solemnly assert that not only are the annual yields growing smaller and smaller, but that the sizes of the fish caught are growing less and less. Worse yet, they assert that illicit practices, or those which should be made illicit, result in the catching and destruction of millions of fish which are too small to market. I do not believe that any man of leisure could find a more benevolent or worthy cause in which to enlist than in that of a crusade against the use of small-meshed nets in Lake Superior. I will not, on my present knowledge, say that the planting of fish fry is a waste of time and energy, but it certainly is regarded by many as ineffectual in the present crisis. Government had better direct its energy to that ounce of net-cutting that is better than a ton of fry.

At present there are trout a-plenty in the streams that flow into the great lake through the beautiful forests which clothe that enormous tract, in which, south of Superior alone, there are said to be between 500 and 600 little lakes. Exactly like it, from the sportsman's point of view, is the region north of the lake, where the land looks, upon a detailed map, like a great sponge, all glistening with water, so crowded is its surface with lakes and streams. In the north are caribou, and all the animals that the fur-traders of the Hudson Bay Company value. South of the lake there are no animals larger than deer, but deer are abundant, and bear are still numerous. In the fishing season a man may feast on trout, black bass, pickerel, muskallonge, partridge, venison, and rabbit; and he may, if he has the soul of a true sportsman, revel in the magnetic, wholesome qualities of the air, and in the opulent and exquisite beauties of the woods. For good sport, however, let him avoid the famous places. There are half a dozen streams near the celebrated Nepigon that are better than they have been for years, while on the south side it is better to go to quiet regions, like Munising or the streams near the Ontonagon, than to whip the more noted waterways. There is a railroad, the Duluth, South Shore, and Atlantic, which dissects this entire region from point to point

THE LOCK AT "THE SOO"

of the lake along its southern coast. The best sport is found south of the railroad rather than between it and the lake. For deer and fowl and fish one can scarcely go amiss along that railway.

Duluth in Minnesota, and Superior in Wisconsin, the two leading ports and lake-side cities of the "great unsalted sea," lie side by side at the western end or head of Lake Superior.

The city of Marquette, on Iron Bay, in the centre of

the most picturesque part of the south shore, gets importance as a shipping port for ore and lumber, but it occupies the most beautiful site and is the most beautiful town, as seen from the water, of all those that have grown up on the lake. It has a large and busy trading district on the sandy shore of the lake, but the finer residence districts surmount a high bluff which half encircles the town. Ridge Street, 200 feet above the lake, may easily become one of the finest avenues in America, and already it numbers among its appointments some of the most artistic and costly houses in the Lake Superior region. With its drives and neighboring forests, its fishing-streams, and the beauties and pleasures offered by the lake, Marquette would naturally rank as a summer resort, but the addition of Presque Isle Park will, when the park is developed, raise it to the first rank among the idling-places in the West. This park covers a bold promontory formed of enormous piles of stone like the Pictured Rocks, which are themselves not far away. The water has eaten several caves into the foot of the sheer wall of forest-capped rock, and into one of these a boat may be rowed. The park is best seen when approached from the lake. The deep pellucid waters in the shadow of its walls form a famous fishing-field.

The greatest commercial activity around the lake is due to the mining. On the north shore gold has been found in the Port Arthur district. The quartz-bearing rock has been followed and the land pre-empted along several veins, but there has been no systematic mining. Silver has been very profitably and extensively mined, the famous Silver Islet Mine having yielded $3,250,000 worth of the metal. There are very many other mines in the district, many of which have proved failures, and a few of which are prosperous, while still others give promise of good futures.

TROUT - FISHING

But, either owing to the greater enterprise and capital of the Americans or to the more valuable and widely diffused metalliferous deposits, it is on the south side that most of the notable mining is found. The names "Calumet and Hecla," "Gogebic," and "Marquette," distinguishing great mines or districts, are doubtless of world-wide fame. There are seventy-three iron mines on the Marquette range, and their output for 1890 was more than four millions of tons. Open-pit mining is largely followed in this district. In the region between Ishpeming and Negaunee are a few gold mines. The richest of these is stopped by litigation, but one profitable mine is being worked. The great copper region of Keweenaw peninsula—a broad, long area of land thrust out of Michigan into the middle of the lake—abounds with copper in the form of conglomerates, or mineral mixed with rock. The census report upon the district declares that 117,800,000 pounds of this mineral yielded 87,445,000 pounds of ingot, showing the percentage of copper to be 74.24. In the census year, 1890, the amount of rock crushed was 2,137,653 tons, and this yielded 86,604,283 pounds of ingot copper. Silver is said to be found in the copper region. The famous Gogebic iron region, or range, marks the western limit of Michigan's 150-mile-wide mineral section, from which, exclusive of gold, copper, and silver, between five millions and eight millions of tons of ore is annually sent away. The logging or lumbering industry, especially on the southern and western ends of the lake, is a gigantic calling, but it is not within my ability to summarize its extent with figures.

All the commerce of Lake Superior that is sent to or from it must pass through the Sault Ste. Marie Canal, until the Canadians finish the parallel waterway, which they are building in order to be in all respects independent of us. Nature made the waters of Superior to flow into Huron by means of the St. Marie River, but in doing so they drop to Huron's level, which is somewhat lower than that of the king of lakes. They make eighteen feet of the descent suddenly by the rapids which give to the artificial waterway built to avoid them the name of the Sault Ste. Marie Canal. "Soo" and "Soo Saint Mary," or "Susan Mary," as it is often called, are Western forms the words take. Commercially speaking, this canal added Superior to the great lake system or route, connected it directly with the Atlantic and the world at large, and shortened very greatly the railroad carriage of ore and grain to the East, and of coal and general merchandise to the far West. The canal accommodates an amount of traffic which for years has been greater than that of the Suez Canal. In 1886 the freighting through the great African canal amounted to a gross tonnage of 8,183,313 tons; but it has decreased, if I am not mistaken; while the tonnage that passed "the Soo" in 1890 was 9,041,313. It is interesting to note that of this sum the proportion of freight carried by Canadian vessels was only 6 per cent. in 1888, and 4 per cent. in 1889. It is also worth while to note that of the 9,000,000 tons floated through the canal in 1890, about 4,500,000 were east-bound, and 2,600,000 were west-bound.

But the canal is inefficient; wofully so in the opinion of the extra-energetic shippers at the Lake Superior ports, who assert that its inability to pass the largest vessels fully laden operates to the advantage of their great rival, Chicago. The depth of water in the canal in 1890 ran from fourteen feet and nine inches to fifteen feet three inches, and during the first half of 1891 it varied between thirteen feet and ten inches and fourteen feet five inches. Such vessels as are now being

ORE DOCKS AT MARQUETTE, THE LARGEST IN THE WORLD

added to the lake service draw sixteen and a half feet, and in view of the present depth of water in the canal it will be seen that they lose several hundreds of tons a trip by carrying only partial loads. The Government is awake to the situation, and the new lock which it is now building, at a cost of more than four millions of dollars, will be 100 feet in width, 21 feet deep, and 1200 feet long.

The fact that the canal does more business in seven months than the Suez Canal effects in a year does not give so clear an idea of its importance as is gained from the consequences of a slight accident to the lock year before last. This necessitated closing the canal temporarily, but it cost the men and companies who use the canal a loss of about one million dollars. There were at that time 183 vessels waiting to pass out of Superior, and nearly as many going in the other direction.

The worst brake on the wheels of the great commerce that strains towards development on the lake is not the "Soo" canal. That will soon be as large as it needs to be. The trouble lies in the inadequacy of the canals far to the eastward—the Welland and Lachine canals. Instead of furthering the ambition of the West, they hold it at the throat and choke it. Until they are enlarged, or belittled by larger canals, the lake commerce with Europe will continue to be greatly limited. It is true that the whaleback steamer *Wetmore* went to Europe from Superior with a load of grain, but had she been the least bit longer she could not have gone through the Welland Canal, around Niagara, and she had to dodge the St. Lawrence canals by shooting the rapids of that river. Were she to return to Superior she would have to be unriveted and pulled through the canal in two parts. Thus it was that the steamships of the Canadian Pacific Company plying on the larger lakes were brought from the Clyde.

It was a valuable experiment, that with the *Wetmore*. It demonstrated the pluck of the far Western navigators and merchants, and it accentuated the demand of the people of the entire Northwest for a practicable water route to the Atlantic. The people of the region around the Great Lakes are chafing and fretting under the chains that bind and hinder them. They demand

LIGHT-HOUSE AT MARQUETTE

the means of reaching the Atlantic either by the St. Lawrence or the Hudson, and they will not be satisfied with less than "twenty feet of water from Duluth to the sea." That is the battle-cry of a people with the will and persistence to achieve whatever they determine upon. They will not long be put off. They are full of the spirit of the present revolution by which we Americans are to recover our prestige on the sea. Thus added force is found in a vast reach of new water-front, which will send upon the oceans of the world not merely men, but ships that hail from the heart of the continent.

The aim of **the students of the situation is not only to** keep **beyond the constant** reduction of railroad rates, but also to secure the carrying **of** the products of Asia. They argue that the Pacific Ocean currents naturally set towards Puget Sound, and put San Francisco out of the natural course of shipping, and also that the Puget Sound coast is six hundred miles nearer the north Atlantic ports than is San Francisco.

There are two sides **to** the contention **for** improved internal waterways, and I propose to present both sides, because both together reflect the influences that are building up the new **West, and show** the strides **that have been** made towards the perfection of transportation **facilities.**

There **is a** conspicuous railroad man in **the West who** argues that water rates will cease to influence rail transportation when the development of railroading reaches the near point towards which it is hastening. For a time in 1891 the freight rate from Chicago to New York was seventeen cents a hundred pounds, and he says that this forced the lake rate down to one and a quarter cents. He argues that when the railroads make a twelve-cent rate, as they must in time, the boats on the lakes **will** not be able to earn their operating expenses.

The form of railroad progress which attracts **every one's** attention **is that** which is marked by the improvement of **the palace cars** through the introduction of baths, barber-shops, and libraries. But the progress which affects earning capacity, and which is constantly lessening the cost of railroad service **to** the public, is that which comes **of the** improvement of the road-beds of the trunk lines by the creation of direct lines from point to point, the reduction or abolition of grades, the easing of curves, the increase in the weight of the rails, and the enlargement of locomotive power and car capacity. The outgo and the income of the railway business are found by considering the train mile and the ton mile as the units or bases of calculation. The cost of running a train a mile is the unit of expense. The amount obtained per ton per mile is the unit of income. The difference between the two is the profit. The resistance, which must be reduced to a minimum, is the law of gravity. But for that a child might draw a train of cars with a piece of twine. But, as the Western railroad man remarked, "the law of gravity is like the poor, whom we have always with us, and the railroad men must see that it is not further weighted by steep grades, weak rails, sharp curves, and indirect routes. Originally railroads were laid on the surface of the ground; now they must find a level, and keep to it, as water does."

The modern railroad must also avoid all possibility of obstruction that can be avoided; and we see in the sunken track of the New York Central Railroad in New York city an example of the lengths to which the best railroads must go to obtain guaranteed freedom from obstruction. With the same aim, this railroad is to pass through Rochester upon an elevated structure, and through Buffalo on a sunken track. Yet, in spite of these strides towards the perfection of railroading, with a consequent lessening of rates, President Depew does not predict the destruction of lake traffic. On the contrary, he says that it will always be carried on. The railroads themselves find it of service; and all those trunk lines which have lake ports on their routes now either own steamers or have made contracts with steamship lines. President Depew says that although his railroad company once opposed the canals, he lives at peace with them, his argument being that the lake boats bring to Buffalo more business than the canals can handle, and the surplus goes to the railroads. Moreover, the

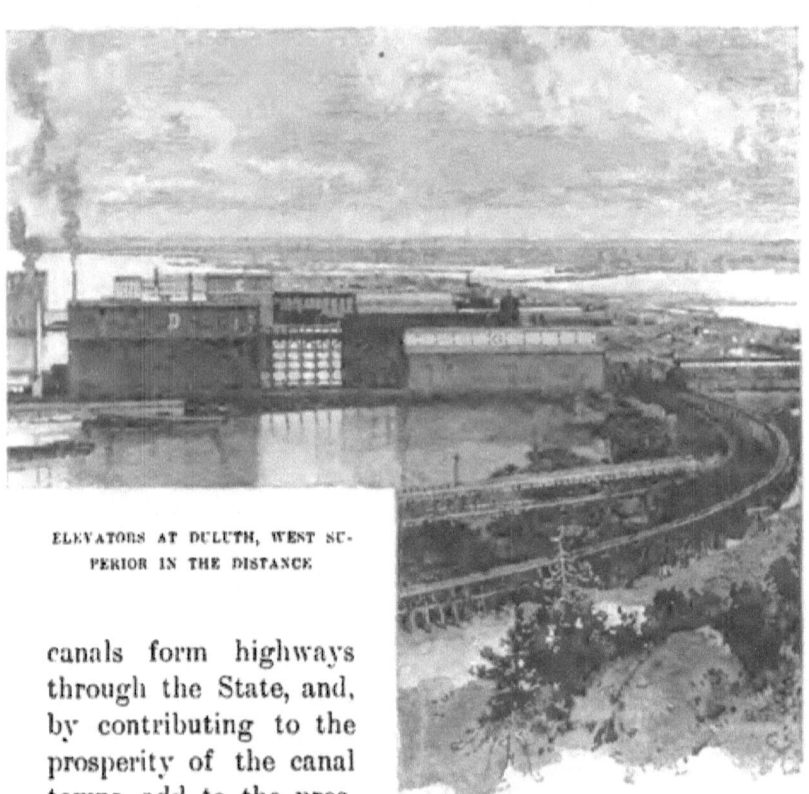

ELEVATORS AT DULUTH, WEST SUPERIOR IN THE DISTANCE

canals form highways through the State, and, by contributing to the prosperity of the canal towns, add to the prosperity of the railroads. Mr. Depew adds, nevertheless, that the canals are no longer formidable competitors with the railroads, as they once were. In the old days a canal-boat carried as much grain as a train of twenty 10-ton cars; but now a train may consist of fifty cars, each one carrying 25 tons. The locomotives have grown from a weight of 30 tons to a weight of 90 or 100 tons, the cars have tripled their capacity, the rails that weighed 56 pounds per yard have been replaced by 80 or 90 pound tracks; and with all these improvements has come a reduction of 50 per cent. in freight rates in the time that he has been interested in railroads.

The leading men of the lake ports admit all this; in fact, they make out a strong case for the railroads in order to emphasize the need of facilities by which those great regulators of transportation rates, the freight-boats, may meet the new conditions. Those who have made the arguments for the various lake ports show that whereas in 1868 the rail rate on grain from Chicago to New York was 42.6 cents a bushel, it was 14 cents in 1885. The water rate in that period fell from 25 cents a bushel to 4.55 cents. It has kept between 25 per cent. and 67 per cent. lower than the rail rate. The value of the waterways to the public is illustrated in a startling way by making use of the Government records of the Sault Ste. Marie Canal traffic for 1889. There passed through that canal 7,516,022 tons, carried an average distance of 790.4 miles, at 0.145 cents a ton a mile. The railroads would have charged 0.976 cents, and the business would have cost the public fifty millions of dollars more if the railroads had transacted it than was charged by the boatmen.

In pressing upon the attention of the country the value of a twenty-foot waterway to the sea, the lake-port business men assert that not only did the Lake Superior traffic through the Sault Ste. Marie Canal amount to three-quarters of a million tons more in 1889 than passed the Suez Canal, but the lake business which was transacted in the Detroit River was more than 36,000,000 tons of freight, or 10,000,000 tons more than the total tonnage of all ocean and gulf ports of the entire coast line of the United States. In view of that fact they ask what would be the growth of this business if, instead of taking this freight out of 3000-ton ships to put it into 200-ton canal-boats, it could go directly and without change of vessels to the sea. As to the expense of the improvements that are asked for, Mr. S. A.

Thompson, of the Chamber of Commerce of Duluth, asserts that in all time the Federal government has expended upon all the lakes above Niagara Falls only $28,038,590, so that the saving at the Sault Ste. Marie Canal, on the business of one lake, amounted to a return of $1 85 to the people for every dollar the government spent upon the lakes.

From the stand-point of the people of the lake ports we have not been either as liberal or as long-sighted as the Canadians, who have a well-defined system of waterways, completed by canals wherever navigation is hindered by nature. They are building a canal around the St. Mary's Falls, and when it is finished their system will be complete. It will only need enlargement to make it serve the requirements of the near future, but, even as it is, it will serve, in case of war, for the intro-

LOADING A WHALEBACK BARGE

duction of gunboats and torpedo-boats by way of the St. Lawrence into those lakes on which we are prevented by treaty from maintaining a squadron. We have upon the lakes only the old wooden sloop of war *Michigan*.

and can put no other war vessels there in case of danger, unless we have the time to build them at some lake port. England, on the other hand, has fifty gunboats and other war vessels of sufficiently light draught to pass through the canals into the lakes.

It is not necessary to weigh the various plans which are offered for a national highway from Duluth to the sea. One looks towards the deepening of the canal between Oswego and Syracuse, New York, and of the canal between Syracuse and the Hudson River. Another plan leaves New York City out of consideration, and proposes direct communication between Duluth and the ocean, or the world at large, by means of a duplication of the Canadian canal system on the American border. Both these plans necessitate the building of an American canal around Niagara Falls.

The provision of twenty feet of water in the new Sault Ste. Marie lock, now undergoing construction, will make possible the employment of vessels carrying 6000 to 8000 tons, in place of the present largest-sized lake boats, which cannot carry their complement of 3000 tons. Such carriers, it is said, can cut down the present cost of water transportation fully 50 per cent. and leave a profit for the ship-owners. In view of the enormous field awaiting development in the Northwest, and in view of the steady lowering of railway rates, the ardor with which the people of the lake ports urge the creation of an American twenty-foot water system, at least as far east as Oswego, does not seem unreasonable.

Upon the 1500 miles of the lake's shore there are living now less than 150,000 persons, and these are mainly in bustling cities like Duluth, Superior, and Marquette, in industrial colonies like Calumet and Red Jacket, or in struggling little ports like Fort William and Port

Arthur. Even there the wilderness and primeval conditions are face to face with the robust civilization which is shouldering its way as capital is accustomed to do rather than as natural growth usually asserts itself. Not that

A WHALEBACK DESCENDING THE RAPIDS OF THE ST. LAWRENCE

it is not a wholly natural growth which we find at all points on the lake shore, for it is all in response to the inexorable laws of supply and demand. Yet the communities there have sprung into being far apart from well-settled regions in answer to these laws.

Thus it happens that to-day one may ride in an electric street car to the starting-point for a short walk to a trout stream, or one may take the steam railroad, and in an hour alight at a forest station, breakfasting there, but enjoying for luncheon a cut of the deer or a dish of the trout or the partridge which he has killed for the purpose. It is, so to say, a region wherein the wholesale fisherman with his steamboat disturbs the red man who is spearing a fish for supper, where the wolf blinks in the glare of the electric lamp, and where the patent stump-puller and the beaver work side by side.

The strange condition is most startlingly illustrated

by a recent occurrence in Michigan, in the same region. Close to a watering resort which is crowded in summer by persons from all over the West, some men were cutting timber in the winter. Two brothers were among them. One hit himself with an axe, cutting open an artery in his leg. The other hurried away for surgical help. When the messenger returned, nothing but the bones of his brother were left. Wolves, attracted by the scent of his blood, had eaten him up.

It is thus that there is forced upon the comprehension the practical newness of this giant fresh-water sea, which geologists would have us believe is millions of years old, and which even history mentions in detailing the exploits of men who died in the seventeenth century. But with the youth of this new civilization have come the vigor and enterprise needed to develop industries and to rear cities of which all the people of all the States, new and old, may well feel proud.

IV

CAPITALS OF THE NORTHWEST

Just as the Atlantic cities were surprised when Chicago distanced all but two of them in population, and challenged all of them by her enterprise, so will they be astonished again and from another quarter, if they refuse to study the forces that are operating to build up new capitals in the West. In another ten years there will be another claim of a million population, and the counting of heads will not make nonsense of it. The new and wonderful assumption of metropolitan importance will be that of **the twin cities** of the wheat region —Minneapolis and St. Paul. They may not be joined under one name and government—opinions differ about that—but all agree that they will jointly possess a million of population. The last census credited Minneapolis with 164,700 population, and St. Paul with 133,000, or, jointly, 297,000. At the time of the preceding census (1880) the **two** cities included about 88,000 souls. At that rate of increase they will boast in 1900 a population of 976,000 and more. But they insisted in the summer of 1891 that they possessed more than 350,000 joint population, and that the million mark will be reached before the **next** census is taken.

Why should men make **such a** prophecy; **or rather,** why have these two towns already gathered 350,000 inhabitants within their limits? We must repeat the study that we made at Chicago. That city we found to be the metropolis of the entire interior between the Rockies and the Alleghanies, but an analysis of its sources of supply and field of distribution showed it to be more particularly the capital of the corn lands. We saw how rich were the returns from agriculture in a country by no means fully developed, and of such vast extent as to be roughly spoken of as a territory one thousand miles square. Chicago is its trading centre, and, from a beginning upon borrowed capital, that city has ceased to borrow, and has begun to amass wealth, to lend money, and to supply its tributary country with manufactured goods in such quantities that it already ranks third in the list of manufacturing centres. In the great amount of rich land that is yet to be redeemed, and in the wide leeway that exists for improved and economical farming, we are able to clearly see a noble, a splendid future for Chicago.

But in St. Paul and Minneapolis we reach the pulse of another region — the wheat lands of America. I understand that in a sense these cities are tributary to Chicago, and that in the same sense their tributary region has in some measure been included in that of Chicago, but the line that is being drawn between the two centres is growing heavier and broader every year. In the possession of home manufactures lies the ability to trade economically and to save a profit, and just as we have seen Chicago emancipate herself from the bondage of Eastern capital through manufactures, so we shall find that the twin cities of Minnesota are setting up for themselves as independent traders. The country they aim to monopolize in trade is far smaller than the corn region, but it is extraordinarily more fertile and profitable to the farmer.

Close to their doors lies the famous Red River Valley, which is by some students of such comparative values declared to be the third agricultural region, in point of fertility, in the world, there being one Asiatic and one African valley in the foreground beyond it. This Red River Valley takes in many counties of Minnesota and the most easterly counties of the two Dakotas. It is prairie land of black soil that once formed the bed or deposit of an ancient sea. It reaches up into Canada, beyond Winnipeg, and is a great deal richer at its southern end in the United States than in Canada. This region pours its wealth of grain (or a great part of it) into Minnesota's twin cities, there to exchange it for merchandise. Other cereals and cattle are produced beyond this valley in the new States, and the valley itself returns the same commodities along with its wonderful output of wheat. In the extra fruitful year just closed—wonderful for its crops and for the world-wide demand for breadstuffs from this country—the predictions that were based upon the results of the sale of the crops seemed fabulous. For instance, it was boasted that the farmers of the Northwest would make sufficient profits to pay off all their mortgages this year.

This boast was not disputed by any of the leaders in trade and transportation with whom I talked, but I gathered from what they said that though the farmers are as well off as this statement implies, the majority will not remove the mortgages, but will be more likely to expend their profits in betterments, in extending their farms, and in redeeming unworkable tracts in their present holdings. This roseate view ends at the valley, so far as the Dakotas are concerned. The Dakotan farmers have suffered some bad seasons, and are not so near the end of their debts.

It is in the Red River Valley that one may hear of a farmer whose profits last season were close to $30,000; it is there that men bought farms of great extent, expecting to pay for them in an indefinite number of years, and then paid for them out of the first crop raised upon the land, the wonderful yield of last year. Such is the region at the very doors of the twin cities of the Northwest. If Ceres left the Old World when the worship of her went out of fashion, it must have been to the valley of the Red River that she came. But if mythology is suggested at all by a study of this marvellous region, it is in the recollection of the fabled river Pactolus, wherein King Midas washed off his power to turn into gold all that he touched. That may well have been the stream that once swelled from side to side of this valley, for, truly, its sediment retains little less than Midas's power.

We realize the majesty of agriculture as we never did before when we learn that in Minnesota and the two Dakotas the wheat crop alone was worth one hundred and twenty millions of dollars last year. Figure for yourself the estimated yield of one hundred and fifty millions of bushels selling at from 75 cents to 82 cents a bushel. In what story of fairyland is there an account of a literal field of gold to equal that?

There are 8,832,000 acres in the valley, and less than a quarter of it was in crop last year. If every acre were put into wheat, there would be no market for the wheat; it would become a drug. As it is, of the portion that is under cultivation, only about three-quarters were in wheat, and the yield of last year was estimated at from 30,000,000 to 37,000,000 bushels, grown at the average proportion of 20 bushels to the acre. The wheat crop of the valley, therefore, fetched about $27,000,000. At 80 cents a bushel, each acre returned $16, at a cost of from $6 to $8. Good land has produced 31 bushels to the acre, and good land farmed scientifically has yielded as high as 47 bushels to the acre, but **20 bushels is the** average product, **and the** farmer is entitled to a profit of $10 an acre, with prices **as** they were last year. Matured farming will raise the yield to an average of 25 bushels an acre.

The Dakotas, **which** are also tributary **to the** twin cities of Minnesota, **do** not offer opportunities for theatrical or bonanza farming. Three-quarters of their territory **is** not wheat land. **More** wheat can be raised upon the six counties in the Red **River** Valley than in all the rest of both Dakotas. The Dakotas will **produce** grain, cattle, horses, sheep, and, **in** ten or fifteen counties, **corn.** These States offer a good reward **for** honest toil, and that would be very high praise of them **were it not that** the opulent valley on their eastern edge forces a comparison between **itself** and them.

The end of one great source of revenue to the region is in sight. That is the lumber production. The trees are all counted; the number of feet in each forest is entered in the lumbermen's books. **In** Michigan, all that is of value in the forests will ha**ve** disappeared in five years, it is said; in Wisconsin, 15 years will end the **industry**; in Minnesota the supply will last 15 to 20 years—a **pin point** in the dial of time. Already capitalists are turning their mercenary **gaze** towards the majestic and virgin forests of the new State of Washington. Montana **is** believed to be another and a greater Pennsylvania, rich in coals, in oil, and in varied metalliferous ores. These resources and the timber and farm products **of the** Washington of a later day are all waited for to swell the importance of the twin cities, for it is not now seen that there is a likelihood that any other very great cities will be developed in the Northwest except upon the Pacific coast. There will be populous district centres, of course, and already three such places are robust, lively towns, but the men who now seem possessed of the most shrewdness and foresight in the Northwest do not believe that the shifting horizon of time is hiding any competitor for the position now occupied by the Minnesotan capitals of trade.

Having noted the resources of the Northwest, possible as well as present, if the reader will turn to his map he will see that the great railway lines of that upper corner of our country present the appearance of a rude diagram of a human hand with the fingers outspread. St. Paul and Minneapolis are at the wrist, and control the fingers that reach out and grasp the trade of the entire Northwest. This double metropolis and this trade have their own ports at Duluth and Superior, while at the twin cities of Minnesota the navigation of the Mississippi begins or ends.

Minnesota's twin capitals in the wheat region are not yet one corporate body, and there are many shrewd citizens of one and the other who assert that they will not unite while the present generation of leading men remains dominant. There has been too keen a rivalry, and each town is too jealous of the other, for union to be possible, they say, until the boys of to-day become the successors of their fathers. Therefore, if for no other reason than that, the cities must be studied separately in this article. They are ten miles apart, but the statement of that fact is very misleading, because they lie side by side like two globules of quicksilver, with a few little drops of the liquid between them. Whoever journeys from one to the other fails to perceive why they may not at any moment shake together into one great glittering mass, with no other division than is created by their separate charters, and no joint border line except that which will require a surveyor's kit to determine.

To begin with Minneapolis, the larger of the two cities, let me introduce the town as that one which seems to me the pleasantest and most nearly perfect place for residence of all the cities I have seen in my country. St. Paul is in the main so nearly like Minneapolis that a slight sense of injustice comes with the writing of these words; yet St. Paul lacks some of the qualities which Minneapolis possesses, and the words must stand. Both cities have arisen amid park-like surroundings, both rejoice in the possession of the lovely Mississippi (for it is a most beautiful river up there), and both are largely made up of dwelling districts which fascinate the very soul of a man from the solid, pent-up cities of the East. But in one minor respect Minneapolis triumphs in being thoroughly consistent with her ruling trait, and at that particular point St. Paul fails. That is to say, Minneapolis is ample and broad and roomy in her business district, while St. Paul is in that quarter narrow, compact, huddled, and old-fashioned.

I cannot force Minneapolis to challenge the world to produce her equal, but it seems to me that it will be difficult to find another influential trading and manufacturing city that is so peculiarly a city of homes. It was after riding over mile after mile of her streets and boulevards, and noting the thousands of separated cottages, each in its little garden, that I came to a locality wherein there were a few — a very few — apartment-houses. They were not what we in New York call "tenement-houses," for the poor seemed superior to the evil, and lived in their own tiny boxes; they were flat-houses for families few in members and indolent by nature. These were so very few that the array of dwellings took on an extraordinary importance. Try, then, to fancy the pleasure and surprise with which I read in the city directory, afterwards, a statement that the city's

164,738 inhabitants occupy 32,026 dwellings. If there were 921 more dwellings there would be one to every five persons, which is to say one to each family.

As these houses are in the main owned by their tenants, the city presents a spectacle of communal dignity, self-respect, and comfort that distinguishes it even in a greater degree than Philadelphia is distinguished among our Atlantic seaboard cities. It was pleasing to hear in the neighboring city of St. Paul, where nearly the same conditions prevail, that when the citizens go to the City Hall to ask for places in the public service, or to demand their rights, they often draw themselves up to their full height and say, "I am a tax-payer," by way of preface to a statement of their wishes. The man who carries that pride in his breast, and who goes home to a house whose every side offers windows to the light and air, should be as nearly a complete and perfect individual as it is possible for the more or less artificial conditions of life in a city to produce. Of such individuals is the great bulk of the population of Minneapolis composed.

It is interesting to know that the motive power of the city has always been pure Yankee. The settlers were in a large degree from Maine, and it is wittily said that they followed the pine westward, until at this point its final appearance east of the Rockies was noted. Here the Maine men rested and set up their saw-mills, using St. Anthony's Falls to move their saws. It was a lumber town during most of its history. The great wheat-handling industry is a new thing by comparison. In 1871 only two car loads of wheat were received here; in 1887 the Great Western Railroad brought thirty-three million bushels to the flouring-mills. It is thought that the summit of fifty millions of bushels will be reached in the twelve months which include the period of receipt of **the** enormous crop of last year. But if **newness** is to be **considered,** what shall be thought of **the city itself?** Its **first** settler marched in a procession through the **streets** last summer. He marked **out** his claim, **in what** is now the thick **of the city, on June 10, 1849.**

A **bird's-eye view of the city is** like such **a** view of one of those parks in the East which rich men dot with **villas.** It is a plain of luxuriant foliage, broken **here** and there by house **roofs.** Trees border the streets and avenues, and deck even the most ordinary building plots. The houses are simply little frame cottages, with here and there a street of pretentious and large residences, also of **wood,** and with **a** few noble **mansions** built of masonry **for the** leading capitalists of the place. **But the same** admirable features distinguish all classes **of homes:** nearly all stand apart one from another; the great majority exhibit that variety which is begotten of individual and independent taste; **and** all are found in districts sacred to domesticity and peace, where a taboo has been put against liquor-selling, and **where** traders of every sort seem loath to jar the homelike tone by intruding **their** storehouses. It is such a town as the average American housewife would plan, and nowhere do the women, both matrons and maids, seem better placed or more thoroughly **the** mistresses of their position in modern city life than as one sees them upon those bowery streets, passing the rows of pretty cottage homes, beneath trees, amid flowers, and beside the rosy children who play fearlessly in the well-ordered streets. We shall see in another article that Minneapolis enjoys a peculiar and admirable liquor license law. Suffice it here **to say that** the dram shops are **confined** to what may **be called** the business districts, where the stores and factories **are** clustered together—a fit arrangement for a woman's capital, an earthly paradise of homes, a settlement of landlords and landladies.

The people of the city have little knowledge of the impression that it makes upon those who compare it with other towns, but they are aware of one effect, while ignorant of the cause; that is, they know theirs is what is called an eminently "healthy" town. The death rate is lower and the sum of the general health is greater (or was in 1890) than in any one of the twenty-six largest cities in the United States.

We have seen in the past, and shall see again and again, that the Western people have not only an extraordinary fondness for public parks, but a positive genius in arranging them. Minneapolis found half a dozen pellucid lakes within her borders, and these she has converted, or is converting, into exceedingly pretty little parks. They are not grand, like the pleasure-grounds which border the majestic lake at Chicago, but they are dainty and bewitching. To go by way of Hennepin Boulevard, for instance, where the electric cars run upon a central strip of grass between parallel driveways, and to see the use that three of these jewel-like lakes have been put to, is to enjoy a treat that will not be easily obliterated from the memory by any crowding of lovelier scenes. First, along the short route is Loring Park, so called in honor of the designer of the city's park system. It is a reproduction in miniature of the most lovely features of New York's Central Park. Then is seen a parkway of woodland beside a great sheet of crystal called Lake Calhoun. In another five minutes Lake Harriet is reached, and there bursts into view a great bowl of mirror-like water, embowered in trees and surrounded by the grove which nature planted there. At one point on the edge of the lake is a graceful casino building, and anchored out in the lake is a floating band-stand, hooded by a sounding-board, under which, on summer afternoons, a band is stationed to play for the people. Light, graceful row-boats are plentiful, and for hire at a low price; the strand is fallowed, and fringed with rows of settees; the scene is distant less than half an hour's journey from the heart of the city, at a passage rate of five cents, and there is no warning or rule against trespass anywhere in the beautiful grounds, which the people maintain, own, and are wisely permitted to enjoy. The parks I have mentioned form but so many links in a glorious chain which compasses two sides of the city, that includes five parks and ten parkways, and that ends

"Where the Falls of Minnehaha
. . . .
Laugh and leap into the valley,"

at what is called Minnehaha Park. The winding verdant route from park to park is a continuous, well-ordered, and beautiful series of parkways, eighteen miles in length.

Many Western cities and towns are interested spectators of the work of removing the railroad grade crossings in Minneapolis, for, although the city has grown to its present size with the railroads entering and crossing it on a level with its streets, the people have not hesitated to force a solution of the problem that confronts Chicago, and, indeed, most of the great cities out West. It was five years ago that the City Council of Minneapolis ordered the City Engineer to prepare plans for the execution of the work. This done, the City Attorney began proceedings in court to determine why the railroads should not lower their tracks. It was fortunate for Minneapolis that the head of one great railroad system was Mr. James J. Hill, whose consideration for the public and eminent shrewdness led him to fall in with the city's project; indeed, he did more—he aided the effort with suggestions that were calculated to lighten and improve the work. Another corporation, using tracks parallel with those of Mr. Hill's Great Northern and Manitoba railroads, fought the authorities; but in time its receiver, who was an officer of the courts, was ordered to accept a compromise between its own and the city's demands, and the great and notable work that is called "The Fourth Avenue Improvement" was agreed upon and begun.

The New York reader will understand the situation clearly if he understands that the case is precisely as if trains were running upon our own Fourth Avenue across all the numbered streets and on a level with them. The danger, slaughter, and discomfort of the citizens of Minneapolis may be imagined; the obstacles against the free and fast handling of the trains need not be described. It is safe to say that if our own New York Central Railroad could return to the old street-level service, and could have back the cost of its sunken track with interest, it would not make the change. It could not if it would; it would not be able to transact its present volume of business under the old conditions. Yet everywhere the railroads fight the efforts towards self-protection that are made by our municipal governments, and out West no subject is now being studied with deeper interest and earnestness than that of the methods by which the railroads can be forced to raise or lower their tracks within the boundaries of cities. Minneapolis's mode of handling the problem is an especially valuable study, because, unlike her twin sister St. Paul, but like most other Western towns, the act of self-defence and self-preservation was postponed until the city had grown great, and the task had become formidable. Along this **Fourth Avenue in Minneapolis run** not merely **the trains of two trunk lines, but on** that narrow avenue in the heart of **the city is** handled the enormous traffic between the **twin cities** and **their** chief summer resort, Lake Minnetonka.

The arrangement **that Minneapolis made was a simple one**—for the city. **It decided that** the railroads were to build the entire viaduct, approaches, bridges, masonry walls, **excavations, and all, and that** the **city** was to stand **between the railroads** and those property-holders who might claim damages for injuries growing out of the improvement. **It** happens that most of **the** buildings whose owners claim damages were old **rattletraps, and** the highest claim for injury is one for $12,000. **In most cases** abutting property was benefited. The city therefore comes out of the affair at very slight cost, while the railroads have been **put to an enormous** outlay. The city establishes all lines and levels arbitrarily, giving the railroads **a** clear space of twenty feet above the tracks. The railroads **must** keep the **bridges** and approaches in perpetual **repair.** One notable concession by the city is the surrender of a street crossing. At Sixth Street, where the work of lowering the tracks begins, and where there are many **rails** and switches, the crossing is closed, and the city gives up its rights in **the street at that** point. Beyond this street, as the city continues **to grow, the people will pay for and build the** bridges that may be **needed.**

The passenger tracks are sunk ten feet at the lowest point; the freight tracks four or five feet. There are six bridges. They vary in length between 100 feet and 500 feet, as the tracks **spread** out beyond the starting-point. One bridge is 100 feet in width, but the others permit of only a thirty-six-foot roadway and a twenty-eight-foot sidewalk. The bridges are approached by a gradual raising of the street levels, and the effort has been to keep the incline of these approaches and bridges within four feet in the hundred, but in one case the grade is a foot greater. The railroads have done excellent work, and the viaduct, with its stone walls and fine freight-houses and passenger station, presents an appearance that is almost ornamental. It will be of interest to those officials of other cities who are meditating work of this kind to know that the railroads which use the new viaduct are greatly pleased with the reform, and would not go back to the old conditions. Moreover, a railroad whose tracks run upon the street level on the other side of the river, in Minneapolis, has made an informal proposition to sink its tracks, if the city will bear a moderate share of the cost. When I was in Minneapolis, in September, the City Engineer had been sent for to testify in behalf of Columbus, Ohio, in a suit growing out of a similar progressive movement in that city; and it is certain that when the whole country knows what Minneapolis has done, her people will be flattered by the attention their enterprise will attract.

To give an idea of the extent of the principal industries of the Flour City, let me say, roughly, that her saw-mills cut 343,000,000 feet of lumber, 162,000,000 shingles, and half as many laths in 1890; that in the upper Mississippi region four billion feet of forest trees were cut down, and that the city received 45,000,000 bushels of wheat, and shipped 12,000,000 bushels away. The city has an assessed valuation of $138,000,000, and nine millions of dollars of banking capital. It boasts a public-school system that is everywhere held to be unexcelled, and a function of the government is the maintenance of a library of 47,000 volumes, housed in a noble building, and having two circulating branches connected with it. In the extent of its circulation of books this library is the seventh in the country. The city is 53 square miles in extent, possesses many miles of granite and cedar block paving, 1500 acres of parks, 49 public schools, and a sufficient number of churches to render the town conspicuous on their account. It carries a bonded debt of seven millions of dollars. Its hotels and theatres are very good, and among its notable office buildings one is the best that I have seen anywhere in the country; that is the Northwestern Guaranty Loan Company's building, an office building that towers above the town, and is peculiar in the fact that its owners surrender more valuable space for the admission of light and air than is given up in any other building of the sort that I have ever seen. At least half the interior is open and roofed with glass, while the offices, which have store fronts of plate-glass, are reached by glass-paved galleries. The building cost a million and a half of dollars, and contains, besides the offices, a Turkish bath, roof promenade and concert garden, a restaurant in the top story, private dining-rooms, ladies' rooms, a billiard-room, a barber's shop, a law library—free to the tenants—locked boxes in fire-proof vaults for all the tenants, cigar and news stands, and a battery of six or eight elevators. The population of the building is 1500 souls.

But the growth of the manufacturing interests is the most important feature of the development of this city. It is rapidly fitting itself to become the main source of supplies for the most opulent farming region in America, and among recent additions to the list of her industries may be noted a knitting-mill; a piano factory; a linen mill; tub and pail, carriage, and macaroni factories; a manufactory for wood-carving machinery, in connection with a street-car construction company; a smelter for reducing Montana silver ore; a stove-works; and additions to the facilities for making boots and shoes, woollens, lumber, and flour. The difference in freight rates enables the manufacturers of the twin cities to hold their own against Chicago in the trade with the Northwest, and they have their drummers in all the cities and villages of the region.

The street-car service in Minneapolis is as nearly perfect as that of any city. Within a year, when the extensions now planned are completed, it will be without a rival in this respect. The electrical system which depends on overhead trolleys is in use there. The cars are elegant and spacious, and run upon 70 miles of tracks. They are propelled at a speed of 8 miles an hour in the city, and at 12 to 14 miles outside. They have run to Lake Harriet in 20 minutes, which is at the rate of 15 miles an hour, and they have made the journey to St. Paul (10½ miles), including ordinary stops, in 32 minutes. At the end of this year the system will embrace 130 miles of tracks.

To the mind that is accustomed to judge of Eastern towns, St. Paul is more city-like than Minneapolis. Its business portion, originally laid out by French Canadians with narrow ideas, is such a compact mass of solid blocks and little streets that it might almost have been a ward of Boston transplanted in the West. One sees the same conditions in Portland, Oregon, but they are rare in the West, where the fashion is to plan for plenty of elbow-room. If we were to imagine the twin cities personified, we would liken Minneapolis to a vigorous rustic beauty in short skirts; while St. Paul we would describe as a fashionable marriageable urban miss, a trifle stunted and lacking color and plumpness, but with more style and worldly grace than her sister. As to which should have the preference, there will be views as differing as the two towns. There are those who prefer hard-paved, bustling streets, faced by ranks of city stores, pressed shoulder against shoulder, with here and there huge, massive office towers breathing crowds in and out to choke the narrow sidewalks; **and there are** others **who like** better the big, roomy avenues of Minneapolis, **even** though **they hang like too** loose clothes against uneven, shrinking lines of fashionless houses. They said to me in Minneapolis that they realized the fact **that** their city was only growing. **If I would call around in** a few years, they said, I would **find all the walls** up and plastered, and the furniture in, and the place cosey. In St. Paul it is just the other way; it looks finished. Its motto is, "While we journey through life, let us live by the way;" but the Minneapolis spirit is that of the man who, to celebrate his marriage, built a four-story house, and lived in the front and back **basement**, saying to his wife, "**We** will lath and plaster the rest, one room at a **time, as the family increases.**" For my part, I find it so hard to **decide** between them that I am not **going to try.** Every **man** to his taste, say I. Minneapolis **has** done wondrous work **for the** future; St. Paul has done more for present improvement than **any other** city in the West that I have **seen**.

The twins are very like or very unlike in other respects, according as you look at them. Minneapolis is very American and St. **Paul** is very mixed in population. She has 65 per cent. of foreigners in her make-up, and the Teutons predominate—in the form of Norwegians, Swedes, Danes, and Germans. There are Irish and Poles, French Canadians and Bohemians, there also, and the Irish and Irish Americans are conspicuous in the government. St. Paul is usually Democratic; Minneapolis is generally Republican.

In eight years St. Paul has made tremendous strides away **from** the habits and methods of civic childhood. Its officials say that more has been done to establish its character as a finished city than will ever need to be done in the future. Its expenditures of energy and money have been remarkable. It has levelled its hills, filled its marshes, and modernized all its conveniences. The water-works, which were the property of individuals, now belong to the people, and serve two hundred miles of mains with pure wholesome water brought from a group of lakes ten miles north of the city. A noted firm of water-works builders has declared that it would willingly assume the city debt in return for the profits of this branch of the public service. No city in the country is better drained than it is by its new sewer system. It had a mile and a half of improved streets and three stone sidewalks eight years ago, and to-day it possesses forty-five miles of finished streets and fifty miles of stone sidewalks. Two costly bridges have been put across the Mississippi, and an important bridge has been rebuilt. In no city in the West is the railroad grade-crossing bugaboo more nearly exorcised. Only one notable crossing of that sort endangers the people's lives and limbs. The public buildings of the city are admirable, and were built at moderate cost, and without sixpence worth of scandal. The restricted saloon system is enforced there, and the residence districts are kept sacred to home influences and surroundings. The streets are thoroughly policed, and the fire department is practically new, and appointed with the most modern appliances. The street-car service consists of nearly one hundred miles of electric railway, and fifteen miles of cable road. There are no horse-cars in use in the city; they would be too slow for such a town. St. Paul is rich in costly and great office buildings. There are a dozen such, any and all of which would ornament any city in the country.

The population in 1890 was 133,000, to which sum

12,000 should, in fairness, have been added. By actual count the city contains 26,942 houses. For its districts of dwellings it deserves the same praise that has been bestowed upon Minneapolis, and only in that slightly modified degree that comes from its having a stronger admixture of foreigners among its citizens and a larger number of houses squeezed close together in its older business district. Once away from that region, trees, grass, and flowers greet the visitor's eyes wherever he rides and walks. On both sides of the river the phalanxes of pretty little homes rise among the trees. There are villas for the well-to-do and tiny frame dwellings for the poor, but the latter are not mere boxes; they are distinguished by prettiness of designing and individuality of taste, and they stand apart from one another so that the people who live in them may get the light and air that are as needful to men and women as to plants and trees. The well-to-do cottagers have gathered in two or three very pretty clusters that were once suburban villages. A notable peculiarity of their houses is their possession of extra large double plate windows. Sometimes a house will have only one such extra large sheet of glass; others will have several. Whether these are backed by drapings of snow-white lace or are filled with plants and flowers, the effect is very beautiful. I was told that in Minneapolis any man may buy himself a home for from $1800 to $2000, selecting a site within easy walking distance of the City Hall. I am sure the same rule applies to St. Paul, which maintains forty-two building and loan societies, with an invested capital of $3,064,310. The stock in these societies used to mature in eight or eight and a half years, but the term has lengthened to nine and a half or ten years, owing to the competition in the loaning of money. The annual growth of the city by the addition of new buildings has long kept up to a remarkable standard. For two years —1888 and 1889—St. Paul was fourth in the list of American cities in this respect. Last year (1890) the permits issued were for 3174 buildings, planned to cost nine and a half millions of dollars. But the wonder ceases after the relation of the twin cities to the rich Northwest is understood. St. Paul is the meeting-point of twenty-eight railroads that crisscross that region. That city will contribute its full share to the million population nine years hence.

With uncalled-for modesty St. Paul's leading men apologize for the absence of a royal series of great parks, and assert that they have now designed and begun work upon such a system. They admit that they possess thirty-two little squares for children and adult pleasure-seekers, and say that the city and its environs are so park-like that the need of great public lungs has not been pressing. The apology should be graciously accepted. It reconciles us with what we know of ordinary humanity in our comparatively torpid Eastern cities to find them weak in one respect. But St. Paul does not lack all elegance and ornament of the highest and most modern order. In one boulevard, called Summit Avenue, it possesses one of the noblest thoroughfares, and the nucleus of one of the most impressive collections of great mansions, in the country. Euclid Avenue, Cleveland, has long ceased to lead the rich residence streets of the nation, for Chicago has more than one finer street of the same character, and so has Buffalo, and so has New York since Riverside Avenue has begun to build up. None of these has the beauty which the Hudson River and its Palisades lend to Riverside Avenue, but a good second to it is Summit Avenue, St. Paul. From its mansions, rising upon a tall bluff, the panorama of a great and beautiful country-side is commanded.

It may be necessary to say to the untravelled Eastern reader that the appointments—and the tenants—of these mansions reflect the best modern attainments of civilization as it has been studied in the capitals of the world. One, at least, among these houses has not its superior in New York, so far as its size, its beauty, and the character of its surroundings are concerned. In its appointments it will be found that the elegances and art triumphs of far more than Christendom have been levied upon to testify to a taste that at no point oversteps the limits cultivation has established. On the walls a number of the masterpieces of the Barbizon school hang side by side with the best efforts of Munkacsy, Diaz, Tadema, Detaille, Meissonier, and many other masters. Barye bronzes have their places in various rooms, and the literature of two continents, freshened by the constant arrival of the best periodicals, is ready at hand and well marked by use. I betray no secret of the Northwestern country in saying that such is the home of Mr. James J. Hill, the president of the Great Northern Railroad, and, despite its ornaments, it is maintained quite as a home, and solely for comfort. It is but one of several mansions in these two far Western cities. They are as representative as the palaces of Fifth Avenue, evidencing nothing of taste that is not shared and reflected in the other homes of those communities.

Once again we come to the heart of any such study of a city's capacity for growth in importance and wealth. St. Paul in 1881 manufactured $15,466,000 worth of goods with which to trade with the Northwest; in 1890 the sum had grown to $61,270,000, an increase of 300 per cent. in nine years. The city is the dairy centre of the Northwest. It has made great investments in the manufacture of clothing, boots and shoes, fine furniture, wagons, carriages, farm implements, lager-beer, cigars, fur garments, portable houses for settlers, dressed stone, boilers, bridges, and the products of large stock-yards. To a less yet considerable extent it manufactures crackers, candy, flour, bedding, foundry-work, sashes and blinds, harness, brass goods, barrels, brooms, and brushes. Its banks have a capital of $10,000,000; its jobbing trade amounted to $122,000,000 in 1890; it did a business in cattle of every sort to the extent of a million head in the same year. It has fine hotels and opera-houses, a typically elaborate Western school system, and is in all respects a healthy, vigorous, well-governed city.

These are the trading centres of the Northwest. But there is another pair of twins, which are the lake ports and shipping-points for that region. They are the baby twins—Duluth in Minnesota, and Superior in Wisconsin. Though they are in different States, they are closer to one another than the cities from which we have just taken our leave. Though babies, these cities feel the impulses of giants. Their growth in so short a time and to such proportions as they possess calls attention to the radical changes that are taking place in the outlets for the produce of the Northwestern States. Not many years ago the grain trade centred at Chicago and Milwaukee, but the demands for economy that led to the development of the present railway systems in Minnesota and the Dakotas have altered the course of the wheat movement, and have led to the building up of the twin ports at the head of Lake Superior. These two ports now receive a large proportion of this business, and have already distanced Chicago in the competition. It is easy to understand why this should be the case. Duluth and Superior are nearer to a large section of the Northwest than either Chicago or Milwaukee, and yet they are not any farther from the Eastern lake ports at the other end of the water route for freight. A glance at the map will reveal the fact that the distance to Buffalo is no greater from the head of Lake Superior than from the head of Lake Michigan, where Chicago is situated. This advantage in position is evident to any one, but the men of Duluth and Superior claim a greater advantage. By drawing circles ten miles apart, with themselves as a centre, they demonstrate the possession of a larger tributary territory than can be shown for Chicago by the same means.

It is humorously said to be as much as one's life is worth to describe or to weigh the comparative merits of these rival inland ports. This was the case not long ago with regard to St. Paul and Minneapolis, but last autumn one of those cities joined in an effort to secure the holding of a convention in the rival town. It will be long before any such amiable and generous self-sacrifice will be shown at the head of Lake Superior. The situation there is intensified by the fact that Duluth was for a long while practically alone in the glorious possession of the advantages that a seat at the head of the great lake brings with it. Suddenly, within five years, a little village a stone's-throw off, on the other side of the St. Louis River, which separates Wisconsin and Minnesota, sprung from the stagnation of a chrysalis condition into a stirring town that began to establish town limits calculated to leave Duluth a very small second fiddle to make music with if the plans were carried out. And when the census-taker came along in 1890, Duluth's 35,000 inhabitants read that, in round numbers, the impudent baby next door had grown nearly half as big as itself. Worse yet, the ambition of Superior is seen to expand with ten times the ratio of its increasing growth, and if the student of the situation reads the official literature of the younger lake port, he will discover that the records of its achievements are arranged to show how it is gaining upon Chicago—upon Chicago, mark you, as if it considered its nearest neighbor, twice its size, too unimportant for consideration! From the point of view of Duluth, fancy such a situation!

There are those who hold that geographical and topographical advantages account for the sudden rise of Superior alongside of Duluth. There are others who account for it on the ground that Duluth was too confident of her position, and adopted a short-sighted policy, which, while it was maintained, gave an opportunity for the development of the rival port. It is not worth while here to discuss these moot points. In considering the relation of the head of internal water navigation to the country beyond it, both cities have a common value. Whether both keep pace in growth with the development of the vast and opulent territory behind them, or whether one becomes ten times greater than its neighbor, the point of interest will still be the head of the lake—the point of contact of lake and rail transportation. Both must gain all that will belong to either solely from their location, which, it seems clear, must become the seat of a great population and of extraordinary activity.

Since this will not be gainsaid, it will be the simplest course to state the arguments and claims of both these rival ports at once. Their leaders assert that whatever of wealth and importance has come to Buffalo, Cleveland, Detroit, and Chicago is due to their advantages as distributing and receiving points for the tonnage of the lake commerce. This it is which has drawn the railways to these cities, and the result of the reciprocal influence of the railway and harbor transactions has been a degree of importance dependent upon the extent and productiveness of the territory tributary to each of these lake ports.

The reader can scarcely be expected, in so rapid a study and upon so brief a trial of results as the history of the head cities of Lake Superior permits, to accept the utmost that has been urged for the future of these cities. Yet the argument is interesting. "If," says the secretary of the Chamber of Commerce of one of these twin lake ports—"if a straight line be drawn uniting Chicago with these ports, and this line be bisected by another beginning near the eastern end of Lake Superior and extending southwestwardly to the Gulf of California, near the 27th parallel, this latter line will represent with geometrical exactness all points that are equidistant from Chicago and the Superior ports." All places north of the line will be in the legitimately tributary territory of the newer ports; and all the railroads in this vast region, which is more than half of the United States, are now pointing towards the newer ports as their ultimate objective, it is said, because they aim to secure the shortest route to deep-water navigation. For an example of the point sought to be made, it is stated that Denver, Colorado, is 125 miles nearer the head of Lake Superior than Chicago. A connection between the new ports and the Union Pacific Railroad at that point is an early probability. The Great Northern System is almost completed to the Pacific coast; and the Canadian Pacific Railroad, which has leased a railway from Duluth to the other end of Lake Superior, is about to dip down from a point in Manitoba to join its new property at Duluth.

These cities have already been sought by eight railways, operating 17,514 miles of roadways. They connect with St. Paul and Minneapolis and their feeders; they bring in the produce of the Dakotas, Montana, Idaho, and Washington; they connect the twin ports with the lumber and mineral regions of Minnesota and along both the north and south shores of Lake Superior. Either projected or in course of construction are other railway lines which will lead into Iowa and the corn belt, and up into the wheat fields of Manitoba and the Canadian Northwest.

These lake-side twins themselves realize some of the benefits of that cheap water transportation which is reached through them. For instance, the coal they use comes to them at the same rate that Chicago gets its coal, and twenty-five cents a ton cheaper than it can be supplied to Minneapolis and St. Paul. And seven months in the year the jobbers in the twin lake ports get Eastern goods at the same cost for transportation that is paid by the Chicago jobbers. Thus they have another advantage over Minneapolis and St. Paul. The flour-milling industry is one that is rapidly growing in the twin lake ports. Duluth has one mill that turns out 2500 barrels a day, and will double its capacity next summer. It has another and smaller mill in operation, and three others are projected. Duluth may yet become a very considerable milling point. The reason is that to ship the flour east from Minneapolis *via* the twin ports (250 miles nearer than Chicago) costs the millers of the Flour City ten cents a barrel—the price of the barrel. This the Duluth miller saves. The big Minneapolis mills are eking out their insufficient water-power with steam, and in the cost of fuel the lake port mills again have the advantage.

At the extreme western end of Lake Superior, where it terminates in a bay called St. Louis, the ancient terrace that marks a prehistoric coast line of the lake rises 500 feet in air beside the narrow beach of the modern level. A river breaks this terrace, and flows into the bay, and across that river and bay is a flat reach of once swampy lowland. The bluff is on the north side of the sharp end of the lake, and the houses of Duluth are perched upon this highland as if they might be a flock of goats grazing upon the face of a steep hill. Thus the land meets the water, and men have built upon it at Quebec, at Bar Harbor, and at minor places in Cornwall and Devonshire, England; but the habit in nature and in man is rare. Naturally Duluth has grown most in length along the foot of the bluff, and the distance from one sparsely built end to the other broken and scattering termination is about six miles. A large fraction of this length is compactly built along streets that climb the hill-side. To prevent a division of the town by a rocky tongue that once ran out into the lake, the formidable barrier has been cut away as if it were so much dirt, and the main street runs by the spot as if the rocks never had been. To get teams and people up the steepest part of the hill-side—and perhaps to demonstrate anew the inability of nature to daunt the Duluth man—an inclined plane, like a massive slanting elevated railroad, is now building, and will soon be ready for the hauling of every sort of load, whether of wagons, cars, men, or beasts, up to the top of the hill. Out there, among those indomitable people, it is impossible to resist the feeling that if the moon were to take a fixed position permanently just over the city, they would annex it, and find a way to travel quickly to and from it.

In this little place, that is only ten years beyond its village condition, if you ascend the hill you will find that a sort of terrace, an ancient beach on top of it, has been laid out as a grand parkway or boulevard twelve miles long, 200 feet wide, and half encircling the city. Unfortunately the larger trees of the one-time forest up there had been all cut down when this was laid out, but there is plenty of slender timber there for future adornment, and, better yet, there are several madcap streams that break upon the edge of the bluff, and would splatter down upon the town had they not been controlled and covered. However, up on the beautiful Terrace Drive they are novel and beautiful ornaments, and ingenious taste and skill have made the most of them. From that terrace one can comprehend and cannot help but admire the city. In the thickly built heart of it are many costly modern buildings of great size, and some of exceeding beauty. The Spalding Hotel, the Lyceum Theatre, the Masonic Temple, the Chamber of Commerce, a great school-house, and a railway depot are among these. Beyond them and the town lies the harbor made by nature in a way man could hardly improve upon, except as he has cut channels to it. A great barrier juts out from Minnesota opposite another from Wisconsin, so that both form a great and perfect breakwater. There are two harbors behind this bar, first Superior and then St. Louis bays. Each city has cut a shipway through the barrier, and each has built upon its side of both harbors an impressive array of wharves, elevators, and coal, grain, and ore bins and dumps. The smoke of the enterprise of both places comes together in one cloud over both, typifying either the united purpose to achieve success in both towns, or the sure result of all efforts to bring about any sort of union there, according as you are poetic or practical.

Across the narrow end of the lake, on the low flat of which I have spoken, you see Superior, Wisconsin, the rival of Duluth, made up of old Superior, West Superior, and South Superior. It is remarkable only for its enterprise. It is not almost unique in the character of its site, as is Duluth, nor is it pretty or picturesque. It has elbow-room on a great level plateau, and it may spread and wax great without the let or hinderance of rocks or bluffs. Its plans, as its chief historian remarks, "are on a magnificent scale. Many miles of streets and broad avenues have been paved for present needs, and a grand boulevard and park system anticipate the growth of population by some years." Then the historian goes on to speak highly of its sewage system, its electric street motors, the fact that it is one of the best-lighted cities in the land; all of which the facts justify. A liberal policy has led to the establishment of a number of important manufacturing establishments in the younger city, and with each such addition the spirits and hopes of the community have risen higher and higher. From the *Evening Telegram's* hand-book upon the subject I gather the following notes of the possessions and achievements of the city: It has an area of 37 square miles, an assessed valuation of $23,000,000, a bonded indebtedness of about $900,000, and a tax list of half a million dollars. It has ten banks, with a million of capital for all, and surpluses and undivided profits amounting to $216,286. Its coal receipts by boat in 1890 were 1,045,000 tons; its oil receipts, 115,000 barrels. Its wheat shipments the same year amounted to 9,318,336 bushels; and in round figures it shipped 1,100,000 bushels of corn, 1,300,000 bushels of barley, and the same number of barrels of flour. It has a coal-dock capacity of 1,500,000 tons, a grain-elevator capacity of eight and a half million bushels, five hotels, twenty churches, seven railways, a street railway, the American Steel Barge Works (where the famous "whaleback" lake steamers are made), the West Superior Iron and Steel Works, a carriage factory, a number of saw-mills, a furniture factory, and many other smaller works of various kinds. The population of what there was of Superior in 1884 was 2000; in 1889 it was 10,000; in 1890 it was 11,983. Now it is variously estimated at from 15,000 to 20,000.

Duluth is said to owe its foundation to the grasping demands of those who held the land on the Wisconsin side of the bay when Jay Cooke sought a terminal point there for the Northern Pacific Railroad. Now Superior has arisen simultaneously with the nearing completion of the Great Northern Railroad, which transfers its grain and other east-bound freight from its cars to its great steamers at Superior.

Duluth had 3500 population in 1880, and 33,115 in 1890, according to the census. This is now called 40,000. Duluth receives less coal than Superior, but ships more grain. Her grain shipments in 1890, and from January 1, 1891, to December 15, 1891, were as follows:

		1890.	1891.
Flour	bbls.	2,589,384	3,220,273
Wheat	bush.	14,090,826	34,492,438
Corn	"	1,453,089	302,503
Oats	"	1,616,635	365,872
Barley	"	130,931	156,497
Flaxseed	"	51,440	308,363
Rye	"	....	20,472

Duluth has extensive iron-works, iron and steel and steel and tin works, a wood-turning mill, lumber mills, a furniture factory, and a woollen mill. The city's grain-elevators have a combined capacity of 21,250,000 bushels. The lumber interest in Duluth is enormous, but the city itself is one of the great consumers of the supply, and receives far more than it ships away. The place is well paved, drained, and lighted, and has a good water supply system. As it would say of itself, it is "a hustler"—but so, also, is Superior.

The key-note and countersign of life in these cities is the word "hustle." We have caught it in the East, but we use it humorously, just as we once used the Southern word "skedaddle," but out West the word hustle is not only a serious term, it is the most serious in the language. One day, as I sat in the lobby of one of the great hotels in the older pair of twin cities, I heard two old friends greeting one another with ardent expressions of friendship and delight. They had not met for a long while, and each asked about the other's Lizzie and Fannie and their respective little ones. All of a sudden I heard one say:

"Well, see you to-night, I suppose. I have got to go."

"Where have you got to go to?" the other inquired, plainly disappointed that the pleasant interview was not to be prolonged.

"Where?" the other echoed. "Why, to hustle, of course. I have lost ten minutes standing here talking to you. I'm going out to hustle."

The word always jars upon the ear of an Eastern man when it is seriously spoken, but it is preferable to that other expression once dominant in the West, but now all but abandoned. That was the word "rustle." The noun a "rustler" and the verb "to rustle" meant precisely what is conveyed by the newer terms a hustler and to hustle. At the first blush, as they say out West, rustle seems the better word. There is a hint of poetry in the suggestion of the sound of moving leaves upon the ground or of the silken dress of a lady moving rapidly. Moreover, that was what the word was intended to convey, the idea being that of a man who moves so rapidly that the dead leaves upon the earth rustled as he swept along. But in its origin it is a word of evil intent, for the cowboys invented it, and applied it to cattle-thieves, rustlers being the swift raiders who stole upon grazing cattle on the plains, and rustled off with as many head, or beasts, as they could get away with. Therefore rustle is the worse word of the two.

But to one who lives where neither word is in familiar use there is little choice, since the actual meaning of hustle is not far different from that of jostle. Both imply a serious and even brutal lack of consideration for other persons, who are elbowed and pushed out of the way by the hustler as rowdies are hustled along by the police.

Both Duluth and Superior are mainly dependent upon the lake system of navigation, and both complain that its limitations greatly retard their growth, and resist the growing demands of the shippers of the Northwest. In another article, upon Lake Superior, the situation in which these cities find themselves, and the need of prompt action by the Government, will receive attention.

V

THE DAKOTAS

In entering upon a study of the newly admitted States, and beginning with those of the Northwest, we are confronted by new scenes, new peoples, and new conditions, in which we shall find far fewer reminders of our Eastern life than greet us in some regions which we regard as quite foreign, as in old Canada, for instance. We are putting a new slide into the American magic-lantern. We are opening a new volume added to our own history, and we are to read of new characters moving amid surroundings quite as new; to them almost as new as to us.

Beginning with the Dakotas, we enter the vast plains country — monotonous, all but treeless, a blanket of brown grass almost as level as the mats of grass that the Pacific coast Indians plait. It is only a little wrinkled in the finishing—at the top edge and down in the southwest corner. On its surface the houses and the villages stand out in silhouette against a sky that bends down to touch the level sward. Here we find the western edge of the lands which the Scandinavians who have come among us prefer to their own countries. Here we come upon the yellow wheat-fields that turned their kernels into millions of golden dollars last year. Here, also, we see the more than half savage cattle whose every part and possession, except their breath, is converted into merchandise in Chicago. The hard-riding cowboys are here "turned loose," and the not less domesticated Indians in their blankets are cribbed in the national corrals. A great thirst would seem to overspread the Dakotas, for the lands are arid, while the people possess prohibitory liquor laws, and water that is poisoned with alkali.

In the Black Hills we prepare ourselves for Montana by a first glimpse of mining. In Montana, where the very first merchant's sign-board announced "pies, coffee, and pistols for sale," we now see the legend "licensed gambling saloon" staring at the tourists, who may walk into the hells more easily than they can into the stock exchanges of the East. In Montana we feel an atmosphere of speculation. Every store clerk hoards some shares in undeveloped mines for his nest-egg. It is natural that this should be. The stories of quick and great fortunes that daze the mind are supported by the presence of the millionaire heroes of each tale. Moreover, the very air of Montana is a stimulant, like champagne. Perhaps it gathers its magic from the earth, where the precious metals are strewn over the mountains, where sapphires, rubies, and garnets are spaded out of the earth like goober nuts in the South, and where men hunt for the diamonds which scientists say must be there.

Montana is a land of ready cash and high wages. Lumbermen and miners get as high as seven dollars a day, and the very street-sweepers get twice as much as politicians pay to broom-handlers in New York to keep in favor with the poor. Here we find wealth, polish, and refinement, noble dwellings, palatial hotels, and numerous circles of charming, cultivated folk. Their mistake has been to despise agriculture. They know this, and with them, to see an error is to repair it.

The mining camps and California-colored characteristics of the mountainous half of Montana spread over into Idaho, a baby giant born with a golden **spoon**. The cattle ranges and cowboy capitals **of Montana's** grass-clad hills are repeated upon **the** gigantic but virgin savannas of Wyoming. In Washington all is different again. The forests of Maine and of the region of the **Great Lakes are** here exaggerated, the verdure of **the East** reappears, **and** passes into semi-tropic and in**cessant** freshness and abundance. Here flowers bloom in **the** gardens at Christmas, small fruits threaten Cali**fornia's** prestige, and the aborigines are bow-legged, boating Indians who work like 'longshoremen. Cities with dozen-storied buildings start up like sudden thoughts, and everywhere is note of promise to make us belittle our Eastern growths that startled the older world.

With surprise we find the New England leadership missing. **Here is a** great corner of America where the list of the *Mayflower's* passengers is not folded into the family Bibles! The capitals of the older Northwest are dominated **by** the offspring of Puritans, **but** we must journey all across the Dakotas and Montana, among a **new race of** pioneers, to have New England recalled to **us again only** in Spokane and Tacoma—and but faintly **there. The** new Northwest is peopled by men who followed the Missouri and its tributaries from Kentucky, Indiana, Iowa, Arkansas, and Missouri. Others who are among them speak of themselves as from California and Utah, but they are of the same stock. Broadly speaking, they founded these new countries between the outbreak of the rebellion and the end of the reconstruction period in the Southern States. They are not like the thrifty, argumentative, and earnest New-Englander, or the phlegmatic Dutch and hard-headed English of the Middle **States.** These new Americans are tall, big-boned, stalwart folks, very self-assertive, very nervous, very quick in action, and quicker still in forming resolutions.

If it would be fair to treat of them in a sentence, it could be said that they act before they think, and when they think, it is mainly of themselves. Their European origin is so far behind them that they know nothing of it. Their grandfathers had forgotten it. They talk of Uter, Coloraydo, Illinoise, Missourer, Nevadder, Ioway, Arkansaw, and Wyóming. The last two names are by them pronounced more correctly than by us. In a word, they are distinctly, decidedly, pugnaciously, and absolutely American.

Because it is impossible to picture the novelty—to an Eastern reader—of life in the Northwest, and because it nevertheless must be suggested, let me tell only of four peculiar visitations that the new States experience —of four invasions which take place there every year. In May there come into the stock ranges of Montana shearers by the hundreds, in bands of ten or twenty. each led by a captain, who finds employment and makes contracts for the rest. These sheep-barbers are mainly Californians and New-Yorkers, and the California men are said to be the more skilful workers. To a layman, all seem marvellously dexterous, and at ten cents a head, many are able to earn $6 to $8 a day. They lose many days in travel, however, and may not average more than $5 on that account. Their season begins in California in February, and they work through Oregon, Washington, and Montana, to return to a second shearing on the Pacific coast in August. Some come mounted and some afoot, and some are shiftless and dissipated, but 'many are saving, and ambitious to earn herds of their own.

They come upon the Montanan hills ahead of another and far stranger procession—that of the cattle that are being driven across the country from Texas. This is a string of herds of Texas two-year-olds coming north at middle age to spend the remaining half of their lives fattening on the Montana bunch-grass, and then to end their careers in Chicago. The bands are called "trails," and follow one another about a day apart. With each trail ride the hardy and devil-may-care cowboys, led by a foreman, and followed by a horse-wrangler in charge of the relays of broncos. A cook, with a four-horse wagon-load of provisions, brings up each rear. Only a few miles are covered in a day, and the journey consumes many weeks. These are enlivened by storms, by panics among the cattle, by quarrels with settlers on guard at the streams and on their lands, by meals missed and nights spent amid mud and rain. That is as queer and picturesque a procession as one can easily imagine.

Then there is the early autumn hop-picking in the luxuriant fields of the Pacific coast in Washington. Down Puget Sound and along the rivers come the industrious canoe Indians of that region in their motley garb, and bent on making enough money in the hop-fields to see them through the rainy and idle winter. They are not like the Indians of story and of song, but are a squat-figured people, whose chests and arms are over-developed by exercise in the canoes, which take the place of the Indian ponies of the plains, as their rivers are substituted for the blazed or foot-worn trails of the East. To the hop-fields they come in their dugouts from as far north as British Columbia and Alaska. When all have made the journey, their canoes fret the strand, and the smoke of their camp fires touches the air with blue. Women and children accompany the men, all alike illuminating the green background of the hop-fields with their gay blankets and calicoes, themselves lending still other touches of color by means of their leather skins and jet hair. They leave a trail of silver behind them when they depart, but the hops they have picked represent still more of gold—a million last year; two millions the year before.

Again, a fourth set of invaders appears; this time in Dakota. These are not picturesque. They come not in boats or astride horses, but straggling or skulking along the highways, as the demoralized peasantry made their way to Paris during the French Revolution. These are the wheat-harvesters, who follow the golden grain all the way up from Texas, finding themselves in time for each more and more belated ripening in each more and more northerly State, until, in late autumn, they reach the Red River Valley, and at last end their strange pilgrimage in Manitoba. The hands and skill they bring to the dense wheat-fields of eastern North Dakota are most welcome there, and these harvest folk might easily occupy a high niche in sentimental and poetic literature, yet they don't. As a rule, they are not at all the sort of folk that the ladies of the wheat lands invite to their tea parties and sewing bees. On the contrary, far too many of them are vagabonds and fond of drink. In the Red River country the harvesters from the South are joined by lumbermen from Wisconsin and Minnesota, who find that great natural granary a fine field for turning honest pennies at lighter work than felling forests.

In area, the half-dozen new States in the Northwest are about the size of Alaska, and they are larger than France, Germany, Italy, and Holland combined. One of the States is greater than Great Britain and Ireland, and one county in that State is larger than New Hampshire, Massachusetts, and Connecticut. The population of those six States is about like that of little New Jersey, yet it is thought that at least half as many persons as are now in the entire country could maintain life in that corner of the nation. Three of the names the new States took are criticised. There are many persons in the Dakotas who now realize that a foolish mistake was made in the choice of the names North Dakota and South Dakota. Both fancied there was magic in the word Dakota, and wanted to possess it. By succeeding in that purpose they ridiculed the noble word, which means leagued or united.

To the traveller who crosses North Dakota in the thoroughly modern and luxurious easy-rolling trains of the Northern Pacific Railroad, the region east of the Missouri seems one dead-level reach of grass. It appears to be so level that one fancies if his eyesight were better he might stand anywhere in that greater part of the State and see Mexico in one direction and the north pole in the other. Everywhere the horizon and the grass meet in a monotonous repetition of unbroken circles. As a matter of fact, there is a slight slope upward from the Red River of the North at the eastern edge of the State, there is a decided valley south of Jamestown, and for fifty miles before the Missouri River is reached the land begins to slope slightly towards that stream. There are hills, too, called by the French the "Coteau du Missouri," and never yet rechristened, to mark the approach to the river. The country west of the Missouri is more attractive to the sight-seer, though far less so to the farmer. It looks like a sea arrested in a storm, with all its billows fixed immutably. It is partly a mass of softly rounded, grassy breasts; and beyond them, in the Bad Lands, the hills change to the form of waves that are ready to break upon a strand. Farther on, the change is into buttes, into peaked, columnar, detached hills. On the light snow that merely frosted this broken country last winter, when I crossed it twice, there seemed not a yard of the earth's surface that was not tracked with the foot-writing of wild animals and birds—that kitchen literature which the red men knew by heart—the signs of coyotes, jack-rabbits, prairie-chickens, deer, and I know not what else besides. It is a 350-mile journey to cross the State from east to west, a 210-mile trip to cross it from the north to the south.

It has been a one-crop State, and the figures that are given of its yield of that crop are not what they pretend to be, for four-fifths of the wheat is usually grown on the eastern edge, in the Red River Valley. In the rest of the State the crops have failed year after year, and even the grazing of stock, for which alone the critics of the State say it is fit, has been attended with some serious reverses. The most extravagant lying indulged in to boom the State has failed to alter nature —just as it failed in Canada, where it was followed by even greater hardship and disappointment. The lying on behalf of North Dakota took the form of applying the phenomenal figures of the rich Red River Valley to the whole State, quoting the earnings of Red River farms and the experiences of Red River settlers as applicable to all Dakota.

Having gone to Dakota because of the marvellous yield of wheat in the Red River Valley, the unfortunate settlers put all their holdings in wheat. It is customary in Dakota for people to say that these poor fellows bought their experience dearly, but they did not pay as much for it as the two Dakotas have paid for the carnival of lying that began the business. A succession of extraordinarily bad seasons followed, owing to lack of sufficient moisture to grow the grain. In one year there was not enough to sprout it. There were five years of dire misfortune, and they brought absolute ruin to all who had no means laid by. Many were ruined who had money, and thousands left the Territory, for it was a **Territory when the wholesale lying was at its height.**

The soil in the Red River Valley **is** a thick vegetable deposit, while that of the remaining nine-tenths of the State is of a mineral character, lime being a notable factor **in the composition. It** is very productive if water **can be got to it. In that case the** Red River country **would be no better than all the rest. And there** is the **rub. With** irrigation, North Dakota **will become a rich** farming **State.** Without it, the State has enjoyed one rich harvest in six years. The irrigation cannot be accomplished by means of any waters that are now on **the** surface of the State; it must be by means of wells, or by "bombs bursting in air," or by Australian alchemy. And yet it is **not** fair to the State to say that it can do nothing without **irrigation.** We shall see that the belief is **that its** worst misfortunes have come from its dependence upon a single crop, and that by diversified farming **the** wolves can **be kept** from **the** doors when **the wheat** crop fails.

Last **year** came **a** change of luck and a **year such as** North **Dakota** has not enjoyed in a long **while.** Between 50,000,000 and 55,000,000 bushels of wheat were harvested; and if the Red River Valley's yield **was** 35,000,000, it is apparent that the rest of the State must be credited with from 15,000,000 to 20,000,000 of bushels. Of corn, 300,000 **bushels were raised;** of oats, 10,000,000 bushels; **of cattle, a** million dollars' worth; and of hay and **potatoes, a very** great deal. This was **good** work for a population **of** 200,000 souls. It is estimated that the money product of the entire harvest **was sufficient** to pay off the indebtedness of the farmers, and **leave an** average of $250 to each farming family. At the beginning of 1892 it was prophesied that the farmers **would free** themselves of only those debts upon which they had been paying a high rate of interest, so as to be in a position to borrow at lower rates and to improve their farm buildings. They have been paying all the way from 12 to 24 per cent. a year for loans. They have also been obliged to give bonuses to the loaning agents at renewal times, getting $180, say, when they were charged with $200. These agents are terrible sharks, and there are crowds of them in the State, calling themselves real-estate and loan agents, getting money from the East, paying the capitalists 6 and 8 per cent. for it, and then exacting as high as 24 per cent., and these stiff bonuses besides. They have made a fine living upon the misery and distress and upon the bare necessities of those around them. An organization of capitalists to loan money at reasonable rates would be a godsend there, and full security for their money could be obtained by them.

How the poor victims lived through these exactions is a mystery. Many did not. They abandoned their farms and the State. A great many came back last year on hearing of the likelihood of a good season. But the best news is that last year nearly all the farmers began to turn their attention to diversified farming and to stock-raising in conjunction with agriculture. North Dakota was always a good cattle State at least three years in five, and the manner in which the farmers are going into the business ought to make the industry successful every year. Those who can afford it are acquiring herds of from 50 to 300 head. In the winter, when the beeves need attention, the farmers will have nothing else to attend to. They calculate that they can raise a three-year-old beef at an expense of from $12 to $15, and market it at from $30 to $40. At the least, they figure on a profit of $5 a head each year. It would appear that cattle thus looked after, with hay in corrals for the winter, may some day be rated between stall-fed and range cattle. In the summer these farmers are advised to put into wheat only that acreage which they can handle without **hired** help, for help is hard to get in the western part of the State. The mysterious nomads of **the** wheat belt do **not go there.**

On the Missouri slope, where **most of the** corn was **raised** last year, that crop never was a failure. It **has been** cultivated there for twenty years. **In** fact **in some Indian** mounds above Bismarck corn-cobs **are found along** with the pottery **and** trinkets for which the mounds are constantly ravaged. Potatoes also **grow** well on the Missouri slope. **Starch is** being made from them at a factory started by a New England man **at** Hankinson, **in** Richland County. From eight to ten tons of starch is being made daily at that place.

The range land for cattle is in that district which may be roughly described as the last three rows of counties in the western end of the State. Dickinson, on the **Northern Pacific** Railroad, is the shipping-point for the **stock.** In order to exact a revenue **from the cow-men, the people** have agreed to reconstruct into five **organized** counties the whole country west of the Missouri and the extreme northwestern counties. By the time this **is** published, the change will, in all probability, have been accomplished. There are thirteen counties west of the Missouri on the present maps, and only four of these have county governments. The new arrangement will complete the political machinery for assessment and taxation in the grazing lands. The cattle-men are supposed **to be** taxed for their cattle **as** upon personal property, **but they** have hitherto evaded the **impost.** The cattle business **in** these counties is rapidly being revolutionized. All **the** stockmen agree that the most return is gotten from small holdings with winter corrals. There are five horse ranches west of the Missouri. At one point Boston capitalists are raising thoroughbreds from imported stallions. The rest of the stock is of the common order, herded loose on the ranges.

But there is some farming even west of the Missouri. Corn, wheat, and oats are successfully raised in Morton County. Mercer County produced a splendid quality of wheat at 25 bushels to the acre, and across the river, in McLean County, a farmer succeeded in getting 31 bushels to the acre. In these two counties we come upon that vast bed of coal which underlies parts of eleven counties in North Dakota. In Mercer County this coal crops out on the river-bank, and a company backed by Chicago capital has been organized to build barges and ship the coal to points down the river. It can be sold at wholesale in Bismarck at $2 40 a ton, and in Pierre, South Dakota, for $3 50 a ton. In Bismarck soft coal now sells for $8 and $8 50, and anthracite for $11 a ton. The Dakota coal is a lignite—an immature coal—but it serves well for ordinary uses, making a hot fire, a white ash, and no soot. Its worst fault is that it crumbles when it is exposed to the air. Dakota coal from Morton County is already marketed. There seems to be an inexhaustible supply of it in that county. The veins that are now being worked are between eight feet and fourteen feet in thickness, and they crop up near the surface. It is in use in the public buildings of the State, in the flouring-mills, and in many hotels and residences. It sells in Mandan for $2 50 a ton. It is said that there are 150,000 acres of these coal beds east of the Missouri, and the coal area west of the river is almost as great. The veins vary in thickness from half a dozen to thirty feet. Farmers find it on their lands close under the surface, and with a pick and shovel dig in one day sufficient to last them all winter. It is a most extraordinary "find"—a bountiful provision of nature. It greatly alters the former view of the future of North Dakota—and of South Dakota also, since there is enough for both States. It adds to the comfort of life there, it provides a coal at least half as good as anthracite at one-quarter the cost, and it would seem that it must become the basis of manufacturing industries in the near future. A good terra-cotta clay in great quantities is found near the coal in many localities.

In showing that the future of the State depends upon diversified industries, and in calling attention to the newly exerted efforts of the people to meet this condition, I have omitted to mention the fact that many capitalists who had loaned money to farmers west of the Red River country are now supplying sheep to their debtors. Between 75,000 and 100,000 sheep were put upon farms in the State in that way last summer in herds of from 50 to 100 head. The plan generally adopted is for the farmer to take care of the sheep for five years, taking the wool for his pains, and at the end of that term for the farmer and the capitalist to divide the herd between them, increase and all. I do not find it to be the general opinion that this will turn out well in most cases. Sheep require constant attention, and the raising of them is a business by itself, not to be taken up at hap-hazard by men who are not experienced. Moreover, the land east of the Missouri is said not to be the best sort for that use.

The proportion of unoccupied land in the whole State is one-third. The western grazing counties form a third of the State, but much of their land is taken up by farmers—along the streams and the railroads. In all probability one-quarter of it that is not taken up is arable land, but until railroads reach it there will be no profit in tilling it. The land yet obtainable is part railroad and part government land. It fetches from $1 25 to $4 an acre. Two railroads cross the State from east to west, and two new ones are in process of construction across the State from the southern border over to Canada.

North Dakota is a prohibition State; that is to say, the making and selling of alcoholic stimulants are forbidden there. One effect of the operation of this law was the driving of thirty-six saloons out of Fargo across the Red River into Morehead, Minnesota. Another effect was the transformation of a brewery in the Red River Valley into a flouring-mill. The reform was asked for more earnestly by the Scandinavian element than by any others, and their votes, especially in the Red River Valley, greatly assisted in making it the law; but intelligent men, who are in a position to know whereof they speak, assert that hundreds of votes were cast for the reform by men who had no idea that it would become a law—men who promised to vote for it, or who voted for it because they thought nothing would come of their action. The Scandinavians are alcohol-drinkers, and many who serve as spokesmen for them frankly declare that their countrymen need prohibitory laws because they are not mild and phlegmatic beer-drinkers like the Teutonic people, but are fond of high-wines, and are terribly affected by the use of them. If an attempt be made to alter the law or repeal it, the process will consume five years. It is impossible to say what the temper of the majority of persons in the State now is, but the exodus that has taken place from the Dakotas, as it is recorded in the archives of Western general passenger agents, tells of one damaging effect of such a law; the disinclination of Europeans to take up land in prohibition States tells of another; and the failure of mankind to enforce the law in any State in which it has been included in the statutes would seem **to make a mockery of** the principle that underlies it.

The local geologists say that the Red **River Valley** is the bed of a former sea. Enormous rivers poured into it, and washed a great depth of alluvial deposit there, **to** make **the** extraordinarily rich soil that now supports the **most prosperous** farming population of the West. **The valley forms the** eastern face of North Dakota, half **of its** width **being in that** State and half in **Minnesota. The** outlines **of** the valley are traced **over** a region nearly 300 miles long, and between 50 and 100 miles wide. It extends from a point 100 miles above **the** Canadian border down to the southern edge of North Dakota. The western or Dakota half of it takes in the six easterly counties **of** the **new State;** but **it** is not all typical Red River **soil, for the western** edge is inclined to be sandy.

The soil is a rich black loam. **In** the old days the **hieroglyphs of** the buffalo, written in their trails, seemed **to be lines of** black ink upon the brown grass. This **black soil is 15** to 25 inches thick, and under **that is a** thick clay, which, when turned up by the spade or plough, is as productive as the soil itself. To the eye the valley appears to be level as **a** billiard table, but in reality **it** dips a little towards the unpretentious river that cleaves it in twain. It is not beautiful. No one-crop country can be either beautiful or continuously active in life and trade, no matter how rich and productive it is. In summer this **is a** wilderness of grain; in winter, a waste of stubble. **But we** shall see further on that this cannot long be the **case.**

The certainty of the wheat crop is the best gift the **good** fairies gave it at its christening. Any farmer who attends **to his** business can make $6 to $8 an acre on wheat at **its** present price, and, considering that he buys his land at about $25 an acre, that is an uncommonly good business proposition, in view of the intellectual ability that is invested in it. I use these figures because the average crop of the valley is 19 or 20 bushels to the acre. That they told me on the ground, where they said, "There's no use lying when the truth is so good." There are higher yields. One large farm near Fargo returned above 30 bushels, and others have done better in the past year, but the average is as I have stated. And this brought a profit of $9 to the acre last year. One man with 6000 acres cleared $40,000; one with 3500 acres made a profit of $25,000. Many paid for their farms; scores could have done so, but wisely preferred to put some of their money in farm betterments.

There has never been a failure of crops in the valley. It sometimes happens that men put in their wheat too late, and it gets nipped by frost, but there is no excuse for that. Barley is what the prudent men put in when they are belated. They raise good barley, and a great deal of it, in the valley, the main products being wheat, oats, barley, some flax, and some corn, the latter being the New England flint corn. Such corn has been raised near Fargo seven years in succession without a failure. Irrigation is not needed or employed in the valley, but artesian wells are very numerous there, as well they may be, since the water is reached at a depth of 20 feet and a cost of $100.

To go to the valley is not to visit the border. It is a well-settled, well-ordered, tidy farming region, of a piece with our Eastern farm districts, with good roads, neat houses, schools, churches, bridges, and well-appearing wooden villages. The upper or northern end of the valley is the finer part, because there the land was taken up in small plots—quarter sections of 160 acres

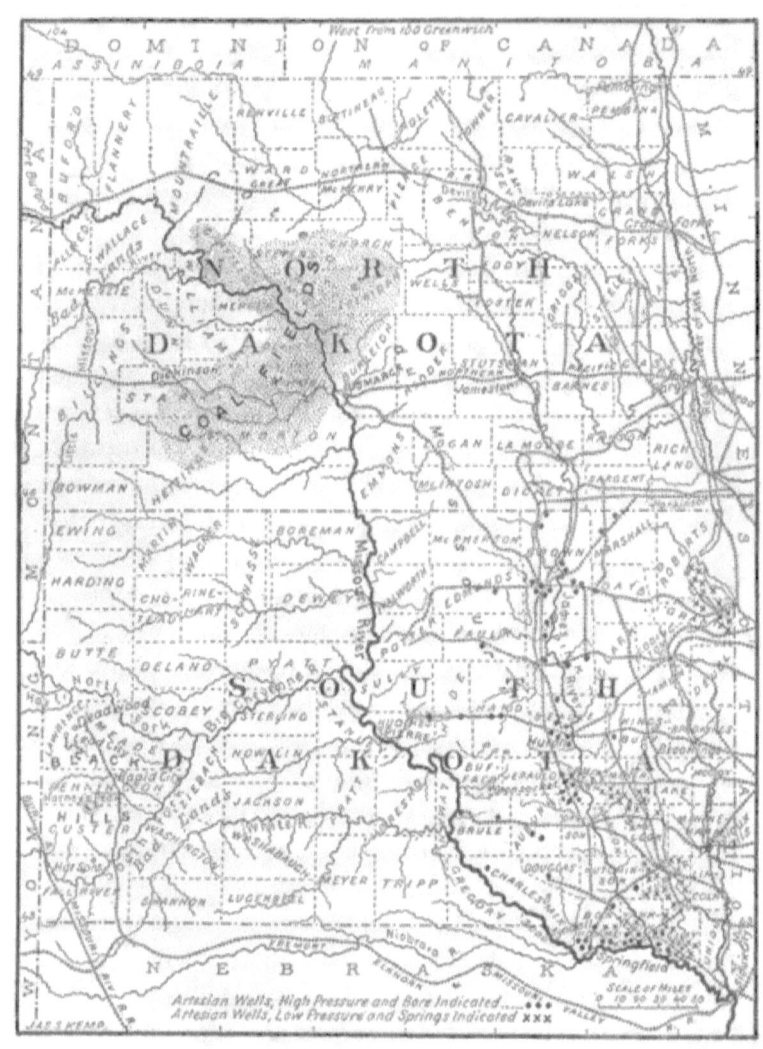

MAP OF NORTH AND SOUTH DAKOTA

each, or at the most whole sections. Therefore that end is the most populous and prosperous, for it is the small farms that pay best. The southern end of the valley was railroad land, and as much of it was sold when the railroad needed money, an opportunity for big holdings was created and embraced. These so-called bonanza properties do not pay proportionately, and are being diminished by frequent sales. In one year (1888) no less than twenty-four thousand acres on one of these farms were sown in wheat.

The present population of the Red River Valley is of Norwegians, Swedes, Irish, English, and Canadians, all being now Americanized by law. It is strange — to them it must be bewildering — to think that in that valley are women who were once harnessed with dogs to swill-wagons in their native cities, and yet are now the partners of very comfortable, prosperous farmers. The Scandinavians are spoken of in the valley as being good, steady, reliable, industrious folk, but eminently selfish and lacking in public spirit, and yet they and all the other residents of the valley have been in one respect both prodigal and profligate, for it has been a rule there never to cultivate or make anything that can be bought. In this respect the people are mending their ways. They are learning the lesson taught in the Southern States, where, to put the case in a sentence, the people were never prosperous until they raised their own bacon. So, latterly, these Red River people have been venturing upon the cultivation of mutton, pork, wool, horses, vegetables, and small fruits. But the first efforts at saving are as hard as learning to swim, and so as soon as these farmers learned that Europe was clamoring for wheat, they lost their heads. It is said that they abandoned 50 per cent. of the dairy farming that had grown to be a great source of income there, and in all the towns where the farmers' daughters were at work as domestic servants, the kitchen industries were crippled by a general homeward flight of the girls. "Our fathers are rich now, and we won't have to work any more," they said.

A leading railroad man in the Northwest, who is noted for his luminous and picturesque way of talking, is fond of calling the Red River farmers "the leisure class of the West." He says: "They only attend to their business for a few weeks in the spring and fall, and that they do sitting down, with splendid horses to drag the farming implements on which they ride around. When their grain is ripe, they hire laborers to cut and harvest it, and then they cash it in for money, fill the banks of the valley with money to the bursting-point, and settle down for a long loaf, or go to Europe or New York." Yet they must find a continuance of their strength and prosperity in diversified farming and in hard work, and this is being taught to the rest by the shrewder ones among them. Such men are making the breeding of fine draught-horses a side reliance, and very many farms now maintain from 1500 to 2000 Percheron, Norman, and Clydesdale horses, as well as pigs, sheep, and poultry. The country is too level for the profitable raising of sheep, however. They need uneven land and a variety of picking; moreover, the soil clogs in their hoofs, and subjects them to hoof rot, and other diseases prey upon them there.

There are nearly 9,000,000 acres in the valley, and one-sixth of it is under the plough. One hundred and fifty million bushels of wheat could be raised there if every acre was sown with seed, but there is no such demand for wheat as that would require to be profitable. As it is, less than a quarter of the valley is cultivated, and only three-quarters of that fraction are given up to wheat, so that last year's yield was about 30 to 37 millions of bushels. That would have brought $27,000,000 had it been sold, but while this is being written (in the holidays of '91-2), a great many farmers are holding their grain in the firm belief that Russia's needs will determine a rise of 20 cents in the price. Those who sold got 80 cents; those who are holding back want a dollar a bushel.

The climate is, of course, perfect for farming. Some very lively tornadoes go with it, and in the winter it is sufficiently cold to freeze the fingers off a bronze statue. But these are trifles. The wind-storms do their worst damage in the newspapers and the public imagination, and the cold of the winter is not as intense or disagreeable as the cold of more southerly States. It is a dry cold, and plenty of glorious sunshine goes with it. There are plentiful rains in the spring and the autumn, with intensely hot weather at midsummer. The moisture is held in the soil by the clay underneath, and in hot summer weather the surface cakes into a crust, still leaving the moisture in the earth.

I am so explicit about this great "bread-basket of America," as it is called, because it is by far the best part of North Dakota—so very much the best that in the valley the people are heard to say that they wish they were not tied to the rest of the State. "What a marvellous State it would have made to have taken the eastern half of the valley from Minnesota, and put it all under one government!" they cry. And others say that the whole valley should have been given to Minnesota, and North Dakota should have forever remained a Territory. But even in view of the excellence of this Red River region there would be little use in exploiting it were it all farmed and populated. On the contrary, there is room for thousands there—for many thousands.

The land now obtainable cannot be purchased for less than $25 an acre, but not more than $30 need be paid. Money down is not needed. The system called "paying with half crops" obtains there. The farmer pays half of what the land produces each year until the sum of the purchase price is met, with interest, of course. Under this system the land cannot be taken away from him unless he fails to farm it. He will need to house himself and buy horses and tools. However, one owner of 910 acres came to the valley with nothing but an Indian pony and a jack-knife. A great many others brought only their debts.

All that I have said about the productiveness of the valley applies particularly to the six valley counties of North Dakota. The Minnesota land is not so good.

Here, then, is a region that must feel the greatest increase in population that will come to any part of North Dakota. The river that curves and twists its way between the farms has been rightly nicknamed the Nile of America. In the twelve counties that border upon it in Minnesota and Dakota are 61 banks, with deposits amounting, in last December, to $6,428,000, or $65 for every man, woman, and child in the region. The farmers are the principal depositors, and they had this amount to their credit when a very large fraction of their grain crop had not been sold. The valley has two thrifty towns—Fargo, with 7000 population, and Grand Forks, with 6000.

I have spoken of the custom in the valley of relying upon a swarm of nomad harvesters to fall upon the wheat and garner it in the autumn. They make a picturesque army of invaders, led by the men from the Minnesota forests and Wisconsin pineries, in their peculiar coats of checked blanket stuff, but far too many of them form a hardened lot of vagabonds—"a tough outfit," in the language of the country. They have been in the habit of dictating how much help a farmer shall employ when they are in the fields, their idea being that the fewer the laborers the more work for those who are employed. They will abandon a farm on half a day's notice, and between the laziness and drunkenness of numbers of them there is little chance for either good or hard work. Prohibition gets more praise here than in other parts of the State, because, even with bottles hid in the fields, the harvesters only get a thimbleful where they once got a quart of rum. Another thing that eases the strain of prohibition is the plenteousness of rum just across the river in Minnesota. The system which relies on these harvesters is a bad one, and in time, with smaller holdings, the farmers will mainly harvest their crops with their own hands and neighborhood help.

North Dakota has many attractive towns, those that I have mentioned in the Red River country being the largest. Bismarck, the capital, on the Missouri River, has 2500 population. It has more than its share of brick buildings, and in its numerous pretty villas are families of a number and character to form an attractive social circle. By great enterprise it secured the position of capital of the Territory in '83, raising $100,000 for a capitol building, and adding a gift of 160 acres for a park around the edifice, as well as 160 acres elsewhere "wholly for good measure." Mandan is a flourishing railroad town across the river, with about 2000 population; Jamestown, near the eastern end of the State, is as big as Bismarck; and Devil's Lake, in the northern part of the State, is the same size. North Dakota has 1500 free schools, supported by a gift of 3,000,000 acres of public lands, set apart for the purpose when the State was admitted. As these lands cannot be sold for less than $10 an acre, the schools would appear to be certain eventually to have the support of a fund of $30,000,000.

South Dakota is 360 miles long and 225 miles wide. It contains 76,620 square miles, and is therefore larger than North Dakota by 2308 square miles. The population is estimated at 325,000, or more than half as much again as the other half of the old Territory. It is another blanket of grass like North Dakota, a little tattered and rocky in the northeast, and slightly wooded there and in the southeasterly corner. Just as North Dakota has a vastly wealthy strip called the Red River Valley, and triumphing over all the rest of the State in its wealth, so South Dakota has its treasure land, the Black Hills mineral region, a mountainous tract in the southwestern corner of the State, 120 miles long and 35 or 40 miles wide. But North Dakota's bread-basket netted $27,000,000 last year, whereas South Dakota's precious metals are worth but $3,000,000 or $3,500,000 a year. Right through the middle of the State runs the Missouri River, with its attendant hills of gumbo clay and its slender groves of cottonwood to relieve the dreadful monotony of the plains, and to give a beauty that no other settlements in the State possess to such towns as lie along it.

Both States have the same story to tell. The people of South Dakota rushed into exclusive wheat-growing, leaving themselves nothing to carry them along if the crops failed; and fail they did in 1887, '88, '89, and '90. Then came a prohibitory liquor law, which is already set at naught in the cities, and settlers left the State by the thousands. But last year brought great crops, and good-fortune was never, perhaps, better deserved. Estimates made before the threshing showed a wheat yield of 31,178,327 bushels, but the editor of the *Dakota Farmer* at Huron, a first-rate authority, told me he believed time would prove that 40,000,000 bushels had been reaped. The other yields were as follows: oats, 33,000,000 bushels; corn, 30,000,000 bushels; barley, 6,000,000 bushels; potatoes, nearly 5,000,000 bushels; flax, nearly 4,000,000 bushels; and rye, 750,000 bushels. This astonishing agricultural success in an arid State was achieved in 50 counties, nearly all east of the Missouri River. Some farming in the western or cattle-grazing half of the State was done in what may be loosely called the Black Hills region in the southwest, where there are railroads and local government and numerous settlements.

But little new sod had been broken to produce these crops. The wheat acreage had decreased by 70,000 acres. The acreage in flax also decreased, but in all the other cereals the acreage was more than in 1890. Notwithstanding the flight of so many farmers, there were only 400 acres less under the plough than during the preceding years. In the middle of the agricultural or eastern half of the State is a fertile, great, and well-watered valley. It is the valley of the James, but is seldom spoken of otherwise than as "the Jim River Valley." It passes through both Dakotas from Devil's Lake in northern North Dakota to the Nebraska border of southern South Dakota. It is watered by artesian wells, of which there is much to be said later on. There are many little streams in the rocky northeastern corner of the State, and here is the best sheep-raising district in South Dakota. Around Sioux Falls, in the southeastern corner, the farmers who had grown flax to rot the sod and to harvest the seed are now growing it for its fibre, and a company proposes to put up a linen-mill in that little metropolis. There is a notable industry in granite there, the stone being pink, red, and flesh-colored, and susceptible of as high a polish as Scotch granite. Hogs, too, are being raised down in that part of the State, and a packing concern is under way. Pierre also has a packing establishment.

Hundreds of thousands of sheep are being taken into central South Dakota. It is called a common thing to keep 95 per cent. of the lambs, because there are no cold rains there to kill them. There are few diseases, and foot rot is unknown. The farmers hope to be able to make from $2 to $3 50 a head in the sheep business. I have their figures, but I will spare those readers who know what a complex, delicate, and precarious business sheep-raising is, except where the conditions are exactly right as to climate, ground, and skilled ability on the part of the herders.

I have a friend, a lawyer, who, whenever he visits the farm on which he was born, vexes his father by asserting that there is a higher percentage of profit in farming than in mining or banking. He cites the enormous profit that attends the birth of a colt or a calf, or the sale of a bushel of corn gained from planting a few kernels. It is far easier to figure big profits in the sheep business. A lamb costs $2 50, yields wool worth 12 shillings a year, sells for $5, and creates several other sheep of equal value. Unfortunately there is another side to the story—but this is not the place for telling it. It is devoutly to be hoped, however, that sheep-raising may be a success in the Dakotas, as, indeed, it has already proved with some extra intelligent and careful men there.

The Black Hills are cut off from the rest of the State. I could not find any one to tell me anything about them until I went to them. The Black Hills business is mining, while that of the rest of the State is all transacted on the surface. Between the Missouri and the Black Hills was, until lately, the great Sioux reservation of twenty-three millions of acres, or practically one-third of the State. That was cut in two a little more than a year ago, and eleven millions of acres were thrown open for settlement. But no railroad yet bisects the tract; no governments administer the affairs of the counties; there are no schools or post-offices there.

The newly opened land lies between the White and Big Cheyenne rivers. The land had offered such rich pasturage that the Interior Department found it next to impossible to keep the cattle-men out. Some white men actually were making use of it; but the greater number of men who had cows in there were squaw men, remnants of a band of French Canadians who came thither in the fur-trading era, married squaws, and grew to be more Indian than the Indians. One rich old squaw man in that region, who caches his wealth rather than risk it in a bank, lives close to Pierre, the capital, but has only once visited the town. To-day white men have 50,000 cattle there.

It is a superb range cattle country where it is watered, and the stock keeps seal fat all the time. Shipments from there have gone straight to Liverpool on the hoof. But, on the other hand, other parts are too dry for use; the springs that are there dry up in early summer. The bother of it is, so far as the cattle-men are concerned, that settlers are taking up the land by the streams, and eventually wells must be sunk in the arid country or the stockmen must retire from it. The farms there are fenced, as the law requires, while east of the Missouri there are no fences, and what cattle or sheep are there must be herded and guarded by day and corralled at night.

The Government is selling this reclaimed reservation land at $1 25 an acre for first choice during the first three years, for 75 cents during the next two years, and for 50 cents for all lands not taken after five years. After that the Government will pay the **Indians for what remains.** The money obtained by **the sales** goes to the Indian fund, and the plan is designed to help to make the Indians self-supporting. What **it** means to the white **men is that the** people **who have** been the most distressed **and** unfortunate **class in the** Northwest are practically subjected **to an especial and** additional tax **for the support of Indians who** are not their wards, but **the** wards of the **nation.** One small **and poor county has already** paid the red men $570,000.

What the Indians think of **it and** of the entire **behavior** of the white men is illustrated by the best Indian **story** I have heard in **a** long while. An old grizzled Sioux dropped into a bank in Pierre, and upon being asked what he thought of the Government purchase of half his reservation, **made an attempt to reply in** broken English as **follows:**

"All same **old story,"** said **he.** "**White** men come, build **chu-chu** [railroad] through **reservation.** White **men yawpy-**yawpy [talk]. **Say:** 'Good Indian, good **Indian; we** want land. We give muz-es-kow **[money]; liliota muz-es-kow** [plenty money].' Indian say, 'Yes.' **What** Indian **get?** Wah-nee-che [nothing]. Some day white man want move **Indian.** White men yawpy-yawpy: 'Good Indian, good **Indian;** give good Indian liliota muz-es-kow.' What **Indian get?** Wah-nee-che. Some day white man **want half big** reservation. He come Indian. Yawpy-yawpy: '**Good** Indian; we give Indian liliota muz-es-kow.' **Indian** heap fool. He say, '**Yes.**' What Indian **get?** Wah-nee-che. All same old **story. 'Good Indian, good Indian.'** Get nothing."

What the white men of South Dakota want now is to **have the Government** of the United States spend a little **of the muz-es-kow it** is getting from the sale of these **lands in driving wells** in the newly opened lands for irrigation and the support of stock. It is not positively known that there is an artesian basin under the land in question, but wells have been successful at both sides of it, in the east and the west, and many students and experts have declared that water will be found there. As the wells will cost $5000 each, no one is going to risk the experiment of driving them, unless it be the Government. The only arguments that reconcile those who dislike all approaches to Federal paternalism are that the Government is charging for what should be public land, and that since it seeks to sell the land, it will be a good business proposition to improve those parts of it which cannot otherwise be sold. It is believed that wells will work there, and it is certain that once the fact is proved, the whole great tract will be settled and made to blossom like a garden.

The story of the artesian basin under part of South Dakota seems fabulous. It is even more astonishing than the wealth of coal that underlies the farms of North Dakota. God does, indeed, move in mysterious ways His wonders to perform when to the poor farmer, amid the cold blasts of the Northern winters, He distributes coal that is to be had for the taking of it, and when under the South Dakotan soil, that would be as rich as any in the world were it but moistened, He seems to have placed a great lake or, as some would have us believe, a vast sea.

On a foregoing page I have given the location and dimensions of that basin which the Dakotans affectionately speak of as the Jim River Valley. Under it all, in both States, there is said to lie a vast lake of crystal water. The fact is amply proven in South Dakota, where, between the northern and southern boundaries, there are already more than fifty high-pressure wells, or "gushers," as they call them there. A hundred, or perhaps more, low-pressure wells, reaching a flow closer to the surface, are at the foot of the same basin. In Sanborn, Miner, and McCook counties almost every farmer has his own low-pressure well. But the wonderful wells are the high-pressure, deep ones, wherein water is struck at from 600 to 1200 feet. The pressure in some of these wells is 200 pounds to the square inch. One at Woonsocket supplies 5000 gallons a minute. One at Huron serves for the town's water system and fire protection. One at Springfield has force enough for more than the power used in a sixty-barrel flour-mill. One at Tyndall is expected to irrigate 800 acres. It is calculated that a two-inch well will water 160 acres; a three-inch well, 640 acres; and a four-inch well, 1280 acres or more. Eight miles above Huron a well is used on a farm that produced 53 bushels and 20 pounds in wheat to the acre, as against 15 bushels in the unirrigated land of the neighborhood. Some who profess to know say that the great basin is inexhaustible, and that the opening of one well near another does not affect the first one. Then, again, I read that this is not wholly true. But, at all events, no one doubts the presence of a vast body of water, and no well, even among those that are five years old, shows any sign of giving out. A law called the Melville Township Irrigation Law, approved on March 9, 1891, authorizes townships to sink wells for public use, and to issue bonds to defray the cost. This aims to make the mysterious basin the property of the people. For farming, the flow of water is not needed during half of each year. It is said that if the subsoil is wet, the crops will need no more water. The water should be turned on to the land after the harvest, and kept soaking into it for four or five months. The drilling of wells goes on apace. In one county where there were eight wells a year ago, there will be one hundred this summer.

The James River Basin is 400 miles long and 40 to 50 miles wide. Well-boring has been a failure to the eastward of it, but to the westward there are several splendid wells, some even as far away as Hughes County, near the Missouri. The boring is very costly, some wells having cost $5000, and even more. At first a soft shale rock of white sand is pierced, and then there is reached a sticky clay like gumbo. Minnows of brilliant colors and with bright and perfect eyes have been thrown out of these wells, as if to prove that the water comes from surface streams somewhere. The theory is that its course is from the west, and an official of the Department of Agriculture holds that several rivers to the westward lose all or part of their volumes of water at certain places where they meet the outcropping of this same sandstone which is found by boring. The Missouri, for instance, is said to lose two-thirds of its bulk after its flight over the cascades at Great Falls. The Yellowstone diminishes mysteriously in bulk. Three or four streams in the Black Hills run their courses and then disappear in the neighborhood of this outcropping of sandstone. When I was at Great Falls in Montana, I was not able to prove that the Missouri loses the greater part of its bulk below there, but it was said that engineers have investigated the subject, and are to report upon it to the Government. I was told, however, that several streams which seem to be heading towards the Missouri in that neighborhood suddenly disappear in the earth without effecting the junction.

With water thus apparently plenteous; with cattle-raising, flouring-mills, linen manufacture, wool, and diversified farming, all newly started; with the coal of North Dakota brought cheaply down the Missouri, and with better coal in the Black Hills, to be brought eastward when railroads are built across the State — the prospect is that South Dakota will stride onward to a degree of prosperity that her people cannot have expected, and yet richly deserve.

It is said that there is more mineral wealth in the Black Hills than in any other territory of the same scope in the world. Gold is the principal product, but silver, nickel, lead, tin, copper, mica, coal, and many other valuable sorts of deposits are there. The output of gold has been about $3,300,000 a year, and of silver from $100,000 to $500,000. The Black Hills are so called because the pine-trees which cover them look black from the plains. The numerous villages of the region are agricultural settlements or mining towns, and are connected by two trunk lines among the foot-hills and by three narrow-gauge roads in the hills. These smaller railways turn and curve through the valleys amid very beautiful and often grand scenery. It is wonderful to see the enormous machines at the greater mines, and to know that they, and nearly all the principal appointments of the buildings of every sort, were packed across the plains in ox carts; for the first railroad — the Fremont, Elkhorn, and Missouri Valley Railroad, of the Chicago and Northwestern system — reached the hills less than two years ago. It was in February of last year that the Burlington road came there.

The great gold-mining company, the Homestake, is said to have taken fifty millions of dollars' worth of gold out of the hills. The Homestake Company is the name of a group of five or six corporations, all under the same ownership. Messrs. J. B. Haggin, Lloyd Tevis, and the Hearst estate, all of California, are the principal owners. They have the largest gold-reduction works in the world. For labor alone they pay out

$125,000 a month. Their mills contain 700 stamps. The last year was the first one of notable activity outside the Homestake plants, and one or two very much smaller ones, because the railroads have only just made it possible to get the ore to the smeltery, or to effect the construction of such works. The ores are all low grade, and will not pay the heavy tolls for wagon transportation. The profits in the free milling Homestake ores have been found in their quantity and the cheapness with which they have been reduced. Five smelteries have been put in within a year, others are projected, and others are being enlarged. It is said that within two or three years no ore will be sent out of the hills, but it will all be reduced there by fifteen or twenty smelteries that will then be operated. It is further predicted that when both reduction works and means of transportation encourage activity in all the districts, the yield of the hills will amount to twenty or twenty-five millions of dollars a year.

The tin in the Black Hills is almost as much a bone of contention there as it is in the columns of the political organs throughout the country. But in the hills all question of the existence of the metal is lifted from out of the controversy, and the only subjects of discussion are the quantity of tin and the reasons why the marketing of it has so long been delayed. There is no doubt that there are surface indications, to say the least, to mark a tin deposit along two great belts. More than 7000 locations have been made, and "development work" (required by law from those who would hold their claims) has been done to the extent of nine miles of drifts, shafts, cuts, and tunnels. The famous Harney Peak Company works as if it had great faith in its future, its work being in the construction of an extensive plant in readiness for the prospective mining. The railroads also, by a rivalry in building spurs to the mines, give signs of perfect faith in the new industry. The local criticism on the situation is best expressed in the pamphlet issued by the merchants of Rapid City: "The reason why tin has not been produced for market is that those who can produce it do not seem disposed to do anything except development work. The men who own 90 per cent. of the valuable claims are poor prospectors, who are unable to erect mills and reduction works. So far, it has been almost impossible to enlist capital in the purchase or development of Black Hills tin mines. With the exception of the Harney Peak and Glendale companies, no money has been invested in the mines of the Black Hills. Why it is that American capitalists refuse to invest in or to investigate the tin mines is a question that yet remains unanswered."

The Black Hills smelteries are closely connected with the coal of the hills, one mine at Newcastle (in Wyoming) being worked to the extent of 1500 tons a day. It is a soft coal, and makes a high-grade coke. It is coked at the mines. A great field of coal, estimated at 4000 acres in extent has been opened at Hay Creek, in the north. It is said to burn with only 7 per cent. of ash. It awaits the railroads, whose lines are already surveyed to the fields. The financial and mining capital of the hills is Deadwood, a very picturesque, active, orderly, and modern city of 3500 souls, caught in a gulch, and obliged to climb steep mountain walls for elbow-room. It has a lively rival in Rapid City, in the foot-hills. Lead City is another place of importance, and Hot Springs is a resort of the character implied by its name. Pierre, the capital, on the Missouri River, is very enterprising and modern, and has a fine district of stores, and a still finer one of residences. Huron is a lesser place, and Sioux Falls is the industrial capital, a lively and promising town of more than 12,000 persons.

South Dakota is diversifying her farm industries, and insuring them by utilizing nature's great gift, artesian water. It is said that central South Dakota has the climatic conditions for the successful cultivation of the sugar-beet, for ripening it while it contains the greatest proportion of sugar. One sample grown in this region last year showed $19\frac{1}{2}$ per cent. of sugar. In 100 samples the sugar averaged above 15 per cent.; in Germany the average is less.

But the best news about both the Dakotas is that the moisture in the soil last New-year's day was said to be such as to warrant firm faith in another splendid year like the last. With that to put the people and their industries upon their feet, and with all the new lines of development and maintenance that are being tried or established, the outlook for both States is very encouraging.

VI

MONTANA: THE TREASURE STATE

Two anecdotes told in Montana as characteristic home-made jokes illustrate the spirit of its people. The first one is about ex-Governor Hauser. It is said that, like many another true Montanian, he begins to feel a new and strange regard for small change once he gets east of the Mississippi, a consideration unknown to any man in the Treasure State. It happened, therefore, that when on one occasion he handed two bits—which is to say, a silver quarter—to a Chicago newsboy, and when the boy gave him a newspaper and moved away without making any change, the Montanian called out: "I say, stop! Give me my change." At that the boy looked wonderingly at him. "Oh no," he replied; "you don't want no change; you're a Montana man." The other story is to the effect that a party of well-known Butte and Helena millionaires were enjoying a quiet and friendly game at poker, when a commercial traveller—a stranger to all in the party—manifested a considerable interest in the game, as an outsider. The gentlemen were "chipping in" white chips to admit them to the betting on each hand of cards, and then they were stacking up red and blue chips in great profusion to attest their faith in what cards they held. The drummer found the game irresistible, and taking out a one-hundred-dollar bill, he flung it on the table and said: "Gentlemen, I would like to join you.

There's the money for some chips." At that one of the millionaires looked over at the banker and said, "Sam, take the gentleman's money, and give him a white chip."

These are characteristic Montana stories, and they reflect the spirit of the dominant handful of leaders in the State. If these men are not all too used to the making of big fortunes, they are at least bent upon making them, and very familiar with seeing them made. Years and years ago there was just such a condition of affairs in California; now it is peculiar to Montana.

Think of it! Montana, speaking very roughly, is so large a State and with so small a population that it may be said to contain one inhabitant for each square mile of its surface, and yet it has been the boast of those people that no similar band of human beings in the world has approached them in the amount of wealth *per capita* that they have produced. As long ago as 1889 Montana contained less than 150,000 souls, and produced $60,000,000 — that is to say that, exclusive of what was consumed at home, the ore, cattle, horses, and sheep sent out of the State brought a sum of money equal to $400 for every man, woman, and child it supported.

It is mainly a mining and a stock-raising State, and these industries have so amply rewarded those who are engaged in them that agricultural and manufacturing development have been unduly retarded. This cannot long continue. So great a State cannot be long given over to grazing herds of cattle, and dotted here and there with mining camps, and when we come to understand what rich farming lands the State contains, and of what vast extent are these parks and valleys, it takes no uncommonly prophetic eye to see the State in the near future checkered with the green and yellow of well-worked farms to a greater extent than it is now ribbed with mountains. The frequent and often easy making of great fortunes has had its natural consequence in causing the postponement of the cultivation of the soil. It has been left for Chinamen to make the valleys laugh with the bloom and verdure of small fruits and vegetables, and the fact that Chinamen were thus employed has tended to make such labor seem so much the less worthy of the white inhabitant. But now the white man has begun to take note of the wonderful results which have followed even this petty farming, and his eyes have been opened to the wide and varied capabilities of the soil, and to the fortunes that lie in it awaiting the great agriculturists who are to come—who, indeed, are beginning work. They earned a million and a half from wheat last year, and nearly two millions of dollars from oats.

But the conditions that have caused mining and stock-raising to monopolize the energy of the original people there have resulted in making Montana a very forward State, a very progressive and interesting fraction of the nation. It will not do for the reader to jump to the conclusion that because mining camps and cattle ranges have been the chief fields of industry, that the population is one of cowboys and shovel-men. On the contrary, Helena, the capital, is one of the most attractive cities in America, and is perhaps the wealthiest one of its size in the world. And scattered all over the State are other fine towns, in which will be found a very cultivated and cosmopolitan people, fond of and accustomed to travel, holding memberships in the clubs of New York and London, living splendidly at home, well informed, polite, fashionable, and intimately related, socially or in business, with the leading circles in the financial centres of the country. It was not long ago in point of actual time that our children were taught to regard the region of the Missouri as peopled by redskins and enlivened by the presence of the buffalo. But it will seem to the tourist of to-morrow that such a characterization of the country cannot have been true in the time of men now alive, so utterly are all traces of the old condition obliterated. As far as such a traveller will be able to judge by what he sees, the Indian will appear to have gone with the buffalo. As a matter of fact, the savage is there still, but he is corralled on reservations as deer are in our parks.

The tourist in Montana will find along his route a chain of thoroughly modern cities, appointed with fine and showy storehouses, the most modern means of street travel, excellent newspapers, luxuriously appointed clubs, good hotels, and all the conveniences of latter-day life. In Helena he will meet something more nearly approaching a leisure class than I saw anywhere else in the Northwest—a circle made up of men who have retired upon their incomes, or who thrive by the shrewd use of capital obtained from industries that do not monopolize their attention. In this respect little Helena is more forward even than great Chicago.

But over and through all of this progress and accomplishment there shines the mysterious and romantic light of a rude era that was so recent as to have involved even the middle-aged men of to-day. It was of the type of that of '49 in California. It was an era of new mining camps, of swarming tides of men thirsty for nuggets, of pistol-bristling sheriffs, of vigilantes, road-agents, Indian fights, stage-coaches, and all the motley characters that gave Bret Harte his inspiration. You may meet some of the men who helped to rid the State of outlaws by the holding of what they gayly spoke of as "necktie parties," and the application of hemp. They are apt to lounge into the clubs on any night, and with them you may see the best Indian "sign-talker" who ever lived, or that quick-handed, "scientific" ex-constable who proudly asserts that in the worst days he arrested hundreds of desperadoes bare-handed, without pulling his gun more than once or twice in his whole constabulary career. They represent the days of the founding of Montana. And yet in the same city where I met such men I encountered others from London, New York, Sitka, San Francisco, and many other capitals; for, as I have said, the new Montana is in close contact with all the world.

Montana is the largest of the newly admitted States; in fact, it is as large as Washington and North Dakota combined. It is one-sixth larger than the United Kingdom of Great Britain and Ireland. It is the third State in the sisterhood, ranking next after Texas and California. It contains 143,776 square miles, and is therefore the size of the States of New York, New Jersey, Pennsylvania, Maryland, Virginia, and West Virginia all rolled together. It is about 540 miles in length, and half as wide. As it is approached from the east, it seems to be a continuation of the bunch-grass plains land which makes up all of North Dakota. But almost all at once upon entering Montana the monotony of the great plateau is relieved by its disturbance into hills, which grow more and more numerous, and take on greater and greater bulk and height, until, when one-third of the State has been passed, the earth is all distorted with mountains and mountain spurs. These are the forerunners of the Rockies, which, speaking roughly, make up the final or western third of this grand and imperial new State. A glance at the map will call to the attention the apparently contradictory fact that the principal seats of population in the State are directly in the Rocky Mountain region. This is difficult for the majority of readers to account for. They think of the

Rocky Mountains as great bastions of bare stone—and such, indeed, the main range is; but the spurs and lesser or side ranges are grass-clad or wooded elevations, and even amid the veritable Rockies themselves are innumerable valleys coated with the richest, most nutritious pasturage to be found anywhere in the world. In or beside such valleys are the cities of which I speak, built there to be close to the mines that are being worked in the mountains.

Helena's history shows how such conditions came about. In 1864, after the discovery of placer gold in Alder Gulch had caused a stampede of fortune-seekers to Montana, the second scene of mining activity was Last Chance Gulch. That gulch is now the main street of Helena. The miners began washing the dirt at the foot of the gulch, and the saloon-keepers, gamblers, and traders built their places of business close to where the miners were at work. When the whole surface of the gold-bearing runways had been passed through the pans, and $25,000,000 had been taken out in nuggets and dust, the mining ceased, but the town remained. It did not shrivel and languish like Virginia City, the town that had grown up in Alder Gulch, but being at the crossing of all the old Indian trails of the Northwest, and a natural centre of the region, it waxed big, and began a new lease of life as a trading, political, and money capital.

Let me begin a detailed description of Montana by saying that its future as an agricultural State will be dependent upon the extent and number of irrigation ditches that shall be cut in it. The average rainfall upon the eastern end of the State is only about nine inches a year; in the central part, still east of the mountains, it is nowhere more than fourteen inches, I believe. West of the mountains there is a very different country, one that is locally described as "green;" that is to say, the verdure has its natural term of life, and the rainfall is greater there. But that is a small part of the State by comparison with the rest. Yet all over the State, on the great eastern plateau as well as in the valleys among the mountains, the soil is of extraordinary fertility, and it is said that at least three-fifths of it can be laid under the ditch. A glance at the map will show the reader the great lines of the Missouri and Yellowstone rivers, and the fine lines of their branches and feeders, which literally vein the chart. It is, of course, by means of the supply in these waterways that it is hoped the future farms of Montana will be founded and maintained.

Governor Toole, in his last annual message, says that "there was a time when it seemed not improbable that the general government would take hold of this proposition, and under its supervision control and manage the water supply to the advantage of all. It is perfectly apparent, however, at this time (January, 1891) that influences are co-operating which will eventuate in destroying whatever hope we may have had in that direction. Eastern communities, which have set this opposition in motion, appear to be mindful only of local interests, and not of the prosperity of the whole country. Their protest is based upon the claim that the reclamation of these arid lands would subject the settler in the Eastern and Middle States to undue competition, retarding relief from agricultural depression. . . . The homes which we propose to make," he continues, "are not for us alone, but for every citizen of the United States who has the courage to come and take one. If we are to receive any substantial or speedy benefits from our arid lands, I believe the State must first acquire a title to them, and then undertake by appropriate legislation to reclaim and dispose of them. The Government should select, survey, and convey these lands to the State upon such conditions as would secure their occupation and reclamation."

Independent of any such Federal action as is suggested by the Governor, individual enterprise has made itself greatly felt in the provision of irrigation canals, reservoirs, and ditches. If it were not that I fear being credited with a desire to criticise, I would say that the rush and mania for water rights in Montana closely resemble in their impetuosity and greed the scramble for rich lands wherever they are newly opened in the far West, and the not altogether patriotic desire to build new cities in the State of Washington. In Montana irrigation schemes are expected to pay even better than mining; hence the scramble. I ventured to speak of this to a man who was planning to control certain valleys, which he described as being of the size of dukedoms, by "corralling" the waterways in them, by which alone they could be made fit for farming.

"Well," he replied, "we who are on the ground are going to get whatever there is lying round. You don't suppose we are going to let a parcel of strangers preempt the water rights so that we must pay taxes to them? No; we prefer to let them pay the taxes to us."

That was eminently logical, and thoroughly human as well. But it still seems to me that either the State or the general government should own and control the water rather than that a few corporations should seize it, and thereby tax how they please that vast and general industry which will be the chief dependence of and source of wealth to the State. I am old-fashioned in this, since I but borrow the ideas of those central Asian kingdoms whose irrigating systems belonged to the governments, and yet I fancy this repugnance to a

MAP OF MONTANA

monopoly of water will prove a new and controlling fashion when the monopolists begin to fatten on their rents.

As it is, water rights can be taken only by those individuals who mean to and do utilize them for the public. Such a person, or such persons, can file a claim for a water right at the district United States Land-office, but must improve such rights within a reasonable time. These rights are given in perpetuity to the owners, their heirs, assigns, etc., forever. They tap a stream of any part or all of its water if they want to, and run their ditch through what land they please, having the right to go through the land of a non-purchaser to reach that of a purchaser. Then they sell the water at so much per acre per year. The rentals vary between 50 cents and $1 50 an acre. Each farmer taps the ditch with lateral canals, gates being put in to divert the water into the side ditches. A farmer may also lay pipe from the ditch and carry water to his house and farm buildings, arranging an adequate and townlike system of water-works for domestic and stable uses; thus, at what should be a trifling expense, the farmers on irrigated lands may obtain this modern convenience. An important recent decision of the courts is that a man cannot buy water and allow it to run to waste in order to deprive a neighbor of it.

A company preempting a water right takes it on a mountain slope, tapping the stream high above the land to be irrigated. As a rule, the water is not brought to a reservoir. In most instances on the east slope of the Rockies this cannot be done, but the ditches start above the basin land, not only to get a "head" or impetus for the water, but because in Montana the streams are apt to run in the bottoms of deep-water channels. It is a tempting business, because, since the rights are eternal, a company can afford to start **even where** the first outlay is large; indeed, the more **extensive** the system and the larger the ditches, the better the profits. The country is certain to grow to meet such improvements, and to pay a handsome revenue as the years go **on; and in** the mean time the ditches **constantly** cement themselves and diminish their waste.

The result has been that when a call was issued for data concerning irrigation in **Montana, preliminary to a** convention for the study of the subject **at the** opening of this year, it was found that there were already somewhere near 3500 irrigating ditches, the property **of** 500 owners. Some **of** these **schemes** are gigantic. In some instances the project has been to secure **not only** the water, but the land it is to irrigate, and the water lords expect to reap fancy prices for the land from settlers, in addition to rents which their great-great-great-grandchildren may fatten upon. In other cases, only the water is got by the men or companies, and they are **content to confine** themselves to the taxes they will impose **on the land as** fast as it is taken up. The **cattlemen of** Montana decry these schemes, and beg the officials and editors of the State not to discuss irrigation and small farming, as, they say, settlers may be induced to come in and spoil the stock or grazing business; yet I am told that one company of cattle-men has secured miles of land and the adjacent water rights along the Missouri against the inevitable day when— But the cattle business shall have another chapter.

The largest irrigation scheme that is reported is that engineered **by** Zachary **Taylor Burton, a** notable figure in Montana. **It is in** Choteau County, and taps the **Teton River. The main** ditch is forty miles long, four**teen** feet wide at the bottom, and eighteen feet at the **top.** The ditch connects and fills two dead lake basins, which now serve as reservoirs, and are fully restored to their ancient condition, not only beautifying a now blooming country, but having their surfaces blackened with flocks of wild swan, geese, ducks, gulls, and other fowl in the season when those birds reach that country. Drives are to be laid around the lakes, and their neighborhoods are likely either to become pleasure resorts or the seats of well-to-do communities. This scheme looks forward to putting 30,000 acres under the ditch. Thus far the cost of preparing the land for cultivation has been five dollars an acre, and the charge for maintenance of the ditches will be about fifty cents an acre a year.

A very peculiar and interesting scheme is that of the Dearborn Company, in the valley of the same name. Here is a valley containing half a million acres, a sixth part of which may be cultivated. The rest is hilly, and will always be grazing land. The valley is between Great Falls and Helena, alongside the main divide of the Rockies. Here are a number of little watercourses—the Dry, Simms, Auchard, and Flat creeks—in themselves incompetent to water their little valleys. These are all to be utilized as ditches. By tapping the Dearborn River with a six-foot-deep canal, thirty-eight feet wide, and only four and a half miles long, this natural system of watercourses is connected with a supply of water fed by eternal springs and frequent mountain snowfalls. The scheme embraces a hundred miles of main waterways and hundreds of miles of laterals. The greater part of the land benefited is obtainable by homesteaders.

I have spoken of the rush for water and land. Let me explain it with an illustration. One of the most lofty and ambitious grabbers in the State was not long ago observed to be engaging in a most mysterious business. He was **taking** women out **into** the wilderness, a stage-load **or** two at a time. They were very reputable women—school-teachers, type-writers, married women, and their friends. They were taken to a large and pleasantly situated house, upon the pretext that they **were to** attend **a** ball and **a** dinner, and get a hundred dollars as a **present. It** all proved true. Excursion party after excursion party went **out in this** way, and when the ladies returned to the town that had thus been pillaged **of its** beauty, they reported that they had fared upon venison **and** wild-fowl, with the very **best of** "fixings," and that at the ball a number of stalwart and dashing cowboys had become their partners, tripping their light fantastic measures with an enthusiasm which made up for any lack of grace that may have been noticed. The reader may fancy what a lark it was to the women, and how very much enjoyment the more mischievous wedded ones among them got by pretending that they were maidens, **heart-whole** and free of fancy! But while those women **were in the** thick **of** this pleasure, they each signed a formal claim **to** a homesteader's rights in the lands thereabout. **And as they** "prove up" those claims in the fulness of time, **each will** get her one hundred dollars. The titles to the land will then be made over to the ingenious inventors and backers of the scheme, and the land will **be** theirs. "Thus," in the language of a picturesque son of Montana, "a fellow can get a dukedom if he wants it." This is an absolutely true account of the conquest of a valley in Montana, and the future historian of our country will find much else that is akin to it, and that will make an interesting chapter in his records.

Governor Toole, in his message for 1891, abandons all hope of Federal supervision of this potentiality of wealth, **and concludes his** remarks with the statement that he assumes it to be the province of the Legislature to provide "against excessive and extortionate charges by individuals and companies engaged in the sale, rental, or distribution of water, and to prevent unjust discrimination in the disposal of the same to the public." He thinks the right of the State to regulate this matter should be asserted and maintained. He does not discuss the project of having the State develop and maintain the ditches, nor does he touch upon the next best alternative — of insisting that the farmers who own the land shall inherit the water plants after a fixed term of years.

But in considering Montana as it is, the main point is that there are thousands of ditches laid, and to-day a bird's-eye view of the State reveals valley after valley lying ready for the settler, like so many well-ordered parlors awaiting their guests. These parklike grassy bowls needed only the utilization of the water that is in or close to each one. There they lie, under sunny skies, carpeted with grass, bordered by rounding hills, rid of Indians, and all but empty of dangerous animals, waiting for the hodgepodge of new Americanism, to be made up of Swedes and Hollanders, Germans, Englishmen, and whoever else may happen along. What the State particularly needs is men of the Teutonic races, whose blood will not be stirred by the El Dorado-like traditions of vast and sudden wealth made in mining. It wants communities that will not be swept off the farm lands as by a cyclone at the first news that a new "lead" of gold or a new deposit of sapphires has been found in the mountains. Of such inflammable material, sent there in search of gold, and prone not to surrender the hope of finding more of it, has the State thus far been made up. The change is under way; the new people of a new and greater Pennsylvania are coming in, as we shall see. **Five years** from this, the politicians of Montana will be kowtowing to the farmer vote.

The northeastern corner of Montana is all Dawson County — a tract **as** big as Maryland, Vermont, and Connecticut. It **is all** high rolling plains land, now in use for stock-raising. It is well watered **by** tributaries **of the** Missouri, and abounds with little valleys, which will **yet** be very profitably farmed. Custer County, **which** takes **up the** remainder of the eastern **end of Montana, is** the same sort of land, and is a stock-raising **country,** but is yielding **to** the inroads of the farming element. It surprised the people of the State by **the** exhibit sent from there to the State fair last August. Wheat, oats, tomatoes, cabbages, potatoes, pumpkins, and squashes were in the yield, which was wellnigh complete, and of a high quality and size. All the lands that are watered are taken up, and this is true of the greater **part** of the State. The bench lands form the bulk of **what** remains. It has been demonstrated that they **are** very productive if water can be got to **them, and since** the streams are tapped on the mountain **slopes, it** is certain that they will, **to** a large **extent, be** irrigated.

Choteau County, in the north, and the next one west of Dawson, is a little empire in itself. It is slightly larger than Massachusetts, Connecticut, and New Hampshire. **It is 100** miles **wide and** 225 miles long, and, to **borrow a** Western expression, the entire population of **the** Northwest could be "turned loose in it." It is like Dawson County in character — a high rolling plateau given over to cattle, sheep, and the growing of the hardier grains. Rich "finds" of magnetic and hematite **iron are reported** from there. Park County is a very **mountainous, crumpled-up,** and rocky area, and is the **northern extension and neighbor** of the Yellowstone

National Park. Sheep and cattle raising and mining are its principal industries, and, on account of the wonderful mining "finds" that have recently been made there, the little county is knocking at the doors of Congress for a favor. Cook City, down on the southern edge of the county, is the beginning of a wonderful mining camp—that is to say, it is wonderful in the amount of ore there that could be profitably worked if coke and coal and transportation facilities could be had at reasonable cost. But, apparently, the only practicable route to the camp is through a corner of the National Park, and the miners are asking Congress to allow the rails to be laid there. They have had a discouraging experience thus far. The mines are principally in the hands of the discoverers, and since a prospector is usually the poorest man in the world, they cannot afford to spend much to make their needs known to the public. The prospector, the reader should understand, is the indefatigable Wandering Jew of the mountains, who prowls about amid every sort of danger, hammer in hand, and dining on hope more often than food, and who, after discovering a "lead," gives an interest in it to capital, and then is very fortunate if he is not frozen out. The metals that have been found in Park County are silver and lead. There is very little gold, but coal has long been very profitably mined at several points in the county.

Gallatin County, next to the westward of Park, is a mountainous and mineral region also, but it contains the Gallatin Valley, which, to the agriculturist, is just now one of the most interesting districts in the United States. This great valley has more snowfall than any county in the State—at least the snow lies there longer than anywhere else. The result of the moisture, in conjunction with the character of the soil, is that the valley is one of the richest grain-producing regions **in the State**. For years barley has been raised there for the use of the brewers of Montana. When some samples of this Gallatin Valley barley reached New York, the brewers there refused **to** believe that any such barley was or could be grown **anywhere in** the world. They thought that what was shown to them **was a lot** of carefully selected samples. They deputized a committee to visit the valley, **and** found that the barley which had so astonished them **was** the common barley **of** the country. The grain is very clear, almost to the point of being translucent, and **is** in color a golden yellow. The brewers declare that **no** better grain for their use **is** grown in the world. They have organized a company, taken the water right, bought various tracts of land, amounting to 10,000 acres, and are going to try to make the valley the great malting centre of the continent, if not of the world. They have put up malting-houses at two points, have established **some** twenty miles of irrigating ditches already, and by furnishing the seed and buying the yields are encouraging the farmers of the valley to grow barley. They cultivated 2500 bushels in 1890, and raised sixty bushels to the acre. Last year they had 10,000 acres under cultivation. They expect in a few **years to be** selling barley to all the brewers of the country **who** value what the New Yorkers think is the best grain obtainable. This is the nearest approach to what is called bonanza or big-scale farming in the State of Montana.

All that central district of the State, including Meagher and Fergus counties, and more besides, has been slow in the development of its mining resources. Mines have been held for years since they were discovered, because it has been hard to make capitalists and railroad men see what **was** in the country. It is almost always the case in such a wealthy mining region as Montana that news of rich finds is published every day, and capitalists hear the tales of prospectors with fatigued and half-closed ears. But now two routes have been surveyed into Meagher County by the Northern Pacific Company, and the Great Northern and Burlington and Missouri roads are expected to go in. All will head for Castle, the great mining camp of the country, where two smelteries are already turning out lead and silver, and freighting bullion 150 miles to the nearest railway.

Thus we reach the county of which Great Falls is the seat of government and of many interesting industries and operations. This is Cascade County. It is here that the noted and majestic falls of the Missouri occur in a succession of splendid cascades. Here a company, controlled by wealthy men of New York, Helena, and Great Falls, have taken up something like twelve miles on either side of the river at these falls, and have thus possessed themselves of what is undoubtedly the finest and greatest water-power in the West, comprising in all at least 250,000 horse-power, and more easily handled than that of Niagara. An auxiliary company owns a large town site there, and a very promising and considerable town has already grown up to handle the wheat and wool and beef of the region, and to be already the site of smelting-works, factories, and other establishments which have been attracted by the cheap and abundant water-power. In the shrewdness and reasonableness of the management of Great Falls lie much of the hope for its future. The town has never been "boomed." It is planned with broad avenues and streets, and even now contains several blocks of really notable stone and brick buildings along its main street. It has a fine opera-house, club, hotel, and strong banks. Its population is above 7000.

This Cascade County is a very new part of Montana.

A small proportion of the land is all that is yet taken, but experiments with this have led the people there to believe that there is no richer land in the State. Thus far the settlers are chiefly Americans. It has been and is yet a grazing country, but it is seen that as civilization pushes into it, the cattle business is being hurt. The difficulty in obtaining cowboy assistance is noticeable wherever farms and well-governed towns spring up, and this difficulty is increasing in this region. The cowboy and civilization are neighbors, but not friends. But it is a good grass country, and the grass is vastly better than that in Dakota, which becomes frozen and loses its nutriment. Here the Chinook winds from the Pacific come in at all times in the winter, never failing to blow upon all except twenty or twenty-five days in each winter. They clear off the snow like magic. Twelve thousand cattle were shipped from Great Falls during 1891. But the wool business exceeded that. From the same point last year nearly three millions of pounds of wool—more than were sent from any other point in the United States —were shipped from the backs of the sheep. Because of the rich soil and good grass, very little sand blows about to load down and damage the fibre of the wool. That is the case everywhere within 150 to 200 miles of the east slope of the Rockies. Sheep in this country have none of the destructive diseases which assail them elsewhere. The sheep and wool industries are going to be enormous in Montana on that account, whether the herding be upon the ranges, as at present, or in small herds managed by farmers, and raised upon the benches and side-hills that will not be brought under the ditch.

But in view of the future of the State, the experiments in agriculture are even more interesting than the harnessing of the cascades of the Missouri to the wheels of manufacture. The sugar-beet grows finely, in answer to the generally discussed project in most of these new States to render that form of sugar-making a leading industry when the lands are well settled. Fine, luscious strawberries grow right out on the plains wherever they have been planted, and one man on Belt Creek sold $170 worth of currants, raspberries, and strawberries from one acre of ground last year. Barley thrives in the soil, and has no dews or rains to bleach or "must" it when it is ripening. Wheat that is graded "No. 1 Northern" in Minneapolis grows thirty to fifty bushels to the acre. There is an orchard there already, producing fine apples; and here we get the first news of the astonishing potatoes of Montana—"the terrapin of the State," as they have been wittily called.

There are no such potatoes in the world as are grown in Montana. They attain prodigious size, and often weigh three, four, or five pounds apiece. Eighteen such potatoes make a bushel. To the taste they are like a new vegetable. The larger ones are mealy, but the smaller ones are like sacks of meal; when the skin is broken the meat falls out like flour. It must very soon become the pride of every steward in the first-grade hotels, restaurants, and clubs of the cities here—and even in Europe—to prepare these most delicious vegetables for those who enjoy good living. As these potatoes of the choicest quality can be cultivated in all the valleys east of the Rocky Mountains, there will soon be no lack of them. To-day the only ones that have left the State have been the few bushels sent to gourmets in New York, Washington, and San Francisco.

All this country east of the mountains must be irrigated to insure good crops. An early and general development of the farm lands is relied upon, because the great mining camps of the State will consume nearly all the products of the farms as fast as the farms increase in number. There is no danger that the mining camps will not grow and multiply to keep the demand strong. The miners are the best people in the world to farm for, because they produce money and they pay cash. The southern end of Lewis and Clarke County is a succession of fine valleys. Here is Helena, the capital of the State. Six miles away a cluster of gold mines is being reopened, after having produced millions. In this county the largest mine is the Drum Lummon, an English property that has paid dividends for many years. And here are the famous ruby and sapphire fields, on the bed-rock of former benches or bottoms of the Missouri. Strawberries of a large and luscious variety will yield 10,000 baskets to the acre, and have sold in the past at a fixed rate of twenty cents a basket for home consumption. Apples, plums, crab-apples, grapes, currants, and all berries grow in wonderful abundance, and find an eager and high-priced market close at hand. Oats weigh forty and fifty pounds a bushel, as against thirty-two pounds in the East, and a yield of sixty bushels to the acre can be obtained. All wheat that is brought out here for seeding produces a soft grain. It has been sent to Minneapolis to be ground into flour for pastry and cracker bakers. The Cracker Trust is building a big bakery in Helena, to be near this product. It is not a bread-making grain. But a new population is needed to reap the wealth that is offered from small fruits. The Chinamen are harvesting this money now, but they do not meet the home demand. It is a rich country, and will some day dry and can large crops of fruits and berries. The side-hills will graze small bands of cattle. If the bunch-grass sod is ploughed up, there follows a growth of blue-joint grass that is like timothy, and that is very high, heavy, and nutritious. The same result follows irrigation wherever it is permitted.

Jefferson, Madison, Silver Bow, Beaver Head, and Deer Lodge counties, in the mountains, are all very nearly like what has just been described. Mining is the principal source of revenue, and wheat, oats, potatoes, and stock are the other products.

West of the Rockies is quite a different country. It is all practically in Missoula County. The mountains are full of minerals; the valleys will produce anything, apparently, that grows in the temperate zone—even corn. Irrigation is not so absolutely necessary, and is not necessary at all in a great part of it. The land is lower; the rains are heavier; the winds from the Japan current blow there with frequency and strength, and are almost uninterrupted. Verdure remains green there all summer, and the abundance of timber, the many streams, and the verdant hills render the scenery more like what the Eastern man is accustomed to than that which he sees east of the Rockies in Montana. The southern part of Missoula County has been settled many years, largely by thrifty French Canadians, and it contains as fine farms as will be seen almost anywhere. Here are orchards, and small fruits grow in abundance for shipment to the Cœur d'Alene mining camps in Idaho. Here is a milling company that produced seventy-five millions of feet of lumber last year. In the north is a new country wrested from the Flathead reservation. The Flathead Valley is forty miles long and one-half as wide, possessing a deep soil and a clay subsoil. It is farmed without irrigation. Several tributary valleys of the same quality open out of the main valley. Large crops of grain, hay, vegetables, and fruit have been harvested there, but the farmers have heretofore been without a market, and have subsisted by raising horses and cattle, and driving them abroad for purchasers. The entrance of the Great Northern Railroad, now accomplished, will open up this rich territory, **and will** develop the timber resources as well as the deposits of coal, oil, and natural gas, which seem to be very extensive there. The mountains are practically unprospected, and have only just **been mapped by** Lieutenant Ahern, U.S.A., who has philanthropically devoted his summers to that **arduous and dangerous work.** Indications of quartz are **seen on every hand in the mountains.** Taking the county **as a** whole, two years ago not **a** mining prospect was **continuously** worked, **while now** four mines are shipping **and** paying profits of **$40,000 a** month. The "**leads**" in **the county** are continuations of those in **the Cœur** d'Alene country in Idaho. Coal as good as the Lethbridge product of Canada is found there in vast quantities. It is a fine sporting region. The Flathead Lake, which has 318 square miles of surface, is cold and clear, and so deep that it has been sounded to a depth of 1000 feet. It is full of landlocked salmon and big trout, and harbors millions of ducks and geese in their season, while deer and winged game are plenty in the country around it. **The** Flathead Indians, south of the lake, **have nice** farms, and raise cattle besides. They are self-sustaining, and **at** least a dozen can be named who have accumulated between $20,000 and $50,000. They are a fine, stalwart people. They are not in reality Flatheads; they have no knowledge that the tribe ever followed the practice of compressing the heads of the children, as **was done** by the tribes at the mouth of the Columbia River.

It is in this county that Marcus Daly, the mining millionaire, has invested a million dollars in horses and land, **and maintains a horse** farm that ranks next to Senator **Stanford's Palo** Alto farm in California. Here also **Daniel E. Bandmann, the** actor, has 1000 acres of land, and is raising imported Percheron horses and Holstein cattle. Other farmers are in the same business. It is an enormous county, and is so well populated that its people cast 4000 votes at elections. With its ore, timber, horses, cattle, coal, petroleum, grain, and diversified small crops, it is unquestionably the finest county in the State. It would be the richest were it not for Silver Bow, with its one industry of mining.

There is plenty of coal in Montana. It crops out in all the northern counties and in several of the southern ones. It is most profitably worked when the owner is interested in the railroad which carries it from the mines. In all probability, the best coal is found in the Sand Coulee fields, in Cascade County. The Rocky Fork mines, in Custer County, are part of a vast deposit which has all been secured by Eastern capitalists. One hundred coke ovens near Livingston, in Park County, provide coke for use in the smelteries at Butte. Also in Park County are the Timber Line and Horr mines. The coal of the State is semi-bituminous. Only a mere speck of what the State contains is being mined.

We have seen that cattle-raising is a conspicuous industry—if industry it can be called—and is carried on in, I think, every county of the State. Large cattle herds are already things of the past in the western end of the State, and it is evident that farming and settlement will soon drive them out of Gallatin and Cascade counties. It is cause for jubilation that this is the case. It seems strange that cruelty should distinguish this branch of food-raising wherever it is seen and in whatever branch one studies it. From the bloody fields of Texas, where the ingenious fiends in the cattle business snip off the horns of the animals below the quick, to the stock-yards in Chicago, where men are found who will prod the beeves into pens, there to crush their skulls with hammers, it is everywhere the same—everywhere the cattle business has its concomitants of cruelty and savagery.

The reader would not suppose there was cruelty in the mere feeding of cattle on the plains, but let him go to Montana, and talk with the people there, and he will shudder at what **he hears.** The cattle-owners, or cow-men, are in Wall Street and the south of France, or in Florida, in the winter, but their cattle are on the wintry fields, where every now and then, say once in four years, half of them, or 80 per cent., or one in three (as it happens) starve to death because of their inability to get at the grass under the snow. A horse or a mule can dig down to the grass. Those animals have a joint in their legs which the horned cattle do not possess, and which enables those animals which possess it to "paw." Sheep are taken to especial winter grounds and watched over. But the cow-men do business on the principle that the gains in good years far more than offset the losses in bad years, and so when the bad years come, the poor beasts die by the thousands—totter along until they fall down, the living always trying to reach the body of a dead one to fall upon, and then they freeze to death, a fate that never befalls a steer or cow when it can get food.

Already, on some of the ranges, the "cow-men" (cattle-owners) are growing tired of relying upon Providence to superintend their business, and they are sending men to look after the herds once a month, and to pick out the calves and weaker cattle and drive them to where hay is stored. By spring-time one in every fifteen or twenty in large herds will have been cared for in this way. In far eastern Montana range-feeding in large herds will long continue, but in at least five-sevenths of the State, irrigation and the cultivation of the soil will soon end it. The hills and upper benches, all covered with self-curing bunch-grass, will still remain, and will forever be used for the maintenance of small herds of cows and sheep, properly attended and provided with corrals and hay, against the times when the beasts must be fed. The farmers will undoubtedly go into cattle-raising, and dairy-farming is certain to be a great item in the State's resources, since the hills are beside every future farm, and the most provision that will be needed will be that of a little hay for stocking the winter corrals. Last year the cattle business in Montana was worth ten millions of dollars to the owners of the herds. "Providence was on deck," as the cowboys would say.

But the sheep there brought twelve millions of pounds of wool on their backs in the same year. They are banded in herds of about 2000 head, and each band is in charge of one solitary, lonely, forsaken herder, who will surprise his employers if he remains a sane man any great length of time. In the summer these herders sleep in tents, and the ranch foremen start out with fresh provisions at infrequent intervals, and hunt up their men as they follow the herds. In the winter the grazing is done in sheltered places especially chosen. On the winter grounds a corral is built, and thirty to forty tons of hay are stored there for emergencies when the snow lies thick on the ground. It is a prime country for sheep. They get heavy coats, and are subject to no epidemic diseases. The grass is rich and plenty, and the warm Pacific winds soon melt what snows occasionally cover the ground. The wool ranks next to that from Australia. The tendency of the sheep-herders to become insane is the most unpleasant accompaniment of the business, except the various forms of mutilation of the sheep for business reasons. The constant bleating of the sheep and the herder's loneliness, spending weeks and months without any **companionship except that of** a dog and the herd, are the causes **that** are commonly accepted to account for the fact that so many herders go insane. Since I found insanity terribly common among **the** pioneers **on the** plains **in Canada,** where no **sheep** were raised, I prefer to leave the incessant bleat-**ing of the** sheep out of the calculation, and to call it loneliness—and **yet, in my opinion,** that is not the sole reason.

The horse market has **been** very poor for some time, and mules are being raised for the market with **better** results. The substitution of electric for horse power on street railways has lessened the demand for horses, and so has the use of steam farming implements. There has been an over-supply of horses as **well. But** the Montana men find horses a good investment. It costs nothing to raise them, and all breeds **seem to** improve there. They get great lung development, and acquire no diseases. When they cannot be sold for from $50 **to** $100 apiece, **the** owners keep them until they do **fetch** those **prices.**

The great wealth of the State is in its mines. **Butte,** in Silver Bow County, is the greatest mining centre not only in Montana, but, with the possible **and** doubtful exception of one **town** in Australia, in all the world. The Butte output is of lead, silver, and copper. **The** total dividends paid by **all the** mines in the United States which make public their affairs was $16,024,842, and of that sum Montana's **mines paid** one-quarter, or $4,059,700. That amount **was paid in** 1891, up to the end of November. Yet the richest mines are owned by **private** corporations which do not make **known** their profits. The Granite Mountain mine, in Deer Lodge County, yielding silver, lead, and some little gold, paid its owners, who **are** mainly in St. Louis, $1,300,000 in the same eleven months, and has sent to St. Louis about ten millions in dividends since it began to pay. Eight years ago the stock in that mine was held at 25 cents a share, and men played pool for it in Helena and Butte.

Butte first attracted the miners in 1864. They did nothing except wash dirt for five years, but they washed out eight millions of dollars. Then they found the quartz, and went down on it, only to find a great deal more silver than gold. As they went down farther, they came upon the copper, and started a "boom" that shows no sign of diminution at this date. Butte has added to the world's wealth $140,000,000 in gold, silver, copper, and lead. The largest producers are the Anaconda, Boston and Montana, Colorado and Montana, Butte and Boston, Parrott, Lexington, Alice, Butte Reduction Works, Moulton, and Blue Bird. Those companies operate forty mines, and all have their own works for the reduction of ores. They are all high-grade ores, but some are high-grade in copper and some in silver. The Anaconda people, for instance, get enough silver and gold to render their vast output of copper all profit. As their capacity in copper is the greatest in the world, and as it does not cost them a cent a ton, they control the copper market of the earth. The principal owners of this property are the estate of Senator Hearst, J. B. Haggin, and Marcus Daly. Marcus Daly, who is known in the East as the foremost patron of the turf, came to Montana first on his feet, and worked at washing with a pan. That was less than twenty years ago, and now he is called "The White Czar" in Montana. He is an influential and shrewd politician, the owner of the second largest horse-breeding farm in the world, the greatest employer of labor in Montana, maintains a metropolitan hotel in a little town in the mountains, disregarding the loss it incurs in order that he may have a place in which to entertain his friends, and finally he maintains a first-class newspaper in the same town or village of Anaconda—a newspaper as good as is published in any city of the second class. The town of Anaconda is where the company reduces its ores. The profits of the company are never made public.

The camp next in importance after Butte is Castle, in Meagher County, sixty miles from a railroad. Barker and Neihart are camps in the same county. The mining is for silver and lead. The biggest mine in the Castle district is the Cumberland, which is known to be a heavy shipper of bullion, but is a close corporation. The mines in the district and in the county need railroads to open them up. Jefferson County is next to Silver Bow in richness, but though it has more paying mines than any other county in the State, the mining is all on a small scale. The Holder Mine, owned in England, is in this county. It paid $400,000 in 1891. There are about thirty districts in Lewis and Clarke County, as against seventy in Jefferson. The richest of the thirty is Unionville, five miles from Helena. The ore is free milling gold. The Whitlatch Union Company has produced $20,000,000 there.

As I have said elsewhere, Deer Lodge, Madison, Beaver Head, and Missoula counties are rich in mine "prospects," but the need of railroads in all except Missoula County hinders work there. The future in mining is not yet in sight in Montana. The mineral veins have been but scratched. For every developed mining district in the State there are ten that are not developed, and that promise as well as any that are now being operated. Moreover, vast reaches of the mountain country have not even been explored. Of copper Montana produced 50,000 tons in 1890; of gold, $3,500,000; of silver, $19,350,000.

A few of the many stories that are told of miners' luck will enable the reader to understand how and why the heads of whole communities may be turned in mining regions. Jim Whitlatch, the discoverer of the Whitlatch-Union mine, near Helena, led a typical Western miner's life. The mine in question is now owned in England, and has produced $20,000,000 in gold. After Jim Whitlatch had sold the property for $1,500,000 he went to New York "to make as much money as Vanderbilt." He was a rare treat to Wall Street, which fattened on him, and in one year let him go with only the clothes on his back. He returned to Montana, began "prospecting" again, and discovered a mine for which he got $250,000. He went to Chicago to rival Mr. Potter Palmer in wealth, and returned just as he did from New York—"flat-strapped," as he would have expressed it. He made still another fortune, and went to San Francisco, where he died a poor man. Another Lewis and Clarke County mine—the Drum Lummon—provides another such story. It was discovered by an Irish immigrant named Thomas Cruse. Although he owned it, he could not get a sack of flour on credit. He sold it to an English syndicate for $1,500,000. But he remains one of the wealthy men of Helena.

There is an ex-State Senator in Beaver Head County who owns a very rich mine, the ore yielding $700 to the ton net. He is a California "Forty-niner," who came as a prospector to Montana, and since discovering his mine has lived upon it in a peculiar way. He has no faith in banks. He says his money is safest in the ground. When he has spent what money he has, he takes out a wagon-load of ore, ships it to Omaha, sells it, and lives on the return until he needs another wagon-load.

There is a queer story concerning the Spotted Horse Mine, in Fergus County. It was found by P. A. McAdow, who sold it to Governor Hauser and A. M. Holder for $500,000 three years ago. They paid a large sum down in cash, and the other payments were to come out of the ground. The ore was in pockets, each of which was easily exhausted. Whatever was taken out went to McAdow, who got about $100,000. Then the purchasers abandoned it, on the advice of experts, and Mr. McAdow took hold of it. He found the vein, over which rails had been laid for a mining car. He has taken out $500,000, and it is still a good mine. One of these children of luck came to Helena with money, picked out a wife, who was then a poor seamstress, hired a hotel, and invited the town to the wedding. The amount of champagne that flowed at that wedding was fabulous, and it is said that the whole town reeled to bed that night.

Butte is the principal seat of the mining work. It is what they call in Montana "a wide-open town," and he who thinks he knows the United States because he can name the buildings which face the City Hall Park in New York would open his eyes and confess his astonishment were he to visit Butte. The old California mining spirit, the savor of the flush times of '49, was transplanted to the Treasure State during the war of the rebellion, and it still leaves strong traces everywhere in Montana. The smallest coin in circulation there is the nickel, or five-cent piece, but the shilling or "bit" is the unit of calculation. Shoeblacks and barbers charge two bits for their work; a drink at a bar costs a bit, and drinks go in pairs at two bits. Whoever wants a postage-stamp will either get no change out of a ten-cent piece, or will have the stamp given to him. Domestic servants are paid no less than $25 a month;

waiter-boys in the hotels get $10 a week and their keep; the lowest wages paid to labor are paid to street-sweepers, and they receive $2.50 a day. This is all an inheritance from California and the precedents set in Virginia City, Nevada, long ago. The little one-story and two-story square cottages that dot the suburbs of each city are of a type otherwise peculiar to the Pacific coast—a type that is seen at its best in San Francisco, San José, and Oakland.

The disproportionate size of the vicious quarters in each Montana city, and the fashions in these quarters, are inheritances from the era of the California gold fever. The outcast women, who were originally the only women in each camp, have a ward or district to themselves, and there the variety theatre (which is descended from the original Bella Union) and the "hurdy-gurdy houses," or dance halls, and the gambling hells are all clustered. The women have streets to themselves in Butte, Helena, Great Falls — and, for that matter, in Seattle also — just as they do in San Francisco. And, as is the case in California, each house in such a quarter is a one-room or two-room shanty, harboring one occupant. For the true women and the children of each city that end of town is *taboo*.

Butte has more than 30,000 inhabitants, and 5000 of its men work in the mines to produce a mineral output which is within five millions of dollars of the value of the total yield of Colorado. The laborers who repair the streets get $3.50 a day, and the miners earn from $4 to $7. When the shifts or gangs of men change at night — for the work never ceases — the main street of Butte is as crowded as Broadway at Fulton Street at noon. At two or three o'clock in the morning the city is still lively. There is no pretence about the town. It has few notable or expensive buildings, and it is without a good hotel. Deadwood and Butte are the only considerable towns I saw out West of which that could be said. It gives the reader a hint of the "beginnings" of Butte to be told that the site of the best brick and granite building on the main street was won by a man who happened to hold only two "Jacks" at the time he was "called." There are sixteen licensed gambling hells in Butte, and the largest ones are almost side by side on the principal street. They are as busy as so many exchanges. They are large, bare rooms, with lay-outs for faro, craps, stud poker, and other games on tables at every few feet along the walls, each table faced by a knot of men, and backed by a "dealer" and "watcher." The gambling hells keep open all the time except from Saturday midnight to Sunday midnight. In summer the doors stand open, and the gambling may be seen from the pavement. The liquor stores never close, neither do the barber-shops, nor—I fancy—the concert halls.

Montana has a saloon to every eighty inhabitants. It has more saloons than Alabama, Georgia, Kansas, and Indian Territory, Maine, Mississippi, South Carolina, West Virginia, Vermont, or the District of Columbia. "One thing I have noticed," said a liquor-dealer of Butte, "is that if a man quits drinking here, he will be dead in a month." This peculiarly businesslike observation veiled a reference to the sulphur fumes, which are the consequence of the presence of many smelteries. The city is at the bottom of a well, the walls of which are tall mountains. High up above the town, around one side of the well, are these smelteries, whose pipes emit smoke and sulphur. In addition to this, they were "heap-roasting" the ore in the open air when I was there, and the sulphur weighted and jaundiced the atmosphere. The people rose in anger and stopped the nuisance.

There are fine schools there, attended by 5000 children. The Catholic parish includes 10,000 souls, and is the largest west of the Mississippi. Butte is the only Montana town that maintains a club of university graduates. Its other club, the Silver Bow, is one of whose club-house appointments and membership any city might be proud. The people there maintain such elevating societies and chapters as those of the Epworth League, the Woman's Christian Temperance Union, the King's Daughters, and the Society of Christian Endeavor. There is a cricket club there, and a rod-and-gun club, and a strong Turnverein, or German athletic society. They have some notable displays in those stores which are the head depots of great trading companies that operate far and wide. Whatever is best in London, Paris, or New York can be duplicated in Butte, and it is said that when strawberries are a dollar a basket in New York, this strange city is one of the purchasers of them. Butte has six banks, with a capital of a million dollars, and a million of dollars are paid out there in wages every month.

It is impossible to make room for that which should be told of the cities of Montana generally. It is my opinion that Butte will grow steadily as long as the present mines pay and new ones continue to be developed. It will be a large city, judging from present appearances. Great Falls should, in the logic of its merits, become an important city. Miles City cannot be threatened by any changes in its vicinage except such as will cause it to grow. Missoula will in all likelihood be the capital of a great and rich farming district, and perhaps of a mining section as well. The Great Northern Railway, now completing its highway through the northern counties, must develop at least one sizable town on either side of the Rockies, but the names of those towns are not in my ken. There are going to be many more inhabitants in the State than there are in Pennsylvania — possibly **twice as many** — and they will build cities.

Though Helena **is** the capital, **it** must still **fight to retain** that honor, **the** permanent seat of **government not yet** having been chosen. But it seems almost **a** foregone conclusion that Helena will remain as it **is, for as Butte** is the industrial centre, so Helena is the **social** and financial headquarters. It has most of the concomitants of a **chief** city—all, in fact, except a first-class theatre. It is commonly credited with being the wealthiest city **of** its size in the world, and it does boast more than a dozen citizens each worth more than a million of dollars. But **it** gains that reputation most creditably **as** the backer of the principal enterprises in the State. **In its** best residence quarters are many fine and **costly** houses, and the people **in** them know the luxuries and refinements of cultivation and **wisely** managed wealth. Helena has three daily newspapers, which **receive** the despatches of the chief news associations of the country. **A** very commendable spirit in Montana finds expression in **a** State historical society, whose already imposing collections **are** housed in one of the public buildings in Helena. President Stuart and Secretary Wheeler, in gathering the early newspapers, diaries, photographs, and biographies **of** the pioneers, are performing **a** work which will **swell in value** faster **than** compound interest enhances the **value** of money.

All the principal religious bodies are well represented in Helena in **church** buildings and membership; the schools and other public buildings are the subjects of popular **pride**; the **stores** are fine and well stocked.

The Montana Club, now building a palatial stone clubhouse, is very much more like an Eastern than a Western club in all that makes a club attractive. There are other clubs — Scotch, German, literary, musical, mercantile, and athletic; there are military organizations and the lodges of half a dozen secret fraternities, and there is a State Fair Association which maintains a fine race-track. Helena has many manufactures, and eight banks, with a joint capital of two and one-third millions of dollars. Already three transcontinental railways meet there — the Northern Pacific, Union Pacific, and the Great Northern. Among its hotels, the Helena is a most cozy and metropolitan house, and in summer the Hotel Broadwater, in the suburbs, gives to Montana the finest hotel and watering-place in the Northwest. It is the property and venture of Colonel C. A. Broadwater, a pioneer and millionaire, and comprises a park, a hotel of the most modern and elegant character, and the largest natatorium in the world—a bath 300 feet long and 100 feet wide, of natural hot water, medicated and curative, yet as clear as crystal, and without offence to taste or smell. The beautiful Moorish bath-house, with its daily concourse of health and pleasure seekers, its band of music and atmosphere of indolence, is the pleasantest holiday spot in the new States. But, in my opinion, still stronger attractions to Helena are its surroundings and its climate, its 300 bright, sunny, golden days in every year, its crisp, clear, healthful atmosphere, and its picturesque belt of soft, rolling mountain breasts encircling it.

Speaking from the stand-point of physical human pleasure, none of the new States has a climate to compare with that of Montana. There the air is always tonic, even magnetic. It rains on 65 days in the year, but the sun manages to shine more or less even on those days — which come in April, May, and June. The valleys are 4000 to 6000 feet above sea-level. Upon them the soft warm winds of the Pacific slope blow after they have emptied their moisture upon the mountain ranges of Washington. These winds temper the climate of Montana so that it seems not to belong in the cold belt of our most northerly States. It is nothing like so cold as the Dakotas; indeed, there are only a few cold days at a time, mainly in January, with little skating or sleighing, and an assurance that the Chinook breezes are always close at hand. Montana is a sanitarium. No account can be given of the attractions of the State without putting the climate high in the list. It has a magic power to breed enthusiastic love in the hearts of all who live there, even if their stay is of but a few months' duration. The inhabitants all went there to make money, and now they remain to praise the country. A spell, a mania, seizes all alike, and each vies with the other in overestimating the vast number of ox teams that would be required to pull him back whence he came.

Close to Helena, on ledges which mark two former levels of the Missouri River, are the world-famous sapphire and ruby beds, 8000 acres of which, with 2000 other acres under water, have recently been acquired by an English company of noblemen, bankers, jewellers, and others for $2,000,000, the mere value of the gold which it is thought will be taken from the dirt. That sapphires and rubies were there has been known for twenty years or more, some miners having kept the finer specimens, and others having thrown them out of their pans into the river by the hundredweight as pebbles of no value. The truth, as I get it from experts, is that these stones are true rubies and sapphires, and the only opportunity they afford for criticism lies in the fact that very nearly all of them are much lighter in color than the Asiatic gems of the same sort. In other words, pigeon's-blood rubies and sapphire-blue sapphires are found there, but not often. And yet these stones of the lighter shades are of far greater brilliancy than the Asiatic gems that fashion has approved; indeed, they are often like diamonds, and as their hardness is next to that of the diamond, their lustre must prove enduring. The gems are found on the bedrock under eight or ten feet of soil, along with crystals, nuggets of gold, gold-dust, garnets, and pebbles. The land was bought by two Michigan lumbermen, brothers, who now treasure a million in cash and a million in shares of the new English company—rewards for their foresight.

One of the English experts who examined the gem fields announced it to be his opinion that the diamond must sooner or later be found in Montana. All the conditions warrant its existence there. What a State Montana is! Gold, silver, copper, lead, asbestos, tin, iron, oil, gas, rubies, sapphires, and a possibility of diamonds—all locked up in her ribs and pockets!

I see a vision of Montana in the future, yet in the lifetime of the young men of to-day. I see half a dozen such mining centres as Butte, and they are all noble cities, set with grand buildings, boulevards, and parks. I see at least two great manufacturing towns besides. I see scores of great valleys, and other scores of little ones, all gay with the blossoms of fruits and grain, supporting a great army of prosperous farmers. I see tens of thousands of rills of water embroidering the green valleys, and I dream that the men who need that water to make the earth give up its other treasures are not obliged to pay more than the conduits cost, merely to enrich a set of water lords who seized the streams when no one was there to protest. I see the brown hills and mountain-sides of the eastern part of Montana dotted with cattle and sheep in small herds. The woollen industry has become a great source of wealth, and Montana has robbed New England of some of her factories. I see in western Montana great saw-mills and mines that were not dreamt of in 1892. I see car-loads of fruit and vegetables and barley malt rolling into the cities, and out to other States. I see no Indians except those who work or who serve in the army, and where there were reservations I see the soil laughing with verdure or tracked with cattle. I see statisticians calculating the value of the annual product of the State; the figures are too stupendous for repetition here. Montana is fulfilling her destiny. She is one of the most populous and opulent members of our sisterhood of States.

VII

GLIMPSES OF PAST, PRESENT, AND FUTURE

SHOPPING IN THE ROCKIES

I am going to the Rocky Mountains to do my shopping! If any one in the East heard a lady say that he would certainly take a second look at her. But he would scarcely be more surprised than I was, to be in the thick of the Rockies, with Lieutenant Ahern, U.S.A., for a companion, hearing his modest recountal of adventures in the most magnificent wilderness in our country; and then on the westward slope, among the foot-hills, to step from the cars to a store like Whiteley's Necessary Store in London, or one of our "shopping stores" on the Sixth Avenue, New York. That was one of the surprises of my experiences in the far West. It was in Missoula, Montana, that I found the unexpected great bazar. It is only fair to say that Missoula has had sly hopes that she might become the capital of the new State of Montana—if the rivalry between Butte and Helena and Great Falls necessitates a diplomatic tendency towards the choice of some place apart from those. But Missoula, though beautiful and kept almost evergreen by the soft winds from the Pacific, is rather the capital of the thoroughly un-Eastern strip of Montana on the other side of the Rockies than of the imperial eastern half of the State.

When I left the cars at this place I found it a typical Western town, with one street of shops, with a fine hotel, some businesslike banking-houses, a club, and a great scattering of dwellings, sufficient for a population of about 4000 or 5000 souls, if my memory serves me right. I noticed one block of stores in particular. They were distinctly "cityfied" in appearance. They had great plate-glass fronts, and the windows were shrewdly and attractively used for displaying the goods within. One was a dry-goods store, the next was a boot and shoe store, the next was a grocery, and the last was a hardware and agricultural implement emporium. All were brilliantly illuminated by electric lamps. Recovering from the first surprise at finding such modern shops in such a place, I next noticed that all of them were alike and of a piece, and then I saw that they lacked the usual sign-boards of different merchants over the windows.

They were, in fact, but a few of the many departments of the Missoula Mercantile Company's stores, and before I tell more about that, I will intrude a note with regard to such places in general. The first of these great trading companies' stores that I saw in the West were in Butte, the great mining town of Montana, and the liveliest, "wide-openest" town it has yet been my lot to run across—one in which the barber-shops never closed, and sixteen licensed gambling saloons flared open on the main street. Two of these great trading establishments have their headquarters in that city, and a tour of either one reveals an enormous stock and great variety of goods, "cash railways," lines of young men and girls behind the counters, crowds of elbowing and goods-handling shoppers, and more of the atmosphere of Sixth Avenue than one feels in any stores in the generality of Eastern cities that deem themselves quasi-metropolitan.

Those who have done me the honor to follow the reports of my wanderings will recall that I found great general stores of the kind in Winnipeg and Victoria, British Columbia, and that they marked the development of the original trading-posts of the Hudson Bay Company, wherever great towns have grown up around the little original forts of the corporation. These Montana emporiums are not the outgrowth or feature of any fur-trading operations, but they are the result of the same necessity that has developed the fur-trading posts. Here in Montana have come big lumbering companies, mining camps, army posts, Indian reservations, railway divisional headquarters, and one form or another of settlements by or collections of men to be supplied with food, clothing, implements, and whatever. The more enterprising traders have extended their business, until such a bulk of trade has come to them that they can buy in enormous quantities at large discount, and have no competitors except one another.

This Missoula Mercantile Company is capitalized at a million and two hundred thousand dollars. It transacted a business of more than two millions of dollars last year. It has four branch stores in addition to the great central one at Missoula; one being at Corvallis, one at Stevensville, one at Victor, and one at Demersville, at the head of navigation on Flathead Lake, in northwestern Montana, near Kalispel, a divisional point on the route of the Great Northern Railway, the last transcontinental trunk-line that is being pushed to the Pacific Ocean. The Missoula company does a large jobbing business with storekeepers and lumbering and mining camps. It is a country A. T. Stewart concern, wholesaling and retailing all necessaries and luxuries to the people of what may be called Montana-west-of-the-Rockies. This whole territory is in one county of imperial size—about 300 miles wide and 600 miles long, with a population of 20,000 souls. Not satisfied with reigning supreme in that field, the Missoula company does business in the Cœur d'Alene mining region in Idaho.

Mr. A. B. Hammond, the president of the company, was born on the St. John's River in New Brunswick. He went West as a young man, and worked as a woodchopper for a time. He reached Missoula in 1868 as poor as he was ambitious; but to-day, at forty-four years of age, he is a wealthy man, with spare time enough to have become a student and a lover of literature. Indeed, it is said of him that when he had his fortune to make "he used to work all day and read all night." He is more than just to his employés; has made presents of stock to those who have displayed the most enthusiasm and enterprise, and now numbers among the stockholders twenty-one who are employés. Each of the many departments of the big concern is managed by its own headman, who has sole charge of it, buys all the goods sold in it, and reports upon its condition once a year.

The stores or departments are nearly all together in one long two-story block, and as all are thrown together by communicating passageways, the reader will understand that the effect upon a visitor is that of one general shopping store. The various stores or departments are these: a gentleman's furnishing and clothing store; a wine and spirit, tobacco and cigar, department; a dress-making and tailoring department; a dry-goods and carpet store; a boot and shoe store; a grocery store; and an extensive department for the sale of hardware, cutlery, agricultural, mining, and lumbermen's implements, harness, saddlery, wagons, carriages, and blacksmiths' supplies. I noticed that there were displayed large assortments of crockery, upholstery, furniture, and made-up gowns, wraps, and cloaks for the women, so that, speaking widely, and at this distance in space and memory, I do not recollect that these traders left unoccupied any field of barter in Missoula except jewelry, drugs, and fresh meat. And I fancy the business must include a trade in drugs, since they would be demanded in the mining and lumber camps and by the retail dealers at a distance. The purchases of the company are upon such a scale, and it buys so shrewdly, that its profits must be very considerable. It is an indication of how the new Western cities are cutting into New York's trade to know that all that the Missoula Company buys here are carpets, dry-goods, gentlemen's furnishings, clothing, hats and caps, and some cigars. Its imported wines and liquors and its groceries are bought in Chicago, its sugar and canned fruits in California, and its teas in Japan.

One hundred and twenty-five clerks, salesmen, workmen, and department heads comprise the force of attendants and managers of this astonishing country store, and the capital it "swings," to use a Western phrase, finds outside chances for multiplication by investments in the Blackfoot Milling Company, a land company or two, and in a national bank. I have mentioned this concern by name and described it, but it must be remembered that it is but one of many such trading ventures where one would least expect to find them.

THE SAPPHIRE BEDS

There is not a more uninteresting-looking patch of ground in all our Northwestern States than that which a company of Englishmen has just bought in Montana for two millions of dollars. Yet it is a question whether there is a space of equal size that arouses a keener interest when the truth about it is known, for it is a mine of rubies and sapphires. It is eight thousand acres in extent, and would look, to a stranger, like nothing more than a bit of pasture-land.

The tract in question is formed of the river-bank in the elbows of several bends in the Missouri River near Helena, the capital of Montana. All through that Northwestern country, after the great river once has broken its bonds and gushed out from the stony hills at what is called the Gate of the Rocky Mountains, it meanders along a curving route through the plains, always in a deep gutter that it has worn down or eaten through. Just where the gems are found there are hills and lesser mountains in sight, but they also are covered with the bunch-grass of the plains, and grass is all that any one sees in any view from the river, either there or over a territory of imperial size to the eastward and southward. Down in the river-gulch there are two former levels of the river, a low terrace forming the present banks of the stream, and a higher one rising above and beyond it. It is on these former levels, under the sod and the soil that time has heaped upon the old river-bottoms, that the jewels are found. The benches or terraces are most pronounced at the bends of the river, and it is the land in a series of these elbows or curves, extending fifteen miles along the stream, that the Englishmen have purchased.

They did not discover the gems, nor were they the first owners of the land after the Government. They purchased it from two brothers Spratt, lumbermen from Michigan, who managed to get nearly all of it before they permitted the fame of the gigantic scheme they had for selling out to a company to be widely noised abroad. But the Spratts were not the discoverers either.

It seems that the discovery dates back twenty-seven years, and was almost simultaneous with the first practical movement towards a settlement of Montana. At about the time of the outbreak of the Civil War there was a rush to Alder Gulch in Montana, and placer-mining or dirt-washing for nuggets and gold-dust led to the establishment of a camp called Virginia City. Millions of dollars were taken from those diggings, and then the next big find led to a stampede to Last Chance Gulch, which was what is now called Helena. While all the miners were running the pebbles, dirt, and rocks of this new field under their water-jets or through their pans, the men who got no foothold there roamed about the neighborhood — and probably almost all over the State — and some began placer-mining on the banks of the big river close by. Among those who washed the edges of the river-banks was an Irishman, who soon came to be dubbed "Sapphire" Collins, because of a monomania that seized him. This was nothing less than the collecting of the sapphires, rubies, and garnets which he found in his pan every time he washed there. He carried the best specimens out of each lot around in his pockets, and came frequently to Last Chance Gulch to show his treasures. It is said that he had more than an ordinary knowledge of gems in the rough. At all events, he insisted that he had found a bed of sapphires and rubies. He bothered everybody with news of his "find," and with his efforts to secure capital for pre-empting the river-banks, until he came to be dubbed "Sapphire" Collins, and was laughed at by every one.

Eventually, as the matter is remembered, he became really deranged, and his talk showed that disappointment in failing to find any purchasers for his claim was what had turned his brain. But in the mean time he had seen all the financiers and successful miners, and all had enjoyed an opportunity to make the money which **the** English have within eight weeks poured into the purses of his successors. The truth was that Last Chance Gulch was proving one of the richest placer-grounds ever known. Men were at work reaping the harvest that was to reach a grand total of twenty-five millions of dollars. These were not the men nor was that the place to bring to market a handful of dirty-looking and dubious pebbles, when gold was so certain and so plentiful. Thus all that came of the discovery of the greatest gem field in America was the nicknaming of a miner and the wrecking of his intellect.

Although "Sapphire" Collins was the discoverer, other prospectors found the stones at other places, for a great deal of washing was done along the edges of the land that the Englishmen have just bought. The majority of the miners, remembering the fate of Collins, and supposing the peculiar pebbles to have no value, dumped them out of their pans by the bushel and the barrel into **the river,** along with all the dirt and stones that were **left** when the gold was picked out.

But a great many who noticed that the stones **were** translucent carried the prettiest **and** largest ones **as** pocket-pieces, while still **others** sent their best collections to New York to be cut. It is a peculiar fact that most of the stones that were treasured in this way, and nearly all that were sent to lapidaries to be cut, were the white and colorless crystals which are plentiful in the beds, but are of no value. The only colored stones that were thought to be worth keeping were the garnets. It is to this strange chance that is ascribed the fact that the lapidaries of the East continued in ignorance of the existence of the true sapphires and rubies. Some of the pretty stones that were saved were chrysolites, which are technically described as being "a silicate of magnesia and iron;" and others were corundums, hard stones of nearly pure alumina, used for polishing steel and cutting gems. Both are found in the Montana beds.

There next appears in the history of this fascinating discovery another man with a faith in the gems that was as strong as that of "Sapphire" Collins, but this new character was a man whose intelligence could not be questioned. His name is George B. Foote, and he not only collected the gems and talked about their value, he wrote about them in the local newspapers, and, later still, published an article about them in a conspicuous Eastern periodical. Then seven years passed, and Mr. George F. Kunz, of the house of Tiffany & Co., jewellers, of New York, wrote for HARPER's MAGAZINE an article on "Precious Stones in the United States." He knew what Foote had written, and had been investigating the matter; and when he came to speak of the Montana fields, he said that the sapphire was found there of a lighter color than the Asiatic variety, but that a few small gems of the true ruby and sapphire colors had been found there. In the *Engineering and Mining Journal* for January 2, 1892, he reviews his later knowledge of the subject, and says, "The colors of the gems obtained, although beautiful and interesting, are not the standard blue or red shades popular with the public." Mr. Kunz is considered to be the highest authority upon the subject of gems in America, and his verdict attracted a great deal of attention, and brought the first honor to the memory of poor Collins.

It was at about the time of the publication in HARPER'S MAGAZINE that the brothers Spratt appeared in this slow-moving history. F. D. Spratt, of Michigan, bought a placer claim on Trout Creek, near "Eldorado Bar." This so-called Eldorado Bar is the last of the benches in the London syndicate's purchase, but it is the bench on which the first discoveries were made, the one which has been concerned in all the talk and writing upon the subject, and is to be the scene of the beginning of the prospective mining. This is all because it has happened so. As I understand it, the Eldorado is no richer than the other bars. Mr. Spratt became interested in the discussion, and at once selected a lot of gems from those he found on the bar, and sent them to various places to be cut and classified. A few were of the darker tints, but most of them were light. However, the reports upon all of them were that they were true sapphires. From the Helena *Independent* I quote the following account of the next steps towards the introduction of these jewels in the world's markets:

"Satisfied that there was a future for the Montana gems, Mr. Spratt began to buy up all the gem-bearing land that he could get hold of. The placer-miners and ranchmen thought it another case of Collins, ran up their prices, and sold to the man from Michigan. Besides buying, Mr. Spratt entered land under the mineral laws, and finally he controlled, with his associates, about four thousand acres of gem-bearing ground. For about one-half of this he obtained a government patent. The miners were glad to unload, though they pitied Spratt. But Mr. Spratt had the son of the most noted English gem expert come all the way over from the African diamond fields to look over his ground. This gentleman, G. K. Streeter, satisfied himself that the gems were in Montana, and took numerous samples back with him. They were subjected to every test, and then pronounced genuine. Then it was determined to organize a company in England for the purpose of developing the fields and placing their product on the European market. News of this reached Montana, and ground on the Missouri River which was thought to contain gems was taken up and held at thousands of dollars where previously it had been considered worthless."

I was in Helena at the time that the English commissioners were making their final examination of the grounds and closing their purchases, and I was told that river-side lands for as far as forty miles up the river were held at extravagant prices. Moreover, stones brought to town by prospectors, such as had been selling for two bits apiece, were now held at $5, and even $25. And cut stones on exhibition in the jewelry stores were offered for sale at the rate of $50 a carat, and even higher, that is to say, at almost the prices of diamonds. All this was a natural result of the unexpected discovery of the value of the gem beds, but it was none the less interesting. We shall see that the Englishmen may expect to realize such prices in the future, but in buying the treasure they valued it in a widely different way.

The caution with which the Englishmen advanced into the work of organizing their company and making their purchase was, to the Americans at least, a notable feature of the affair. Perhaps they were afraid that the so-called gem lands were "salted"—that is to say, sprinkled with genuine jewels brought in the rough from somewhere else—or perhaps they but exercised their customary caution. At any rate, they first obtained a report from a well-known engineer. He made a voluminous and exhaustive statement, in which he said that the sapphires are found to be numerous over a large area for nearly three miles on both branches, and from the river-bank to the foot-hills wherever openings were made. Then two experts from England went all over the ground and made their reports, which, as it turned out, confirmed that of the American. Then the Englishmen proceeded to obtain views upon the character, quality, and value of the jewels from English gem experts. Professor A. H. Church, Professor of Chemistry at the Royal Academy, S. P. Thompson, professor in the London Technical College, and F. W. Rudder, curator of the Museum of Practical Geology in London, were all asked to examine stones that were brought to them from Montana. They all, happily for the owners of the river benches, pronounced the gems sapphires and rubies. They said they found them to be pure alumina, with very slight traces of iron. Their crystalline form, hardness (which is next to that of the diamond), and specific gravity were all proofs of their genuineness. As one expert phrased it, "some of them exhibit shades of pink and red, and may be scientifically designated rubies." Then the Englishmen got a report from **Edwin W. Streeter**, the well-known jeweller of London. He found the Montana stones admirable in every way. He found that, "taking a hundred carats in the rough, twenty-five carats would be cuttable gems, and the **remaining 75 per cent. only valuable for mechanical uses and watch-work. Of the cuttable gems there would be returned from the lapidary, say, eight and three-fourths carats of cut gems."

Thus equipped with these expert opinions, the promoters undertook to get subscribers **to the** stock of the company. This is done in England through the work of a person called an underwriter, who receives a commission for the services he contributes. The underwriter begins his task with an effort to secure as officers and founders of the company men of title, high social position, distinction in commercial life, or fame in **the** professions. With these names, and the merits of the scheme set forth in prospectuses and circulars, he begins to advertise the company and take subscriptions to the stock. In the case of the "Sapphire and Ruby Company of Montana" such **names as** that of the Duke of Portland, the millionaire Marquis of Tweeddale, Sir Francis Knollys, secretary to the Prince of Wales, Sir Arthur Sullivan, the operatic composer, Frank C. **Burnand**, editor of *Punch*, and a great many lords, earls, baronets, secretaries to dukes and duchesses, **railway** officials, brokers, and well-known business men were put down among the officers, founders, or early subscribers to the company.

The subscription-books were closed in London on November 2, 1891, and that is when the deal for the land in Montana was practically closed. The property purchased by a preliminary payment in cash some weeks later was bench land to the extent of about 8000 acres on both sides of the Missouri River for a distance of twelve or fifteen miles, together with all the water rights in the district. It is said that not all the gem-bearing lands nor all the water rights have been purchased outright, but all that have not been bought have been leased for a long term. The company is stocked for £450,400 in £1 shares, and is understood to have paid £400,000 (or $2,000,000) to the brothers Spratt, one-half in cash, and one-half in fully paid-up shares. I was told by one of the gentlemen in the English party that in appraising the land the basis of calculation was the amount of placer gold that would be found upon or in it, so that the gems would be considered a second source of income or by-product. It is said that although the brothers Spratt receive a million of dollars for the land, this is by no means to be considered as a windfall. They spent a very great deal of money in securing the bulk of the land, and held options on a lot more, which they paid for, or will pay for when they receive the English money. The money was not to be paid until an examination of all the titles to the land had been made by a firm of reputable lawyers.

The mining that was being done when I was in Helena was of the most primitive sort. The gems lie on or close to the bed-rock, which is covered with ten feet of soil on the lower benches, and perhaps twenty feet on the upper benches, or second terrace. The workmen dig down through the soil and sand, which they throw away until they are within a few inches of the rock. That rock is practically smooth, and is like a shelf, upon which the gold and gems are found. The gravel or dirt close to the rock is passed through a coarse sieve, and then through a fine one. What the coarse sieve holds is thrown away. The second sieve lets the dirt through it, and the stones rattle down the screen into a box. The contents of the box are put into a sack and carried to the river, where the stones are washed and sorted. Besides the gems, they find in the washings quartz pebbles, slate, alluvial gold, and nodules of iron. Between 2000 and 3000 carats in sapphires and rubies have been taken out in this way daily without machinery. According to the figures of Mr. Streeter, the London jeweller, who is now a stockholder in the company, this rate of mining would produce $8\frac{1}{4}$ carats of marketable gems in every 100, or about 250 carats a day. It is understood that the mining on Eldorado Bar will continue in this primitive way all winter, but that next spring (1892) hydraulic washing will be introduced. There is not likely to be any very rapid work upon the mines. The owners know enough not to flood the market with the stones, either all at once or in any manner.

I have seen a great many of these gems; indeed, I have seen pints of them at a time in the company of experts or in my wanderings among those who had them to sell. They are very disappointing to look at in the rough. Were any person who is accustomed to spend his summers upon the sea-coast to see a hatful of them, his first impression would be that they were very like the chromatic and translucent pebbles that are mixed with the sand on the ocean beach, the pretty stones which children pick up and carry to the hotel verandas to play with. A closer look at the gems would reveal the fact that nearly all except the garnets look green or pale blue, and are of many-sided crystalline shape, or at least have evidently been of that shape before some or all of their sides were worn smooth by the action of the water in rolling them along upon and among the rocks. An expert would point out a singular mark upon nearly all of them—a raised triangular piece upon their ends, the outlines of the triangle being very clearly defined. This, I believe, is what is called the signature of the sapphire. After that, when the stones were held up to the light and looked through, interest in them would increase, for unexpected colors would be found in them, and there would be seen a nameless quality about them which is due to the subdued luminousness which cutting will reveal in all its force. The colors they are seen to possess are all shades of green, all shades of blue except the indigo shade, all shades of yellow and red, and a great many pink and violet hues. The shapes they take are those of bits of pipe stem, perfect crystal, and a queer flat form like the body of a flat-iron, though not as large as an ordinary masculine thumb nail. The flat ones are thin; the cylindrical and hexagonal ones are thick. As a rule, I should say they vary between the size of half a carat and less than four carats. This attempt at a description is an effort of an untrained memory and an absence of technical knowledge, and must be taken, as it is intended, as a general suggestion.

And what do I think of them? They are very beautiful when they are cut. They sparkle and almost flame as the original or fashionable Asiatic sapphires do not begin to do. In fact, the Asiatic sapphires, when put beside them, appear like highly polished colored glass beside a flaming jewel. I am assured that this fiery quality of the Montana stones will endure forever, because of their very great hardness. The diamond, being classed as 10 in point of hardness, is only one-tenth harder than these Montana stones. I have not been so fortunate as to see any Montana rubies, and therefore will not speak of them. I have not the least doubt in the world that rubies are found there, though they are very uncommon. A peculiar thing about some of the sapphires is that they look red from one point of view and blue from another.

But now as to the sapphires. They are genuine and very beautiful, but they are not, except in very rare examples, of the color of the true sapphire. Therefore they are at a disadvantage. If they were all sapphire blues, they would still have the diamond to fight against — that brilliant plague of all owners of other stones, since it persists in remaining fashionable year after year in spite of every effort to dethrone it. But in addition to the supremacy of the diamond, these home gems are of many colors, and yet not of the right colors. I think they are, next to the diamond, the most ornamental stones I ever saw. But what will others think? What will fashion decree with regard to them? There is their situation in a nutshell. To it there can only be added a glance at the titles of the noblemen interested in the company. If they can induce royalty to don Montana gems, and if their own duchesses and countesses and grand dames all put them on, Dame Fashion will certainly deign to cast an eye upon our offering. Then we shall have to wait and see whether she frowns or smiles.

THE GREAT FALLS OF THE MISSOURI

It can scarcely be possible that time adds to history so fast anywhere else in the world as it does in the new Northwestern States of this country. To very much the majority of Americans the marvellous Falls of the Missouri are thought of as Captains Lewis and Clarke so graphically described their discovery, ornamenting a vast rolling wilderness of plains-land in what might be with poetic license described as the shadow of the Rocky Mountains. Those gallant explorers made their famous excursion across the continent in 1804-6. When they mapped the country they traversed, they thought of the lands through which the Missouri runs only as the territory which had been the subject of the Louisiana purchase. Montana was thus part of Louisiana in their time. Then it became part of Missouri Territory; next it was part of Nebraska Territory; and after that it was part of Dakota. That, however, was slow-paced history, and in that region the people do not think that the recent organization of Montana as one of the sisterhood of States was accomplished any too quickly.

Later events of a minor character have been much more rapid in that region. That is markedly illustrated by two little pamphlets that lie on my desk as I write. In one the author, Mr. William F. Wheeler, now secretary of the Montana Historical Society, says, under date of 1882, that the Falls of the Missouri are in Choteau County, 100 miles from the Northern Pacific Railroad at Helena. There was then no railroad to them. In the other pamphlet, issued by the business men of "that prosperous centre of industrial activity" called Great Falls, the rapids and cataracts in the Louisiana purchase are described as being near the county-seat of Cascade County, on three railroads—the Great Northern, the Montana Central, and the Great Falls and Canada. In so short a time a new county, a prosperous industrial centre, and three railroads altered the local conditions out there.

I visited the falls last winter, and am both free and

IN COTTON-WOOD PARK, GREAT FALLS

frank to confess that in thinking of them the thrilling and fascinating experiences of their discoverers, Lewis and Clarke, were uppermost in my mind. On the way there, it happened that I met an energetic and valiant successor to those military officers in the person of Lieutenant Ahern, who has of late years done much valuable work in exploring and mapping the Rocky Mountains in Montana. It fell out, most appropriately, that he told me of an adventure during this work wherein Lewis and Clarke may be said almost to have returned to the virgin territory in which they risked and often nearly lost their lives. Lieutenant Ahern had cut out from a copy of their printed journal those leaves wherein they describe their journey over and through the Rocky Mountains. The lieutenant was in a part of the mountains with which he was unfamiliar, and, happening to meet a hunter, he talked with him about the forward route to be taken. The hunter professed intimate familiarity with the trail, but speedily acknowledged himself lost. As night was falling, a camp was made, and Lieutenant Ahern whiled the time away by rereading his pages of Lewis and Clarke's journal. He found in them an accurate description of the country around him, and in the morning enjoyed the satisfaction of becoming guide to the hunter, and leading him to a landmark which both were seeking. Later still, when I stood beside one of the falls of the majestic river, I was informed that though it is nearly ninety years since the explorers visited and described the cascades and rapids, their descriptions and even their measurements apply to them accurately to-day.

I did not have the journal of the explorers with me, but I recollected how they separated, and Captain Lewis took one water route while his companion followed another stream, each being most anxious to come upon the falls in order to distinguish the main current from its feeders. I remembered Captain Lewis's hearing the noise of the great fall from a distance of seven miles. I recalled his description of numerous great but abandoned Indian camps, and the notes he made of the scene near the falls, where the vast grassy plain was dotted with great herds of buffalo. I remembered how a bear chased him into the river, how three buffalo bulls charged upon him, how a rattlesnake came near to making his acquaintance in a most unpleasant manner, and how the hardy explorer wrote that at the end of all these adventures he felt his mind crowded with a host of memories of the uncommon and astonishing scenes and occurrences he had witnessed and experienced.

Leaving out the buffalo, or perhaps exchanging for them the Texan steers of to-day in far fewer numbers, and excepting the big-horned sheep and the wolves and eagles and deserted Indian camps, the scene near the Great or Lower Falls cannot be so different from what it was in their day as Messrs. Lewis and Clarke might expect. To-day, as then, the everlasting, rolling blanket of brown bunch-grass reaches incessantly away in every direction except where the Belt Mountains and other spurs of the Rockies raise their blue and sometimes snow-capped masses. To one who has seen the Missouri elsewhere, in Montana, the Dakotas, or Nebraska, the falls, where they occur, impress the spectator as being entirely outside of the staid and dignified character of the noble stream. But scarcely anywhere along the whole course of the river could they create greater surprise in one who was not on the lookout for them than where they are found. It is true that there the plains are very hilly and contorted, but this very irregularity of the earth's surface helps to hide the river, and one may often ride close beside it, and look over it

LOWER FALLS

at the hills beyond, without getting a glimpse of the lordly stream. The Missouri, before it comes to the first falls, is only about 300 yards wide, enormous enough in itself, but, as seen by an eagle, a mere thread of silver and suds bisecting the plains.

The best way to see all the falls and the rapids is from below. It must be remembered that for a distance of more than a dozen miles the river battles with its slanting bed, or, if it be not battling it, is racing and frolicking down a steep hill. There are five falls and a score of rapids in that madcap descent. It is five hundred feet nearer to the level of the sea at the end of that run than it was at the beginning. Approaching the river from below the lower falls, it is found to be compressed into a third of its former and after width by towering walls of sandstone, which form a magnificent cañon. In the bottom of that it races along, now smoothly and now in myriads of fretful wrinkles, white-capped here and there, as it passes over the rocks that it has hurled along and formed into semi-blockades against its own headway. It is not here a muddy river. It is a mighty course of crystal when you sample it; of emerald where it is shallow; of molten sapphire where it has great depth. The sheer and mighty walls suggest the Palisades of the Hudson in places; but in other parts they are broken, and terraces of bunch-grass rise one above the other, each toothed with an outcropping of rough or jagged rock.

It seems at first as though the river must once have filled up the great gutter along the bed of which it runs, and must there have been many times as deep as it is now; but the farther up the ascent is made, as fall and rapid, rapid and fall, are passed, the more evident it becomes that the river descends at a greater angle than the land slopes, and that the effect this produces is heightened very greatly where the hills that accompany its course press close upon its sides. It is everywhere a noble stream, but to the eastward and southward of the falls, in other States, it has an indolent, patient, stolid character. To understand its might and mastery, it must be seen not only where it carves a roadway through the bed-stone of the plains but higher up still, where it bursts the Rockies asunder, and scattering the solid masses like a Hercules fretted by granite bonds, leaps out from the gloom and shadows of the hills into the open and sunshine of the plains. It has always seemed to me a gigantic theft and outrage that we committed when we gave to the more famous part of this royal river the name of one of its tributaries; for it is the mighty Missouri that begins in the Rockies, that divides the southern part of our country, and that discharges its waters into the Gulf of Mexico at New Orleans. That to which we give the name of the Missouri is 2900 miles in length. At the point at which the Mississippi joins it the Mississippi has run 1300 miles, and has 1300 more to go; but the Missouri, everywhere possessed of the same characteristics, is 4200 miles long between its birthplace in the mountains and its ending in the Gulf.

I was not so fortunate as the first Americans who visited the Falls of the Missouri, and saw the greatest of the cascades sending up clouds of fog-like spray to catch a golden sunburst and turn it to a rainbow. They came upon the falls in June, when the river had been swollen by heavy rains. Yet, but for that and the sunshine, it was last winter just as they had described it. The great fall is somewhat disappointing as seen from above, and most majestic when viewed from below. It may be said to have two parts, one of which is a sheer leap of a third of the river's bulk from over the edge of a flat sharp-edged rock down about 90 feet to the lower

PART OF LOWER FALLS FROM BOTTOM OF CAÑON, LOOKING NORTH

level; the other and **major** part plunges interruptedly, at a lesser angle, down upon other **rocks, there to lash and pound itself into a fury.**

There **are four** distinct falls above **this, at** some of which **the walls of the** river cañon slope towards the water, **at others where** the walls **are** precipitous. Everywhere the grass and **the dead and** lifeless-looking rocks **edge** the chasm. **Everywhere the walls show either ledges** and **terraces or lines of stratification. Small cottonwoods and bushes cling to what shelves they can find,** islands of **rock or small timber divide the swift current,** rapids **almost innumerable break the intervals with** veritable stairs, **and** the thunder of cascades or the **low** roar of swirling waters fills the **air.** But wonderful **as** the aggregation of water-washed declivities is, there is one spot in the river which I would eagerly select **were** I to know that I could visit but one of its many points of **interest** again. That is the point from which **one may view** both the Crooked **Falls** and the Rainbow Falls. **The Crooked Falls are** most peculiar. **To imagine them, not having seen them,** the reader must **fancy a deep and rugged cañon bedded** with troubled, **racing water, and in the middle a** great water-fall **shaped** like **the** blade **of a hatchet,** whose hammer end points up stream, while the extreme corners **of** the blade touch either shore. It **is not a** high **fall.** It is not 20 feet high at the deepest part, I think, **but it** presents the spectacle of waters falling towards **each** other sidewise, **and at** right angles and obtuse angles **and in** curves; for the hatchet **form,** the reader must recollect, is the shape **of** the **placid water, and the** water-falls **are** around its **edges, playing their** majestic streams upon it.

There **may be other such** falls in the world, but I never saw **one. That part at** right angles to the course of the stream, which **I have** represented as the blunt end of the

239

hammer, is that which would naturally be the main cascade; but in the Crooked Falls it is the least part—it is a tiny fraction of the cascade. One bank of the river is rocky and precipitous; the other is low and sloping. From the high bank across a slight curve the spectator sees the Rainbow Falls—only 48 feet high, but the most perfect and beautiful of all the leaps the great river takes. All the falls are straight and sheer to the left of the middle of the river, and are more or less broken and terraced on the other side; but where the Rainbow Falls are thus interrupted by projecting rocks the disturbance is slight, and enhances the splendor of the effect.

From the Rainbow Falls the visitor sees the first sign that Lewis and Clarke's diary is far behind the times, for in the distance are the chimneys of the smelters and other works that belong within the confines of that new disturber of the maps of our school days called Great Falls, a town which has grown up above the plains in acknowledgment that man's conquest of the wilderness is a thing of so distant a past that cities now are growing up in his honor. Almost among these evidences of man's complete domination of the land is a freak of nature even more surprising and unique than the combination of other wonders in the neighborhood. It is, apparently, a river bursting up through the earth alongside of the Missouri. The spot is called the Giant Springs, but one wishes he could know what the Indians used to call it, for they were the happiest of all folk at such christenings. It is a Devil's Caldron, if you please, or a Spouting River, or a Big Fountain. Over a great space the water of these springs forms a pocket at one side and close to the river. It looks, at the first glance, as if it were a big pool that has been held apart from the river by a chain of rocks, over which it has risen and is leaping; but a second, longer glance shows that

CROOKED FALLS

the middle of the surface of the pool is very much higher than the water around it; a still closer look makes it clear that the water is bubbling up not only there, but in many places, in many aqueous mounds made by many streams of water that spring with force and volume from under the pool they create. Piers or bridges have been built out over this extraordinary fountain, and one may walk far out upon them, and see not only the powerful disturbances of the water and the majestic body of it that pours over the rocks to add another and nameless river to the Missouri's bulk, but something besides, and far more beautiful. That is the vegetable life under the water. The water is as clear as any that was ever seen, as colorless as that in Lake Superior's bays, and far down on the rough rocky bottom are weeds and plants that lift their slender many-shaped leaves to be swayed ceaselessly to and fro by the commotion of the water. All the vegetation is green, but none is so vividly and brightly green as the water-cress plants. There are millions of these, fields of them. They are the largest, tenderest, most succulent cresses I ever tasted, and are always as cold as the water, which is the next thing to ice, whether it be tasted in midwinter or in July. Like everything else pertaining to this playground of nature, the spring was discovered by the first white men who visited it. They said of it that "the water of this fountain is of the most perfect clearness and of rather a bluish cast, and even after falling into the Missouri, it preserves its color for half a mile." I did not notice this peculiarity, and cannot say whether it continues to-day or not. But, quite appropriate to this sudden upspringing of a body of water equal to that of a river, is the fact that I was told that in the country adjacent to the Missouri more than one river, after advancing for miles towards the

Missouri, suddenly ceases to exist, ending in a bed of stones, as if the water sank through the earth's crust or dried up.

Colter's Falls and Black Eagle Falls complete the chain of great cascades. It would be tedious to write or to read a list of the rapids. Colter's Falls are formed by a combination of rapids and cascades, and are scarcely worthy of separate mention, but the Black Eagle Falls, by which the great river leaps down a distance of nearly 32 feet, in a skip of five feet and a jump of nearly 27 feet, are great and roaring and beautiful. At these falls is now to be seen a great dam with buildings on either side of the fall, one a power-house for running an electric railway and lighting plant in the city of Great Falls, and the other a huge smelting-works for the reduction of copper ore. This dam and these industries are but the beginnings of the projected utilization of all the vast water-power which the falling river creates, and which in other lands and eras would have squandered itself upon the incompetent air, as Lewis and Clarke described the charms of the great fall that "since the creation had been lavishing its magnificence upon the desert."

Above the Black Eagle Falls and the dam is the city of Great Falls, a place not yet five years old, but boasting 7000 population, two newspapers, an opera-house, a club, good hotels, electrical service, several railroads—and a desire to become the capital of Montana when the votes of the people of that State determine the permanent seat of the State government. We will return to another view of this ambitious little city after a further sweep of the eye along the Missouri. It dawdles along above the first falls all the way to the gate of the mountains, as if unconscious of the tumbling it has to go through, or as if tired after its hard-fought

PART OF RAINBOW FALLS, FROM THE SOUTH SHORE, LOOKING NORTH

contest with the Rockies, that press upon it, and even squeeze and try to barricade it before it breaks away from them. The distance from the mountains to the first falls is thirty miles or more, and instead of savages and buffaloes and wolves, the country is inhabited by farmers, sheep-herders, cattle-men, horse-ranchers, and the station-men and track-tenders of the railroads. Strawberries, potatoes, barley, wheat, oats, apples, and butter are some of the products of the region; three million pounds of wool were shipped from Great Falls last year, brownstone is quarried there, and coal is mined there. The transformation from the conditions that Lewis and Clarke found is complete and tremendous. Since I have come back from there, I remember that the discoverers of that region said that strange noises, as of explosions, frequently rolled over the plains from the mountains, and a foot-note in the *Journal of Lewis and Clarke*, published in 1842 by Harper & Brothers, declares that the Indians of Brazil accounted for such noises in the mountains of that country by saying that nature has a way of enclosing colored stones "like jewelry" in cases or shells the size of a man's head, and then exploding them, when they came to maturity, "to scatter about abundance of beautiful stones." However this may be, one must go in precisely the opposite direction, to where the Missouri has left its rocky cañon and begun to earn its reputation as a muddy river, before its beds of sapphires and garnets are come upon, near Helena.

Just as Niagara Falls is being harnessed to manufactures by those who have estimated the force that it has been wasting, so is this series of cascades and rapids along the Missouri River beginning to be manacled to the car of industrial progress. It is estimated that the descent of the Missouri affords an opportunity to secure

250,000 horse-power of the cheapest and most reliable sort, and a company that is largely made up of New Yorkers has secured the land on either side of the river for a distance of twelve miles beside the falls and rapids. Mr. Paris Gibson, then a resident of Fort Benton, is said to have been the first man to think of utilizing this wasted power. He interested James J. Hill, the great railroad operator of the Northwest, and then the steps necessary for securing the land and the water rights were taken, and four years ago a company with $5,000,000 capital was organized. Messrs. D. Willis James, J. Kennedy Tod, J. S. Kennedy, Smith Weed, John G. Moore, and General Samuel Thomas are mentioned there as among the New-Yorkers who are interested in the venture. The Montana Silver-Lead Smelting-works, in which other New-Yorkers have an interest, was the first company to put up works on this tract, and coincident with the building of the first dam at Black Eagle Falls was the construction of the works of the Boston and Montana Smelting-works for the reduction of ores brought from Butte. About 20,000 horse-power is obtained at this dam, and as the demand for more power necessitates it, the work of building other dams will be pushed farther and farther along the river. It is more than the ordinary mind can conceive to estimate the surprise of Messrs. Lewis and Clarke, could they return to earth and see, a few years from now, the banks of that cañon lined with factories backed by clusters of the homes of workmen, the falls and rapids each seconded by dams, and all the water-power, which they regarded only as productive of scenic effects, trained to turn the modern spinning-wheels, the turbines of to-day. And who shall say whether they would envy the owners of the power, or mourn the practical tendency of the age?

CAÑON OF THE MISSOURI RIVER, BELOW GREAT FALLS

At about Christmas-time last year there was an obvious and palpable stir among the older men of the city of Helena, the capital of Montana. It was not seen in any movement or gathering of these people; indeed, it would be difficult to say in what way it was made manifest, and yet there was plainly a strong influence at work that disquieted and monopolized the leading men. These citizens when they met asked one another, "Have you seen him yet?" or, "How does he look?" or they expressed a wish to shake the hand or to get a glimpse of some one—always the same person, evidently, and always referred to as "he" or "him." It was plain that some one of extraordinary importance, and whose presence was a novelty, was in the city and in every one's thoughts. I, who did not especially deserve such good-fortune, was among the first to see him. Mr. Hugh McQuaid, one of the pioneers of Montana civilization, though still a young man, was impelled by his former training as a journalist to take me to see this pervasive personality regarding whom he said, "I wish to make you acquainted with a man from another world. I wouldn't on any account have you miss talking with him."

"A man from another world?" I repeated; "miss talking to him? I should say not. But who is he?"

"Why, it's Johnny Healey, one of the finest and bravest men who ever lived, and a pioneer and pillar of the old days; ex-sheriff of Choteau County when that county was the size of New England—an old Indian fighter and trader and hunter. He has been in Alaska six years, and has just come back to see the folks he used to know and the places where he made his mark. Everybody is crazy to see him; I tell you he is a very remarkable man. He used to be a terror to road agents and Injuns, and he is back again. To us of Montana it is like the reappearance of a man who has died. But come along. I've told him you are here, and made a date with him to see you, now, at the club."

"But why do you call him 'a man from another world?'"

"Because it was another world that we had here in his days, when Montana contained only a few raw mining camps, miners, traders, women of only one kind; stage-coaches and no railways, shootings, hangings, highwaymen, Indians. When mining was about the only business, and the only law that amounted to anything was miner's law."

On the way to the attractive and almost metropolitan headquarters of the Montana Club man after man stopped us to ask Mr. McQuaid whether he had seen Mr. Healey, or "Johnnie." It was evident that the excitement would not abate until all had seen the hero of the life that had departed.

I found Mr. Healey in the office of the secretary of the club, stowed away behind a closed door, as if he were too precious to be allowed to move around the rooms where the card-tables and the newspaper files and the "loaded" tumblers were in busy use. He seemed to me to be about fifty or perhaps fifty-five years of age, a plain citizen who might have been taken for a soldier in civil dress; very spare and hard of flesh, light in weight and slightly Celtic in facial features, with brown hair and mustache and a grizzled goatee. He was dressed distinctly like a man of the present world

MANITOBA RAILROAD BRIDGE, GREAT FALLS.

in what we call a "business suit." As I studied him more and more closely I saw that he had very steady and intense blue eyes, a sun-browned complexion, and a strong chin and jaw, to betoken great firmness. He showed but one scar, a little one on one side of his nose, where a cur had bitten him as he stooped down once upon a time to enter an Indian tepee. That scar made a great impression on my mind, so often have I stooped down to enter tepees, and so abundant and vicious are the dogs wherever there are tepees.

Mr. Healey would not talk about "the other world" from which he had come. He said it would look like boasting, "and," he added, "what's the use?" He was willing to tell me all about the people and resources of Alaska. He has a trading station at Chilcat, in that territory, and for six years he has studied the less poetic people of that region precisely as he once studied the Sioux, Crows, Bloods, Blackfeet, Piegans, Crees, and Stonies of our plains. But a lucky accident or intervention sent his thoughts and talk back to early Montana. Some one passing along the hall outside the room called out, "Whose voice is that I hear? Can I come in? Why, bless me, if I didn't know you by your voice, Johnnie. How are you, old fellow? You look first-rate."

"Why, hello, Tom?"

The new-comer was United States Senator Power, another old comrade and old-timer with Mr. Healey. The two men sat down, and I could not help contrasting the appearance of my companions. Mr. McQuaid and the senator were both men of full habit, soft-faced, fat-handed, with every appearance of leading easy, placid, in-door lives, accompanied by rich meals regularly obtained. They were the men of to-day, and they sat facing the man of yesterday—the wiry, browned, nervous, muscular, out-of-door semblance of what they had been. It was the scene of the famous painting of "The Return of the Missionary" repeated. As the missionary looks, surrounded by the cardinal, his retinue and the magnificent trappings of his palace, so looked Mr. Healey for the next hour in the Montana Club. Senator Power felt this, for after a pause, during which he looked Mr. Healey over from head to foot, he asked him a question that seemed inspired by the situation — the one question that could fetch an answer to epitomize the entire gamut of contrasted conditions.

"Johnny," the senator inquired, "you don't mean to say you are still at it, with your hand on your gun and the border life around you?"

"That's what I am," said Healey; and then he hastily added, "but it ain't what it used to be, Tom; not near."

A flood of recollections—pleasant, exciting, tragic, and fierce—must have surged over the senator's mind, for he sought relief and expression by turning to me with a testimonial to Mr. Healey's virtues such as any old Montanian would be proud to have earned, and such as it never was my fortune to hear spoken of any man before.

"Healey was the best man we ever had here in the early days," said he. "He was afraid of nothing and no one. You could not scare him with a gun. He was as quick as a cat, and as scientific as Sullivan. If you pulled a gun on him he would grab it with one hand and knock you down with another. The rough element wanted no trouble with him, I can tell you. If he was out of reach of a gun that was pulled on him he would simply laugh, and wait his chance at the man who threatened him. He has made hundreds of arrests, and never used a pistol once in taking a man. Is not that so, Johnny?"

"No," said the hero; "I pulled a gun once."

"What time was that?"

"Dutch Bill's gang."

"Oh."

I got Mr. Healey to tell me that story, but it was by no means the equal in old-time flavor of others that I heard and heard of. He and a companion were out after thieving Indians near Fort Benton, and they were tired and hungry. They saw some horses and two mounted men and rode up to them. Mr. Healey rode close to the men, and they slipped off the beasts they were riding and rested their rifles on the saddles in a decidedly threatening manner. "Who are you," one cried. "We're white men," Healey shouted, riding closer. "But who in —— are you?" the stranger insisted. By this time Mr. Healey was so close to the men that he could see what sort of rifles they were "heeled" with. "Quick! who are you?" "Healey," said the hero of the story. "Then throw up your hands, —— you," was the answer. Instantly Mr. Healey threw himself sidewise over his horse so as to expose but one foot, and dashed away for his life. His companion followed suit. As they rode away Mr. Healey said, "They've been stealing horses, and I'm going back to stampede the horses and get them away. Come on."

"You'll get killed—and that's all you'll get," the other replied. But Mr. Healey on his superb horse was dashing back as if the grass was on fire behind him. Both men rode right up to the bunch of stolen horses and began firing at the men, who were still behind the barricades they had formed of their horses. Mr. Healey shot both their saddle horses and stampeded the stolen steeds, getting them away with him. Next day one of the thieves was captured and brought into Fort Benton by some one else, and on the day after that Mr. Healey rode out for the other scamp. He rode up to a shack, or rude house, where he suspected the other desperado would hide, and learned that the man he wanted would soon return; that he had gone away for water. When the man did return, Healey, standing in the doorway of the shack, covered the man with his gun and remarked:

"It is my turn, now; hold up your hands."

That was the only time that, as constable or sheriff, he had occasion to threaten a man's life in order to make an arrest.

I talked with Mr. Healey then and afterwards, and found my appetite for stories of the old mining-camp life keenly whetted. In the course of my quest for the recollections of the pioneers, I learned that one who had a knack at writing had made a book of what he knew, and that this book had been declared by no less a person than Charles Dickens to be "the most interesting volume he ever read." It was on his second visit to this country that the famous English novelist had obtained and read the work; at least that is what the most reputable men out there believe and declare. Very eagerly I sought the book, and after but little trouble obtained a copy. As I had suspected, it left little else to look for by one who wished a clear reflection of the mining-camp scenes in the early "sixties," when Alder Gulch and then Last Chance Gulch (Helena) sent the fame of their gold yields broadcast and attracted a host of miners, prospectors, traders, and adventurers from California, Utah, Nevada, Missouri, Arkansas, Kentucky, and many other States, into the new region of diggings.

It is called

THE VIGILANTES OF MONTANA

OR

POPULAR JUSTICE IN THE ROCKY MOUNTAINS

BEING A CORRECT AND IMPARTIAL NARRATIVE OF THE CHASE,
TRIAL, CAPTURE, AND EXECUTION OF

HENRY PLUMMER'S ROAD AGENT BAND

TOGETHER WITH ACCOUNTS OF **THE LIVES AND** CRIMES OF MANY OF THE ROB-
BERS AND DESPERADOES, THE WHOLE BEING INTERSPERSED WITH
SKETCHES OF LIFE IN THE

MINING CAMPS OF THE "FAR WEST"

BY

PROF. THOMAS J. DIMSDALE

SECOND EDITION

VIRGINIA CITY, M. T.
D. W. TILTON, PUBLISHER
1882

I had intended to quote liberally from the professor's book.* I wrote to his publisher at his printed address in Virginia City and at another address to which it was said he had removed, but I got no reply. Then I interested some friends in Montana in the task and they failed. It is a pity, for no substitute can be made for the charms of the plain and direct tale which thrilled the great novelist.

It is indeed an interesting and a very peculiar book. It is not true, as its title indicates, that it is an impartial account of the scenes and contentions it records, but

---

* A more modern and comprehensive work upon the times and characters of the Vigilantes has been written by Nathaniel P. Langford, of St. Paul, Minn., and is called *Vigilante Days and Ways*.

perhaps it is as nearly fair and frank as it would be possible to find a history written by a spectator of, if not an actor in, a drama of such heated and desperate action as that which began with wholesale murder, robbery, and arrogant vagabondism, and ended by tasseling the trees with the swinging bodies of desperadoes executed by an excited populace. The time has scarcely yet arrived when a history of the vigilance committees of either California or Montana can be absolutely impartially set down, because many of the participants in those movements are yet alive, and because some among those who took part in them were little better than or different from the men they chased and shot and hung.

In the presence of a company of these heroes of that other and boisterous era, I explained the conditions that render such a work unlikely by an interrogation that I put to them—though not without some hesitation and timidity.

"Gentlemen," said I, "in reading about these necessary and righteously conceived uprisings in the far West, it has several times struck me that the Vigilantes were not all of them better than the outlaws. Am I right about that? Were all the Vigilantes wholly deserving of the admiration the people bestow upon them?"

"Well," one old settler replied, "I guess you are right. You see, things were red-hot when they came to the pass where vigilance bands were organized, and some men who saw that right was going to triumph over wrong were induced by their shrewdness to take sides with law and order."

"There is one thing that you must make note of that is not put down in the records," said another, "and that is that in these mining communities there were many weak and shifty characters who were not bad at heart, and did not want to be bad in deed, but who found themselves siding with the outlaws and did not know how to break away. Sometimes these were men who were asked or forced to give some little assistance to the desperadoes—to shelter them, or outfit them, or perform some other act that they did not dare to refuse. After having done it they never had the courage to shake off the relationship that grew up between them and the outlaws. Then there was one notable but unique case of a man who trailed with the bad men when he was drunk and with the decent ones when he was sober. But the majority of men who became Vigilantes after having more or less dealings with the desperadoes were the store-keepers and tavern-keepers and others who had trade relations with every class in each community, and who knew their bread was buttered by sticking to the stronger side. Until the Vigilantes were organized and set in action the thugs ruled the roost, and these politic persons kept in their good graces. As soon as they saw that order and justice were climbing up on top they came over to us. The cases of actual 'state's evidence,' where outlaws joined us, were very few indeed, for the reason that if they had been notorious we were after them to hang them, not to associate with them.

"Our mining communities all go through the same processes between the first stage of 'the stampede' to the new finds and the last stage when the yield of metal and the interests that grow up around the mines become so important that lawlessness and tomfoolery cease to be possible, and then the men of will and worth get together and enforce good order. It will surprise many persons to know that one kind of law—and it is a very strict kind—obtains from the very outset at every new camp that is started. That is the law governing the interests of miners to one another in their pure character as mine-holders and mine-workers. This law or set of laws originated in California, and has become the basis of justice as regards mining property all over the West. It is the law in California, Montana, Idaho, Wyoming, Utah, and Colorado, and a separate class of lawyers has been developed in consequence. A lawyer who is famous for his knowledge of mining law soon becomes a rich and important character in these States. Such specialists are the only ones who are retained in suits over mining property, because the ordinary lawyers do not pretend to understand this peculiar system of legislation. It is as different from the common law as is the Code Napoleon. It grew up out of the commonsense, every-day rules that every camp established at the beginning when the men first began to stake out their claims. By common agreement they were to make claims of a certain size, announce and protect them in certain ways, and retain possession of them by the performance of certain obligations. As time went on numerous complications arose, and these had to be adjudicated by local arbiters or referees, there being no courts to try the suits. For instance, a lead of ore running through several claims would set all the owners of those claims by the ears as to whose rights controlled the situation. There are hundreds and hundreds of possibilities for contention, and new ones arise all the time. As mining claims were all the property that most of the men in a camp possessed, equitable rules had to be established and enforced. This was done, even though the civil law was left hundreds of miles behind and forgotten.

"No one who is given to reflection will wonder at the lawlessness of the mining camps. The stampedes to such scenes were always by motley crews of men among whom the bad ones formed a greater proportion than they do in civilized and **settled places.** Men who had failed **at** everything else, deserters **from** the army, gamblers, **outlaws,** tramps, and men **who had** forever forsworn **the** fetters of organized society, were in the **crowds** along with the earnest and reputable men whose **sole hope** was that of bettering their poor or perverse **fortunes.** The desperadoes in all new camps are **free to carry** weapons, are equipped with money, and have resorted to such a region solely because of the opportunities it affords them to **live and** do as they please without let or hinderance by **the** restrictions which civilization imposes upon mankind. Terrible indeed would be the consequences of such conditions **if it were not** for the character of the men whose reasons for going into such regions are not such as make them sympathize with outlawry. Rough and rude the law-abiding men may appear, but their instincts are right, and they are as fearless, to say the least, as the desperadoes. They soon learn **that their** power and safety lie in acting justly but sternly and quickly whenever, in the absence of other law, **they** need to take **laws** of their own making into their hands. Men who go to the mining regions have to draw a fine line as to the character they propose to exhibit there. They must be good or bad, and must declare themselves quickly, there being no loose line or latitude between the **two sorts of men.** Where every sense is keen, and judgment of **character** is unerring, the mass of the people quickly place a new-comer where he belongs, if he is slow about making up his own mind.

"Long after a mining camp has purged itself of ruffian rule, and has set up the civil law, there still remains **a tendency** towards prodigious drinking among the peo**ple of nearly** every class. What must have been the amount of drinking **when** there was neither law nor order you can perhaps imagine. Men without the restraint of law, indifferent to public opinion, and unburdened by families, drink whenever they feel like it, whenever they have the money to pay for it, and whenever there is nothing else to do. Gin-mills of the vilest sort, in great numbers, spring up in such regions, and do a thriving business. Bad manners follow, profanity becomes a matter of course, and with that goes the tendency to let speech become too free and personal. Excitability and nervousness brought on by rum help these tendencies along, and then to correct this state of things the pistol comes into play, and it is understood that if certain words are uttered blood is likely to be shed. To call a man a liar, a thief, or a coward, or to apply a too common expression that reflects upon a man's ancestry, is to court a bullet from his pistol. 'Thief' is a particularly criminal word according to the miner's code, because actual thieving is a capital crime. No one is punished for killing like a dog any man who is caught stealing.

"Where there is some pretence of the existence of law it is usually ridiculous in its injustice. Part of what is called 'law' in a wide-open mining camp is the recognized rule that shootings are justified for the causes here mentioned, so that, just as in some so-called civilized communities no jury will find a verdict against men for duelling or for killing the destroyers of their homes, here in the mountains men are discharged from custody if they have murdered those who questioned their veracity. Under such conditions the bully of a camp goes scot-free, no matter what he does, and so does the swaggering, 'flush' gambler, whose friends applaud him because he runs a fair game, befriends the poor, has killed a man for insulting an unprotected fast woman, and who, in various ways, has made himself a local hero able to defy the mockery called law. It is not necessary to add that in such communities another class of **men who** do as they please are the rich men, who may not be popular, but are able to discover means for escaping punishment when they earn **it**. In a word, **all** the law there is finds itself enforced only against the poor, the shift**less, and** the unpopular. I am speaking of the **new** camps, before the orderly citizens take control."

"In the settlement of New England," said another of these graduates from **ruder** conditions, "it is said that the first thought of a new community was towards the establishment of a school-house and a church. In the mining regions the first institutions **of a public character** were a piano and a billiard-table. Of course, in **the** mountains (and especially before the railroads began to run all over them as they do in Colorado and other States) such bulky things were not hauled in, and a hurdy-gurdy or a banjo took the place of the piano, while a roulette-wheel **or a** simple lay-out for faro or craps served instead of the billiard-table. The billiard-table represented the gambling-house, and also served, in some **places, for** a theatrical stage, if a strolling company of actors or minstrels happened along. The musical instrument was the mainstay and advertisement of such a house as harbored the first women who came to **the** camp. With gambling saloons run wide open, and outcast women the only females (or almost the only ones) in the camp, one can perceive how such men as once possessed refinement were almost certain to lose it, while such as were hardened became all the more callous and reckless. The women are, and always used to be, among the first-comers after the noise of the starting of a new camp got abroad. It is their habit to leave a place as soon as it begins to grow dull, and they jump for the next new camp about which they hear talk among the men. They are by no means tramps. Even in the wildest days of early mining they spent large sums of money to get transportation from place to place, and to have houses built for them as soon as they arrived. Then they would make a great display of feathers, silks, gay colors, and frescoed faces on the streets. So long as they continued free they were treated with rude deference and respect, and the dust (gold) was showered upon them. They kept good accounts at the bankers—sometimes mounting up to the thousands—and had costly jewelry and clothing that the rough miners thought the Queen of France would give one of her fingers to own. It really was costly finery, though I wouldn't vouch for its strict compliance with the Parisian fashion in make-up.

"Since all that was softening and gentleizing in the camps proceeded from these women, it is worth while to halt a moment at a public dance-hall in an old-fashioned camp. In these days such places are far fewer than they used to be. The variety theatres, where the female performers visit with the audience between their appearances on the stage, have taken the place of the old-time resorts where the miners used to dance with the 'hurdy-gurdies,' as the girls were called. There might not have been a church or a reputable resort of any kind in one of these camps, and the dance-hall was really the most orderly and the least harmful place in the outfit. To be sure, rum, jealousy, old feuds, and any one of a dozen causes might start a row in such a place. And rows were not infrequent. Pistols, dirks, fists, and bottles were used; frightened men hid behind women; the women screamed or laid down on the ball-room floor, and there was much excitement whether any harm was done or not. But fights took place, as the wind blows, wherever they happened, so that this feature was not the fault of the dance-house. There the dancing-floor was beyond the bar, and it cost a dollar to go upon it and to pick out a partner from among the women who sat around the sides of the room. In some places they wore *décolleté* dresses, in some their skirts were abbreviated; in some all were dressed alike, and in some they were simply clad as any other women might have been, according to their varying tastes. There was a band of music in the corner or at the end of the room, and when each man had selected a partner the floor-manager called out what sort of dance he pleased: a polka, a schottische, a Virginia real, or a quadrille. The waltz was not danced out here in those days.

"The men would have impressed a tenderfoot as a very queer lot. Some wore buckskin coats and cloth trousers and others wore cloth coats and leather trousers. Trousers, a flannel shirt, boots, a bowie-knife, revolver, and leather belt, satisfied others. As a rule, all were bearded, wore their hair long, and carried both knives and pistols. Gamblers, mine-owners, miners, store-keepers, clerks—all the sorts of men there were in the camp were in the place. At the close of each dance every man led his fair partner up to the bar for a drink, and she took 'soft stuff,' or hard liquor, or what she pleased—even champagne, at from ten to fifteen dollars a bottle, if she wanted it, and if her partner was 'flush.' Drinks came high, but the prices varied according to how far from a railroad the place was and how well the camp was panning out. It did not cost less than a dollar in most places for two drinks, no matter what they were or how cheap the proprietor bought them. The hired dancers were paid according to the number of times they were invited out upon the floor. The prettiest and most popular ones made the most money, of course, but in those rough places where the women were so few, I never saw one so ugly or unshapely or ill-mannered that there were not plenty of men eager to pay for the right to enjoy her company for the few minutes that a dance lasted. Coming right from the effete East, you might not have thought all the men polite to them, especially if you chanced to hear a low-browed, ruffianly fellow call out, 'Here, gal, let's you and I have a spin,' in a voice like that of a fog-horn. Nevertheless, every man was as polite as he knew how to be, and the women had little to complain of, all things considered. It was only when they linked their fortunes with some gambler or bully, who then thought he had the right to abate his tenderness, that they were abused — and not then, in most cases. It was not safe or healthy to notoriously abuse anybody weaker than yourself—man or woman —and it ought not to be safe to do so anywhere in the world."

Professor Dimsdale wrote that what he called "the mountains," by which he meant the mining camps, "circumscribe and bound the paradise of amiable and energetic women." He asserted that they were treated with the greatest deference and liberality, and that there was an unwritten law that gave such women a power for good that they could never hope to attain elsewhere. But while I was in Montana I heard of an era earlier than that which he wrote about, when there were practically no such women in the camps, and when the only women who were there were treated as only good women should be treated. The men even took their hats off to them in the streets. A tale is told of a happening in a place called Pioche—I think that was the town. A powder-barrel exploded in a cellar under a store and a number of men received dreadful injuries. The only women then in the place tore up their linen for lint and bandages, and applied themselves to the care of the wounded. They took the injured into their houses and nursed them. Soon afterwards the house of one of these humane creatures was burned to the ground, and, in remembrance of her good conduct, the men made up a purse, built her a new house, and sent to San Francisco for a piano that cost twelve hundred dollars by the time it got to her.

From a historian who has not yet published his collected notes I got some queer memoranda respecting the dancers above referred to, and to many others who sought the new camps, both men and women. They made their slow and uncomfortable way to Virginia City, in Southern Montana, by stage-coach, and the journey cost sometimes as high as fifteen hundred dollars from Omaha. The fare by way of Denver and Salt Lake was $575, and all baggage was carried at $1 50 a pound. Ornaments, dresses, everything, had to be brought; for practically nothing except food, powder, pistols, guns, mining implements, and men's clothing could be bought in the camps. When a woman reached a camp she was obliged to order the building of a log-house or cabin. These were very rude buildings, in the walls of which mud was used to fill up the chinks between the logs. It was a woman's work to put these finishing touches to a home; it mattered not what her character or standing. The women made the mud and patted it in place with their hands.

When the house was ready for use the floor was covered with green cow-skins staked to the earth with wooden pegs. They made a fine carpet except while they were "curing," then it was not pleasant to be in such a house. Cow-skins were put on the roof and covered with mud to keep out the cold, the heat, and the rain; but when it rained the women went out of doors and stood in the rain to save their dresses from the mud that leaked through and fell in the houses. Beds were made by building a framework of wood and fitting the ends of one side of the frame into auger-holes in the logs of one wall. Ticking was bought and filled with straw and a buffalo robe was laid over the mattress. Candles were the only lights at first, but by-and-by, in Virginia City, oil-lamps were introduced.

Professor Dimsdale speaks of the certainty of a shooting scrape in the dance-halls. The women were not unused to such occurrences, and one who has added her recollections to the notes I have read, declares that, when men began to shoot, she made it a rule to throw herself flat on the floor and scream. Women were not shot at, struck, or maltreated; no man dared to misbehave in that way. On the contrary, a man who admired a woman's dancing or beauty or amiability would take out his chamois bag of gold-dust and say, "Hold out your hands and tell me when to stop pouring." Overcome by such a tribute, they found it impossible to speak in order to interrupt the flow of dust. So, I fancy, would a prima-donna in the merry old days in St. Petersburg have found her voice choked if it were commanded of her that she should cry "Enough!" while the nobles were flinging jewels and roubles at her feet upon the stage.

Gold-dust was the money of the era in which "The Man from Another World" figured in the Montana mining camps. "Weigh out," was what the bar-tenders used to say at such times, as men of to-day would say "pay up," or "settle." Wherever business was done, a pair of light jewellers' scales was at hand, and, as every man carried his dust in a bag, the gold was weighed out to close each transaction. The price of admission to the theatres was a pinch of dust. Many men, fearing robbery or the loss of all their dust through drink or gambling, made it a practice to give the treasure to a woman to keep. The women did not steal; not because they were honest, but because it did not pay to do so. The "shacks" or cabins of which I have spoken are still plentiful in Montana. Even in Helena several are yet to be seen. They are very much smaller than the reader would imagine, not very much higher than the crown of the head of a man of ordinary stature. They contain only one room as a rule; and, if my recollection serves me, are often without windows.

Mr. John Maguire, the famous Western actor and manager, now at Butte, Montana, told me some of his early theatrical experiences. He went from Salt Lake to Pioche in Nevada by stage under an engagement for a week's performances. Instead of a theatre—this was in the "sixties"—he found a big shack of logs, chinked up the sides and roofed over with canvas. There was a rude stage, and the benches were down in a graded pit with mother-earth for the floor. He was to have $100, and two women in the company engaged for $60 and $40. The stock company of the place gathered around a big stove in the middle of the theatre, shivering in their overcoats. They had been sleeping under the stage and on the benches. They did not earn enough money to live at the hotel. Lodging at the hotel cost $12 a week; cocktails cost four bits (50 cents), and so did a shave. A week's bill at the hotel averaged about $30. The local actors were wofully incompetent—indeed, one of them told Mr. Maguire that "the only thing he could play was a cornet." The actors of ability, like Mr. Maguire, were treated with respect; the actresses received chivalric attentions, but, alas! in this particular town the manager every night gambled away the money taken in at the door.

Sometimes, during and at the close of the War of the Rebellion, theatrical folk played upon billiard-tables, or in dining-rooms where the tables were massed together to make a stage; or in any empty building there happened to be. Each travelling company carried curtains and a few rolled-up, painted scenes, representing a kitchen, a parlor, and a street or forest. They hung these scenes from copper wires stretched from wall to wall and fastened with screw-eyes. For an actor's dressing-room, or a dressing-room for the ladies, they strung up blankets before or behind the curtain, in a corner. They got light by massing candles in many parts of such an auditorium.

The good companies made almost as much money as they do now because the price of admission was high. It was a pinch of gold-dust, and that was worth $2 or $2 50. The miners offered their bags at the door, and the ticket-takers pinched the dust. A room might hold 150 to 300 persons, and there was sufficient money in the business to tempt the best talent. Mr. Barrett and Mr. Jefferson, Miss Eytinge and Lotta have all played in such camps. If a performer, particularly a lady, pleased the crowds, they threw slugs and nuggets of gold and coins upon the stage. Singers who could "touch the heart" were in great demand, and a certain Maggie Moore coined money on this account.

The mention of Miss Moore brought to the memory of Mr. Maguire the fact that the music of the orchestras was atrocious.

"The orchestras were usually composed of a fiddler and a pianist," said Mr. Maguire, "and while one played in the key of G the other played in the key of K."

This Maggie Moore was heartly encored on one occasion but would not respond. An old actress who was dressing behind the blankets that separated the retiring room from the auditorium said, "Go on, Maggie." "Oh,

I can't," said the younger **actress, bursting into tears;** "I can't sing to such horrid music." **Every word** was heard by the audience, and one man arose **and** called out: "Go ahead, **miss; if he don't** play better I'll **fill** him **full of bullets."**

In time, when the terrible reign **of the outlaws of the Montana** camps had **begun** to prove unendurable, **the line** drawn between **the lawless** and the reputable men **in** the camps became so **tight that** the tension was frightful. It was felt that neither **life nor property** were safe; that the "bad" **men** were not willing **to** stop at anything, and that, **if only from self**-interest, the decent folk **must** band together and make relentless war upon the evil-doers until the latter should see that the country had become too hot to hold them. Nine men, some in Virginia City and some in Bannock, led all the rest in the Vigilante movement. The word "vigilante" is used because the same sort of bodies that were called Vigilance Committees **in** California were never spoken of **in Montana otherwise** than as **Vigilantes.** Just as **there** had **been too** many weak **and impassive men when the** evil-doers **were** having all things their own **way, so** there instantly **was** formed a general and common courage and unity for the reform when it was **felt** that punishment **and** protection were about to be extended to all who **needed either.** Professor Dimsdale says that in the swift, stern work of the Vigilantes twenty-four wicked lives **were** sacrificed; but he adds that before the outlaws were thus brought to terms they had caused the loss of **at least** one hundred lives in that sparsely settled country.

The **ways of** the outlaws and the methods by which justice **was administered** to them were both peculiar. The **chief of** the road agents was Henry Plummer, "a **perfect gentleman," after the** manner of the heroes in

California's records of a similar period in that State. We can imagine him perfectly without asking for any man's recollection of his appearance: a slight, well-formed, dapper man, modestly and well attired, careful to be barbered whenever it was possible, and always armed to the teeth. As a matter of recorded fact, he could empty a revolver in an incredibly short time. When he or any of his friends were in need of money, the practice was to intercept a stage or an express load of bullion, or to lurk beside a highway for the purpose of robbing the first person who came along. They very frequently added murder to the lesser crime. One of Plummer's former companions had robbed and murdered a man, and, riding into town with his booty, was killed by Plummer, who had broken friendship with him some time previously. The murderer brought on his own death by too much boasting, and Plummer, after remarking that he was tired of hearing the man's self-praise, emptied his revolver into his head and body. The murderer begged for his life, but got no mercy. It was bad enough to have such acts committed in a settlement where innocent folk ran many chances of being shot, and where others were frightened half out of their wits, but it was worse to think that these ruffians were more apt to find victims among the honest folk than to kill one another.

These men of the Plummer stripe would shoot or maltreat a man whom they had never seen before, simply because they did not like his looks, or his dress, or because he would not drink with him. They sought quarrels where they dared, on any pretext, and literally terrorized all but the men of undaunted courage. They took part in politics, and managed to get public offices that gave them the greater power and opportunity for evil. Plummer, the leader, was actually elected sheriff, and it is easy to imagine what sort of aides he drew around him, and what use he made of his office. So long as he was unopposed by any combination of upright men the people whom he terrorized aided him in his ambitions, and suffered from his crimes in silence. He proved a wretched poltroon when the Vigilantes caught him and put him to death on the gallows. He had been a marked man from the moment the reformers began their work. He was caught with difficulty, and then there seemed nothing that he was not willing to promise rather than die. He said his prayers—an act which to his ruffianly comrades must have seemed both annoying and ignoble—and he confessed all his crimes. Others cried "like women," as the saying goes, when they were confronted with violent deaths that were more humane than they had meted out to their unoffending victims. Short, sharp work, by no means unattended with danger to the Vigilantes, was made with the wretched lives of all who were captured, and the reign of order that has since prevailed in Montana was thus inaugurated.

Such were some of the conditions in that "other world" from which it seemed to the people of Helena that Johnny Healey returned the other day. He mixed with that strange life the still more strange career of a trader with the wild Indians of those days, but, as Mr. Kipling would say, "that is another story."

VIII

WASHINGTON: THE EVERGREEN STATE

I have called Montana the Treasure State, and have shown that it is vastly larger than Pennsylvania, with prospectively many times its wealth in minerals and in the variety of its resources. But much that we find promised in Montana is amplified within the territory of Washington. The hopeful inhabitants of the former boldly adopt the motto, "The last shall be first," as if to say that amid the riches of which they find suggestion and promise all around them, they see for themselves a greater wealth-producing future than is boasted at present by any of the older States. I cannot follow them so far. There is a certainty that Washington has more varied resources than Montana, and I think that, with or without irrigation, Washington will support a larger population; but with both States it is too early for closer comparisons. The vast treasures of precious metals in Montana are sufficiently worked to give as definite a basis for hope as is found in the marvellous soil and forests of Washington, but in both States there are great areas of thirsty soil whose future is a moot point in Washington, and of which in Montana it is only certain that they yield a good return from their present use as grazing-grounds for cattle.

The Evergreen State is a huge block of land. It is as large as New England and Delaware, as Pennsylvania and West Virginia. It contains 69,994 square miles. It is 360 miles **wide between** the Pacific coast and the Idaho **border,** and to journey over it from British **Columbia** southward is to travel 245 miles. It is the most populous of the new States, and its inhabitants outnumber those of Oregon. In 1890, according to **the** last census, it contained 349,390 souls, but its people now assert that they number 360,000. **They** have suffered some **losses in** certain cities, or the increase would be from 15,000 to 20,000 greater.

The State shows to poor advantage for those who cross it upon **the** Northern **Pacific** Railroad, because the **route** taken by that great and well-equipped line **lies across an** extensive desert of sage-brush, and then **cross**es a vast reach of usually brown bunch-grass before **it** plunges into the mazes of the Cascade Mountains and rushes out from them upon the perennially green Pacific slope into the Puget Sound country. But the necessities of railway construction compel a disregard for such choice of territory **as** would be made by an agriculturist **or a** scenery-hunting tourist, **and,** in this case, even the land granted to the railway, along its route, is in great part **very** valuable, though its richer parts are **not** always **close** beside the rails. Washington **is in** every material way a grand addition to the sisterhood of States. With **the easy and** rich fancy of the West, her people say **that** if you build **a** Chinese wall around Washington the State will yield all that her inhabitants need without contributions from the outer world. Nevertheless, the Chinese wall they think of oftenest is the true one, and that they wish to break down, for a trade with Asia is a thing dear to their hopes.

"**If I** could only have half an hour with the Emperor **of China,**" said a talented son of Washington, in whose veins the blood **of one of** our most gifted orators is flowing, "**I would make** this the richest State west of the Mississippi. I would tell him we wanted the trade of Asia as New York has that of Europe. I would explain to him that we entertain no prejudice against his people, and mean no insult in shutting them out of our territory. I would make it clear to him that our dislike is only for his coolies, but that as for his merchants and scientists and scholars—we welcome them, we want them, especially the merchants."

Now let us look at this great State in detail, keeping in mind that it is by nature divided into two parts by the Cascade Mountains, which bisect it along a line to the westward of the middle of the State. West of the mountains is the seat of the great timber industry of the future. There the land is all heavily timbered except in the bottom-lands and at the deltas of the streams, and agriculture, though a future source of great wealth, is yet but a small factor. East of the Cascade Range there is smaller, inferior timber, but it cuts a minor figure in the wealth or character of the State, for in the main we have returned to land something like that of the other new States—we are at the end of the plains that have crossed the Rocky Mountains, and we are again in a bunch-grass country. But in crossing the Rockies the plains have partaken of their character, or rather of the disturbance that produced them. A large area of eastern Washington has been several times overflowed by lava, and it crops out in a disorder that is sometimes abundant in the Big Bend country and in the sage-brush lands. The powder or decay of this lava makes rich land, and where it is driest and most forbidding, the addition of water will turn it into a blooming garden. The Columbia River flows through this country in a deep gorge far below the level of the adjacent land; and there are other great gorges, like cracks in the earth, where you may see

MAP OF WASHINGTON

marked in the side walls eight or ten distinct strata or flows of lava. At the bottom of these "coulees" there is generally good land underlaid by lava. It is used for range land for cattle. For the rest, a great part of eastern Washington is in hills and mountains with valleys between them, with grassy or wooded slopes, profitable always to the fruit-grower, the farmer, or the cattleman. Gold, silver, copper, lead, and small coal basins are found all over the northern tier of counties. This is part of that extraordinary treasure belt that reaches from the Cascade Mountains across Washington, across the Rockies and Idaho, and far into Montana. It is a vast tract of once-convulsed nature, a sweeping ocean of timbered billows of rock and soil. Where man has scratched the western end of it—and he has nowhere done more than that—is in the Kootenay country, but everywhere its productiveness is thought to be fabulous.

Its western end, at the Cascades, is a marvellous scenic region. For grand desolation, ruggedness, vastness, and primitive wildness, it is unparalleled in our country. Below the ever snow-clad peaks that raise their white heads above the black solitudes of the forests are unnumbered glaciers, some of them even ten or twelve miles long, and many of them a quarter that length. The forests on the west slope of the Cascades are bewildering, stultifying to the mind, in their magnitude and denseness and stupendous individual growths. The entire western slope of the main range is a solid belt of cedar and Douglas fir. There is spruce among the fir, and in the bottoms a little cotton-wood and maple, but these lesser woods are unconsidered. The Douglas firs attain a size of from eighteen inches to eight feet in diameter. They shoot 100 feet in air without putting out a limb, and then, above the first limbs, they tower 100 feet higher, and often more than that. The cedars vary between a **foot and a** half **to fifteen** feet in thickness. **The** larger trees are hollow at the butt for many feet above the **ground,** but this still leaves from one to three **feet of solid** timber around each hollow core. Over thousands of square miles upon the forest **bed lies** the débris of another forest prone upon the ground, **as if a** tangle of toothpicks from 200 to 300 feet in length had been strewn upon the earth, and through and over this giant lace-work grows the forest of to-day.

The roots of the **new trees** straddle and ride the trunks of the old ones. **The fallen** firs are **rotten, but** the cedars are as stout **and sound as** when they reared their topmost branches beneath the eagle's path. Amid **the** dense moist undergrowth the dampness has forced coats of moss upon the prostrate giants. It is a solemn and an awful forest. It might be likened to a graveyard in which every upright column is the head-stone for a fallen fellow. Absolute silence reigns there, and daylight becomes twilight over the earth. It is a task to see **the sky.** Far above his head **the** prospector in those pathless **woods** sees the wind swaying **the** tree-tops, and half hears their gentle murmuring, without being sure **of the sound.** There is no bird life **in that** oppressive solitude, no animal life, except that now and then a bear is seen. He who would penetrate the forest must be content to make two miles **a** day in a straight line, and then only by seesawing many miles to and fro, clambering from tree trunk **to tree** trunk, and patrolling the lengths of what fallen trees lead nearest to the course he **would** pursue. The forest has only been penetrated by the waterways. The Indians, the most expert canoe-men in the world, know nothing of it. Travel there is only where water takes it. The streams are the roadways, and canoes the red men's horses.

Hunters and prospectors upon the eastern, more lightly timbered, slopes of the mountains report that great herds of mountain-goats may be seen feeding close to the glaciers. The wool of these animals is used by the Indians. The skin is clipped close, and the wool is given to the squaws, who card it roughly, and then roll it on their bare thighs with their bare hands. They weave it with rude looms into blankets, and out of the finer yarn they knit stockings and mittens.

And now for the pastoral regions of eastern Washington. This table of the production of wheat in the State in 1891, prepared for the Government, will, if the reader consults the map while he studies it, reveal what farming lands are now in use and where they are situated:

Counties	Acreage.	Average bush. per acre.	Total.
Whitman	320,000	23	7,360,000
Walla Walla	150,000	20	3,000,000
Garfield	100,000	27	2,700,000
Columbia	80,000	27	2,160,000
Asotin	20,000	25	500,000
Lincoln	20,000	15	300,000
Douglas	16,000	15	240,000
Spokane	25,000	18	450,000
Klickitat	20,000	20	400,000
Kittitas	12,500	20	250,000
All other counties, including those west of the mountains.	5,000	20	100,000
Totals	768,500	22.71	17,460,000

These figures tell the whole story of last year's wheat crop in Washington. They are the best that could be obtained as early as last Christmas. The Washington wheat fetched seventy cents a bushel, or about twelve and a half million dollars. The same authority from whom the above figures were obtained is of the opinion that without irrigation—that is to say, outside the lands that must be watered—the **State will** eventually produce between forty millions and fifty millions of bushels of wheat. In a pamphlet issued by the State Board of Trade, and written by President N. **G.** Blalock, of the Washington World's Fair Commission, the advantages of **the soil and** climate for the cultivation of cereals are **clearly** set forth. The soil is very deep, and is a sedimentary deposit of volcanic origin, made up of a sandy loam, distintegrated basalt, **and ash.** It is porous, readily takes in and yields moisture, **and allows the salts to rise to** feed the growing crops. **From year to year** the climate **varies** but slightly, **and where** the **rains** are sufficient, they bring up and mature the grain without its being scorched. This writer has known wheat to be sowed in every month of the year. In the summer the ground is covered with dust thick enough to keep the moisture in the soil underneath. Wheat sowed in the dust between the months of June and September will spring up only after the autumn rains have set in. From September 15th to December 1st is the best time for seeding. **There is no** necessity for haste in harvesting. The wheat **need** not even be stacked. **If** left standing it does not suffer. Though the harvesting begins in early July, "the machines are in the field until December, and occasionally the crop is left standing **until the** following spring." Thus a man in Washington **can** cultivate more land than he could in many other **States** where wheat is grown. The Federal statistics **for** 1890 showed that Washington's average yield per acre **(23.5** bushels) was the highest in the United States. Mr. Blalock made a calculation of **the cost** and profit of wheat-raising, taking **three successive** crops that averaged thirty-two bushels **to the acre.** He found that the labor made it cost **nineteen cents a** bushel. To this he added interest on the value of the land **for** two years, and thus brought the cost to twenty-nine cents a bushel. As the crops sold for an average of fifty-five cents a bushel, he found a profit of eight dollars and twenty-eight cents an acre. These statements, which accord closely with my own deductions from all that I heard on the subject, are so remarkable, and reveal conditions and results so different from any that obtain in most parts of the other new States, that a study of Washington would be incomplete without them.

Spokane is the principal city of eastern Washington, and a good point from which to view the agricultural and mineral resources of the lands east of the Cascade Range. It used to be called Spokane Falls, after the falls in the Spokane River, which attracted the first settlers as a rallying-point, but the people dropped the word "Falls" in June, 1891, and Spokane is the city's full name. Long before its settlement the trails and roads from every point of the compass met there, and seemed to mark it as a natural distributing centre. Eight railroads meet there now. It is a dozen years old as a settlement, and now extends its broad streets and battalions of brick and stone buildings over a considerable part of the bowllike, level-bottomed basin in which it has been built. There are evergreen hills all around it, and upon one slope overlooking the town the well-to-do citizens have massed a considerable number of villas, many of which are both costly and handsome. Milling, the lumber trade, and jobbing in all the necessaries of life are its mainstays, and possibly by the time this is published it will have started up its smeltery to lead the new industry which many think must become its main one when, amid the development of the innumerable mines of eastern Washington, it shall have become a great mining town. Its jobbing trade in 1890 amounted to $21,565,000.

Spokane is very enterprising. It has an opera house that is the finest theatre west of the Mississippi River, and its Board of Trade, under the tireless energy of Mr. John R. Reavis, is incessantly at work to strengthen and enlarge the industries of the city. The place has 25,000 population. It lost 3000 last year as a result of the general monetary depression, but its gains continue, and the agricultural country tributary to it has grown steadily and suffered no set-backs. It trades with 200 towns, and talks with 60 over its telephone wires. Its water-power — having a minimum power of 32,000 horses—runs its electric cars, electric lights, cable-cars, printing-presses, elevators, and all its small machinery. It is not rampant in its vices as most Northwestern cities are. Gambling is done under cover, the variety theatres are closed on Sundays, and there is even broached a proposition to close the saloons on Sunday. In justice to Spokane, I should explain that the leading men ascribe this mastery over public vice to the unique and high-toned character of the leading citizens, who embrace a large proportion of Eastern blood, and good Eastern blood at that. Such an explanation is highly necessary here, for in the new Northwest public morality is sometimes regarded as a concomitant of failing business powers. Happily I can vouch for the fact that Spokane society is leavened by a considerable class of proud and cultivated men and women, who live in charming homes, and maintain a delightful intercourse with one another. They make it a very gay city—they and the fine climate—and are fond of high-bred horses, good dogs, and bright living, with dancing and amateur theatricals, good literature and fun. San Francisco is no longer peculiar in this respect, for Spokane shares her brilliancy among our Western cities.

Close to Spokane is the famous Palouse country. The

1,300,000 acres of Whitman County, and 1,000,000 acres of Spokane County form this rich region, which bears various names in its minor extensions, but is all alike in its extraordinary fertility. It was settled early by a class of immigrants known in the West as "Pikes," who came in 1844-54 from Missouri, Kentucky, Arkansas, Tennessee, and as far east as the Piedmont region. They were poor whites, and were a tall, angular, drawling band of blond men, lazy and shiftless, but of dauntless courage. They took up the bottom-lands between the rolling, timber-topped hills, beside the streams. In time they were driven to the hills, and then they discovered that more and better wheat could be raised there, without irrigation, than on the bottoms. This Palouse country is about 150 miles long, and averages 30 miles in width. It is said that in summer the soil is covered with a thick dust, and that in place of rain they have heavy dews. It is reputed to grow an extraordinary amount of wheat, and its yield really did reach 30 bushels in 1890. Wheat, barley, and flax are the great crops, but melons, all vegetables and fruits, both large and small, grow there as profusely, perhaps, as anywhere in our country. Berries of every kind, peaches, plums, apricots, apples, pears, and grapes all grow in abundance and of superfine quality. Land fetches $36 an acre, and will soon sell for $50. Eight hundred thousand acres of it is the rich land of which I speak, and of this 389,000 acres are in cultivation, 320,000 acres being in wheat. The land is all taken up. Farming has been done with small holdings, but moneyed men are now buying large tracts. In Colfax, the main town, the principal loaning brokers report that they know of no single failure there in the payment of interest upon loans last year.

Walla Walla County, down in the same corner of the

State, ranks next after **the Palouse** country. Its basaltic soil has been cultivated for **forty years**, and **one** farm of that age produced forty bushels of wheat to the acre last year without fertilizers, of which, **by-the-way**, not **any** have ever been used. They irrigate there **for small fruit**, but not for wheat. They have 200,000 acres **under** cultivation, all **but** 50,000 acres being in wheat. Prunes, pears, **enormous** yields of strawberries, blackberries, and the finest **(because the oldest) orchards are their** most important **products** after the wheat. Walla Walla, the principal **town, bears a** name familiar even to the school-boys of thirty years ago. **It is the seat of an old army post, is a beautiful town, and boasts a cul**tivated society. **It** has 5000 population, and though at **one** side of the main tide of travel, is growing slowly. It was once the great outfitting point for the mines of Idaho and Montana, and pack trains left there daily.

A heap of nonsense is spoken and written about the Big Bend country in order to dispose of **it**. It is simply a fairly good wheat country, difficult **to** irrigate, and bound to be uncertain in its products until it is irrigated. How this shall be done is one of the great problems before the people of Washington—the greatest that confronts the people of the eastern part of the State. Else**where** I have spoken of the strata **or** flows **of** lava that underlie it. The trouble **is** that this crops out in fields and bunches all over the region, as **we** see ice-floes in a harbor at the time of a thaw in the spring. There are pieces of good land between the outcroppings of volcanic rock, and some of these bits of good ground con**tain as** much as twenty square miles of land all covered with **grass. It is a** high plateau, rolling far above the Columbia, which cuts a cañon through it. It has scarcely any other streams, and but few springs. It embraces the two large counties of Lincoln and Douglas. There are in it a million acres of land that can be cultivated. Only a small part is yet so utilized. In 1890 about 80,000 acres in Douglas County and 7000 acres in Lincoln County were under the plough, but it is believed that last autumn (1891) this sum of cultivated acres was doubled. There is some government land there, offering what is perhaps the best chance left in eastern Washington for "the homesteader," but he must irrigate or be prepared for great uncertainty in his crops. In 1890 the Big Bend wheat lands produced nearly 30 bushels to the acre; but in 1891 the yield was not over 15 bushels, dryness being the cause. An effort to get artesian water is being made near Waterville in Douglas County. If they find water, and it is abundant and not too far underground, the result will promise redemption to a great belt of soil that is second to none when it has moisture.

The problem what to do with the sage-brush country is a greater one. It embraces Adams and Franklin counties, and lies between the Big Bend and the Palouse regions. It is sage-brush from end to end—nothing but sage and cactus and basalt rock, except that in Adams County there is some good land. The region has a rainfall of only nine inches. It too is all good land if water can be got to it. Vegetables and fruits grow well in it.

The great Yakima tract across the Columbia is very promising. Small farmers are rapidly putting it under settlement and cultivation. They are growing fruits, vegetables, and alfalfa, the last to be marketed as hay. Hops also are grown in great abundance, and since this part of the country has not known the hop-louse, and is not damp enough to invite that pest, the outlook for a great hop industry there is most encouraging. The whole Yakima country was divided between railroad

and government lands. The latter **have been** thrown open, and are all taken. The railroad lands were offered for very little before the Northern Pacific company experimented with its admirable schemes for irrigating the **soil.** Now the farms command high prices, **and fetch them** so easily that it is predicted that within 25 years Yakima Valley and County will be in as high state of cultivation **as any part of the** State. The rainfall is only about **ten inches a** year, and irrigation is necessary. The Northern **Pacific** Railroad is building a ditch sixty miles **long, to be** fed by **water** taken from the Yakima **River at a** point **below** that at **which the** river issues from the mountains. **The ditch is an enormous** one, and was built at great expense across ravines and all the irregularities of the country. Seventeen miles of it was ready for water in December, 1891. **It** will moisten thousands of acres that once were purchasable **at** $1 50 each, but now are held at $45 an acre or more, because no lands in the State will be more productive, **if the best** judges reason correctly. With the sale of the **irrigated** lands, stock in the irrigation company is offered, and the scheme is so planned that when the land is all sold, the stock will all be in the hands of **the** farmers. **It is likely** that the farmers will then continue to pay water rents, and will divide the profits after the expense of **maintaining** the ditch and its laterals is defrayed each year. **A** second canal, 250 feet higher than the present one, is said to be contemplated, and an added supply of water is expected from three large lakes on the eastern slope of **the** Cascades. Thus the highland district of the Yakima country will also be brought under the ditch. This is the most extensive irrigation-work that **I** know **of** in the new States. It may not **make** the Yakima the richest section of eastern Washington, for it may not excel the Palouse or Walla

Walla tracts, but it will be highly productive, and uncertainty about crops will be reduced to a minimum. Perhaps time will show the richest land to be in the future clearings of the big timber on the Pacific slope.

I have spoken of the prospect of a great yield of hops in Yakima County in the future. The cultivation of hops is a source of large income to the State. The hop was first cultivated in the Puyallup region in 1866, and with such results that in 1890 the crop was 50,000 bales, about half of which was grown in the Puyallup fields. That crop was marketed for two millions of dollars. The industry has spread into the valleys of the White, Stuck, Snohomish, and Skagit rivers, all to the westward of the Cascades, at the feet of which rich valleys of alluvial soil of great depth have been formed. Since it is known that one hop-yard in England has been uninterruptedly cultivated for 300 years, there is no reason to look for a wearing out of the rich soil of West Washington. The Washington hops are of a high grade, and the yield, averaging 1600 pounds to the acre, is almost threefold that of the fields of England, Germany, and New York State. The hop-louse has now made its devasting presence felt in western Washington, and must be fought there as it has long been fought elsewhere. On account of this pest the Puyallup yield was reduced to 50 per cent. of what had been expected last year, and since the price was low, it was thought that the revenue from hops would not be above one million dollars. Hops have fetched more than a dollar a pound in the past; of late the prices have run from twenty cents to thirty cents. To produce them costs less than ten cents a pound in Washington.

North of Yakima is the Wenatchee Valley, reaching from the mountains to the Columbia. It is prophesied that this will prove an extremely rich fruit country. And this is measurably true of all the very numerous valleys that seam the mountains west and north of the Columbia, all the way around to Kettle Falls in the northeast part of the State. Washington is going to be a great fruit State, and the time must soon come when she will do with her fruits as California does with hers—export a great deal, dry a great deal, and can and bottle more. Perhaps the best business done in Spokane to-day is that of handling provisions for the mining camps of Idaho and British Columbia, and fruit is an important factor in these supplies. For a time, as the mining lands are extended, there will be this market for Washington fruits, but the outlook is that the production of fruits will eventually far exceed this so-called home demand. The Wenatchee lands, owned by the Government and the Northern Pacific Railroad, are just beginning to be settled. As the Great Northern Railroad, which is to give a tremendous impetus to the development of northern Washington, is to pass along that valley, its lands will soon reach their full value.

North of the Wenatchee Valley is the great Okanagon country, and east of that is Stevens County, or "the Colville district," as the miners call it. It is mainly viewed as the scene of future mining activity, and of that we will tell further on; but it is all guttered with rich valleys for fruit and vegetable raising, and it is to-day as fine a sporting region as there is in the United States. In the Okanagon country, west of the Columbia, is Lake Chelan. It is a beautiful sheet of blue-black water 70 miles in length and from half a mile to three miles in width. It starts at its Columbia River end from a noble bunch-grass valley, already fairly settled, and farmed for fruit, wheat, and vegetables. Mr. Frank Wilkeson, who is familiar with the country, describes the lake as practically landlocked. Soundings to the length of 700 feet have not touched its bed. Its waters teem with trout of from half a pound to six pounds weight, and of several varieties. Suckers and chubs, and an unclassified fish that attains a weight of 14 pounds, are also plentiful. The lake terminates with an eight-foot water-fall, up which no salmon seem to have swum, for none has been found in the lake. Many creeks empty into the lake, and almost all show the distinct marks of old glacier basins at their heads. In the Stehegan belt these departed glaciers have left their former rocky confines bare, and prospecting is done with a glass, the prospectors scanning the rocks, and easily perceiving the metalliferous ledges. In the trails or ridges of bowlders left by the melted glaciers are seen masses of galena ore that have been torn from the leads. It is the sight of these that directs the prospectors to follow up the glacier beds. There is a wealth of ore in these glacial deposits, and doubtless the day will come when it will be worked.

In the rugged, wooded mountains that rise precipitously from the lake and wall it in, the mountain-goats are so numerous that they will long provide sport for the hunters. Black-tail deer are plenty, and so are black and cinnamon bear. A packer in that country reports having seen twenty-seven bears in one day last autumn. The grouse there are without number, and include the blue, the gray, and the ruffed varieties. Smaller birds are equally numerous. A hotel-keeper near the lake, wishing to explain why he only charged seven dollars a week for lodging and the luscious fare that weighted his table, said that venison and bear meat only cost a cartridge now and then, and for trout he used the same fish-line that he brought into the country years ago.

Mining in Washington, **though its promises are vast,** is in its veriest infancy. The production of metals is insignificant. The first discovery of the precious metals was made by placer miners along the Columbia River, and this ground is still worked, by Chinamen now, with trifling results. Recent discoveries have been, first, in **the** Colville district, Stevens **County.** It **is a** mountainous region, an extension of the rich Kootenay country of British Columbia. Silver and lead are found there, but not yet in such large or promising leads as those **north** of the boundary. Development-work is being done there, the ores are being sent out, and concentra**ters** are building. In the Okanagon country, east of the Cascades and west of Stevens County, silver and gold without lead are found. It is smelting ore, and cheap transportation facilities are needed for the development of the mines. One railroad operator is ready to build **from** Marcus on the Columbia, north of Colville, **along the Kettle** River, to the Boundary Creek mines of silver **and** gold, which show splendid prospects. The Colville Indian Reservation hinders him from tapping the Okanagon country, and, as we have seen wherever there are similar conditions in other States, there is a strong movement to have the reservation reduced, and the upper part thrown open. The railroad could be built across it **as it** is, but there is no money in a railroad on a reservation land where settlers may not come nor towns spring up. It is apparent that the reservation must be reduced in response to this pressure, because it is a vast tract, bigger than some large counties in the State, and yet it contains but **a thousand red men,** remnants of several tribes. The notorious **Chief Joseph, who** harried several of our generals, is there, **and so** is Chief Moses, whose people once inhabited the Okanagon country before it was "bought," and

President Grant set aside the Colville Reservation for them. An argument used to help to open this land is that the reservation leaves sixty miles of our frontier unprotected. The Spokane Chamber of Commerce is bending all its energy to the redemption of this border land, and what that body sets out for it generally obtains.

The Lake Chelan prospects, so called, are of argentiferous galena. At least 700 claims have been taken, and this summer's work will prove the value of the district, though all miners qualified to judge of it express confidence in its great richness. The Stehegan belt of hills, where the ore is found, runs northeast beyond the British border. In addition to the galena, other ores are found, though not yet in sufficient quantities to excite the cupidity of the prospectors. But the belt contains more limestone and white marble than the world can use. It is proposed to build a railroad to Lake Chelan, whereon the ore can be boated seventy miles, and then carried by short rail to the Columbia, and thus to the Great Northern Railroad at Wenatchee.

Western Washington is another proposition, as its people would themselves say. All over the Evergreen State inanimate nature would appear to be divided in two parts, so that whatever is not a "proposition" must be an "outfit." One word or the other applies to and describes whatever you may speak about. A new town is either a good proposition—that is to say, it has good chances to grow—or it is not. The Nicaragua Canal is a good proposition, and so is the prospective million-dollar hotel in Tacoma. I several times heard the word "outfit" applied to men, particularly when they seemed to deserve to be called "queer outfits," but I never heard the word proposition applied to anything animate. I did hear a waterfall called a "proposition," however.

Up to **that time, I confess, I had regarded it as an "outfit."**

The chief city in western Washington is Seattle. **It has a** population of about 40,000. It is a remarkable city, perhaps the most enterprising one in this country. When the odds against which it has fought are taken into consideration, and when it is understood that **its** progress has been made against railroad opposition, instead of with the aid of that usually powerful influence, its progress, size, and accomplishments seem marvellous, and its leading men deserve to be called the most indomitable and plucky **organizers that** any city, even **in** the West, can boast.

Seattle is metropolitan. It has that indefinable tone that marks the city from the town, and that when amplified belongs only to the chief city in a State or industrial district. It has the crowds of hurrying men and women, the lounging, staring groups of yokels, the daily battalions of tourists and drummers and strangers generally, bent on selling or buying, and driving about with **heavy** baggage piled on their cabs; it has large and fine hotels, theatres **of** several grades, beer-gardens, **and** an unduly large vicious quarter on the Pacific coast **plan** of a myriad little cabins each with one frescoed occupant. It makes the visitor feel that it is a bustling capital town, and that is a character and influence that cannot be simulated or made to **order.** From the harbor Seattle makes an impressive appearance, because **it is** built on the side of a steep hill, and is uplifted **and** spread out in a manner peculiar to itself. In a lesser degree all the chief cities of Washington send portions **of** themselves up steep hill-sides; and though Seattle is not the city in which I saw cleats on some sidewalks, to make the **pavements** even more like ladders, its streets **are so steep** that one feels sorry for the horses of its cab system—which, by-the-way, is the best I know of on this continent outside of Montreal. Towering buildings do not make a city. London has not one steeple of offices within her limits, while Seattle, on the other hand, has many and to spare. But it is the districts of wholesale stores, whose merchandise and customers crowd one another on the sidewalks, it is the bustle at the depots and wharves, the activity in the harbor—if it is a seaport—the flurry of people in the retail quarter; such are the telltales of a city of importance, and Seattle has them, and has kept them in a great degree after the financial crash in London, which disturbed the cities of Washington more than it might had it not been that in them an effort was making to reverse the natural order of things by which territorial development creates city extension. Seattle's jobbing trade in 1890 was in goods of the value of $35,000,000. The town is strengthened by neighboring coal mines, has built up a large shipping trade, and boasts several manufacturing industries.

Since the above was written news despatches from there tell of the discovery of slavery among the Japanese in Seattle. The slaves are the women in the singular rows of one-story cottages by the water-side in what is locally known as Whitechapel—the vicious quarter. In that strange district and still stranger community are women from Mexico, China, Japan, and France, as well as American blacks and white women. The police say that of them all the Japanese are the least troublesome, since they alone refrain from adding theft to their other outlawry. It is more than likely, as the news despatches relate, that they are owned by men who purchased them of their parents in Japan, and brought them to this country for the purpose to which they appear to lend themselves. The "tough end" of Seattle, as the Western vernacular would have it called, is very much like the pestilential parts of Butte and Helena, and all the other Northwestern towns of considerable size of which mention has been made in this series, but it is livelier than most others, in addition to having the most motley population. It is said to be well under police control, and I was told that the gambling there is above-stairs, and not too public.

Tacoma, an hour and a half away by water, and also on the sound, seems a substantial town. It has great wealth, and is the financial, though not the trading or popular centre. It has about 35,000 population. Its homes seem to me the proudest possessions of Tacoma. Separate dwellings of tasteful design, and costing from $3000 to $20,000, are to be seen there in great numbers, and I am told that the proportion of still less costly cottages owned by the families which occupy them is also considerable. Any Eastern city—any city anywhere—might well be proud to show a club-house like that in Tacoma, wherein the most perfect taste prevails throughout. The city is the seat of a large circle of wealthy and cultivated folk. Though the place is nothing like so showy as Seattle, it has shown great enterprise—a force which there has always felt the backing of a great transcontinental railway. Some of the capitalists are building a floating dry-dock 325 × 100 feet in dimensions, and to be extended by smaller docks of the same sort, so that almost any vessel on the Pacific can be handled upon it. Tacoma has hopes of being at the eastern end of a transpacific line of steamers at an early day, and of being the seat of the iron industry which must certainly spring up somewhere on the coast. What Tacoma is most sure of is that she is at the end of a great railway line, and that she is at the gate of, and indeed is surrounded by, a very rich country, part of which—the Puyallup region—is already forward in development.

I have not mentioned the electric lights, electric cars, water systems, and such modern conveniences in speaking of either of these chief cities. It would be an omission due to familiarity with the entire new West if I failed to say explicitly that almost wherever one may travel in that country the same conveniences are at hand that one is accustomed to finding in New York. If there is a difference, it is that the West is the more progressive, and the more quickly takes up whatever is good as well as new. Seattle has cable as well as electric cars, but all the cities have the latter sort of vehicles. The traveller who steps from the newest Pullman car on the Northern Pacific Railroad suffers no jar when he is in such hotels as the Tacoma, the Rainier or Denny in Seattle, or the Fairhaven in the hopeful little city of that name, near the head of the sound. Appointed with that most artistic furniture in the world which is turned out of Michigan factories as pins are produced in Birmingham, provided with elevators, electric lights and calls, offering great public rooms richly decorated and draped, with French cooks, with the best food in the markets of the world (refrigerated and whirled from place to place), the hotels of Washington are in the same list with the leading hotels of London and New York. Need I say that the same is true of the public schools? That also goes without saying in any study of the West. The State of Washington expended $932,000 for its free schools last year.

The steamboats that ply between Seattle and Tacoma and up and down the sound are also unexcelled. One called *The Flyer* is the most admirable vessel of its kind that I have ever seen. It is of the build of a fish, and is almost as swift. Its two saloons, one above the other, are carpeted, and provided with soft plush-covered reclining-chairs. The walls are, to all intents and purposes, plate-glass. The machinery is exhibited like jewelry, in a glass case. By day the panorama of nature is uninterrupted in the view of the passengers; by night the little *Flyer* is all aflame with electric light, like a glass boat or a lantern shot over the water from a cannon.

These boats are not the prettiest products of the Pacific slope, because nothing animate or inanimate can be more beautiful than the women there. I will not commit myself to a decision whether it rains there six months in the year, as I think, or all the year around, as the critics of that country insist; but the effect of that warm, soft, moist climate upon the complexions of the women is magical—is worth going to see. The effect upon the ladies' gowns of one of the concomitants of the rainy season, as the wearers climb and descend the muddy hills of those cities, is not nearly so admirable. If ever Mistress Fashion will permit dress reform to be undertaken by women, it will be hailed with joy on the shores of Puget Sound. But with regard to the beauty of the women of the coast, all that need be told is that the women of the interior insist that the Puget Sound belles all have web-feet, the result of the frequent wet weather on the coast. The reader may judge from that how captivating the coast women must be.

Western Washington comprises nearly one-third of the State. It contains 25,000 square miles west of the Cascades, as against eastern Washington's 45,000 square miles. Through a part of this western end of the State, tearing a great mouth in it, is Puget Sound. It is a majestic harbor, and no one who sees it can criticise its human neighbors for the store of hope they rest upon its future. It has a superficial area of 2000 square miles, a shore line of 1600 miles, an average depth of 70 fathoms, and, lying north and south 90 miles back from the ocean, it is all within the State. Its first surveyor, in 1841, reported to the Government: "I venture nothing in saying that no country in the world possesses waters equal to these. From the mouth of the strait to the head of navigation, 200 miles inland, not a shoal nor reef nor hidden danger exists. At times it narrows to a river's width, and again widens into the majesty of a sea, but is everywhere free to navigation, the home of all craft, blue, deep, and fathomless." The quotation is hackneyed, but it describes this wonderful body of water better than any other words that can be chosen. Yet it but helps to distinguish an equally wonderful country—a country with the climate of England, and better than the best qualities of California and Florida.

I have described its amazing forests of giant timber. They cover the greater part of it. It is said that they contain two hundred billion feet of marketable wood. It is very valuable wood. It will continue to supply the country when all other timber is gone. For a long while the great stringers used in the flooring of the Pullman and Wagner cars have come from these forests, and a shrewd railroad man is quoted as saying that out of the wood in the cedar stumps that the lumbermen have left standing in the present clearings he can build the walls and roofs of freight cars that will pay for themselves in three years in the saving of weight. The Washington timber competes with Georgia pine and Eastern oak in the uses to which those woods are put. Lumbering is the chief industry in western Washington, but it is small to what it must be when reduced rates are brought about by competing transcontinental railroad companies and by the Nicaragua Canal. This lumber has already found good markets in South America, China, France, Australia, and the Sandwich Islands.

The coal measures **of the** Puget Sound basin **come** next in importance. The coal and **the** iron, which is also abundant, lie side by side. Limestone is also found, and although practically nothing has been done with the iron, some most excellent coking **coals** have been found, **and** the happy combination must soon prove alluring to capital and enterprise. The coal supply seems inexhaustible, and already its development is a great source of income to Seattle, **as** it will soon be to Fairhaven and other ports near the coal beds. All the coal of the coast, including **that at** Nanaimo, on Vancouver Island, **may be classed as** lignite, **but** it **is often of so high a** grade that the operators do not greatly strain the truth in classing it as bituminous. The Seattle coals do not make coke or gas, but are excellent for general domestic use and steam-making. Large mines are being opened in the Skagit country west of the mountains. The coal **lies** in the cretaceous measures, and is in dipping seams of from four to eighteen feet of clean coal. Farther down the river are the Fairhaven mines, opened by the Great Northern Railroad Company and by Montana capitalists. All this Skagit coal makes a coke that **is** held to be only second to the Connellsville (Pennsylvania) **coke,** if **it** is **not** fully as good. Coking ovens are being erected, and a large market in California, Mexico, and South **America** is looked for. Other coal in this region, now used on the sound steamboats, is superior to the Nanaimo product. The South Prairie coal, near Tacoma, makes a fine coke that is used in a smeltery at the latter place. There are mines and coke ovens at Wilkeson also. The coal product of the State in 1890 was nearly a million tons, worth at the mines $2,203,755. When it is known that California has but little **coal,** and only of an inferior quality, and that Oregon **is** but slightly better off, the value of the superabundant coal measures of Washington will be understood. Then again, the Washington coke will displace the Eastern and English material on the coast. At San Diego these other cokes are received for distribution among the smelteries of northern Mexico, New Mexico, and Arizona at $13 a ton; indeed, they are sold in Victoria, British Columbia, at $20 a ton.

Capital is needed to take hold of the iron. There is talk of iron and steel works near Seattle, the enterprise of Eastern men; and in Tacoma an effort is making to found a business in the making of steel bars, plates, and rods from imported blooms, as is done in San Francisco. In time, whether these projects rise or fall, fortunes will be made from the iron industry in that new country. Asbestos is plenty; and there are clays that must yet be the foundation not only for rude wares, but for good white ware. Sewer-pipe is already made in Seattle. The reader sees that all these resources are practically in embryo. In spite of the fact that the first settlements in the east and west were in the forties, the State is nearly as new, so far as all except its farming is concerned, as if the date of its admission to Statehood—November 11, 1889—were the date of its first settlement.

Whoever passes along the main retail street of Seattle and happens to notice the counters in the principal fish store will be astonished. In the chromatic display of the captive creatures of the sea is the text for another chapter on future wealth for Washington. They have the salmon, though that catch is credited to Oregon and Alaska. There are in the northern waters cod banks thousands of miles in extent; halibut, codfish, rock-cod, sole, sea-bass, smelts, shrimps, herrings, and oysters are all abundant. Apparently the fisheries outweigh those of the East as the timber belt excels that which once enclosed the Great Lakes. Candor compels me to say that the Pacific fish, with one exception, are inferior to the same kinds of fish in the East, yet they are not wanting in fine qualities. The halibut of Washington and the North is, I believe, the finest sea fish for the table that is known in America. The tiny muddy oysters, the size of a dime or a quarter, are the meanest product of that sea, but they find a ready sale and are admired. Since that is so, hope for all the rest should be rampant. Their crabs, on the contrary, are not mere samples; they are wholesale products, regular marine monsters; and all the better for that, since they make good food. The fishing that must in a few years fleck the waters of the Pacific with sails is scarcely begun. There is only a million invested in it, and only a million a year is produced by it.

The new transcontinental railroads that are expected to cross to Puget Sound—the Great Northern and a spur of the Union Pacific—are thought to be going to work wonders. They will find many present industries controlled by the older companies. They will encourage the development of new industries and the extension of others. Mr. Hill's road, the Great Northern, is to be pushed through the mountains in what is described as "a scenic wonderland." It is thought that Fairhaven will be its terminus; but whether that prove true or not, a feeder all along the sound, at right angles to the main road, will tap all the country between the Cascades and the great harbor.

And what of the land which these railroads will open up? What of it, apart from its minerals and timber? It gives a name to the State—it is evergreen. Roses, nasturtiums, and chrysanthemums may be seen blooming in the gardens the year around. The ocean, and especially the Japan current, keep the climate equable. The mercury seldom rises above 90° in the summer, and to see it at zero in the winter is to see an extraordinary thing. The rains produce semi-tropical abundance of vegetation. Agriculture cuts a small figure yet, but where it is carried on, in the valleys and reclaimed marshes, oats grow higher than a man's head, and so does timothy. Oats will run from 60 to 100 bushels to the acre. Men have been known to make more than $800 from an acre of strawberries. If good land is chosen, and a market is handy, five acres will support a family well. Raspberries, currants, gooseberries, orchard fruits, all do well. There are some who think the sound country may yet supply the whole United States with prunes, so fine and abundant are those that are but just beginning to be grown there. Tobacco does well; and, by-the-way, it is being grown and made into cigars in the Yakima country, in East Washington. Wherever the big timber is cleared—and many of the farms are abandoned logging camps—there is found the richest soil imaginable. It raises hay, potatoes, oats, barley, wheat, hops, cherries, apples, berries, and all which that list implies. It is a natural grazing land. The grass is forever green, and cattle and sheep keep "hog-fat all the year."

East of the sound the land that can be farmed is practically all taken, but west of the sound is the great Olympic Peninsula, until lately almost uninhabited, and even now but little known. It has not been surveyed. Out of the heart of it rise the eternally snow-clad Olympic Mountains. On their sides roam the elk, black bear, cougar, and other more or less noble beasts. Over the earth is a mass of timber, and at its feet a jungle. Fir, spruce, and white cedar are in the woods, and in the many waters wild-fowl abound. Frost is said not to know the country. On the Pacific coast side are many valleys, and some small prairies. In this absolutely new country the homesteaders are appearing in such numbers that it is said that between 700 and 800 settlers went in there last year to pre-empt the lands along the streams and on the prairies. There, entirely cut off from the world, they will wait until the lands are surveyed, and they can file their claims. They believe that a railroad from Gray's Harbor or Shoalwater Bay to the Strait of Juan de Fuca will soon be built past all their holdings. It is likely, for, in addition to the timber, that is the best dairy country in the State. As one citizen put it, "They have more rain than we on the east of the sound, but the presence of water has never yet been considered an objection in the dairy trade."

A question which agitates the minds of many persons in western Washington is whether it is possible for both Seattle and Tacoma — lying so near one another as they do—to become great cities; and if not, which will eventually become the chief and gigantic seaport whose development is so confidently looked for. I wish I could say. Indeed, since everywhere that I travel I find these rivalries between neighboring cities (Bismarck and Mandan, Rapid City and Deadwood, Helena and Butte, and so on through the list, which rightly begins with St. Paul and Minneapolis), I find myself constantly wishing that I could postpone the publication of these articles for a trifling term of ten or a dozen years, so as to avoid this series of conundrums. In this case, in western Washington, there is a little speck upon the horizon. It calls to mind the small black cloud that shows itself in all well-regulated nautical tales as the herald of frightful disaster. It may be a hurricane or only a teacupful of wind. It is called South Bend, and it now pretends to threaten great mischief to Seattle,

Tacoma, and Fairhaven, along with all the other points on Puget Sound.

It is on the Pacific coast, on the front of the Olympia peninsula, only four hours from Portland by rail, and very much nearer to Asia, Nicaragua, and Europe by water than the sound ports. South Bend is a yearling, and where it rubs its juvenile eyes the map shows only the words Shoalwater Bay, but that, being a libellous name, is now changed to Willapa Harbor. It is 57 miles north of Astoria, and is said to be a harbor of the first grade, variously credited with offering 29 to 32 feet of water at its bar. It is the only generally useful harbor between the Columbia River and the Strait of Juan de Fuca. South Bend is about to be connected with the Northern Pacific Railroad system. In the region tributary to it is an extraordinary wealth of timber and of agricultural lands. The founders of the town insist that if there is to be an export trade in Washington products, no other port in the State can compete with it, since vessels from Puget Sound ports must double the Olympia peninsula before they reach the point at which South Bend shipments begin. South Bend is several hundreds of miles nearer to San Francisco, Nicaragua, and Cape Horn than any Puget Sound port. But it is too early to say more. The best possession of the new little seaport thus far is that essence which was deserted by all its companions in Pandora's box.

With a mention of those considerable islands in the Northwest which are, from a military point of view, the key to the British possessions in the North, we must end this view of the forty-second State in the Union. Of the islands, be it known that they are thinly wooded, but rich for agriculture. Sheep are raised there in great numbers, and more wool than they grow is shipped to the main-land, smuggled over from Vancouver Island. Smuggling wool, opium, and Chinamen are profitable callings up in the extreme northwestern corner of our country. San Juan Island is the seat of a great lime deposit that is of considerable value, and is already marketed all along the coast.

There is a peculiar feature of the affairs of Washington upon which I have not dwelt. The critics of the State think it an important element, but I cannot see that it cuts any figure in the future of the great commonwealth. It seems to some critics as if several regiments of our nomads, who keep moving West in the belief that they "must succeed there because they failed in the East," are gathered in this last of the States, principally at its jumping-off edge, in the cities on Puget Sound. Town-site gambling is what attracted these persons. The booming of new towns, that vice which swept the Northwest like an epidemic, ran all along the Pacific coast. The snap of the whip took place at its end in southern California, but the whole of what they up in Washington call "the sound country," felt the strain and the final catastrophe in some degree.

"You could not expect us to develop our soil or our mines," said a leading spirit in one city, "when we could buy a town lot on one day, and four days afterwards could sell it for fifty dollars more a front foot than we gave for it." And that is true. Wiser behavior was not to be expected where, after all, a great many persons went at first rather to make money than to establish homes and found families. The fever for town-lot gambling has abated, and we can look back on it as an episode. It must have raged marvellously, for before it ended some cities were far overbuilt. This was not peculiar to Washington; it was the case from Vancouver, in British Columbia, all the way down to southern California. A cruel but useful reaction came, and now one hears little more about the matter. The talk now is of smelteries and furnaces, of the possibilities of the trade with Asia, of the blessed prospects of new railroads from the East.

I rode up to Fairhaven, near the head of the sound—a very likely town, now that it too has lived down the epidemic—and I heard of only one boom in progress; that was in the "city" of Everett; but I passed many dead boom towns, extinct volcanoes, so to speak, and they were often wonderful to look at. They were, for the most part, mere acres of stumps, clearings hastily made in the forest, with suggestions of streets and avenues laid out at right angles among the stumps, and dotted at long and irregular intervals with cabins, frame saloons, and perhaps a brick building or two—all rendering the scene the more confused and unkempt.

Everett is regarded as a place rich in promise. It is the seat of the Pacific Steel Barge Company, a branch of the company that builds the "whalebacks" at West Superior, Wis. Everett also boasts a milling company, heavily capitalized, for the manufacture of paper from wood-pulp. That which gave occasion for the excitement over Everett was the belief that it might become the west coast terminus of the new transcontinental Great Northern Railroad. This belief proves to have been well founded, for at Everett the new route reaches tide-water. The millions invested there on this account were not sunk, therefore, but were "planted" by shrewd men who now expect them to bear golden fruit.

We have seen something of the scramble for public lands in the other States; the companion picture in Washington was this mania for town sites—or rather for city sites, since a settlement in Washington is either a city or it is nothing at all. Some of the greatest corporations in the State—the railroads—**were** not above setting **the example.** Sometimes it **was a** railroad which, as a corporation, essayed to "**boom**" **a** tract of land **on** its route—a terminal station, a divisional point, or a **junction.** Sometimes one of these corporations would strain not only to "boom" a city of its own creation, but to crush or cripple a near-by town which had grown up without leave.

It is as interesting **a chapter as any** in our new history, that which tells of how the planning and sale **of** new towns goes **on in** these new States; I now refer **to what** may be called the ordinary and customary method, **such** as obtained **before** the thing became a craze, and such as will obtain as long as there are virgin districts for men to rush in upon. Suppose a number of fine "leads" of ore are struck in any new neighborhood, the town-site man is soon on the ground. Something akin to nature used to build towns in the older States, wherever **towns were needed,** but in the **new** Northwest the speculator is up earlier than nature. **Men have to** nudge the **slow old dame** along out there. They note where the new mining prospects are, and then they **look up** the most likely town site. Often its natural position is self-evident; it is **at the** head of the valley below **the** mountains, or it is **where two** streams join. The capitalist "locates" **the spot, and** goes home for friends, relatives, and employés to claim homestead or timber lands where he wants the town **to be.** They make their claims. He sets up a store and post-office; **a** hotel also, if **he has** the means. He employs some of the squatters; the others go away, and only come back to "**prove up.**" He pays them a hundred dollars **each or two hundred** dollars for their trouble, and they **turn over their land to him.** In one case that I know of two such **land-grabbers thought** better of their opportunity, and determined to hold on to the land they had preempted. That is considered the next worse thing to horse-stealing out West. Fancy, if you can, how society could exist were such men common! The theory and policy are to this effect, that a man shall accept for such services what sum will repay him for the trouble he has been put to, without computing the value of his services or of his claim to the land baron who employs him.

But suppose that all works smoothly, as it usually does. The capitalist establishes his store, has one of his clerks empowered as recorder and notary, and opens a hotel. The miners come the second year to do that "improvement-work" which the law requires that they shall perform each year in order to keep their titles to their claims. They need giant-powder for blasting; they need picks and shovels and barrows; they need food, tobacco, and rum. They gravitate to the only place at which these commodities are obtainable—the new town site. A blacksmith sets up a shop, perhaps a saddle-maker comes, several saloon-keepers equip their establishments, a few painted women order shanties put up, and a "hurdy-gurdy" (dance-house) or variety show is started. The transition from wilderness to town is rapid and wonderful. The founder asks all he can get for his lots, and coins money like a mint. His customers stop at the hotel and gamble with the building lots they have bought. The revised maps contain the name of another city, usually called "So-and-so City," or "Such-and-such City," in order that there shall be no mistake about its really being a city.

When it is carried to an excess, town-lot and townsite gambling hinder the development of a region and bring together a great many unscrupulous and irresponsible men; but in the State of Washington, in the presence of the vast and varied resources of the soil, the mountains, and the waters, the epidemic that brought communal tragedy elsewhere can here be called only an incident.

So much, then, for Washington. It would seem to share with all the others many of their greatest resources, as if it were the essence and epitome of them all. If it is not "the last which shall be first," it is the one in which we see the summing up of all the rest. A sweeping glance over it, in the mind's eye of one who knows it well, is like the transformation scene at the end of a Christmas pantomime, wherein we see gloriously some hint of all that went before—of all the climates, forests, metals, fruits, cereals, and vegetables of our entire country; of the men of all the world, the fishes of both oceans. But the scenes that are hurried along the grooves were never hung before a paint bridge. They are real.

IX

COLORADO AND ITS CAPITAL

If its people had not already called it "the Centennial State" and "the Scenic State," I might have done better by it. I would have called it the Palace-car State, because it is the only one in the West where palace-cars are run all over the tallest mountain ranges, and to the gold and silver mines as fast as they are discovered, and because the general style and finish of the cities and pleasure resorts are of palace-car luxury and thoroughness, while nature provides an endless gallery and museum of gorgeous scenery and magnificent curios that would seem extravagant anywhere else, yet are in keeping there.

Colorado is sufficiently settled and developed to form a valuable object-lesson for the study of the early results of the forces we see at work in the brand-new commonwealths near by. They are seizing the water rights in Montana, Wyoming, and Washington, but in Colorado the water is being sold and used. In the newer States wiseacres are prophesying what will be done with imperial reaches of bunch-grass and sage-brush land, but in Colorado county fairs are being held upon such lands. In Montana the leaders are wishing for an agricultural battalion of neighbors to the miners, but in Colorado agriculture has already distanced mining as a wealth-producing factor.

Denver's peculiarity and strength lie in its being all

alone in the heart of a vast region between the Canadian border and the Gulf of Mexico; but it has been brought suddenly near to us. Not all the fast railway riding is done in the East in these days. The far Western steeds of steel are picking up their heels in grand fashion for those who enjoy fast riding. On a palace-car train of the Union Pacific Railroad between Omaha and Denver the regular time is nearly fifty miles an hour, and the long run is made in one night, between supper and breakfast. Denver is only fifty-three hours of riding-time from New York as I write—twenty-five hours from New York to Chicago, and twenty-eight hours from Chicago to Denver.

I am going to ask the reader to spend Saturday and Sunday in Denver with me. Instead of dryly cataloguing what is there, we will see it for ourselves. I had supposed it to be a mountain city, so much does an Eastern man hear of its elevation, its mountain resorts, and its mountain air. It surprised me to discover that it was a city of the plains. There is nothing in the appearance of the plains to lead one to suppose that they tilt up like a toboggan slide, as they do, or that Denver is a mile above sea-level, as it is. But a part of its enormous good fortune is that although it is a plains city, it has the mountains for near neighbors—a long peaked and scalloped line of purple or pink or blue or snow-clad green, according to when they are viewed. There are 200 miles or more of the Rockies in sight in clear weather. As there are but fifty-six cloudy days in the year, and as these mountains elevate and inspire even the dullest souls, I think we can forget that it is a city of the plains, and ever associate it with the mountains hereafter. I plighted my troth to the sea near which I was born, but in Denver and Salt Lake City, loveliest of all our inland cities, I felt a straining at my loyalty;

and when I saw in the dining-room of Mr. W. N. Byers the great square window that his charming wife ordered made so that she might frame 200 miles of the Rockies as in a picture, I admitted to myself that there was much to be said for "t'other dear charmer," and that, in the language of Denver's poet, Cy Warman, "God was good to make the mountains."

We have looked on Denver's patent map, and know where we are. Every Western city has its own patent map, usually designed to show that it is in the centre of creation, but Denver's map is more truthful, and merely locates it in the middle of the country west of the Mississippi. It shows the States east of that river without a single railroad, while a perfect labyrinth of railroads crisscross the West in frantic efforts to get to Denver. Gravely a Denver man says to us afterwards, as he holds the map in his hand, "If those Dutchmen and Puritans and things who settled the East could have landed out here on the plains, the thirteen original colonies would have been a howling wilderness filled with savages to-day." And that in turn reminds me of the remark of a man in Utah, a Mormon, who was a member of a colony that pre-empted an alkali lake, washed out the salt with a system of ditches, and succeeded in growing crops. "Eastern people make a great mouth about irrigation and farming in the arid belt," said he, "but we folks 'd rather scoop out a ditch than have to clear out forest stumps and blast rocks to get room for farming." The moral of both these tales is that we may have our own opinion of the West, but we can't prevent the West's having its own opinion of us.

In all other respects the patent Denver map is reliable. It shows that this city of 135,000 souls stands all alone, without a real rival, in a vast rich region. It is 1000 miles from Chicago, 400 from Salt Lake City, 600 from Kansas City, and the same distance from the Missouri River. If you drew a circle of 1000 miles diameter, with Denver in its centre, you would discover no real competitor; but the people have adopted what they call their "thousand-mile theory," which is that Chicago is 1000 miles from New York, and Denver is 1000 miles from Chicago, and San Francisco is 1000 miles from Denver, so that, as any one can see, if great cities are put at that distance apart, as it seems, then these are to be the four great ones of America.

Denver is a beautiful city—a parlor city with cabinet finish—and it is so new that it looks as if it had been made to order, and was just ready for delivery. How the people lived five years ago, or what they have done with the houses of that period, does not appear, but at present everything — business blocks, churches, clubs, dwellings, street cars, the park — all look brand-new, like the young trees. The first citizen you talk to says: "You notice there are no old people on the streets here. There aren't any in the city. We have no use for old folks here." So, then, the people also are new. It is very wonderful and peculiar. Only a year ago Mr. Richard Harding Davis was there, and commented on the lack of pavements in the streets, and I hear that at that time pedestrians wore rubber boots, and the mud was frightful. But now every street in the thick of town is paved with concrete or Belgian blocks as well as if it were New York or Paris. The first things that impress you in the city are the neatness and width of the streets, and the number of young trees that ornament them most invitingly. The next thing is the remarkable character of the big business buildings. It is not that they are bigger and better than those of New York and Chicago—comparisons of that sort are nonsensical—but they are massive and beautiful, and they possess an elegance without and a roominess and lightness within that distinguish them as superior to the show buildings of most of the cities of the country. The hotels are even more remarkable, from the one down by the impressive big depot, which is the best-equipped third-class hotel in the country, to the Brown's Palace and the Métropole, both of steel and stone, which are just as good as men know how to make hotels.

The residence districts are of a piece with the rest. Along the tree-lined streets are some of the very prettiest villas it is any man's lot to see at this time. They are not palaces, but they are very tasteful, stylish, cosey, and pretty homes, all built of brick or stone, in a great variety of pleasing colors and materials, and with a proud showing of towers, turrets, conservatories, bay-windows, gables, and all else that goes to mark this period, when men build after widely differing plans to compliment their own taste and the skill of originating draughtsmen. The town spreads over an enormous territory, as compared with the space a city of its size should take up, but we must learn that modern methods of quick transit are so cheap that they are being adopted everywhere, and wherever they are used the cities are spreading out. Denver has cable and electric cars, but it is the electric roads that are the city-spreaders. They whiz along so fast that men do not hesitate to build their homes five or six miles from their stores and offices, where they can get garden and elbow room. We are going to see all our cities shoot out in this way. It promotes beauty in residence districts, and pride in the hearts of those who own the pretty homes. It carries the good health that comes with fresh air. But it entails a great new expense upon modern city government, for the streets and the mains and sewers and police and

MAP OF COLORADO

fire systems all have to be extended to keep pace with the electric flight of the people, who, in turn, must stand the taxes. Not that they are high in Denver, or in those other electric-car-peppered capitals, Minneapolis and St. Paul, but they are higher than they would be if the people were crowded into smaller spaces. In Denver the government has spared itself and the people one source of anxiety by ordering that, no matter where the houses reach to, it shall be a fire-proof city. The fire lines follow the extension, and every house must be of brick or stone.

As we walk about the town, noting the theatres that are absolutely gorgeous, observing that the Methodist church is a quarter-of-a-million-dollar pile of granite, seeing the crowded shopping stores that are almost like our own in New York, heeding the bustle of people and vehicles, stopping to look at the precious Colorado stones that are heaped in the jewellers' windows, and the museums of Indian curios that are peculiar to the town, a marked and distinctive secret of the place is forced upon our attention. It is that though the signs of great wealth and liberal outlay are in every view, there is no over-decoration, no vulgar display, no wasteful ostentation (except in that saloon that has silver dollars sunk in the floor, and that other one where the mosaic floor slabs are set with double eagles). There is upon the show-places of the town that restraint which we call "taste." To be sure, the bar-rooms cost the price of a prince's ransom, and the walls and bars are made of onyx. But there they stop. A little spray of silver arabesquerie, necessary to save such a room from bareness, is all the ornament one sees. In the high-class hotels, for some reason that appears inscrutable to an American who has been surfeited with bold paintings and dubious bric-à-brac from Madison Square to Nob

Hill, there **is the same** extraordinary good taste. The walls **of** all the rooms, **both** public and private, rely on the harmonious blending **of** soft tints, and on mere lines of fine beading **on** the hard-wood fittings. **Why that** taste which makes the apartments of the Japanese **our** marvel and delight should reappear in Denver, and **nowhere** else out West, is certainly remarkable.

"There is in Denver," says **a** man who meets me in the Hôtel Métropole, "**what** is shockingly called 'the one-lunged army.' **I am a member of** it, and may **repeat the** nickname without **shame, for we** are proud **of ourselves.** This army comprises 30,000 invalids, **or** more **than** one-fifth of the population **of** Denver. Not **by** any means is this a host of persons with pulmonary ailments, but of men in physical straits of many sorts, who find the rare air of a place a mile on the road to heaven better than medicine. These are men of wealth, as a rule, and of cultivation and of taste. They have been more important **factors in** the making of this unique city than **most persons, even** in Denver, imagine. The stock and **oil and gold and** silver millionaires point to their opera**tions as the cause of Denver's** importance; and they are right. But importance **is one thing,** and good taste, good society, and progressiveness **are** quite different things. **It** was not mining that begot **the taste which** crowds our residence quarter with elegant dwellings, **or that** created a demand for clubs like the Denver Club. It was not oil that gave us college-bred men to form a 'Varsity Club of 120 members, or that insisted upon the decoration of the town with such hotels as ours. The influence of the invalids is seen in all this. They are New-Yorkers, Bostonians, Philadelphians, New Orleans men, **Englishmen** — the well-to-do and well-brought up men **from all** over the country—architects, doctors, lawyers, and every sort of professional men being among them."

After that we caught ourselves constantly looking for invalids, but without success. Even those who told us that they were members of the strange army of debilitated æsthetes did not look so. But we came upon many queer facts regarding them, and the air, and the customs of the place. One very noticeable peculiarity of the people was their habit of speaking of the East as "home." "At home in the East we call that Virginia-creeper," said one. "I go home to New York every few months," said another. "We long to go back East to our homes, but when we get there the climate does not agree with us, and we hurry back to Colorado." Thus was revealed the peculiar tenure the place has upon thousands of its citizens. But among them are very many who say that it is customary for Eastern folks to let their regard for the East keep warm until the moment comes when they seriously consider the idea of leaving Colorado. At that juncture they realize for the first time the magic of the mountain air and the hold it has upon them. Few indeed ever seriously think of leaving it after one such consultation with themselves. But I must say it is a very queer air. It keeps every one keyed up to the trembling-point, inciting the population to tireless, incessant effort, like a ceaseless breathing-in of alcohol. It creates a highly nervous people, and, as one man said, "it is strange to fancy what the literature of Colorado will be when it develops its own romancers and poets, so strong is the nervous strain and mental exaltation of the people." One would suppose alcohol unnecessary there; but, on the contrary, there is much drinking. It is a dangerous indulgence. Among the dissolutes suicides are frequent. "If you stay here a week you will read of two," said a citizen. And I did. It was found that when the saloons were allowed to remain open all night, violent crimes were of frequent occurrence. Drinking too deep and too long was the cause. The saloons were therefore ordered shut at twelve o'clock, and a remarkable decrease of these crimes followed.

We shall see that on its worst side the city is Western, and that its moral side is Eastern. It will be interesting to see how one side dominates the other, and both keep along together. But in the mean time what is most peculiar is the indifference with which the populace regards murder among those gamblers and desperadoes who are a feature of every new country, and who are found in Denver, though, I suspect, the ladies and children never see them, so well separated are the decent and the vicious quarters. It is said that not very long ago it was the tacit agreement of the people that it was not worth while to put the county to the cost or bother of seriously pursuing, prosecuting, and hanging or imprisoning a thug who murdered another thug. It was argued that there was one bad man less, and that if the murderer was at large another one would kill him. The axiom that "only bad men are the victims of bad men" obtained there, as it did in Cheyenne and Deadwood, and does in Butte. To-day a murder in a dive or gambling-hell excites little comment and no sensation in Denver, and I could distinctly see a trace of the old spirit in the speech of the reputable men when I talked to them of the one crime of the sort that took place while I was there.

The night side of the town is principally corralled, as they say; that is, its disorderly houses are all on one street. There is another mining-town characteristic— wide-open gambling. The "hells" are mainly above-stairs, over saloons. The vice is not flaunted as it is in certain other cities; but once in the gaming-places, the visitor sees them to be like those my readers became acquainted with in Butte, Montana—great open places, like the board-rooms in our stock exchanges, lined with gambling lay-outs. They are crowded on this Saturday night with rough men in careless dress or in the apparel of laborers. These are railroad employés, workers from the nearest mines, laborers, clerks—every sort of men who earn their money hard, and think to make more out of it by letting it go easily. Roulette, red and black, and faro are the games. Behind each table sits the imperturbable dealer—sometimes a rough cowboyish-looking young man, who has left off his necktie so as to show his diamond stud; sometimes a man who would pass for a gray-bearded deacon in a village church. By each dealer's side sits the "lookout," chewing a cigar, and lazily looking on in the interests of such fair play as is consistent with professional gambling. All around each table, except on the dealer's side, crowd the idiots, straining and pushing to put their chips where luck will perch. These places are orderly, of course. It is the rule with them everywhere. There is very little conversation. Except for the musical clink-link-link of the ivory chips, the shuffling of feet, and the rattle of the roulette marbles, there is little noise. But the floor boards hold small sea-beds of expectoration, and over each table is enough tobacco smoke to beget the fancy that each lay-out is a mouth of the pit of hell.

Queer characters illustrate queer stories in these places, just as they do in the mining regions, but with the difference that all the stories of luck in the mines are cast with characters who are either rich or "broke," while in the hells they seem never to be in luck when you happen on them. They were flush yesterday, and will be to-morrow—if you will "stake" them with something to gamble with. The man who once had a bank of his own and the one who broke the biggest bank in

Leadville were mere **ordinary** *dramatis personæ* **when I** looked in, but the towering giant of the place was the man who at twenty-six years of age had killed twenty-six men, all so justly, however, that he never stood trial for one episode. This is part of the "local color" in any picture of Denver; but, on the other hand, the best of that color is, as I have hinted, of the tone of lovely firesides, elegance, wealth, and refinement.

From the gaming to the fruit fair, that happens to be in progress, we are eager to go. The fruit or orchard **exhibition was an** unlooked-for consummation in so **new a State**. It was a sight of the dawn of the fruit industry **where** the best orchards were not five years **old**. Indeed, some of the finest fruit was plucked where **Indians** were guarded not long before. There were apples, pears, peaches, plums, quinces, grapes, and ground-cherries. It was too late in the year (October) for berries, but they are grown in Colorado in great abundance, and the strawberries are said to be big and most delicious. The fruits I saw displayed at the fair were of large though not Californian size. Their most remarkable quality to the eye was their gorgeous coloring—the richest and deepest I ever saw except in paintings. I found afterwards that all the fruit grown in the valleys of the Rockies is equally gorgeous. But of more practical import **is** the fact that this **Colorado** fruit is of delicious flavor. In Denver and in other parts of the State I tasted every product of the orchards. I cannot recall my experience in California clearly enough to say more than that they pick their fruit green to ship it away, and so they miss the credit they deserve abroad as growers of luscious fruit. I would like to encourage the Coloradans in their boast that theirs has higher flavor than the west-coast product (if it were true, and I had both kinds **to prove it by), and I** will say that I think I never enjoyed any fruit more than most of that which I ate in Colorado. The only melons at the show were muskmelons, but it is a great State for melons, particularly for watermelons. One place, Rocky Ford, in Otero County, is celebrated for its observance of what is called "melon day" every year, when the idle people, tourists, and pleasure-seekers gather there to eat free melons in a great amphitheatre built for that purpose. This affair is not altogether unique. 'At Monument, in Douglas County, the exuberant villagers dig a great trench and cook potatoes—as the Rhode-Islanders do clams—for the multitude, without charge. The fruit at the Denver show was grown in the following counties: Arapahoe, Boulder, Delta, Grand, Jefferson, Larimer, Mesa, Montrose, Otero, and Weld.

The wild flowers at this show were very interesting. No account of Colorado would be complete if it omitted at least some mention of these gorgeous ornaments which Nature litters with lavish hands all over the State —far up the mountain-sides, where the very rocks are stained with rich colors, and up and down the valleys, where even man's importation, the alfalfa, turns the ranches into great blue beds of thickly clustered blossoms. It may have been the flowers, or it may have been the beautifully stained rocks, or, as some say, the color of the water in the Colorado River, that gained the State the Spanish name it bears, but whichever it was, the flowers alone were sufficient to justify the christening, so multitudinous, lovely, varied, and gay are they. Fortunately for the fame of the flowers, certain Colorado ladies are skilled in pressing them so as to reproduce and preserve the natural poses of all the flowering plants, as well as to make them retain their colors unimpaired. The work of these women is now known in every part of the civilized world.

It was interesting to read the progress of Denver in the remarks of those who were presented to me during that visit to the fruit show. One gentleman was interested in the electric-light plant, and said that it is so powerful that during a recent decoration of the streets in honor of a convention that was held there, no less than 22,000 incandescent and four 5000 candle-power search-lights were used in the display. In few cities in the world, he said, is this light so generally and so lavishly used. He added that few of the dwellings, except in the poorest quarter, are without telephones.

A public official volunteered the information that since 1870 the percentage of increase of population has been greater in Denver than in any other city of the land, it being something more than 2000 per cent. A bevy of smiling young women was pointed out as representative art students; for there is a Denver Art League which has sixty members, and aims to maintain classes in oil and water-color work and sculpture. Two of the classes, one for each sex, pursue the practice of drawing and painting from the nude. This institution is the pride and care of the leading business and professional men of the city, who give it ample funds, and are encouraged by the eagerness of the youth of the State, as well as of the city, to enjoy its advantages. A merchant spoke of the Chamber of Commerce, to the enterprise and kindness of which, and especially of the secretary, I was afterwards indebted. I learned that this watchful organization of promoters of the commercial welfare of the city maintains a fine free library, containing a collection of books that now numbers 20,000 volumes, and is constantly increasing. No less than 77,000 volumes were read in the homes of its patrons last year. The reading-room is kept open on all the days of the year, and the city government has passed an ordinance appropriating $500 a month, from the fines imposed by the police magistrates, for the benefit of this valuable institution. Another new acquaintance urged me to see the public schools of the city. The high-school building cost $325,000, and is the second most costly and complete one in existence. Many of the ward or district schools cost a fifth, and some cost more than a fifth, of that large sum. I could not then nor there further insist upon the opinions that have engendered the only criticisms that have passed between myself in these papers and the new West which I am describing. The report of the Denver Board of Education is before me, and if I read it aright, it declares that the common-school system embraces a course of twelve years of study, eight in the common schools and four in the high-school. Drawing, music, physical culture, and German are mentioned as among the studies in the grammar grades, while the wide gamut between algebra and Greek, with military training for the boys, comprises the high-school course. The 700 high-school pupils are said to be of the average age of seventeen years. I reiterate that this is education for the well-to-do at the expense of the poor. If Denver is like any other town of my acquaintance, the poor cannot release their children from toil during twelve years after they are of an age to be sent to school. The disparity between the sum of 9500 in the common schools and the sum of 700 in the high-school makes it appear that Denver is no exception to the rule. I will not dwell upon my belief that the wide range of studies in these latter-day schools gives children a mere but dangerous smattering of many things and no thorough grounding in any study, and that the result is to produce a distaste for honest labor and an unfitness for anything above it. It is unpleasant to criticise at all where a community is so enthusiastic as this, but I believe the whole system, whether we find it in New York and Boston, as we do, or in Denver, is undemocratic, unjust, and unwise. The "little red school-house on the hill," which has been glorified as the chief pride of Puritan New England, is the seed that has grown into the $300,000 palace of learning for 700 children, at the expense of the parents of more than 9000 other children. The little red school-house was grand indeed. It taught the "three R's" thoroughly, and when a boy or girl wanted more, he or she managed to get it, at such pains and in such a way as to cause him or her to value all that was acquired. Honest work was the portion of all but the rich, who paid for their children's higher schooling. However, the spirit in which Denver maintains and elaborates her school system is beyond all criticism; it is, indeed, creditable and wonderful. If we do not agree about the result, I can at least testify to the impression I received—that the whole people are honestly and enthusiastically proud of their schools, and that of their elaborate kind they are among the best in the country.

Denver has other than her public schools—the (Methodist) University of Denver, the (Catholic) St. Mary's Academy, the (Episcopal) St. John's College for boys; an Episcopal school for girls, called Wolfe Hall; the Woman's College, and the Westminster University, the first a Baptist and the second a Presbyterian institution. I should have mentioned the fact that a second fine public library is maintained in connection with the public-school system. It goes without saying, in a study of a city like Denver, that musical, dramatic, literary, and kindred coteries are numerous.

Away from the fruit display, out in the brightly lit streets, were the crowds of Saturday-night shoppers. Of these many more were persons employed in manufacturing industries than those would imagine who know no more of Denver than I have told. The fine and varied building stones that will yet become a great asset in Colorado's inventory of wealth are cut and dressed in more than one establishment. The notable buildings of Denver are built of Colorado red sandstone, granite, and other beautiful materials found in the mountains. The main or parent range of the Rockies loses its striking configuration soon after leaving Colorado in the south. Then it becomes a broken, ragged chain. They have some good stones in the territories to the southward, but not the assortment found in Colorado. Already Colorado stones are shipped to Chicago, the Nebraska and Kansas towns, and Texas. These are brownstones, granite, a so-called lava or metamorphic stone of great durability and beauty, and a variety of sandstones. Some red sandstone that I saw being quarried in the Dolores Valley, where it is abundant beyond calculation, is said to be well adapted for fine interior decorative uses. Others in the crowds were workers in the cotton factory; in a knitting-mill that has been removed there from the East; in the three large establishments where preserves, fruit pickles, and sauces are made; in the making of fire-brick, drainpipe, jugs, jars, churns, and other coarse pottery; in the manufacture of the best mining machinery in the world, whole outfits of which have been shipped to China and South Africa, to say nothing of Mexico and our own mining regions, which are all supplied from Denver. Other operatives work upon the hoisting machinery and pumping machines, of which the Denver patterns are celebrated. Still others in the streets work at the stock-yards, where there are two large packing companies, and where nearly 200,000 hogs, cattle, and sheep were slaughtered last year. A mill for the manufacture of newspaper has been in operation for a year, and now (October, '92) three other paper-mills are about to be erected, the aim being to make book and letter paper, Manilas, coarse wrapping-paper, and flooring and roofing papers, as well as to produce the pulp used in these manufactures.

The three smelting-works employ nearly 400 men, and handled 400,000 tons of ore, producing $24,500,000 in gold, silver, lead, and copper, last year. In addition to the twenty foundries and machine shops of whose work I have spoken, there are thirty other iron-working establishments, making tin and sheet-iron work and wire-work. In another year a barbed-wire factory and a wire and nail making plant will be in operation. There are sixty brick-making firms. Leather-workers are numerous, but all the leather is imported; there is no tannery there. Paint and white-lead making are large industries; there are six breweries; and eight firms engage in wood-working and the making of building material. In a sentence, this busy metropolis is manufacturing for the vast territory around it, with 339 manufacturing establishments, employing 9000 operatives, and producing $46,000,000 worth of goods.

The Chamber of Commerce advertises the need of woollen mills, stocking factories, tanneries, boot and shoe factories, glue factories, and potteries, but declares that Denver will give no subsidies to get them. "The natural advantages of the centre of a region as large as the German Empire, without a rival for 600 miles in any direction, combined with cheap fuel, fine climate, abundant supply of intelligent labor at reasonable prices, unutilized local raw materials, a good and ever-growing local market, protected against Eastern competition by from 1000 to 2000 miles of railroad haul—these are the inducements that Denver offers to new manufacturing plants."

And now we will fancy it is Sunday in Denver. The worshippers are coming out of the churches. But in the streets rush the cable cars with their week-day clanging of bells. On the car roofs are the signs, "To Elitch's Gardens," where, according to the papers next day, there are "music and dancing and bangle-bedizened women." Other cars rush towards the City Park, where the State Capital Band is to play. "Oho!" thought the critical Eastern visitors; "we are in the presence of the usual American Sunday, with the gin-mills and the gambling-places all wide open." Not so. So far as I could see, not a bar-room was open. The shades were up, and the desolate interiors were in plain view from the streets. The gambling-saloons were tight shut. No one loitered near them. Here, then, had reappeared the Sunday of the Atlantic coast, for the local ordinances are enforced, and require the closing of the saloons and "hells" from Saturday midnight until Monday morning.

Except for the cling-clang of the street cars, an Eastern-Sunday hush was upon the town. Just as we see them in New York, country couples, strangers there, walked arm in arm in the business quarter, looking in the shop windows; German families, children and all, in stiff Sunday best, streamed along in queues behind the fathers; idle young men with large cigars leaned against the corners and the corner lamp-posts, and the business streets were nine-tenths dead. Thousands gathered in the park, just as they do on such a Sunday in New York. Beyond that the silence and stagnation of Sunday were on the town. In the Denver Club the prosperous men loafed about, and looked in at the great round table in the private dining-room with thoughts of the grand dinners it had borne. In the pretty homes were many circles wherein the West was discussed just as it is in New York, with sharp words for its gambling, its pistol-carrying, and its generally noisy Sundays. It was strange to hear in the West such talk of the West. It was easy to see the source of the influence that brought about that quiet day of worship. Yet in the same homes, in the same circles, was heard the most fulsome lauding of Denver and Colorado—praise that seemed to lift those altitudinous places even nearer to the clouds. With only the happiest memories and kindest wishes, then, adieu to Denver.

I made a journey of more than two thousand miles in Colorado without seeing half of it, for it is as large as New England and New York. Upon the famous "Scenic Route" (the Denver and Rio Grande Railroad) I rode from Denver to the New Mexican border, through southern Colorado, and back through the middle of the State, over the famous Marshall Pass. I took in, on the way, the full lengths of the Silverton and the Rio Grande Southern railways, which, in quest of mining towns and agricultural settlements, are laid amid some of the most gorgeous, stupendous, and varied scenery in the State. It will surprise the reader to hear that on these mountain railroads rock ballast, heavy steel rails, and gas-lighted palace-cars are provided. Yet the greatest surprise comes with seeing how the railroad-builders have flung their steel in loops upon the mountain sides and tops, where one would suppose no engines could ever haul a train, or trains could ever yield a profit, and where it is no uncommon thing to see three and even four lengths of the same railway above or below your car, as the rails "tack" to and fro towards the top of a steep mountain. "Yachting round the Rockies" was what the party on the trip with me resolved to call our journeying. There is not sufficient room in a chapter for a description of the scenery of Colorado. I had not supposed that, after enjoying the mountain scenery of British Columbia, I would find anything to delight me as much in any other part of the Rocky Mountain chain. Even now I think there are grander views in the North, but they are not as numerous, nor as beautiful and warm and full of color and variety, as the mountain scenes in Colorado. The railway tourist in British Columbia merely crosses the mountains, whereas in Colorado it is possible to start from Denver and, riding only by daylight, to spend a week of nearly continuous mountaineering. At the end it will be difficult to determine which is the prettiest scene that memory retains for the mind's eye to return to. Perhaps it will seem that, taken altogether, the wondrous cañons were most worth seeing; those of the Rio de las Animas Perdidas, of the Grand, of the Dolores, of the Rio Grande, and that at Toltec, in New Mexico. Perhaps the surprising views of innumerable far-reaching, snow-clad mountain peaks—seen at many points when the cars cross a divide—will be most delightfully remembered. Or it may be that the choicest recollection will be of the superb region between Trout Lake and the Cathedral Peaks, followed by a valley view of great beauty beyond. Then strangely beautiful mining towns, built in blind valleys between towering mountains, will come to mind, and Telluride, Pandora, Ouray, and other villages will seem the most enchanting bits of the grand experience. Their neat houses, shaded streets, and glorious surroundings gain much from the added novelty of mining paraphernalia in action. The pack-trains of long-eared burros, which the people call "Colorado canaries," the trolley railways, the heaps of ore, the Welsh miners—all these lend added value to the scenes. Each day is crowded with views of fearful gorges, of mountain-sides stained red and blue and green, of valleys cultivated to the degree of an Illinois prairie, of vast irrigation-works gridironing the plains with silver threads, of Mexicans and their huts and villages of adobe, of myriads of sheep on southern ranges. It is not necessary to go to Europe for scenery or for unfamiliar peoples and conditions.

I shall say even less about the mining than about the scenery. Colorado is generally known to possess both in abundance. Let it be my part to show that already the surer, more lasting resource of agriculture is the heaviest asset of the State. The Denver smelteries treated four and a quarter millions of pounds of Colorado copper, 100,000 tons of Colorado lead, twelve million ounces of silver, and 120,000 ounces of gold. The total value of all this was fifteen and three-quarter millions of dollars; but much of the Colorado ore is of the free-milling variety not treated at the smelteries; and besides, there are other smelteries at Pueblo, Rico, Leadville, and Durango. The total revenue from mining in 1891 was thirty-three and a half millions of dollars. And yet the Denver Chamber of Commerce estimates the income from agriculture at forty millions, derived from the cultivation of two millions of acres of land. If the value of the live-stock were added as a farm product, the sum would be increased by at least $15,000,000. A wonderful showing for so new a State.

It is estimated that at the end of another hundred years Colorado will boast a population of four millions of souls. Her stone quarries, her petroleum, her mineral paints, her cement, which is already classed as equal to the best, her clays, found in tremendous banks, and suitable for the production of fine china, as well as pottery of all the coarse grades, her coal and iron, her natural parks, scenic wonders, mineral waters, farm and fruit and pasture lands, her vast stores of metals—all these, and many resources that I have not mentioned, will more than support a population of that magnitude.

The range cattle business and civilization, with its fences and farms and towns, cannot exist together, and as Colorado is civilized, this rude business is almost at an end there. Cattle are being held in small bunches and with winter corrals—an infinitely more practical and humane industry. The present grade of cattle is higher than before. Every farmer sells a few head each year, and thus makes a little money where a few used to make (or lose) large sums.

One-third of the State is plains land, and two-thirds are cut up by mountains. These are separated by valleys of varying degrees of value for farm land, and the mountains are not so rocky as to be to any great extent unavailable for pasturage. Farming and orchard culture are making great headway in Larimer, Arapahoe, Boulder, Jefferson, and Weld counties, in eastern Colorado. Farmers are pushing into the valleys of southern Colorado, especially those in the southwest, that were once thickly peopled and well cultivated by the cliff-dwellers. The Mormons and other thrifty folk are taking up valley lands in the western part of the State.

Colorado's 66,560,000 acres of land lie upon either side of the continental divide and upon many secondary ranges, forming mountains, parks, and valleys, of which not 5 per cent. is bare of vegetation. Long ago the Mexicans began, with petty irrigation-works, to borrow from the eight principal rivers and their tributaries the water that came down from the mountains in those channels. The mean yearly precipitation west of the mountains is but 25 inches; east of them it is only 18.7

inches. At Denver the highest rainfall was in 1891, and amounted to $21\frac{4}{10}$ inches. The lowest was in 1890, and was $9\frac{1}{3}$ inches. All over the State irrigation companies have been formed, or farmers have banded together as ditch-owners, and, as we shall see, a vast acreage is under irrigation or ready for it. The destruction of the forests, and consequent loss of water, through its unequal distribution, have hurried the necessary building of reservoirs, of which there are many, and some very large **ones, in use.** Colorado is forward in **this** respect. The **importance** of reservoirs **where water is** scarce **will** be seen when the reader understands that the winter's stores of snow, **and even** the heavy rainfalls, are apt to rush away in one great flood, robbing the State of a large fraction of the too little water that comes upon it. The gauge records of the Cache la Poudre River show that 82 per cent. of the total annual discharge passes down the river in May, June, and July, whereas in August the discharge is only 6.6 per cent., and in September it is only 2.6 per cent.

Artesian wells add comparatively little to the wealth of the State, although this source of supply has been so successfully tried in the San Luis Valley that there are **now** more than 2000 wells there.

On the eastern slope, **out** to the eastern boundary of Colorado, there are nearly thirty millions of acres of arable land, of which four millions of acres are "under the ditch," and only a million and a half are actually cultivated. Of what remains unditched it is difficult to say how much may be redeemed. It depends upon the situation of the land and the extent of the water supply, and the latter **factor** is dependent on future developments.

For one thing, the **irrigable** land is constantly being **extended** and increased by the storage of the water of spring freshets in reservoirs that are usually formed out of natural depressions at the base of the mountains. The custom is to use the stored water on the near-by land, while the stream carries its own quota, undiminished, to distant fields. Thus the area of irrigable territory is greatly increased. Moreover, time has demonstrated the strange but important fact that, after three or four years, water used in irrigation goes twice as far as it did when the work was begun. The ground under the ditches becomes a vast reservoir, from which the water that sinks into it "seeps" or drains back into the natural waterways. Mr. Maxwell, the State Engineer of Colorado, finds that at the eastern line of the State, far beyond the ranches and farms which drain the river, the Platte carries 600 cubic feet of water per second as against the 200 cubic feet it brings out of the mountains. There is, therefore, a far better supply in the eastern plains country than formerly, and this will increase as reservoirs catch the spring floods, for it is certain that however much water be spread on the land, none is lost except by evaporation. The least hopeful outlook in eastern Colorado is for the land on the divide between the Platte and the Arkansas. There is no water there; the land is higher than the distant rivers, and wells have not succeeded there.

West of the Rocky Mountains there are more and larger streams, but there is less rainfall than on the eastern slope. It is estimated that there is a drainage area of twenty-five millions of acres in western Colorado, but that only nine millions are arable. These nine millions are mainly irrigated, the country being the field of rapid development. The principal streams flow through well-cultivated farming districts, and these form the region already noted for choice fruit-raising.

In the celebrated Greeley colony, north of Denver, the

ditches are owned by the men who own the land. They bought and pre-empted a large tract (now as rich as a typical Illinois district, by-the-way), took the water rights, constructed a large canal, and distributed the water proportionately with the various holdings of the land. Thus the water has become **part and** parcel of the land, and costs only the trifling sum each owner **is** assessed for repairs and superintendence. This **is** as near to the perfect and **ideal** method **of** irrigation **as** mankind has come in this country. **It is** the **method of** the Mormons also. But, alas! practically the **whole water** treasure and **irrigation-work is** in the **hands** of speculative corporations. All the newer schemes are of that sort. In the San Luis Valley, the Arkansas Valley, and along the Platte River corporations have built the ditches, appropriated and diverted the water, and are selling the liquid to farmers with a superimposed annual tax for repairs—a tax of such proportions that the plan may **be justly** described as making the farmers pay down at the **outset** for the privilege of having water afterwards **by** paying **for** it over again every **year.** Like cows who come home **to** be milked at nightfall, **the** settlers of Colorado must "**give** down" each year **or go** dry. **The** first payments vary **between five,** eight, **and ten** dollars an **acre** for the land—usually eight to **ten** dollars—and the annual dues (for " maintenance," as this Colorado method of producing water-barons is called) are from a dollar to two dollars and a half an acre.

In each State I have visited where irrigation is necessary (and this **is** the case in something like one-fifth of the land of the United States) the conditions are about the same, and their unjustness causes thinking men to predict excessive irritation and trouble in the future. An eminent lawyer in Denver has reached the same conclusion **that I announced in one of my** papers on the new

States in the Northwest. "Eventually and surely," said he, "the States must control the water supply within their borders. They will have to take the water by right of eminent domain, and pay the present owners for it. They must pay a great deal, for the owners count on becoming wealthy and on bequeathing Fortunatus purses to their descendants. Once in the possession of the Government, the water must be distributed for the benefit of the greatest possible number. It will not be in our time, but it will be done, and it will result from the very great discontent, and perhaps even violent disorder, that are certain to breed out of the present unjust, selfish, and primitive methods."

The coal of eastern Colorado extends the whole width of the State in a belt that reaches an average distance of twenty miles out into the plains. It is an accompaniment of the Rocky Mountains, and has been thought to extend from the Gulf of Mexico to Alaska. An equal field lies to the west of the mountains, and is worked in Utah, Wyoming, and elsewhere. It is by no means uninterrupted or continuous. Glaciers and floods have worn away great reaches of it, and other lengths are overlaid by such thicknesses of rock that they are unworkable. But there are vast fields of it in Colorado—thirty thousand to forty thousand square miles, one official report declares. It is bituminous or lignite, and varies in quality, but even that which shows the lowest of these stages of development is valuable. The southern coal area is the better. There the coal is firm, does not slack, or slacks but slightly, breaks up into large blocks, is freer from impurities, and is found in thicker veins than elsewhere, as a rule. It is to get this coal and supply it to Kansas, Nebraska, New Mexico, and other States and Territories that several railways have extended their lines into Colorado, to the incalculable benefit of the State. A remarkable and indubitable "find" of anthracite coal is the gem of this vast double field of fuel. It is mined at Crested Butte, in Gunnison County, in the Elk Mountains By the fossil remains found with it geologists determine it to be of the same origin as the lignite of the foot-hills and plains, altered by heat into anthracite. It is now known to occur in more than one large bed, and close to it are beds of semi-anthracite, as well as much bituminous coal. There is a great deal of coking-coal here, and other coking-coal in large quantities is found in the Trinidad region—a plateau of 750 square miles in southern Colorado and New Mexico. It is also found in lesser quantities near Durango, in the San Juan district.

The field of petroleum oil in the State is in Fremont County, near Cañon City. The supply of oil is reported to be practically unlimited, and the wells are called more prolific than any others of the same number and size in the United States, yet the production of the whole field is kept down to the requirements of a very limited market. I found but one opinion in Denver, and that was that the Colorado output of oil is limited to the demands of Colorado, Wyoming, Montana, Utah, and New Mexico.

Along the entire foot-hills are geological conditions more or less similar to those at Florence, and it is not at all certain that the present wells are in the best place. That is the general opinion in Colorado, and it is also believed that natural gas will prove a factor in the State's assets some day. With varying success, nearly ninety wells have been drilled in the Florence oil-field. Fifty-two and a half per cent. have proved productive in greater or lesser degree, and some have produced constantly for five years. Out of the 30,000 barrels produced up to October, 1891, one-third of the amount was refined into oil, and 5000 barrels of lubricating oil were made, both products being excellent, for the oil is rich in illuminant and lubricating qualities.

There is among Colorado capitalists a project for operating a four-million-dollar iron and steel producing company, and this company has for a long time kept experts in the field in an endeavor to find suitable coal and iron in such proximity to one another as to warrant the establishment of furnaces for the making of pig to blend into the Bessemer product afterwards. I went to the chief personage in this great prospective industry and asked him as to the quantity and kinds of iron that were supposed to exist in the State. With rare tact, and a quality of courtesy not often met with in the West, he said that exactly what I wished to know was precisely what I should not find out. What was vouchsafed to me by this custodian of the bad manners and the knowledge of the iron deposit in Colorado was as valuable as it was churlishly given.

There is, it seems, but little development-work in iron in the State, though the iron is found scattered in large fields on both sides of the mountains, some being magnetic and some hematite, not to speak of the more or less worthless ores. For twelve years iron has been made at Pueblo of ore from the San Luis Valley, Leadville, and other points. There is in the State a great deal of ore free from phosphorus and sulphur to make Bessemer steel, ore of good quality being found in many places, the only question about any of it being with regard to its quantity and availability. "But," said the gruff sage who told me this, "there is not a pound of fuel east of the Rockies that is fit to use in making iron, and to use what there is would bankrupt whoever did it." Iron is going into Colorado from Alabama at seventeen dollars a ton, ten dollars being the market price and seven dollars the freight charge. **In** another **year** Lake Superior pig-iron will enter the Colorado market. The problem in Colorado, then, **is to** find iron to market at a less **price.** Fifteen-dollar iron would do, on a basis of thirteen dollars cost, leaving a margin for profit and interest on the plant. There is required a combination of the right ore, the right fuel, and satisfactory transportation facilities, and that combination is yet to be made. **An** exhaustive, energetic investigation is going forward, and the men interested hope to work at **many** points to produce mixtures **for Bessemer.** They believe that there. is a good prospect **of** success **at an** early day. They are looking into the **fuel** question in Wyoming, **where** the **iron** supply is no longer debatable.

Second to Denver among Colorado's cities is Pueblo, in the county **of** that name. It claims 40,000 population, and is a substantially built and very busy town, with **a** banking capital of a million, and mercantile operations that amount to $35,000,000 a year. Its three smelteries **produce** $14,000,000 **a** year. It has five railroads **running** through it, a $400,000 opera-house, a public library, immense iron and steel works, oil-refineries, thirty miles of electric street railway, and a solid, orderly, and prosperous appearance. It is 4700 feet **up in** the air, and surrounded by **a** delightful country, either cultivated or naturally picturesque. The mineral palace for the display of the mineral resources of the State, the artesian magnetic mineral baths, the near-by lake-side summer resort, and the really fine hotels **of** the city **have** attracted tourists and invalids in great numbers.

Colorado Springs is another important place, of which **it** has been said **that** it presents the anomaly of **a** bustling town of **fine** buildings, banks, clubs, palatial hotels, and **yet** manufactures nothing at all, and does no business except with itself. The place has 12,000 inhabitants, and is a winter and summer resort, 6000 feet above sea-level. Residence there is advertised as a "sure cure" for consumption, which explains the mystery of its size and character. The town has electric cars, a college, the Childs-Drexel Printers' Home, hospitals, churches, schools, banks, clubs, an opera-house, and a casino, which includes a fine restaurant and an orchestra. The place is surrounded by resorts and scenic points that have been widely advertised. Pike's Peak, Manitou (another resort famed for its springs), the latest sensational mining camp, called Cripple Creek, and many other noted places are all close to Colorado Springs, which is perhaps the most finished and elegant health resort west of the Mississippi.

Colorado is dotted with springs of medicated water of various kinds—hot, cold, sulphur, soda, iron, magnetic—a great variety, and existing in almost every county. At Glenwood Springs, an especially beautiful resort, hot springs are utilized to fill an open-air bath 600 feet long, in which men and women may bathe in midwinter without being chilled while in or beside the bath. A hotel to cost $400,000 is building there.

The southwestern part of the State, called the San Juan country, has for its capital a place named Durango, which is sufficiently far from any competitor, is in a sufficiently rich country, and has a sufficient reputation for "hustling" to make it a very promising place. It is 6000 feet above the sea-level, in the Animas Valley, and includes some fine buildings, good hotels, several banks and churches, a free-and-easy, electric lights, gambling layouts in all the saloons, and, indeed, everything that goes with a high-spirited Western town. The United States land-office there has sold 102,000 acres of land, at $1 25 an acre, and has given away 50,000 acres to homesteaders. It has issued receipts for about 3000 gold and silver mining claims, and has sold 7000 acres of coal land. Here is the San Juan Smeltery, which cokes its own coal, and a smeltery that treats ore from Red Mountain and Rico. The Porter Coal Company, whose mines are near by, turned out 70,000 tons last year. The San Juan Company mines 150 tons a day; the Ute Coal Company mines twice as much; and there are still other companies in the business. The place supports three banks and a savings-bank, an iron foundry and machine shop, two flour-mills, saw-mills, a brick-yard, a lime company, a stone-quarrying company, and the inevitable brewery. Timber for charcoal, gypsum for plaster of Paris, fire-clay, and fine building stones are found near by. The farm land yields, in the local parlance, "everything from peanuts to persimmons," viz., wheat, oats, apples, pears, cherries, plums, melons, grapes, and many sorts of berries. Over in New Mexico peaches are said to do well, and they raise thirty-five varieties of grapes. There are many streams, and irrigation-works are numerous. Montrose is the likely town at the northern end of the San Juan country. Montrose County has 500 miles of ditches, and is rich in the production of wheat, corn, potatoes, hay, and very fine fruit. Here again flour-mills, lumber-mills, banks, an opera-house, a club, and the other monuments of a prosperous community are to be found. It would be interesting to glance all over the State in this way, but since I must choose, I have told of this region—distant and backward until very lately—to illustrate what is true of the whole State.

Aspen and Leadville are no longer bold, bad mining camps. Both are solid, sober places. Creede has moved out of the original gulch to what was "Jimtown," and is also an earnest, orderly town. Greeley is a thrifty, prosperous, and beautiful farming centre; and Grand Junction, in western Colorado, is an ambitious and inviting place.

X

WYOMING—ANOTHER PENNSYLVANIA

YOUNG AMERICA builds bigger than his forefathers. Wyoming is not an exceptionally large State, yet it is as big as the six States of New England and Indiana combined. Indiana itself is the size of Portugal, and is larger than Ireland. It is with more than ordinary curiosity that one approaches Wyoming during a course of study of the new Western States. From the palace cars of the Union Pacific Railroad, that carries a tide of transcontinental travel across its full length, there is little to see but brown bunch-grass, and yet we know that on its surface of 365 miles of length and 275 miles of width are many mountain ranges and noble river-threaded valleys of such beauty that a great block of the land is to be forever preserved in its present condition as the Yellowstone National Park. We know that for years this had been a stockman's paradise, the greatest seat of the cattle industry north of Texas—the stamping-ground of the picturesque cowboys who had taken the place of the hunters who came from the most distant points in Europe to kill big game there. We know that in the mysterious depths of this huge State the decline of its first great activity was, last year, marked by a peculiar disorder that necessitated the calling out of troops—but that was a flash in a pan, much exaggerated at a distance and easily quieted at the time. For the rest, most well-informed citizens outside the State know nothing more than the misnaming of the State implies, for the pretty Indian word Wyoming, copying the name of a historic locality in the East, is said to mean "plains land."

Excepting Idaho, it is the newest of the States in point of development. It waits upon the railroads to open it up. The Union Pacific Company have done this for the southern part, but until three years ago no other railway entered the State. Even now the other roads merely tap its eastern and northern edges. The Burlington and Missouri Railroad, of the Chicago, Burlington, and Quincy system, is pushing its rails into the northeastern part, having come up from Nebraska. It is finished to the Powder River in Sheridan County, and is graded to Sheridan, which is in a region of rich agricultural promise. This railroad must soon, one would think, push on to the Big Horn country, as we shall see. The Fremont, Elkhorn, and Missouri Valley Railroad, of the Chicago and Northwestern system, is also building into the eastern part of the State, and so a beginning is made. But the old-fashioned stage lines are far more numerous than the railroads, and are the sole links between the railways and many interior communities. The State has a population of only about 65,000, and only one town that is well known all over the country. That, of course, is Cheyenne, long the headquarters of the stockmen of the West, and once a very wild and "wide-open" city. It is not easy now to see where it stowed its wickedness as one walks its tree-lined streets bordered by pretty homes and trod by a sober and self-respecting population. Cheyenne has 12,000 population, strong banks, good schools, notable churches, some large and enterprising mercantile establishments, a fine park, and a great State capital. The town languishes. Not that the people regret the loss of the dance-houses and gambling layouts, but because the vim has gone out of business. The range cattle industry is failing, and the railroads have opened up other centres where mining and agriculture are the chief interests. But Cheyenne is like Wyoming itself, in a transition state, and its future is far more glorious than the noisy, profligate, and unnatural past.

The people call their State a second and Western Pennsylvania, because it contains such great stores of coal and iron among many another sort of natural wealth. They are right in asserting that coal and iron such as theirs have been the bases of great wealth for many powerful commonwealths and nations, but we shall see, in making a hasty tour of the State, that a still surer and greater asset is Wyoming's soil. Agriculture and stock-raising combined will surely give birth and impetus to a degree of development that will produce many a thickly settled, prosperous district, where now there is little else than the magic soil itself.

It must not be thought that its conditions are more primitive than they are, merely because I have called it next to the newest State. There are twenty banks in the State, and nine or ten are national banks; there are five daily and two dozen weekly newspapers; there are several scores of settlements, and seven of these are of the grade of cities, and provided with water-works and lighted by electricity. The school system is a thorough one capped by a free university, and representing a million dollars' worth of school property. Free public libraries are also maintained there. But it is the future of such a State that is most interesting, and it is the future that we have looked towards throughout this series.

The best maps of Wyoming, issued by the Department of the Interior at Washington, are almost as useless as no maps at all. Because what is called "mountain work" in surveying pays better than mapping the plains, this map was heaped with mountains, like the surface of a potful of boiling water, and where there should be a few well-defined chains and parallel valleys, there are more mountains, scattered higgledy-piggledy, all over the map, than there are in British Columbia or in Switzerland. To make a tour of the State and see it as it is, let us begin with the northeastern part, that corner which is bounded by South Dakota and Montana. The mountains that are here form the Bear Lodge Range—broken spurs and isolated mountains not higher than timber grows, and not sufficient in number, extent, or height to produce much water. This is now a great range cattle country, of course. Around the bases of the mountains, where there is an appearance of more moisture than elsewhere, there are great reaches of fine grass land, on the benches and elevated plateaus where the soil seems formed of decomposed gypsum. Big beds of gypsum are exposed in this region. Here, on these inviting benches, farming to a considerable extent has crept in, pushed by a population that is thought to be an overflow from Nebraska. There is no market, so the farmers farm only for food for themselves and cattle. Note, however, that they fence in their cultivated land and keep cattle of their own to be fed in the winter. Thus the character of Wyoming and of the stock business both change—quietly, steadily, surely. The agriculture centres around Sundance just now. The stockmen do not consider it a serious invasion of the ranges yet. Cow companies as large as any in the State headquarter to the west of this farming country on the headwaters of the Belle Fourche. The historian of the next decade will, almost surely, write the reverse of this, that agriculture is the mainstay, and cattle deserve a passing notice.

Passing along to the middle of the northern part of the State, in Sheridan and Johnson counties—famed as the seat of last year's "war" between the rustlers and the cowmen—we find the Big Horn Mountains dominating the region. The east slope of these mountains almost duplicates the rich plains country around Denver or Cheyenne. It is more broken, and the ridges between the mountain streams are higher, yet the narrower benches and smaller mesas are of the same fruitful character, well watered by just such sparkling, crystal-like streams as one sees leaping from the sides of the Rockies in Colorado. The Big Horn is a noble range of the Rocky Mountain system. From its tallest point at Cloud Peak, 13,400 feet in air, in the heart of Johnson County, it sinks, in one distinct chain, into nothingness in Montana. Its bold granite knobs and points tower far above timber-line, maintaining a direct northwesterly course with few spurs and side ranges, and with the eastern foot-hills taking the form of an inclined reach of plains land. Already on this slope, in both counties, agriculture is the principal reliance. This is most true of Sheridan, the border county, because there are still immense herds of cattle on the Johnson County ranges. There is a larger percentage of farmers among the people in these counties than anywhere else in Wyoming. It is not that the land is the best. It is very good, indeed, but it owes its advancement in value to the fact that whereas in other parts of the State the big cow companies pre-empted the water, here it was the farmers who took the first claims of land, and water with it. The Burlington and Missouri Railroad, now being pushed to the heart of this region from the Nebraska border, will, before this is printed, connect these farms with Christendom, but up to this time the farming has been only sufficient to satisfy the home demands of an army post, a few villages, and an Indian reservation in Montana. Yet it has been enough to prove that the land is sure of a great future. Barley that is said to be as rich as any grown in Canada; very good wheat, oats, and rye; luscious big strawberries, fine cherries, and apples, and, in short, all the common fruits of that zone, except peaches, grow well there. The farm land is between 3800 and 5500 feet above sea-level, and but a small portion of the best of it has been taken up.

Westward again, across the Big Horn Mountains, we find a superb country between those mountains and the Yellowstone Park. It is a great basin, walled in on the east by the Big Horns, on the south by the Wind River Mountains, and on the west by the Snake or Shoshone range of the national park. The Big Horn River, a splendid stream, runs northward through this region, on its way to pour its waters into the Yellowstone in Montana. Two large streams—the Gray Bull and the Shoshone—enter it from the west, and the No Wood, also a large stream, runs into it from the east; all these have their own smaller tributaries. The Big Horn, at its best, is $12\frac{1}{2}$ feet deep and 300 feet wide. The arable lands here are at elevations between 3600 and 5500 feet above sea-level, and they constitute the largest mass of unoccupied arable land in the State. Much of it is comparatively low, and it is all sheltered by great mountain ranges. It is not a corn country, of course, yet good corn matured there last summer, proving an unlooked-for length of the warm season. Surveys have resulted in determining that there are 172,000 acres of irrigable land on Gray Bull River, that south of this strip is a piece comprising 100,000 acres on the Big Horn, and that on the Stinking Water there are at least 100,000 acres that can be watered. In addition, there are a dozen large and small streams, on all of which are valley lands capable of irri-

MAP OF **WYOMING**

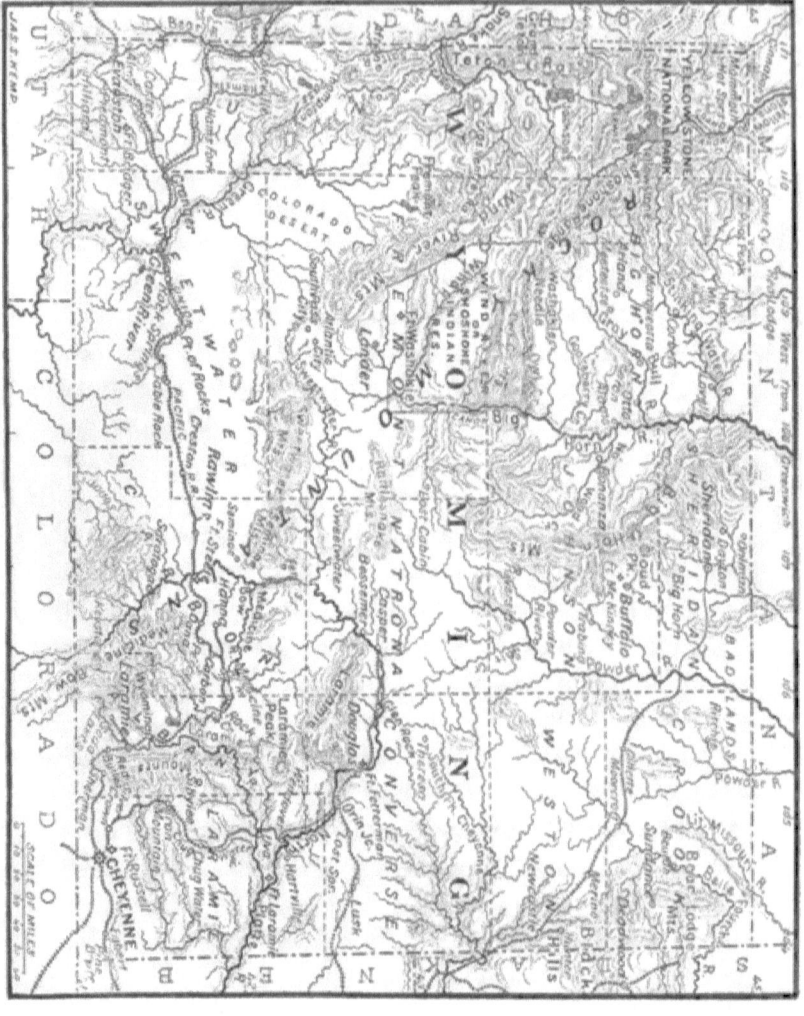

gation. They are in tracts of varying sizes, but they are bottom lands and good. This Big Horn basin has an apparent measurement on the maps of 7800 square miles, which, considered as a field for the combined industries of farming and cattle-raising, is one of the largest in the mountainous States of the West. The biggest bit of irrigable land along the Gray Bull is a great and uncommon prize for future comers. Not above 500 persons now live in this entire basin. There is a little town, called Otto, near the junction of the Gray Bull and the Big Horn, and there are solitary settlers here and there along the river, as well as a few tiny settlements ("bunches of houses" they would say out there) on the foot-hills in the shadow of the mountains. The basin is, therefore, practically unoccupied. The land is Government land, obtainable by homesteaders. One man, who grew forty acres of oats there, succeeded in obtaining sixty-five bushels to the acre, it is said. But there is no market, there is no railroad, and there are no wagonways. The good land of which I have spoken is that near the streams; the rest of the region is a wilderness of deep gulches, high broken plateaus, sage-brush country, and "bad lands."

I have dwelt thus at length upon this brand-new bit of America so desolate now, so inviting to speculation, because it is plain that its future must be grand. How strange a thing it is to be able, after reading the signs of development everywhere in the far West, to point to a vast bowl, unpeopled except by half-wild cattle, and to say, with more confidence than one may prophesy of his own life to-morrow: "Here will come thousands upon thousands of men and women. Here will soon be seen vast areas of land fenced in, set with tidy farm-houses and out-buildings gay with green and yellow grain, dotted with orchards, lively with teams upon a tangle of wagon roads. Railroads **will** thread the scene, and somewhere" **(ah!** that would be great prophesying to say just where) "in this same basin there is certain to arise a city of wealth, size, and importance, with factories **and** wholesale and retail shops, high-schools, stone churches, parks, and **mansions."** Yet it must be so, and **the** days that **are near at hand** will see **this basin so** peopled that the force of **this** prediction will even **then** be lost, for its force lies in the fact that there is nothing of all this in the region **to-day.**

Wyoming is so **very** new a State that there are many **regions very** similar **to** the Big Horn basin in present status and future likelihood. Look **on the** map. Below this basin is the great Wind River Indian Reservation. This great reserve is practically the same sort of country. Below it, where the Big Horn River is new and slender, is another fine farming country, and one that is already beginning to be settled. The army post —Fort Washakie—on the reservation, is a market that has **developed a** comparatively settled **region.** The town **of Lander is the** capital of this small but thrifty section, **which is made** valuable by reason of the rich **but** narrow little valleys of the tributaries of the main river—there called the Wind River, though it is the Big Horn none the less. The farms support two flour-mills. There is some land for new-comers, but not much.

West of the Indian Reservation **and** south of the Yellowstone Park is what is called the Snake River Country—a very mountainous territory, but with several fine valleys and an abundance of water. Its defect is that the arable land is very elevated. The value of the land has not been determined, but it is superior to its present limited task of growing hay for small holders of cattle who are feeding their stock in corrals in the winter.

South of this is the Salt River Valley, at one time an ancient lake-bed, but now a level plain at the bottom of a bowl—a little isolated world among the mountains, and a place of exceeding great beauty. The Mormons. 1500 strong, have pre-empted it all. Originally they began taking quarter sections of 160 acres under the Homestead Law, but later they filed claims for 640 acres at a time under the Desert Land Act. Many of the holders of large tracts are the sons of rich men, but they will find, what every one else has discovered, that the greatest profit is not in large holdings, but in tracts that a man can grasp, so to speak—twenty to forty acres—on which the owner works, and every inch of which he studies. These thrifty saints have a vast amount of stock in this valley, and produce cheese, butter, and meat, which they ship into the outer world. They raise grain and make flour. Theirs is fine and very productive land, and yet it is more than 6000 feet above sea-level.

All of this great belt that I have been describing, south of the Yellowstone Park, is called Uintah County, and at the bottom of it is the Bear River Country, which is largely taken up by great cattle corporations. One man in this region owns the river-side land for twenty miles on either side of the Bear River. The main use he makes of this is to grow hay for live-stock, the whole region being principally taken up by great stockmen's corporations. The Desert Land Act offered a very convenient instrument for wholesale land-grabbing. Altogether one person could take up 1120 acres, and it was easy for cowmen to employ their cowboys to file claims upon great tracts. The employers provide the nominal land-office fees and the Government price of a dollar and a quarter an acre. This act when it was in force operated in the arid belt, and affected any land that had to be irrigated. **The amount** upon which **a claim can be** filed has been reduced to 340 acres, but the principle **is** very mischievous, because the only hope for a land where soil **is** plenty and water is scarce is to limit the individ**ual** settlers to small holdings, that there may be as many of each as the land will support. Of course these large holdings will in time be broken up, and the region will be thrown **open to the multitude.** This will happen when the grabbers can make **more** money by selling the land than by holding **it** for stock-raising. This is fine farm land in a narrow valley fifty **or** sixty miles **long.** Behind this good **land, on either side of the** valley, **is** broken land that **is no use** for **farming,** but which with the farm land forms the happy combination so frequent in Colorado, Montana, Wyoming, and Idaho, by means of which agriculture and stock-raising can be easily and profitably coupled. In the southwestern part of the State is the Green River, a large stream that drains a wide country. This is yet a great stock country, and **the** farming along the tributary valleys is for **hay** for the cattle.

But times **and conditions are** changing. **The Mormons,** for instance, **are pouring** into the land around Fort Bridger, where there are **at least** 50,000 **acres of** irrigable land on half a **dozen** little streams. The Mormons are single-minded. **They want** land only to till it. Along the entire southern end of the State there had been but one flour-mill, and that (at Laramie City) had failed. As I write, three mills are building; one at Evanston, one at Douglas in Converse County, and one at Saratoga on the North Platte River. There were four flour-mills in **Wyoming in** 1890, but when this is published there **will be nine.** Moreover, the new mills are of a character **and** capacity far superior to the first ones.

The **story of** the transformation of Saratoga from a

cow outfit to a farming settlement is, in great measure, the same as the story of the transformation of the entire State from a stockman's paradise to a nineteenth-century commonwealth. And one such story is worth ten pages of argument and explanation. In the valley of the North Platte River, seven or eight years ago, there were twenty-five herds of cattle, large and small, owned by men or corporations. Fifteen bore the brands of large companies. Then the valley and the country around it were open and unfenced. The soil was uncultivated. The people who lived there bought even the potatoes—indeed, they bought everything—that they used. Hay, however, was wild, natural, plentiful. They did not know that they could raise anything; in all probability they never gave the matter a thought. It was an axiom that Wyoming was only fit for grazing; even to-day there are plenty of stock owners and store clerks who say that potatoes and hay are the only forms of vegetation that can be cultivated in the State. The first man in the valley who planted a garden was ridiculed by all the others; but ridicule will not affect the laws of nature, and as the soil was excellent, his garden was a success. Then others followed suit, all in an experimental, groping way, beginning with potatoes, following with turnips and beets, and so going on through all the grades of general garden truck. At last came experiments with grain, until to-day single fields of wheat and oats comprise 200 or 300 acres, and, as I have said, a thirty-barrel flour-mill is now going up there. So rich is the soil that oats have been grown there to weigh forty-five pounds to the bushel, though the number of bushels to the acre has not been exceptional. The people have learned to cultivate alfalfa (lucern), the rich and beautiful plant that serves for grass and hay in the arid region, and already it yields two crops in a summer.

The agricultural **development is closely associated** with the changing **of the stockmen's methods. The** Eastern men who had gone into the valley to grow cattle on the open range had supposed the conditions would for an indefinite period remain as they were, based upon plenty of pasture and water. During the first four **years** they came gradually to admit that the range business was not profitable. They **saw that the first** prices they got for their stock were "boom" prices. **These depreci**ated rapidly. Then came a reduction **in the range area.** Men began to fence **for pasture for** horses and for winter hay Each **man as he fenced in land also fenced in** water, and made it difficult for cattle in **the open to get to water**. Then settlers began to arrive in numbers, **al**ways to locate on water, to fence it in, and to cut off more of the open range. The stock no longer wintered as it had done; wanting water and food, the animals died to an extent that piled up losses to the owners. At last it was necessary **for** each cowman to maintain an outfit of riders through the winters to look after the stock. That **was expensive, but it** was still more expensive to feed the animals in winter, putting ten-dollar hay into fifteen-dollar beasts, for the hay could be sold **for ten** dollars **a ton.** It gradually **dawned on** the stockmen that they had better have one hundred **head** of cattle, and care for them well, than keep a thousand, with the risks and cost attendant upon large herds **The big** herds were gradually driven out and sold off, and **the** places of most of the early range operators were taken by men who took up land and stayed there with smaller herds, farming as well **as** beef-raising. The result is peculiar and unexpected. There are **as** many cattle in the valley as there **ever were,** but they are owned by a great number of persons, and these **persons** are cultivating the soil. Against fifteen herds, say, **of** 2000 heads each, under the range system, there are still 300,000 cattle, but they are in 150 herds of 200 heads.

There is only one large cow company left in the valley. It has to keep six or seven riders out in the winter looking after the she-stock. It has to take the precaution, early in each autumn, to make a cow and calf round-up, in order to gather the cows in one pasture and the calves in another, so as to wean the calves. The winter shelter that the cattle get is generally in the natural brush, but it is sometimes necessary to drive them into a long shed, which has had to be put up against the severest storms—the cruelty of which is in the winds that rage there. This valley, or rather the range which goes beyond the valley, is sixty by sixty miles in area. The cow company herds 3500 to 4000 head. It has to hire a ranch for growing its hay, and this it piles around the cow and calf pastures in the winter. Thus is the business now managed by what is spoken of as "the only company that has withstood the revolution" in that valley. It will look to the reader, if he knows about the range stock industry, as if the company has its business yet, but the profits of old have vanished. Thus is told the story of the range cattle business in one valley, but it will answer for all Wyoming, since, in every other part of the State, the same things have happened, are happening, or must happen.

The middle southern part of Wyoming is just what it seems from the cars of the Union Pacific Company—of problematical value except for grazing and for its mineral resources. We shall see, further along, that the mineral resources of most parts of the State are extraordinary.

We have now gone over the State in all parts except the eastern end. A study of the progress of the work of irrigation will lead to a more complete acquaintance with it. Over all the State timber is heavily distributed in large areas, which altogether form about 16,000,000 acres. The State comprises about 63,000,000 of acres, and, though more than two-thirds of the area has been surveyed, only 5,000,000 of acres are owned by individuals and corporations, the rest being public land. With so small an amount yielding a revenue, the State has no money with which to develop irrigation; it is as much as it can do to support a government. The State is very forward in progressive legislation affecting irrigation. Its Constitution declares that the waters within its boundaries are the property of the State. If this principle were acted upon, and the State constructed its own ditches and reservoirs, with a single eye to the distribution of the water among the greatest number of landholders, then all that I have urged in other chapters upon the other States in the arid belt would here find its consummation. But, having announced the prime fact that it owns the water, it proceeds to give it away. This is not done in the reckless manner we noted in other States, but it gives it away, and to men who want to make money out of it, saying through its officers, "We are only too glad to give it away in order to invite settlers." Still Wyoming is in advance of its neighbors in even this respect, and too much praise cannot be given to its State Engineer, Professor Elwood Mead, whose views are large and practical, who does all that the laws permit towards the conservation of the water supply, and who would make Wyoming's the best system in the country if he had his way, and if it were not for the mischief that was done before Wyoming became a State.

The State has been at the mercy of water-grabbers nearly twenty-one years, but has only enjoyed its own government two years. Under the Territorial system there were no restrictions, and there was no supervision in respect of the distribution of water. Any one who wanted it took it, not as the Mormons have always done, for the greatest good of the greatest number, but like ordinary white men, solely for individual gain. The grabber filed a claim and stated what he had done and for what purpose he did it, but that was a mere formality. The claims were mainly taken by stockmen who wished to get water on land so that they might utilize great tracts taken under the Desert Land Act. There was a tremendous building of ditches, and some of it was crazy work, as where one company built a $70,000 ditch and only watered 340 acres. Around Lander and a few other places farmers took water for the legitimate uses of farming. Three thousand and eighty-six ditches were run out of 631 streams, and were applicable to 2,172,781 acres under the Territorial system. And that is about how the case stands to-day.

Now, Wyoming is divided into four grand water districts, to meet as many natural systems of surface drainage. In charge of each district is a superintendent, and these superintendents with the State Engineer as president, *ex officio*, constitute a Board of Control, which meets twice a year to try and determine causes growing out of the distribution and use of the water. Wyoming alone among all the States in the arid region aims to limit the supply each water owner may have. This is the next but one most important step that the States in that region must yet take. In the Territorial days men built ditches as they pleased, and then thought that they owned all the water such ditches could take. They were obliged to go before the district courts to get decrees validating their claims, and the courts were supposed to see that each claimant took only what water he needed. As a matter of fact, the courts did as they do elsewhere:

took an affidavit by **the owners as to the** capacity of the ditches, without regard to whether such quantities of water had been, were, or could be utilized, and then issued the decrees. Though the machinery of law courts was not calculated **to** settle those questions the decrees stand, governing 200 of the 3000 ditches of the State, or, to put it in another way, forever disposing **of** the water of six of the streams in the State.

The new Board of Control has decided that the **mere** diversion of water **from its** natural channels shall **not** constitute appropriation thereof. **The** water must be applied **to** some beneficial use, and **if that use is** irrigation, **the water must be** actually applied to the land. The new decrees restrict allotments to actual acreage reclaimed—already watered and growing crops. If a ditch is built to reclaim 10,000 acres, and yet is only watering 1000 acres that are cultivated, the board allots the water for that 1000 acres, crediting the owners with water for the other 9000 acres only when such land is **cultivated.** Where new ditches are built an extension **of** time for development is made; in the cases **of old ditches,** no attention is paid to their future possibilities. In **Wyoming, then,** the land is reclaimed before the water is **parted** with by the **State.** The reader will understand how important and **wise** this course is when he comprehends the evils that result from the absence of such a rule. **In** Colorado, for **in**stance, A taps a stream, and runs his ditches as far as he pleases Then **B** taps the stream above A, and runs his ditches in the same or another **valley or** locality. Farming is carried on along both sets of ditches, but when there exists a scarcity of water, A appeals for his priority rights, and gets all the water his ditches will **carry.** B has his ditches closed, and the orchards and **gardens and** grain fields along his ditches must die of drought, even though A's territory may not be all under cultivation, or though he may have twice the water he needs. Under the Wyoming system priority rights prevail, but only water that is actually benefiting land is at any man's disposal.

It has been determined in Wyoming that a stream of a cubic foot per second shall serve to irrigate seventy acres, but this estimate is considered non-essential there, because every acre which has water can keep it, there being plenty for all who now use it. The law declares that the first comer must have all that he needs, and the second and third comers must follow in their order; but it is said that priority rights have occasioned little trouble so far, owing to the quantity of water, and the fact that the distribution keeps pace with the actual improvement of the soil. The old hap-hazard water-grabbing freedom of the Territorial days has left its evils, nevertheless. I saw on a map of part of "the Little Laramie Country" a place where 150 ditches paralleled and duplicated one another in land which two ditches would have served thoroughly well. Eventually, when water is not so plentiful, there will be great trouble and expense in watching the head-gates in such localities, to make sure of fair play with the water on hand, and in the mean time there will be great loss from the heating and evaporation of the fluid in so many ditches, nine in ten of which must eventually be abandoned.

The surest way to prevent this would be for the State to survey all its districts, and prescribe the route of all ditches, but there is no law for such a course in any State. Nevertheless, in Wyoming whenever proposed ditches are palpably unnecessary, permits are refused; that is to say, if two applications describe one set of lands, the second one is refused until the time set for the completion of the first one has expired.

It is estimated that between six millions and seven millions of acres of land in Wyoming are irrigable from the streams. Of the five millions of acres now held in the State only a little above two millions are under ditches. The great majority of the ditches are small ones, and most of these are owned by stockmen, although a few farming communities operate their own. The stockmen's ditches will eventually be applied to agriculture. In all, in this baby State, ten millions of dollars or more have been invested in these artificial waterways. When the Board of Control came, with its new rulings, the stockmen as well as the farmers saw that the only way to hold their water rights was to make use of their water, and so they have been ploughing their land and seeding it (for hay at first), and thus in the last two years have caused the State to take an extraordinary stride forward in agricultural development. Thus have come the four flouring mills where there had been none before. Between January, 1891, and November, 1892, there were 352 applications for the right to build new ditches, and the State Engineer has been notified that at least one-third of the number have been completed and are in use. Nothing could speak more eloquently of the new forces of civilization and improvement that are at work in the State.

These new ditch companies have not been large ones. The experience of the people of the State has been that such corporations should control the settlement of the land, or—as I believe, and the State Engineer adds as an alternative—the State should own both the land and the water. The rule is seen to be that when great ditches are built squatters pre-empt the land to be benefited in order to bother and blackmail the ditch-owners into buying them out. If the State owned the public lands and surveyed them, and encouraged the building of ditches, it could sell the land for its value as improved land, and could reimburse the local ditch company by buying the shares and joining them with the land thus sold until the water and the shares were at an end. Thus even a State with a low and new treasury could prevent the creation of water barons and avoid the troubles that must come under the grab system of to-day.

A bill has been introduced in Congress for the surrender of the public lands to the State; but before we can consider this proposition clearly it is necessary to glance at the past and present of the cattle business in this one of its former strongholds. The range cattle business is in a bad way there. One of the shrewdest capitalists in the State, himself a former range-cattle owner, told me that not a cow company there made a dollar of profit in 1892. He afterwards corrected himself by saying that he believed a little money had been gained from a new form of the business by men in the northern part of the State who had gone out of the breeding business and were grazing steers exclusively. This safer method, which discounts the risk to cows and calves, has been widely adopted in Montana and the western end of the Dakotas.

The rapid decline of the range business began six years ago. Before that it had been of a character to tempt even the rich. At one time men paid 2 per cent. a month for money, and made 100 per cent. profits. That was when cows came up from Texas at a cost of $7 each, sold in two years for $22, and in three years for $40 and more, when the ranges were not overstocked, the pasturage was good, and all the conditions, including "boom" prices at the stock-yards, were favorable. The men who did the best pushed into new territory as fast as the Indians were crowded off, and kept finding **new** grass and plenty of it. But the risks soon came and multiplied. **If** one man was careful not to overstock a range, he could not be sure that another cow **outfit** would not do so precisely where he had put his cattle. Prices fell, fences cut up the ranges and shut **off** the water, winter losses became heavier and heavier, and the "good old **days" of** this inhuman, devil-may-care, primitive, and clumsy business came **to** an end. The cowboys of picture and story existed in the brilliant days. At first they had come from Texas, **but** in the zenith of their romantic glory they came from everywhere and from every class. They included young Englishmen, college graduates from **the** East, well-born Americans—all sorts who did not "strike luck" at anything else, and who were full of vim and love of adventure. They got $40 a month and good keep during the greater part of each year. They rode good horses, that had as much of the devil in them as the "boys" themselves. They bought hand-stamped Cheyenne saddles and California bits that were as ornate as jewelry, and stuck their feet in grand *tapaderos*, or hooded stirrups, richly ornamented, padded with lamb's-wool, and each as big as a fire-hat. Their spurs were fit for grandees, their "ropes," or lariats, were selected with more care **than** a circus tight-rope, **and** their big broad felt sombreros cost more than the Prince of Wales ever paid for a **pot-hat.**

And then, alas! the cowmen began **to economize in** men, food, wages—everything. The best **of the old** kind of cowboys, who had not become owners or foremen, saloon-keepers or gamblers, or had not been shot, drifted away. Some of **the** smartest among them became "rustlers"—those cattle thieves whose depredations resulted in what almost came to be a war in Wyoming last year. **They** insisted that they had to do it to live.

From the cowboy stand-point it was time for the business to languish. Towns were springing up every here and there, each with its ordinance that cowboys must take off their side-arms before they entered the villages; wages were low down; men had to cart hay and dump it around for winter food; settlers fenced in the streams, and others stood guard over them with guns; it was time such a business languished. From the stand-point of nineteenth-century civilization the same conclusion was reached—the range business was an obstruction to civilization, a bar to the development of the State, a thing only to be tolerated in a new and wild country. And now I am assured that there is not an intelligent cowman who does not know that the business is doomed in Wyoming, and that the last free-roving herds must move on. There is not one who does not know that small bunches of cattle, held in connection with agriculture, must take the places of the range cattle, because better grades of cattle can be bred, better meat can be produced, all risks will nearly disappear, and the expenses of the care of the cattle will not be a tithe of those of the old plan.

And so we come to the much-discussed plan for having Wyoming intrusted with the public domain within her borders. This plan takes account of the fact that she will ever be a great cattle-raising State. The plan is to sell the agricultural or arable land in connection with the water and with the upper or range land, always combining the irrigable bottoms or mesas and benches with the higher unirrigable territory. Then farmers may grow hay with one hand, so to speak (along with whatever else they choose to plant), while with the other they look after their cattle. With thoroughbred bulls, sheltered winter pasture and feed, and an income from farming, the farmers will be rich and the beef will be the finest that it is possible to produce. There is an unexpected opposition to this project, and by the men most certain to be benefited were it carried out. They are ignorant and suspicious, and fear that the plan cloaks some effort towards a land-grabbing monopoly or steal of some sort. Nevertheless, the plan is peculiarly well suited to the natural conditions in Wyoming, and, for that matter, in Colorado and other States in the arid belt. It turns to good account land of a sort that is all too plentiful there that it is not easy to employ otherwise, and that is not attractive or profitable as pasture-land for cattle-owners other than such as own farms in the neighborhood. For such it should be held against wild cattle, and against the devouring bands of sheep that otherwise might and often would pass over the hills and leave them as bare as the back of one's hand.

The number of cattle in the State in 1892 was estimated to be 428,823, and the value of the stock was considered to be $4,654,379, but I was told that the State never gets reports of more than six-tenths of the number actually within her borders. However, in 1886 the number reported was 898,121 head, or more than twice as many as now, and then cows were considered worth $16 31 apiece as against $10 50 now. But this falling off argues no such ill to the State as it would have been to have the range-cattle industry thrive. The auditor's figures show that while there has been a decrease of ten millions of dollars in the valuation of the cattle in the State within seven years, the total assessable value of properties in Wyoming has increased $1,236,713 during that period.

The reports of horses indicate that there are 78,286 of them on the ranges, and these are computed to be worth $2,681,000; but this is also an untrustworthy item. In truth, there are no less than 100,000 head of horses, and many of them are of excellent stock. Sheep exceed all other animals in numbers. The auditor reports 639,205, and there are really close to 900,000 of these animals on the ranges. They are worth, at graded values, $1,750,000.

Wherever the cow business is carried on there exists the most fanatical prejudice against sheep and sheep-herders. The English language fails every cowman who tries to express his opinion about this sister industry. This is worth recording here, because it is true in all the States where cattle are fattened from British Columbia to Texas, and because it is a prejudice without warrant or base, and it is bound to die out. We shall see why, after telling what a cowman said of it when I brought up the topic in Wyoming:

"The sheep-herder is the worst blot on the State," said he. "He is no good, and much harm. He may have his office in New York, Chicago, or London. He fits out a wagon, with a Mexican and a dog and several thousand sheep, and away they go, like an Egyptian scourge, eating the grass down to the ground, and, in sandy soils, trampling it down so that there are great regions where once the bunch-grass grew knee high, but where the country is now bare as a desert. You might search acres in such a place with a microscope and not discover an ounce of grass. These people pay no rent, don't own an acre, send their profits abroad, and are bitterly opposed to the settlement and development of the State."

But new men are constantly drifting into the sheep business, and mutton, which always hung back in the meat markets of America, is coming to be a favorite meat, as it is in England. There is no more remarkable change in our country than this general turning towards mutton after it had been so long and generally disliked. Men who harbored the same ill-will towards the business of sheep-herding are now rushing into it because of the money there is in it. He who was always spoken of on the ranges as "that —— sheep man" is now on top, the subject of the envy of his neighbors. It is not true that the sheep are largely owned by foreigners or outsiders. The three largest sheep-herders in Wyoming are residents of the State. In Carbon County, the largest sheep county in the State, 138,438 sheep are ranging, and they are owned at home. The manner of conducting the business, and the figures of the cost and profit in it, are very interesting.

Five thousand sheep are considered a good holding, because that number divides into two herds convenient to handle. The owner of such a bunch will employ three men—two herders and a foreman who is also the "camp-mover." Each herd will have a wagon, a man, and a dog, or usually two dogs. The wagon in use on the ranges is the typical "schooner" of olden time—a heavy box on wheels, covered with a canvas top, and appointed with a bed in the back, a locker, and a stove. The camp-mover divides his time between the two herds. He has a team of horses, and after he has moved one wagon and herd to new pasture, he leaves that outfit and goes off, perhaps fifteen or twenty miles, to the other herd, to find new pasture for that, and to leave it till the grass is nipped close. The sheep are not exclusively grass eaters. They like to browse on brush and the bark of willows, and they do well on what is called "browse," which is the short white sage-brush of that region. It is estimated that it costs seventy cents a head to maintain a herd, but the wool greatly more than meets this expense. The herders sell the old ewes to feeders in Nebraska and elsewhere to fatten for market, getting $3 50 to $4 a head for such stock. Occasionally, if they think the herds are increasing in numbers too fast, they sell off a bunch of young lambs, and yearlings fetch as high as $2 75 a head. The profits lie in the increase of the animals by multiplication. This amounts to almost a doubling of the herds in a year, the percentage being between 75 and 100 per cent. At an average cost of $3 50 for stock sheep, and a doubling of the animals, with sales at $2 75 to $4, and with an additional margin from the wool, after expenses are met, it is plain that the business is not a bad one. Wool has fetched from eleven to sixteen cents during the last few years, and good sheep yield about nine pounds as an average clip.

The coal and iron of Wyoming form a wonderful treasure. Unlike nearly all the other far Western States, Wyoming's settlement was not connected with mining. The first actual settlements were around forts Laramie and Bridger. Gold was discovered on the route of the old trail in 1867, and there have been many mining flurries in the State since then, but these were as nothing to those which built up the neighboring States or to what must yet draw millions from this one. It was the extension of the cattle business that lifted Wyoming into prominence, and yet it will not do to say that this led to the State's settlement, since that was an industry which rather obstructed than fostered the development of the Territory. Yet the rocks and the earth bear treasures comparable with those of any State in our West. Coal is found in every county. From the northern centre to the eastern end of the State it is a lignite of low grade, which crumbles when exposed to the air. It outcrops frequently and generally. It is in use in the towns of Sheridan and Buffalo, and is found to burn very well. Near Buffalo there is a vein that is said to be seventy feet **thick**. **The nearer** this deposit approaches the mountains, where it has been subjected to more pressure, the more commercial value it has. The coal burned in the settlements around Bonanza, in the western part of Johnson County, is so free from sulphur and phosphorus that it can be used by blacksmiths. Close to the Montana border the same good bituminous coal that is found in that State extends its field into Wyoming. In the eastern part of the State, where the Black Hills enter from South **Dakota, is** Newcastle, a busy coal-mining town, **whose** neighborhood is richly **veined** with a bituminous coal **that** makes high-grade **coke**. Coking ovens supply that material for the Black **Hills** smelters. This is the only coal of the kind in the State. It is of such quality that the Burlington and Missouri Railroad Company uses it for locomotive fuel, mining 800 tons a day for that use and for sale along the line in other localities.

The next best deposit yet mined is at Rock Springs, in **Sweetwater County, in** the southwestern part of the State, and on the Union Pacific Railroad. More than a million tons were shipped from this immense field last **year**. It is the best soft coal in the Wyoming markets, and as good as any in **the West**. The Union Pacific Railroad **is** heavily interested here, but there are some small private mines. In order that the people of the State may have no rose without its thorn, and may not grow too **proud** of their good-fortune, this coal is sold in Cheyenne **at $6** a ton. From Rawlins, to the eastward, comes a good coal, and eastward again is the carbon coal-field, where the railroad again owns producing mines. This coal is not **so** good as that from Rock Springs, and sells at thirty-five cents less per ton. Away down in the southwestern corner of the State are **other great coal-beds, from one** of which the Southern

Pacific Railroad Company gets its supply. It is a lower grade than the Rock Springs coal. The Fremont, Elkhorn, and Missouri Valley Railroad (Chicago and Northwestern system) came into Wyoming for coal, among other reasons, and has a large mine in the Platte River field, near Fort Fetterman. This is not a good locomotive or steam coal, but finds a ready market in Nebraska and elsewhere along this gigantic system. There are at least half a dozen large coal-fields in the central belt of counties of whose merits I find no mention in my notes. Their development doubtless awaits that of the country around them.

Iron is as plentiful. First in importance is the great district around Hartville, north of Fort Laramie. It is theoretically pure hematite—as nearly so as hematite is found, and it has been developed or mined sufficiently for the owners of the present mines to be confident of its value. Duluth and Eastern capital has been invested here, and active operations only await the building of a railway connection with the Skull Creek (Newcastle) coal-mines. Next in promise are the Seminoe, Carbon County, mines to the northwestward of the carbon coal-fields. Here is plenty of fine hematite, with fuel and fluxes close by, and only transportation facilities needed. There is a large soft deposit of mineral paint (oxide of iron), which is being ground and readily marketed. It has been found to be excellent for painting freight-cars, iron and tin roofs, and buildings, is a valuable wood preservative, and retains its color longer than most paints. The Chugwater River runs through an immense field of iron ore, but it is impregnated with what is called titanium. Iron carbonate ore is found in the Big Horn Basin, and in the basin east of the South Powder River. This will be mined, in time, for use in Bessemer steel making.

The tin of the Black Hills extends into Wyoming. The State has some extraordinary soda deposits, some of these being actual lake-beds of soda. Copper is found all along the North Platte River. Lead appears at least twice in large quantities in a survey of the State, and kaolin, fire-clay, mica, graphite, magnesia, plumbago, and sulphur are more or less abundant. Gypsum is found in almost every county, and plaster of Paris is being made of it at Red Buttes on the Union Pacific Railroad. Marbles—some of them very fine and beautiful—are being gathered in every county for exhibition at the World's Fair in Chicago. They are of all colors; but the only white marble is found in the Sibylee region, where, by-the-way, is another undeveloped agricultural section of great promise. The granites of the State are very fine, and the sandstones, which are of unlimited quantity, include beautiful varieties for building purposes and for interior decorative work.

Petroleum appears in several places in the State. There are wells at Salt Creek in Johnson County. The Omaha Company have flowing wells at Bonanza, in another part of the county, and this oil, whose flow is stopped by the company, is a splendid illuminant. A mile away is a spring carrying oil on its surface. Near Lander, south of the Indian reservation, are more than two dozen borings. All have flowed, and all are now cased, but there is a three-acre lake of leakage from them. There are signs of oil elsewhere in the State. The oil production and supply of this country is controlled by one company. If any other company offers to compete with this giant concern, it would be possible for the master company to give oil away until the opposition was starved out. The money of the great company is in its by-products, and it would not suffer greatly by making a free gift of all the oil that is consumed in Wyoming. It is generally believed that the controllers of the oil supply look to the wells of Colorado to piece out the supply if the Pennsylvania wells fail. After that, or at that time, perhaps, humanity will be interested in the oil of Wyoming; but it is noticeable now that this oil excites little human interest, and interests still less capital.

Gold is still being mined where it was first found, below the Indian reservation in the South Pass district. Here is both lode and placer mining, but the principal placer owner is working the quartz. Within the past year many new mines have been opened there, and one shipper claims to be getting from $200 to $400 a ton out of his ore. Another gold district is west of this on the Seminoe Mountains. Others are on both sides of the Medicine Bow range, southwest of Laramie City, and near the Colorado line; in the Black Hills, in the Little Laramie Valley, in the Silver Crown district, and in the Big Horn Country. The gold mining in the State is sufficiently promising to interest a great many miners, and considerable capital; but the best friends and best judges of the new State see the richest future for her in the development of her splendid agricultural lands first, and next in her coal and iron fields.

In certain of the newer States the citizens are especially proud of the constitutions they have adopted as the bases of their governments. In Montana, for instance, the Constitutional Convention comprised an assemblage of men who, it is said, would win distinction anywhere. Wyoming's convention may not have been so notable in its make-up, but its product, the Constitution, is certainly very remarkable. It is *fin de siècle*, if I may apply French to anything so extremely American; it is thoroughly "up to date."

Wyoming had progressed under Territorial government for **twenty years,** when, in January, 1888, her Legislature memorialized Congress for an enabling **act,** in the belief that Territorial government retarded the progress and development of the region. The Congress committee to which the matter was referred reported it favorably, as it also did a bill preparing for the admission of the other Territories which **were so soon** to become full-fledged members of the Union. **In** June, 1889, the Governor, Chief **Justice, and** Secretary districted the Territory, and apportioned **the number** of delegates for **the** convention upon **a just basis.** Then the Governor **directed that an election be held** in July to **choose delegates to a constitutional convention** in **September.** Fifty-five **delegates** composed the **convention,** and drafted the Constitution which was afterwards ratified by a vote of five-sixths of the citizens. There were many precedents for the adoption of **a** Constitution prior to admission to Statehood. Wyoming's assessed valuation **was then** $31,500,000, whereas California, when admitted, **showed** only $13,000,**000 of** assessable wealth. **The** population of the **Territory was** then about what it is **now. It was** admitted in 1890.

It was generally **believed that the** party **in power at that** time effected **the admission of** Wyoming, **Idaho, Montana, the** Dakotas, **and Washington** for **the purpose of** gaining **votes** in Congress, **and of putting the people** of those States under **a debt to that party. This will** not be disputed, **I** think; but **it seems to all the people** of Wyoming, and **to me also,** that **the action has proven very advantageous. It is** true that **the State government is in some degree** more expensive than **that of the Territory had been, but** the expense is more than **offset by the** good **riddance** of the former officials, who were apt to be carpet-baggers—*i. e.*, persons sent there from other parts of **the country,** interested **far more** in drawing salaries and enjoying ease than in developing the resources of the soil and studying the needs of the settlers and the welfare of the whole people. Then again, the county governments are equally improved, and definite moderate salaries for the county officials have taken the places of the wasteful fees by which they formerly paid themselves.

And now for the Constitution itself. In its declaration of rights it perpetuates the right of the women to vote as they had been doing when Wyoming was a Territory, and this was understood when the State was admitted. "Since equality in the enjoyment of natural and civil rights," it declares, "is made sure only through political equality, the laws of this State affecting the political rights and privileges of its citizens shall be without distinction of race, color, sex, or any circumstance or condition whatsoever other than individual incompetency or unworthiness duly ascertained by a court of competent jurisdiction. Article VI., entitled "Suffrage," further declares that "the right of citizens to vote and hold office shall not be denied or abridged on account of sex. Both male and female citizens of this State shall equally enjoy all civil, political, and religious rights and privileges." The age when a citizen may vote is fixed at twenty-one equally without regard to sex, but "no person shall have the right to vote who shall not be able to read the Constitution of the State" (physical disability in this respect being no bar). The method of voting is what is generally called "the Australian system."

I was very anxious, when I found myself in Wyoming, to ascertain what I could of the effect upon women, men, and the politics of the State of this measure, so persistently labored for by the women's rights agitators in all the States of our Union. I am and have ever been in favor of woman's voting, but it has always seemed to me that the women were themselves the obstacles to the general introduction of the practice. I have not lived so entirely in vain as not to see that the women can and do have pretty nearly whatever they want in America, and I know that whenever they conclude that they wish to do so they will vote. The situation in Wyoming is especially interesting, because women cut a small figure in a new State, and what they have got there the men must have given them. Do they vote—now that they may? How many vote? Do they vote as their husbands do or tell them to? Is the voting of women mainly done by the respectable, the intelligent, the ignorant, or the disorderly classes? To what extent, if any, do the women study politics and statecraft in order to vote intelligently? I am drifting to one side of a study of Wyoming's Constitution, but these are interesting questions, and the Constitution is responsible for them.

In the first place, when I put these queries, here and there, I said "women" whenever I spoke of that sex, for which I have the highest respect—the most sentimental, if you please. But I never heard any other man in the State apply any other word to the better sex except the much-abused and demoralized term "ladies." That is a marked peculiarity of the language in the West. It does not contain the noble word "woman." It sickens the ear with the overuse of the word "lady." For my part, I know a woman when I see one, but I find it difficult to determine ladyhood except upon hearsay or acquaintance. When I do find it I compliment it with the dignified word "woman;" a statement which I hope will free me from even a suspicion of rudeness or lack of gallantry here and in what follows.

I found that the great majority of the women in Wyoming are in the habit of voting. Not all of them vote as their husbands do, and as one official expressed himself, "good men pride themselves upon not influencing their wives." Yet it is true, I am told, that very many women, of their own volition and unconsciously, copy the politics of their husbands. Occasionally the men of the State hear of women who refuse to embrace the privilege, who do not believe that women should meddle in affairs which concern the homes, the prosperity, and the self-respect and credit of the communities of which they are a part; but such women are, of course, few.

On the other hand, other women are very active in politics. There is a Ladies' Republican League among the political clubs of Cheyenne. It is seen that the right to vote acts as an incentive to study the principles and records of the opposing parties, and if there are women who blindly vote as their husbands do, there are yet others who fail to agree with the views of their life companions upon public matters.

Among the women who show an intelligent interest and take an active part in politics, a few resort to the stump and speak for whichever cause they have adopted. But there are many who serve side by side with the men as delegates to conventions and voters in the party primaries. In the last State convention of the Republicans there were three women delegates; in that party's last county convention, in Laramie County, the secretary was a woman, and three delegates were of her sex. Women literally flock to the primaries—in the cities, at all events. At the primary meeting in the Third Ward of Cheyenne last autumn, out of 183 who were present at least 80 were women. In the other wards the proportion of women was as one is to three. On election days the women go a-voting precisely as they go a shopping elsewhere. On foot or in their carriages they go to the polls, where, under the law, there are no crowds, and where all is quiet and orderly. There is no doubt that female suffrage has an improving effect upon politicians and their manners. All sorts and every sort of women vote; but it is to be remarked that this affords no criterion for larger and Eastern States, since the proportion of women of evil lives is very small in Wyoming, even in the cities, and, so far as other women are concerned, our new States are nearer like democracies than our old ones. The lines of caste are more apt to be noticed by their absence than by their enforcement.

To return to the Constitution, so remarkable if only because of this recognition of woman's equality to man, it forbids imprisonment for debt except in cases of fraud; it guarantees liberty of conscience, but declares that such liberty "shall not be so construed as to excuse acts of licentiousness or justify practices inconsistent with the peace or safety of the State." (A notice to the Mormons who are already forming colonies there.) It provides that " no money of the State shall ever be given or appropriated to any sectarian or religious society or institution." The old maxim, "the greater the truth the greater the libel," receives its quietus, so far as Wyoming is concerned, in this clause: " Every person may freely speak, write, and publish on all subjects, being responsible for the abuse of that right; and in all trials for libel, both civil and criminal, the truth, when published with good intent and for justifiable ends, shall be a sufficient defence, the jury having the right to determine the facts and the law under the direction of the court." And here is a truly modern clause: "The rights of labor shall have just protection through laws calculated to secure to the laborer proper *rewards for his service* and to promote the industrial welfare of the State." (The *italics* are mine.)

"No power, civil or military, shall at any time interfere to prevent an untrammelled exercise of the right of suffrage.

"No distinction shall ever be made by law between resident aliens and citizens as to the possession, taxation, enjoyment, and descent of property.

"Perpetuities and monopolies are contrary to the genius of a free State, and shall not be allowed. Corporations being creatures of the State, endowed for the public good with a portion of its sovereign powers, must be subject to its control.

"Water being essential to industrial prosperity, of limited amount, and easy of diversion from its natural channels, its control must be in the State, which, in providing for its use, shall equally guard all the various interests involved.

"The State of Wyoming is an inseparable part of the Federal Union, and the Constitution of the United States is the supreme law of the land.

"No session of the Legislature after the first, which may be sixty days, shall exceed forty days.... No Legislature shall fix its own compensation." (The sessions are biennial.)

"No bill (before the Legislature), except general appropriation bills, and bills for the codification and general revision of the laws, shall be passed containing more than one subject, which shall be clearly expressed in its title; but if any subject is embraced in any act which is not expressed in the title, such act shall be void only as to so much thereof as shall not be so expressed.

"No appropriation shall be made for charitable, industrial, educational, or benevolent purposes to any person, corporation, or community not under the absolute control of the State" (nor to any sectarian or denominational institution, as we have seen).

The provisions to prevent bribery and corruption in the Legislature are intended to be especially finely drawn. No legislator may give his vote or influence for or against any measure in consideration of the promise of another legislator's influence in favor of or against any other measure before, or to be brought before the Legislature. To make such a proposition is declared to be "solicitation of bribery;" to carry out such a bargain is to be guilty of bribery. Witnesses may be compelled **to testify in trials of such causes,** and shall not **withhold** testimony on **the** ground that it may criminate them **or** subject them **to** disgrace, but such testimony may not afterwards be used against such witnesses, **except** upon a charge of **perjury** in giving **such** testimony. " A **member who has a** personal **or** private interest in any **measure or** bill proposed or pending before the Legislature, **shall disclose** the fact **to the** House of which he is **a member, and shall not vote** thereon."

" **All fines and penalties under** general laws of **the State shall belong to the** public-school fund of **the respective counties."** This is in addition **to the usual two** sections in each township, to all lands given to the State for purposes not otherwise specified, the proceeds of all property that may come to the State by escheat, or forfeiture, and in addition to all funds from unclaimed dividends or distributive shares of the estates **of** deceased persons.

" In none of the public schools shall distinction or discrimination **be made on account of sex, race, or color.**

" No sectarian instruction, qualifications, or tests shall be imparted, exacted, applied, or in **any manner** tolerated in the schools, . . . **nor shall** attendance be required **at any** religious service therein, nor shall any sectarian tenets **or doctrines be** taught or **favored** in any public school or institution **that** may be established under this **Constitution.**

" **Railroad** and telegraph lines heretofore **constructed, or that may hereafter be** constructed in this State, **are hereby** declared public highways **and common** carriers, and as such **must** be made by law to **extend** the same equality and impartiality to **all who** use them, excepting employés and their families and ministers **of the** Gospel.

" Exercise of the power and right of eminent domain shall never be so construed or abridged as to prevent the taking by the Legislature of property and franchises of incorporated companies, and subjecting them to public use the same as property of individuals.

" **No street** passenger **railway,** telegraph, telephone, or electric-light line, shall be constructed within the limits of any municipal organization without the consent of its local authorities.

"Eight hours' actual work shall constitute a lawful day's work in all mines and on all State and municipal works.

"It shall be unlawful for any person, company, or corporation to require of its employés any contract or agreement whereby such employer shall be released from liability or responsibility for personal injuries to such employés while in the service of such employer, by reason of the negligence of the employer, or the agents or employés thereof." (Condensed to give the mere substance of the clause.)

"No armed police force or detective agency, or armed body or unarmed body of men, shall ever be brought into this State for the suppression of domestic violence, except upon the application of the Legislature, or Executive, when the Legislature cannot be convened."

The laws governing taxation and revenue are equally notable. Except for the support of educational and charitable institutions, and the payment of the State debt and interest thereon, the annual levy shall not exceed four mills on the dollar of the assessed valuation of the property in the State. Twelve mills on the dollar is the maximum levy in the counties for all purposes, exclusive of the State tax and county debt. An annual and additional tax of two dollars for each person in each county is imposed for school purposes. No city or town may levy a tax greater than eight mills on the dollar, except to meet its public debt and the interest thereon.

It will be seen that in preparing this great establishment for the reception of future millions, the furniture is as complete as the variety of attractions in the soil, and the future millions will find, already settled for them beforehand, many of the problems which we in older States are sorely troubled to decide—such as the female suffrage question, the eight-hour law, the Pinkerton problem, the question of religion or no religion in the schools, the mischief of discrimination in freight rates, and the evil of free passes on railways, with fifty other greater or lesser **matters that foment doubt and** contention far to the eastward of this forward and vig**orous** commonwealth, which thus has everything it **needs,** except the trifle called population.

A TALK WITH A COWBOY

The first cowboys I **ever saw** greatly disappointed me by their appearance. All that I have seen since that time have disappointed me equally. **If** I were to **write a play in** which there was a cowboy character, **I would dress** him up in fringed leather breeches and **a** buckskin **coat,** a big drab Spanish hat as stiff **as a** board and as big as the top of a wash-tub, in dainty boots, and beadworked gloves; his pistols should be of mother-of-pearl, and none but the best Cheyenne saddle should he sit on —for of such is the cowboy of the flash literature which has immortalized him; and if the true cowboy does not know enough to live up to his own china, I would ignore the fact. And yet these first cowboys I saw in Montana were a very ordinary-looking lot of young depot-loungers, peculiar only because they wore big flat-brimmed hats, and because they **had a** long line of broncos fettered **to a** hitching-rail near by. **I** would **have** been immeasurably disappointed and disgusted **had** they not been redeemed by a story that was told concerning them as **soon as** our train pulled away **from the** station where they were loafing.

The story was that this same band of plainsmen had long noticed **a** course of behavior on **the** part of **a** Northern Pacific train conductor which they determined not to tolerate. The conductor did the worst thing, in a cowboy's opinion, that any man could do—he acted like **a dude;** he "put on style." He actually went so far as to swing himself off the cars before they stopped, and, with one arm extended and head offensively erect, would shout: "Dingleville! All out for Dingleville!" His whole manner was artificial, affected, and unbearable. This being noticed—and no one is quicker to notice the hollow trickery of an Eastern man than cowboys are—the boys decided to "take him down." So one day they assembled on the station platform in a semicircular line, into the curve of which he must run as he leaped from the moving cars. The conductor did as he was expected to, the cowboys surrounded him, and he was bidden to dance.

"Dance, —— you!" they shouted; "dance, or we'll shoot the toes off you!"

At the words each cowboy pulled his pistol, and began shooting down into the platform planks, not exactly at the conductor's feet, but so as to narrowly miss them. They blazed away and he danced, until, after he was all but exhausted and they had no more shots to fire, they bade him go on with the train, and never "show up" at Dingleville until he could behave like a man.

I heard other stories about cowboys on that trip. One of the best of them was told by a globe-trotting Englishman, whose habit it was to amuse himself and while away life by going wheresoever there was promise of novelty, danger, or excitement. He had been to the African diamond fields, to the Mahdi's realms, to our frontier mining camps, and now he was on his way to Alaska. But one trip he made was to see the cowboys, about whom he had read a great deal.

"They are a very rum sort of beggars," said he—"a very rum sort. But they're not half bad as a lot, d'you know. The first cowboy town I got into was fortunately chosen, for I had no sooner got into bed in the 'otel than a band of the beggars came dashing up the street, firing off their **revolvers** like madmen. **It** happened that **the** 'otel was a very ram-shackle frame building, almost as thin as card-board, and in five minutes the walls of my bedroom were riddled with bullet holes in the most surprising manner. Fancy my satisfaction — for I had travelled five thousand miles to witness that very thing!

"But to show you that they **are not as** bad as they have been painted — in fact, that they are opposed to anything like law-breaking and violence—let me relate an incident that took place the very next day. There **was a** poor clark standing up over his books at a desk **in a** shop **on** the main **street, and there was a** drunken **cowboy** riding up **and down the street. Well,** the cowboy saw the clark, and his sense of humor was aroused by the idea of shooting at him, d'you know. Those cowboys have a very remarkable sense of humor. So the cowboy ups with his pistol, d'you know, and he shoots the poor clark right through the head, killing him instantly. **Well, now,** that sort of thing is very distinctly **frowned upon** by cowboys, as a rule, and in this case the **cowboys held** a meeting, and resolved that the fellow with the lively but dangerous sense of humor should be hanged at once. **They put a rope** around his neck, and there being no tree anywhere in sight, they hung him to **the side** of a Pullman as the train came rolling in. I've seen a number of occurrences of that sort, which makes me quite positive in stating that though they are a very rum sort of beggars, they are really not a bad lot."

Up to date, much **as** I have been in the Western country, I have not **the** close acquaintance with them that was boasted by this Englishman. I have not yet seen a "round-up," or a "trail" coming up from Texas, or a **cowboy** camp, or any part of their life that may be called illustrative or typical. **I** have seen thousands of **them** hanging about depots and saloons, riding like the wind across the open, seated in railway cars, betting their hard-earned money in gambling dens, and punching cattle into stock-pens and cattle-cars. I know them, their horses, their saddles, their clothing, their careless ways, their masterful riding, but I have yet to spend a day with them on the ranges or a night with them in camp.

I know that their unique position among Americans is jeoparded in a thousand ways. Towns are growing up on their pasture-lands; irrigation schemes of a dozen sorts threaten to turn bunch-grass scenery into farm-land views; farmers are pre-empting valleys and the sides of waterways; and the day is not far distant when stock-raising must be done mainly in small herds, with winter corrals, and then the cowboy's day will end. Even now his condition disappoints those who knew him only half a dozen years ago. His breed seems to have deteriorated, and his ranks are filling with men "who work for wages" rather than for love of the free life and bold companionship that once tempted men into that calling. Splendid Cheyenne saddles are less and less numerous in the outfits; the distinctive hat that made its way up from Mexico may or may not be worn; all the civil authorities in nearly all the towns in the grazing country forbid the wearing of side-arms; nobody "shoots up" those towns any more. The fact is the old simon-pure cowboy days are gone already; and when the barber Destiny again has a vacant chair and calls out "next" the cowboy will himself disappear.

For that reason I greatly enjoyed a morning spent with a cowboy of great fame in his business, of twelve years' experience, and who has forced his way upward to a position of prosperity and honor, although he still keeps his seat in the saddle, and officiates at every "round-up" of the cattle of a great cow company. It seems to me that to repeat what he said, as nearly as possible in his own words, will be to make a contribution to history for some future writer. As to its present interest, there can be no doubt.

"Folks in the East think that cowboys are savages, and eat grass," said he; "but I find 'em about the best men I ever knew; by that I mean that they are the manliest and squarest men I ever saw. There's one thing I will say, you put 'em in the best hotel there is, and they'll order ham and eggs three times a day, the reason being that you can't make 'em believe there's any better food than that a-going. They work hard, and they live hard, and when they smash, they go all to pieces. I know one, as smart a cowboy as ever roped a steer, smart at every part of the business—one of your true cowboys, he was, that's too proud to cut hay, and the kind that says, as I heard one say once when a big cattle-man came on from the East, and asked him to saddle his horse: 'Saddle him yourself,' says he; 'if you don't know how, you 'ain't got no business out on a range. Anyhow, I don't have to saddle no man's horse as long as I can ride the way I can now.' This fellow that I speak of was one of the regular sort like that, and yet he is sunk so low that a painted woman is keeping him. I saw him to-day, and he borrowed money of me, which, when I gave it to him, I knew I was flinging it into the gutter. Do you know why I gave it to him? It was because I know hundreds that would do the same for me. They would whack their last dollar with me, for standing by your friends is the cowboy's religion.

"Rum, cards, and women are the epitaphs in the cowboy's graveyard. Some bunches all three, and some cuts one out of the herd, and rides after it till he drops; but however they take 'em, those are the things that rounds up most of 'em. It's curious, but if they quit horseback, and go into business, those are the three businesses they choose from, or the two, I should say, for cards and liquor go together.

"How do I dress when I'm with an outfit? Well, mostly in rags. Truth is, I don't care how I dress so long as I've got a good hat and boots and saddle. I've got shoes on now because I've quit my horse, and am hoofing it. You can't walk in a cowboy's shoes; they fit too much. You see, we wear high-heeled boots, and get 'em as small as we can. When a cowboy goes into a shoe store, if two men can get a pair of new boots on him without a good deal of trouble, he won't buy 'em; he'll say he doesn't want a whole hide to slosh around in, he just wants shoes to fit his feet. Cowboys are very particular about the look of their feet, and have a right to be, because they pay $15 for a pair of boots. A good broad-brimmed hat 'll cost up to $20, and a plain Cheyenne saddle and trimmings is worth $40, but the boys like to get their saddles all stamped up with patterns, and will pay $55 for one like that.

"Folks East think the Indians are such fine riders. We cowboys may be conceited, but we don't think an Indian can ride for sour milk. It is true they are on horseback all the time, but their horses are little played-out old racks that you could mostly put in your pocket. An Indian can ride a horse that I've rode down and quit, but I always say the horse goes to git out of misery. You see an Indian ride once. You often have? Well, then, there's no need o' my tellin' you that he keeps his heels bumping into the horse's ribs the whole time he's riding him, or that he has a quirt, with which he keeps a-whipping and lashing the horse the whole time.

"Indians can't ride. Do you know what they do when they get a horse that's got some spirit? They put a **stake** in **the** ground, and tether **the** horse to **it** with **a** long halter. Then all the squaws and children and **old** men in the **camp** get around with whips and **sticks** and **stones, and** they holler and chase and beat the horse around and around that stake till he's wellnigh dead. When they've broke **his** heart and **got** him nearly dead, **some** buck will **get on** him and **ride him,** whipping him and digging **him with** his heels. **The** horse will go to get out of **misery.** That shows **what the** Indians know about **horses.**

"Cavalrymen are **fairly good** riders—on a road. **They can** move along a **road, if** it's in good condition, **quite fairly.** But, great Scott! what we call riding is to **take** your horse across country wherever a horse can go—down gullies, up bluffs, and just as **it** happens. A good cowboy rider is unconscious that he is riding. A man who is conscious that he is on horseback ain't a good rider. You want to get on your horse and let your legs flop around loose from the knees down; and you must **let your** body **sit** loose, except where it joins the horse **and** is part of him.

"**A** cowboy **is drunk** twenty minutes after **he** strikes a town. We used **to 'shoot up'** the towns, but now they disarm us. Was I ever in **a** fuss? Well, little ones, **once in** a while. When **a man** raises a gun on me, I'm going to do whatever he wants just as quick as I **can.** I've heard men in towns say they **wasn't** afraid of **a** gun. Well, I am; and **so** would they **be if** they had ridden from Texas to Montana **as** often as **I have.** I've also heard **men say they'd like to** see the **Indian** they'd be afraid **of.** Well, **I've seen a** good many **I've** been afraid of, **no** matter what bluff I made to show that I wasn't **scared. As I** say, I like **to oblige** a man that drops a **gun on me,** because the **man is** apt to be drunk, and **when he is drunk he is apt to** be a little mite nervous.

"But there was a time lately when a man pulled a gun on me, and I didn't like to do what he wanted. You see, I don't drink liquor, and I'd refuse $500 sooner than corral a spoonful of it. I was in a bar-room, and a man came in and asked me to drink. He was a stranger or he'd 'a' known better than to ask me, and he was steaming drunk, too. I thanked him, and told him I didn't care to drink. I was unarmed, but he was 'fixed,' and he whips out his gun—a 45-calibre six-shooter—and he says, 'Pour out a glass of rum and chuck it in yourself, or I'll make windows in your skull.' He had me, and I want to tell you that a man doesn't feel first-rate looking along a gun-barrel when he knows the weapon's cocked and the man is drunk, and has only got to press hard enough to move two ounces when the thing 'll go off. A man doesn't get absent-minded under the circumstances; he 'tends to whatever business is asked of him. I replied that certainly I would drink, and that I didn't know he was so pressing. I grabbed the bottle, poured out the poison, and was just raising the glass, with a 'Here's looking at you, pard,' when a friend of mine came in the door. He saw the lay of the land, and he walked up and stuffed the muzzle of his six-shooter right in the drunken man's ear, and he says, 'Drop it!' Up to that time it had been a tableau and not a word spoken, but when my friend said, 'Drop it!' the feller let his gun fall as you would have done with a mouthful of scalding hot coffee."

XI

A WEEK WITH THE MORMONS

Finding myself in Salt Lake City for the first time the other day, I went directly to the heads of the Mormon Church and put myself in their charge. In all probability it was that indefinable thing called "the newspaper instinct" that made me do it—the same that once told me that a man I was hunting New York to find was just disappearing from sight behind a door, although the door was the entrance to an evil place and the man was a minister of the gospel. I had never seen him, but it was he.

That is the same instinct that once caused a friend of mine, afterwards a distinguished editor, to bolt down the yawning staircase of an underground oyster-saloon on Broadway. "A news-current came up out of the cellar—a perceptible current of magnetism—and pulled me down there," he afterwards said, gravely; "and just as I entered the restaurant one man shot another dead."

For further particulars as to this remarkable but undoubted mind current—the newspaper instinct—I refer the reader to the various psychical research societies, or to any newspaper-man who really has a right to be so called. Should I preface my story with any more illustrations of its magic, the reader would prepare himself for a very different tale than the one I am now about to write down.

Being landed in Salt Lake City at daybreak not long before Election Day, 1892, I was surprised and affected by the beauty of the city. Upon seeing Denver in the crystal-clear light of its atmosphere, and with its beautiful view of the Rockies always over my shoulder, I had for the first time acknowledged that it would be possible for me to live away from the sea with at least some degree of happiness.

But Denver is only an appetizer to be taken before seeing Salt Lake City—at least, so far as the beauty of its surroundings is concerned. Denver's mountains are distant, and sometimes have to be looked for round a corner, whereas Salt Lake City is right against its mountains, and they all but wall it in. Not only that, but it is so broad and open and clear a town, and it is so lavishly set with beautiful trees, that there is no comparing it with any other city. It is a city with country improvements. Of course it is not elegant and rich and bustling and crowded with all the latest elegances like Denver, and I have not pretended that it was, but it is first in its own class—a great tree-littered, elbow-roomy, overgrown village, if you please, with all its electric-light and car poles along the middle of its streets, so that the trees and the wires may not interfere with one another; with its everlastingly queer Tabernacle rounding up like a brown roe's egg, and its three-and-a-quarter-million-dollar Temple lifting its many towers of granite above all but the mountains, as if conscious that it and they both elevate the soul and eye alike.

Thinking thus pleasantly of the countrified capital of the Latter-day Saints, I made my way—no cab or 'bus interfering to help me—down a very long, very broad street, under a splendid line of Lombardy poplars and box-elders, to the new hotel which, by-the-way, is one of the two **thousand really** first-class **hotels in** which **the West is** so rich. I passed ever so many scores of tidy little box-like dwellings, mostly frame ones as I recall them, and thought, as I always do when I see many detached homes of small size in a place, what a grand good thing it is that there is no other place in America like New York (where men and women and helpless **little** children are herded in barracks), and that there are so many cities in which whole families feel the pride and joy of independence, of all **that** goes with true homes. Why! I believe that no one thing contributes more **to America's** greatness than her unparalleled **number** of **citizens** who are their own landlords.

Thus further delighted, I reached **the hotel** and was barbered, and got the morning paper and my breakfast. Then it was that I determined to go to **the** officers of the Church of Latter-day Saints and give myself over to their care. Having so decided, the next thing was to think what I should say to the Mormons.

"**I first noticed your** people," I made up my mind to say, "when **I first** crossed the country years ago. **I had** come from San Francisco, and was in a train that **was** rolling over a particularly deserted and wretched **desert**, when all at once the waste, brown, dead-looking land became green with grain-fields and pastures and hay meadows. Neat houses, prosperous looking groups of outbuildings, flower-beds, and happy-faced, well-clad persons sprang up as if I was riding on a magic carpet and had wished myself in **Illinois.** I was told that these were Mormon wonder-workers who had brought about this splendid transformation. Now here I am again in Mormonland, and I would like to see something more than an express-train view of you all."

Next I thought I would say that I recollected reading **an** account by **one of** Brigham Young's daughters of her school-girl days, in which account she sought to show how happy and human and gentle were the pleasures and the training of Mormon children. What she wrote did not affect the main question before the people at that time—which was the question whether polygamy should be practised in violation of our laws—but, nevertheless, she drew a very pretty picture of a very happy household of little folks, who might have existed in New England, except that they would have had more fathers had they been so much farther East. I promised myself I would tell the Mormons about that echo of in-door life in Utah, and would ask to see some of their homes—a good deal to ask if the reader loses sight of the fact that "journalistic instinct" was at work; but keeping that in mind, such a request will seem quite moderate and in keeping.

I found Mr. Angus Cannon, and I said all that I had planned to say. Whether he is an apostle or a bishop or a plain saint, I do not know; but he is a brother of George Q. Cannon, the wisest and most forceful man in the Mormon Church, and a counsellor to the head of that body. "I am not out here to open old sores," said I, "nor to stuff any controversial points with straw, and knock them about for the edification of either Gentiles or Mormons. I have seen all the rest of the people between the Mississippi and the Rockies, and now I want to see the Mormons. It is an old story to say that the results reached by your settlers and the changes brought about on your desert land are among the wonders of the West, but it will be a new story, perhaps, to tell what sort of folks you are, and how you live and think and talk. Therefore let me see some thoroughly Mormon community, where Gentiles have nothing to do with the public management, and introduce me so that I can see the home life of the people there."

Any one might have supposed that **Mr.** Angus Cannon had been approached in precisely that manner three times **a** day for many years, so entirely at ease **was he, and** so calmly and readily did he make answer,

"**The** only difficulty about that," said he, "**is** to hit upon the best town for the purpose."

Afterwards, when **I** employed a photographer and asked him if he was a Mormon, the man of the camera said that he was, indeed, and why did **I** ask? Was it because I did not see his horns? Well, as to his horns, he was sorry to say he had none. He supposed they would begin to grow out when he got older.

"**I** told a man once," he added, "**that I was a Mormon,** and he said, 'You don't say so! **I thought** Mormons were queer-looking people and had horns.'"

Since my reader may wonder what sort of persons they really are, suffice it if it is noted here that they are precisely like the people of the West generally—the Americans **being very** American indeed, the Germans being more **or** less German, the Scandinavians being light-haired and industrious **as** they are at home, and so on to the end. But it is of especial value to say that Mr. Angus Cannon is of old Scotch stock, and that nearly all the leading men to whom he made me known were New-Yorkers or Virginians or Kentuckians or New Jersey born, or perhaps from one or another of the original thirteen colonies. I considered anew that such blood as that is apt to be good, and that this was why they were on top in that Church. Mr. Cannon would have passed for a Mississippi steamboat captain if he had been in St. **Louis.** He introduced me to his sons—four of them, I think—and one **of** them was an Ann Arbor **graduate and a Democrat.** The others were Republicans, **and** so was he. He introduced me to a Captain Young, a West Point graduate and son of Brigham Young, who looked the American army officer all over, though he has retired from the service. To each one of these persons Mr. Cannon told my story, and of each he asked where I had better go. Nearly every one said I had better go to the Cache (pronounced "cash") Valley, but one or two halted over a place called Provo.

Finally we met Bishop William B. Preston, and in his hands Mr. Cannon left me and went his way. Bishop Preston is a Virginian, and of a fine type of sturdy American manhood—a middle-aged, kindly man, gentle but firm and strong in appearance, speech, and methods. In Virginia he would be set down for a well-to-do man in a large country town—a country banker, for instance. His place in the Church is called "the Presiding Bishopric." He has two counsellors, sits in the counting-room of the great tithing depot in Salt Lake City, and I hazard the guess that he has charge of the property of the Church, and is the man of affairs who cares for the material possessions of the great organization.

He also seemed to take me and my errand as a matter of course, just as he would have regarded a flurry of snow or a request for the time of day. It is true that I had now explained myself to half a dozen men, and was going off with another who was also to hear me and judge me. It might be said that I was passing in review before all these persons, and yet that seemed to me to be mere accident. At all events we went to look at the Tabernacle, than which there is not, of all man's handiwork in America, anything more curious and unique. It stands on a square block of grass behind the mysterious but beautiful Temple which cost millions, and in which—though that is for another chapter.

"We used to meet in a bowery here," said Bishop Preston, "in the shade of foliage out-of-doors, but one day Brigham Young said we needed a more serviceable bowery, and he planned and built this Tabernacle. You would call it a church, but we call our society the Church, and our churches we call tabernacles."

I turned and looked at the strange building, so familiar in pictures, with its long low walls cut by doors between each buttress of supporting stone-work, and upon its rounded dome-like roof shaped like half of an egg that has been cut lengthwise.

"There never was a building like it in the world," said the bishop. "It was Brigham Young's idea."

In we went and stood in the enormous interior in which 6000 persons may sit on any day, and 10,000 can be seated if stools are brought in. Not even Henry Ward Beecher's old Plymouth Church is more plain and bare. It is just a great hall with a wide gallery around three sides, with little wooden posts, which look like marble, to support the gallery; with battalions of pews on the floors, and a gigantic organ at one end rising above the greatest choir space I ever saw in a church. And that, in turn, is above a terraced series of platforms leading down to the main floor, like a very broad but short staircase.

A man stood at the end of the church. He said, "Go up in the gallery and walk to the other end of the building. It is 250 feet long and 140 feet wide, yet when I whisper you will hear me, so perfect are the acoustic properties of the building." I walked the length of the church. My footsteps were repeated so many times in echoes that the reverberations sounded like a drummer's roll-call—almost as if I was a regiment a-marching. From where I stood at last the man who had spoken looked like a boy. He held up his hand. "Answer me in a natural tone when I speak to you. I am going to whisper." (Then the whisper came, distinctly, "Can you hear me whisper? I am going to drop a pin on this.

altar rail, see if you hear it.") He held the pin two inches above the rail and dropped it. I heard it as if— as I never supposed a pin could make itself heard a foot away. "And now," said the man, "see and hear what I do now." He rubbed his hands together, and a sound like a loud rustle of silk floated through the hall. Afterwards I sat by that amiable and ingenious man, and saw him go through the performance for others. The only trick was in the building. I offered the man half a dollar.

"Oh no," said he; "we do not sell the attentions that visitors get from us."

I said I would like to give something to the Church.

"We do not want it," said the man; "but you can pay it into the Temple Building Fund, and get a receipt for it."

I did so, and got a receipt on a printed blank like this:

```
  $50/100                                    Series B 5.
                                             No. 307.

            CHURCH OF JESUS CHRIST OF LATTER-DAY SAINTS.
                     OFFICE OF THE PRESIDING BISHOPRIC.
                              SALT LAKE CITY, UTAH, Oct. 15, '92.
  Received from............Julian Ralph..........................
  ...........................................N. Y. City..............
  .....................................50/100 Dollars, in Cash.
  On Account Voluntary Offering        W. B. PRESTON,
       to the Salt Lake Temple.              By N. R.
```

Bishop Preston, seated with me in the echo-haunted hall, then told me what I would see were it Sunday. In the choir space I would see 300 trained singers and the organist. At the top of the terraces of benches would sit President **Wilford Woodruff (the Brigham Young of to-day),** an aged man who knew the founders of the Church, was long an Apostle, **and** now **is " Presiding High Priest."** He has two counsellors, **and** all three compose what is called the First Presidency of the Church. Next below — one step down — **I** would **see** such of **the Twelve** Apostles **as** might be then in Salt Lake City and **their President.** These, I was told, are gifted eloquent preachers **and theologians.** Then would **be seen** on lower tiers " the Seventies," **who now number 100 quorums of seventy ministers** each. **Every** Seventy has seven Presidents, who **are the directors of** the group. The seven First **Presidents of the** Seventies **are the directors of all the Seventies in** the world. They are ministers, spreaders of the gospel. Their work is that of the Apostles, **who** are too few in number to do what is required, and therefore have this assistance. Next below would be seen, on a Sunday, the Presidents of Stakes—a stake being **what** we call a county. These **diocesan rulers have** spiritual control over all the bishops, **whom they** instruct **and** direct. Next would **come** the Eighties, **or elders, of whom there is a host. They are** often called upon **to preach, and are** preparing **to** become " Seventies," or full-fledged preachers. Next would be seen the Presiding Bishops **in** charge of the temporal affairs of the Church. **The** Presiding High Priest, his two counsellors, the Apostles, and the Presiding Bishops, **are the** general officers of the Church. **On** each side of these terraced platforms was an enclosure, railed off. One was for the Bishops of Wards, and the other for High Councillors and High Priests. Ending **the** series of **departments,** between the leaders and the plain saints, was the communion-table, on which the **bread and water rest every Sunday.**

Bishop Preston **went on to say** that in addition to

these officers were many others. Every bishop has two counsellors, for instance. Then there is an army of priests, teachers, and deacons. They are scattered in every ward. The teachers go from house to house among the saints, inquiring into the spiritual and worldly needs of the people. The priests follow if spiritual stirring is needed; others follow if worldly help is wanted. In every ward the women maintain their societies also.

"Why," said I, not irreverently, "it's like the Spanish army. Nearly every one wears shoulder-straps."

"Yes," said the bishop. "In the Mormon Church every man who is earnest and trustworthy and is possessed of ordinary sense is elevated to some office or other. Therefore all such are doubly spurred and interested."

I had been told by some Gentiles that I would not be allowed to enter the great Temple. I was therefore not surprised or disappointed when Bishop Preston said that the Temple was full of workmen, and could not then be seen. It is the *sanctum sanctorum*, and I never dreamed of entering it. But the bishop talked much about it, calling to my attention the fact that its name, "the Temple," was another name for that "Endowment House" of which scandalous things had been charged by the Gentiles in times gone by. It is there that the saints are sealed to their wives and the children are baptized when they reach eight years of age. There, also, the bishop told me, the saints pursue the trying course of being baptized over and over again for their ancestors, in order that the dead who had no opportunity to know the gospel may be saved after all. A saint, I was told, will undergo the ordeal for every ancestor of whom he can learn the name. To be sure, some of us are said not to know who were our grandparents; but, on the other hand, some of us are descended from Brian Boru. And in Utah there are men who trace their line back to famous men of England and Scotland, and must be baptized for scores of dead progenitors, each repetition of the ceremony taking the best part of a day, from eight o'clock in the morning until three o'clock in the afternoon. Perhaps I was deceived as to this, but it will not be easy to make me think that those who were so undeviatingly kind to me for many days were deceivers at the same time.

After being introduced to many Mormons it came to be luncheon-time, and I was invited to join the family circle of one of my new-made acquaintances. I must draw the line at the door of a private house, and cannot say a word to indicate whose it was. The husband, as he approached his garden gate, called my attention to the sparkling water coursing down the street gutter, and then to a bit of board beside it. He took up the board, dropped it into a pair of slots in the side of the gutter, and thus dammed the flow, and turned it instantly and full head into his garden. The performance was a familiar one to me, but perhaps the reader does not understand it. The street gutter was an irrigation ditch. The water was that of a mountain stream, tapped high up in the hills. There was the secret of the rich greenery of Salt Lake City, and, for that matter, of the marvellous transformation of Utah from desert to garden. There, too, was seen the only, yet confident, hope of the people of the Dakotas, Wyoming, Idaho, Montana, Colorado, Arizona, New Mexico, Utah, and Nevada—that vast empire of arid land that looks to irrigation to duplicate in the West the imperial wealth of the agriculture of the East. How simple it was! A stream tapped, a rivulet running in the gutter, a block of wood to dam it, and—result, a laughing garden full of grass and flowers and fruit.

Left alone, in-doors, in my first Mormon house, I noticed only one thing, at the outset, that I had never seen in any other house. It was a scroll of Mormon texts hanging in the hall. It displayed on the outer sheet a text from the book called *The Doctrine and Covenants.* Perhaps 'twas this:

"21. Take upon you the name of Christ, and speak the truth in soberness."

"22. And as many as repent and are baptized in my name, which is Jesus Christ, and endure to the end, the same shall be saved."

"23. Behold, Jesus Christ is the name which is given of the Father, and there is none other name given whereby man can be saved."

But presently being asked to amuse myself for a few moments, I discovered that the burden of literature on the centre-table in the sitting-room was nearly all Mormon. Most interesting of all was a Mormon periodical aiming to publish the early records of the pioneers who came to Utah to escape annoyance and build a world of their own. Strange heroic stories they were — of caravans of Americans pushing out to a point half the width of the continent beyond civilization, to an alkali plain of which their leader said, "This is the place that was revealed to me." Tales of thirst, of Indians, of murder, of misadventure of every sort these were; followed by records of ship-loads of Europeans toiling along over the wilderness. What must have been the sensation of the men of Berlin and Edinburgh and London in that country in those days?

For the rest, the gay carpet, lace curtains, the piano, the canary, the furniture, and the pictures, were all very like the contents of an Eastern parlor in Gentiledom.

Called to follow the host to the dining-room, I confronted the first **wife and daughter of a** Mormon that **I** had **ever met. The mother** was an Eastern woman of prim and matronly appearance, and **with** great strength of character deep-lined in her face. I would have said she was **a reformer, or a** principal of a school. The daughter was very beautiful, of the type of which we think in New York that Miss Georgia Cayvan is the best representative. She was about twenty years of age, full but graceful of figure, with nut-brown hair and great dreamy eyes. She was spirited and witty; her mother was sober and practical. The daughter was already a leader among the women of the **Territory in** ways apart from the Church. **Of the** mother I **learned** nothing. The meal began with an offer of thanks to the Almighty, and was sufficiently bounteous to have warranted a longer and heartier grace. We talked of the Japanese, and I told how I had learned that the characters that stand for words with the Japanese were originally pictures.

"**And** what **do** you suppose was the sign for 'trouble?'" I **inquired.**

No one could guess.

"Two women in one house," **said I.**

"Ah," said the elderly lady, gravely, while the others were still laughing, "our Mormon brethren have found out the truth of that."

Then the conversation turned upon other themes, and I learned that too many Mormon boys and girls were allowed to go to Garfield Beach—the Coney Island of Salt Lake—on Sundays, preferring music and gayety and Sabbath-breaking crowds to the peace of home and the lasting benefits of church attendance.

"This frivolity of the young is a new thing to us," **said the father,** "and I suspect it is in the air, for I hear **the same stories among** all people everywhere."

Out-of-doors, I said to a Morman, "You've dropped polygamy."

"Yes," said he; "we do not teach it any more. We have no wish to prolong the conflict, or to have any conflict, with our Government."

"I have an idea it was not popular with your women."

"The women have never liked it or advocated it," said he; "but they understand that it was sanctioned by the Church, and that it was best for the race. It left no excuse for or possibility of a class of evil women in our communities, it left no surplus women uncared for, since men took wives according to their means, and there were other points to be urged for it in the direction of ensuing healthy offspring—the offspring of the sturdy instead of the offspring of the weak, as in monogamy."

"Were you married more than once?"

"No; but I never had one wife. I was married to two at once. I have been imprisoned for my course in that regard. The law has separated me from one wife, but it could not make me promise to abandon her to distress; it could not prevent me from taking care of her, and seeing that she never wants while she lives. You will not be believed if you quote me," he went on; "perhaps you won't believe me yourself; but we are as good Americans in our loyalty as any in the land. Your flag is mine, and we are the only people in the United States who call the Constitution an 'inspired document.' I would not do a thing hostile to the Government any more than you would. Among us here are men whose ancestors helped to found this country. Can you say any more?"

Back through the streets, under the poplars and elders, the locusts and the cotton-woods, I made my way to the tithing-office and to Bishop Preston. The tithes are paid in kind — that is to say, of ten cows one is given, of ten tons of hay a ton is given. The tithing-place was enclosed by a stone-wall, originally built for possible use as a haven from the Indians. In the enclosure and in the buildings there were cows and horses, kegs of honey, dressed meat, hay, bags of rag carpet, flour, bacon — a thousand kinds of produce. In one place was a sort of salesroom, and men and women were buying provender.

"Notice the money that they use," said the bishop.

I saw that it was green paper money. I changed a half-dollar for a shinplaster of it because of the fine picture of the Temple upon it.

"When we give aid to our poor," said the bishop, "it takes the form of that money. When the poor come here to buy what they need, they hold their heads as high as any. If we gave them orders on the store, they would be betrayed; but as it is, no one is the wiser."

Very pretty, I thought. The more I inquired, however, the more I was satisfied that these industrious, practical church-folks have as little use for pauperism as the West in general has for drones. The poor are assisted only to the near limit of short patience. Then they are made to understand that they will do better by working.

The tithing system puzzled me. I could not — nor can I yet — understand how any organization could succeed in inducing its 200,000 members to give up a tenth of their capital or of their earnings. That it, like so very much else of Mormonism, is based on Old Testament writ, does not explain the latter-day application of the case. I said so to one saint.

"What do you give for a pew in your church?" he asked.

"Forty dollars," said I.

"Well, the average tithe among our people is not so much. We find it to be thirty-five dollars. And as you know what your money goes for, so do we trace ours. As a rule, the bulk of it is spread around among those who give it. It builds ward assembly-houses, temples, tabernacles, and so on; it buys land; it gives to the poor; it employs mechanics, laborers, teamsters; it is all scattered again. To be sure, there are saints whose tithes in a year may amount to a great deal. I have in mind a merchant who paid $2000 this year. But in the same way that he got rich he gets back his tithes—in great part, at least. He contracts to do the church work, to outfit a gang of laborers, to furnish or paint a building. There is no mystery and no hardship about it."

In the evening I went to Logan, in the Cache Valley, by means of a railroad run of a few hours northward from Salt Lake City, and near the Idaho line.

In all my Western travelling, Logan is the prettiest country-place I have yet seen. It would be difficult for me to picture to the reader's mind a more charming, enchanting spot than this Mormon village, that dots a lovely park or bit of prairie that is walled around by chains of stately mountains, whose sides are all deeply furrowed and heavily ribbed. The valley was half sage-brush and half alkali forty years ago—an old lake bed, no doubt—and yet to-day it is a glorious garden. Asbury Park, which has been built in a forest by cutting streets and building sites out from among the trees, has not a tenth so many forest trunks, and not a thousandth part such beautiful or such valuable ones. Trees which no man can reach around have been planted in lines along each curb and within each dooryard. Behind these, in every yard and garden, are still other trees, so thickly scattered that the pretty little cottages of the town are more than half hid among leafage, and a view of the town from the nearest mountain-side is a sight of clouds of foliage, broken only by the towering granite spires of the Mormon Temple and the massive bulk of the granite tabernacle.

The sparkling water of the Logen River, tapped upon a mountain-side, is led so cleverly through the town that each gutter on each side of every street is a rush-

OLD-STYLE HOUSE AT LOGAN, UTAH

ing, plashing mountain rill. Gates, which look to the lay beholder like tiny cataracts, are opposite each garden, and the melody of rippling, singing water fills the air— that air already so freighted with the sweet breathings of the trees and the mingling essence of a million flowers. The great broad streets, with the electric wires on poles in the middle of each roadway, the small and cosey dwellings, the thick orchards, the flower-beds, the shade trees, the walled-in tithing-house, the rat-tat of frequent saddle-horses, the cows streaming through town at dusk, the fierce glare of the sun in the clear sky, the purpling, blushing, ever-changing mountains—these are but a few of the details that memory sends leaping back to my eyes. The busy trading street, the neatly-dressed, hardy men, and plump and rather saucy-seeming Mormon lasses come next in view; and I think that if I had to describe both men and women, I would say that they form just such a population as one finds in out-of-the-way Eastern places like Gettysburg or Whitehall.

Ah! but to climb the near mountain and look down is the best of the things to do. Then the valley is seen to be checkered with villages and farms alternately—now a town, and now great tracts of farm-land. There are twenty-one villages in sight, and each is but the huddling place of so many farmers. They live as their kind do in Turkey and the Orient generally, building all together, and going to the outlying farms to do each day's work before returning to the houses, where the women have had each other's company and that of the old men and children. It was in 1859–60 that seventeen young men, with younger wives, and a baby that came at about the same time, moved into the valley, and built close by one another on both sides of what is now the depot street. Each took ten or twenty acres of farm-land a mile or more up the valley, with five acres for pasturage in yet another locality. Some men wanted more land, even sixty acres.

"How will you cultivate it?" they were asked.

"Why, we are going to have sons," they said.

"Then wait till you get them, and there will be land for them in their turn."

All together the settlers built an irrigating ditch, each digging his part according to the land he held. They washed the salt out of the earth, and it blossomed under the same ditches thus led through the farms. And every year these men, with pick and shovel, cleared out each one his bit of the main ditch after the winter had heaped and choked and torn it. To-day that water goes with the land, and the hired men keep the ditch in repair for the owners. How different from the usual American plan, whereby one man seizes a water right, and calls his "grab" a dukedom, and extorts so many dollars a year from all the settlers—for himself and his children, even unto the fourth and fifth generation!

The Indians—magnificent big Shoshones—came once a week and demanded oxen, or flour, or whatever. They were treated kindly, because Brigham Young always taught that it was cheaper to feed an Indian than to fight him.

"What do they want? Cows?" he once inquired. "Well, is it not better to give up all your cows than to see a neighbor—or even a child—killed?"

But he believed the Indians seldom made exorbitant demands, whereas they certainly did so in Logan on a certain day, when 300 of them, in war-paint, demanded 10 oxen and an immense amount of grain. After that the settlers had to loan their remaining oxen to one another — one working a team consisting of his own beast and his neighbor's one day, the other the next. Thus, from 1847 until now, and from Mexico to Canada, these peculiar people have got along with the Indians, and to-day they have tamed a half a thousand of them near this valley, and have actually taught them to farm in earnest.

It was Brigham Young's idea that the Mormons should remain a pastoral people. He taught that the surest wealth was in agriculture; and so it comes that one sees the valleys peopled and cultivated, while the mountains, that are full of metalliferous ores, are for the most part neglected — to an extent unknown in the neighboring States, each one of which, except Wyoming, was first opened and settled by miners. It was Young's idea to put the telegraph poles in the middle of the streets, but then he believed in enormous streets. In Logan the streets are six rods wide, and the blocks are six times as long. But in Salt Lake City the blocks are forty rods long. The effect is grand. The system has more merits than disadvantages.

I went to the Tabernacle on a Sunday. The general service is at two o'clock, and then at night the saints of each neighborhood assemble in their ward meeting-houses. The service in the Tabernacle disappointed me. The huge plain interior was peculiar in that the galleries were bent down at one end to meet the elevated choir space—which as yet contains no organ, by-the-way. Instead there was a melodeon, and two violinists stood beside the leader. There were thirty-five well-trained voices in the choir, and the singing was good. The service began with the song of "Home, Sweet Home," the words being altered. The President of the Stake sat up on top, and a dozen dignitaries sat below him. Below them, in a solemn row, were sixteen men behind a table on which stood sixteen silver ewers and sixteen plates of bread broken into coarse crumbs. The house was filled, and with a truly good-looking congregation, no whit different from an ordinary mixed Western Methodist assemblage. An old man prayed for a blessing on the bread, and around it went, in the hands of the sixteen. Then a young man blessed the water that symbolized our Saviour's blood, and round that went, in pitchers and goblets. The choir sang again, and then an elderly man made a brief but pointless address, it being a rule, as I understand it, that whoever is called upon may talk as he feels best able to, and on what topic he pleases. Another man—both sat among the officials—spoke about a great conference at Salt Lake City, and the earnest piety that moved it. Then up rose an apostle—a banker named Thatcher—who was evidently a popular speaker. He told how difficult it was to be a good Mormon, and how Mormonism enters every moment of life, and how a Gentile once said "he would rather be damned and go to hell than try to live up to the Mormon faith." Next the apostle spoke of material things; of the home industries, the saw-mill, the boot and shoe making, the necessity for more manufactures. He said the young Mormon men would do anything with their teams, but would not work with their hands, and that he did not blame them. At last he took up the topic of winter fun. He advised all the saints to have a good time, to hold parties and sociables, to gather the young together, and not to grudge them their pleasure or misjudge them for loving it. He liked to see them merry and joyful. It was good, he said. After the apostle came an old man who read a notice calling upon the women to meet somewhere and vote upon a choice of a flower that should be the favorite and emblematic blossom of the Territory. The choir sang, and the meeting ended. Of course no collection was taken up; the tithes are enough. The service disappointed me. It was too practical for my old-fashioned ideas. The one good speaker simply made a business man's address; the others had no fervor. Possibly the fervor came at the ward-meetings that night.

In the houses where I was a guest I saw absolutely nothing peculiar, unless it was that it seemed to me there was a phenomenal number of excessively rosy and robust children. The wives were hearty and healthy, but it was very evident that motherhood brought an obligation heavier than usual upon their sex. Everywhere I was asked to note the children, to see how healthy and fine they were. Fifty times in one week in Utah that was the topic. Not once in any other State was it spoken of. And they may well be proud of their children, for never was solicitude and pride more richly rewarded.

"Our sons are free to fall in love," said one saint, "but they have no right to fall in love with flimsy, sickly girls. They know there is no excuse for that."

Are the Mormon girls pretty? Many are very pretty, mainly with rustic beauty, to be sure, and yet I saw a number who would be called belles in our largest cities. They were the daughters of the well-to-do, and had tasted travel and training in fashionable schools. Are they nice? That was the first question I asked of a young woman at the same hotel with me.

"You bet they are!" said she. "I'm one myself."

But she was not like one in that, for no other girl or woman that I saw in Utah was so enthusiastic, or even a particle slangy in my presence.

I asked what pleasures the girls and boys had, of which the apostle had spoken. I was told that they maintain literary societies "to discuss the poets, and enjoy a light supper afterwards;" that they not only give parties and dances at their homes, but that general assemblies are held in the tabernacles in the little towns and villages. A fee is charged, a supper is served, dancing is the chief delight, and an official of the Church is present to preserve order. These communities are little democracies. All work; all are land-owners, and independent in that respect. All are comfortable, and few are rich. Caste is unknown, and whole villages dance as they pray—in harmony together. For the little children are maintained just such party customs as our own little ones enjoy.

There are three colleges in little Logan—the State Agricultural College (officered by Gentiles), the Brigham Young College, and the New Jersey College (a Presbyterian institution). Four-fifths of the tax-payers are Mormons. They spent $5000 in lawyers' fees to keep liquor-selling out of the town, but the Federal courts ruled against them, and the best the Mormons could do was to put the license fee at $1200 a year. The next thing after that was to "taboo." whoever frequented the saloons. While I speak of these virtues, let me add that they are an honest people. They are taught that they must pay their debts. One of the chief financiers of the far West told me that the losses of his company had been less in Utah than anywhere else.

I asked what there was so trying in their tenets as to lead a Gentile to prefer damnation to Mormondom. I fancy I got only a partial answer. It was to this effect: The Church aims to produce a perfect race of men, and to make each generation more nearly perfect than the last. The perfection that men can reach is of the physical sort; the morals God looks after. He puts good souls only in fit bodies. Therefore Mormons may not drink or smoke or use tobacco in any form. They should not use tea or coffee. They should fast one day in every thirty—at least until dinner-time—and give to the poor what is thus saved. They should keep Sunday holy, and go to church twice on that day. That was all I heard. Alas! it was admitted that not all the saints are as strict as they should be.

"One thing you have not seen," said a Mormon lady. "At any moment a deacon may come to our door, and join our family circle. He will ask us a number of questions as to our religious welfare if we are well to do; as to our worldly condition if we are struggling. Or perhaps it will be a teacher who will call. 'I wish to read the gospel to-night,' he will say; 'is it agreeable to you?' 'Well, no,' I would say, 'we have company this evening.' Then he would rise and bow himself out, saying that he had fifteen houses to visit this month, that he would go to another and come back to us at another time."

Perhaps if some politician reads what I have told of this Church the case will strike him as it does me. Never was there a political organization so thoroughly managed as is this Church. The socialist philosophers hold that Tammany Hall is the most thorough, self-renewing, and complete political machine known to man. But Tammany Hall is clumsy and superficial compared to this Church. Indiana, the State that is raked with a fine tooth comb by two parties every year, is poorly looked after beside Utah. Mr. Platt thinks he has reduced organization and the supervision of voters to a science. He is a bungler compared to Brigham Young. What politicians do for a month, once every four years, this Church does all the time—endlessly. It never takes hand or eye off its people. Not even their houses are castles out of which the Church can be shut. With half the saints dignified by office, and all of the rest under constant scrutiny, conceive the power and order of the Church! Yet remember that nothing that is done is felt so as to be resented. All is as kindly as it is shrewdly devised. The Church of Latter-day Saints is the most complete and perfect human machine (if it is human, which the leaders deny), and Tammany Hall has not reached the primer of the science it illustrates.

I have said that there are 200,000 saints. They are

by no means all in Utah. Their towns and districts almost form a chain north and south of that Territory from Canada into Mexico. They are in Wyoming, Idaho, Colorado, New Mexico, Arizona, the Sandwich Islands, and the countries of Europe. They have four palatial temples, the main one being at Salt Lake City, the Rome of that Church. There is a $600,000 one at Logan, and a more expensive one at St. George, in far southern Utah, where the colonists in the southern Territories and in Mexico must go to perform whatever rites are celebrated in those beautiful but mysterious buildings.

Down in the bottom of Utah the soil is found in little pocket-like valleys and small plateaus, just big enough for orchards or vineyards, but not for grain-growing. Cotton is grown there and coarse cotton goods are made of it. It is said that no other people would have gone there, yet the Mormons are all in comfortable circumstances. Out in the eastern desert end of Utah I heard of Mormons living where a jackal would go mad before starvation brought him an early death. They were huddled on little streams in the sage-brush desert, growing hay and raising sheep that must possess microscopic eyes with which to see their food.

Utah contains nearly 85,000 square miles, and 52,601,600 acres of land and mountains. It is almost 300 miles square, and is as large as New England and New York. Mining is now the chief industry, and gold, silver, lead, and copper are the chief metals that are mined there, the product in 1890 having been $14,346,783. It is the third mining region in the West, and it is said that of all the metals found in the Dakotas, Montana, and Colorado, only tin is lacking in Utah. Men who are familiar with all the new States and the Territories predict a golden and amazing future for Utah. There is water to irrigate thousands of square miles of good land that is embraced in three drainage systems. Wheat, oats, and rye grow well in all the irrigable lands, and corn in some. Orchard fruits and small fruits thrive there. Three millions of acres are said to be irrigable and arable. There is a vast store of timber, and the cattle industry finds plenty of range land, now used for 300,000 horned stock, 100,000 horses and mules, and a million and a half of sheep. Precious stones, mineral springs, inexhaustible and vast beds of coal, natural gas, marbles and building stones of many sorts, health resorts, new mining regions, and a certain-to-be-formidable agricultural product, are the assets of the future in this majestic Territory which now holds but 200,000 population.

XII

SAN FRANCISCO

WHETHER you drop down upon it after crossing the desert and the Sierra Nevadas, or whether you come to it at close of a long voyage at sea, San Francisco surprises you. It is at the edge of an empire of magnificent distances, over most of which the future is a thousandfold more important than the present, and yet you find it a great, bustling, parent city, surrounded by a family of thriving and sizable suburban towns. Its isolation, the difficulties of communication between it and the older civilizations of our country, as well as of those which we copy, have been so tremendous and still are so great that though I should criticise it in cold blood, and should find a million faults in it, there still would remain good cause for the San Franciscans to be extremely vain of their work. And the more one considers the influences that have combined to make that city, the more one thinks of the character and aims of the people who drifted to that coast and clung there, of the discordant extremes of immense wealth and bitter ruin that befell them, of how little suited or minded they were at the outset to build a great city, the more criticism's point is dulled, the smaller the faults seem, the greater grows the meed of praise to the builders.

After a tourist has visited a few far Western "boom" towns, he feels his footing grow unsteady, as if he walked on thin and gaseous clouds. The man who can stop at six such places and boast a clear head in the last one, is of superior stuff. For myself, I had by that time become so confused that I lost all sense of proper values and of the true means of judging the commonest things. Fancy it! In one place I found a great area all built up with streets and dwellings, with real estate at the outskirts going readily at $4000 an acre, and with impressive brick and stone buildings in the business section costing from $30,000 to $60,000 and renting for $100 a year—for which rentals bogus receipts were given for vastly higher sums (the same to be shown to strangers).

After such a tour it is refreshing to find one's self in San Francisco. Every phase of its life seems genuine and substantial. Elsewhere you cannot escape the "price of lots;" in San Francisco you must go out of your way to hear that staple talked of. The people are engaged in a thousand businesses, and are attending to them, precisely as in New York or Boston or Chicago. Genuine business makes the air and the earth throb. The streets in the business portion are crowded with men intent upon their own affairs, the roadways thunder beneath great drays of merchandise, the retail shops display as wide a variety and as fair a proportion of high-class goods as those of any city in the country. The wholesale houses are fine establishments, with a solid and prosperous air about them. The cable-cars that dash through the streets amid the clangor of their own gongs keep even a New-Yorker's every sense wide awake, and, in a word, San Francisco strikes the visitor instantly as being instinct with the metropolitan spirit.

Like thousands of other New-Yorkers, I had constructed my own idea of the place. I had heard that San Francisco was more like New York than any other city on the continent, and as for the country and the climate, I painted them in *couleur de rose*. Therefore I

SAN FRANCISCO BAY

was unprepared for what I was to see, and it hurt me like a knife-thrust—I mean the first sight of the city, not the impressions I got in a month's stay afterwards. The steamship *Walla-Walla*, beautifully fitted within by San Franciscan taste and skill, entered the Golden Gate under a moonlit sky on a calm August night, disclosing a view as beautiful as ever could be formed by a combination of headlands, hills, water, and town. The shadowy hills rose majestically on every hand, the superb harbor was rendered doubly picturesque by reason of its bold islands, and the lights of the city and of Saucelito and Oakland gemmed the horizon as with a myriad of brilliants. It was hard to shut a state-room door against so beautiful a scene. But it was harder to open it in the morning and behold the revelation that the sunlight had to make! It was only the hills that were at fault, after all; everything else was as the moonlight had shown it. But such hills!

They were of dirt—reddish, yellowish, bare dirt hills. They hemmed in the glorious harbor; they composed the islands; they rose above and among the city's houses. And when I plunged into the city, and tried to forget the blow that I had myself invited by picturing home scenery where no one had ever said it existed, it seemed that the hills pursued me and hurled their surplusage upon me in clouds of dust, which, mingling presently with a bank of fog, grimed itself into my clothing, while the cold wind searched out my very marrow. I registered at the Palace Hotel—which I like better than any other, except one in Europe, of all the hundreds I am familiar with—and in a short time was on my way to Oakland. A countrified Brooklyn I had pictured Oakland to my mind, and lo! the stuffy, ill-kept cars carried me through a city of which the most that could be seen was a dust-covered, shabby avenue of cheap houses, drinking-saloons, little neglected dwellings, and low-grade shops. I had a surfeit of disappointment.

When I look back now and recollect how difficult I found it to leave that picturesque and fascinating coast, how many happy days and glorious pleasures I experienced there, I realize as never before the enormity of the crime men and women commit in writing locomotive literature—of the kind that produces the fruit and blossom of positive statement out of the soil of inference, conjecture, hasty opinion, and instant prejudice.

Those hills are just as bare to my mind to-day as when I first saw them, but the thought of them calls up such a flood of remembrance of rich colors and opulent vistas as I have seldom witnessed in any other travel. They were always glorious in color, and were never twice alike, though a rosy blush was ever the dominant tone in their appearance. At sunset every view of the harbor, every scene from the hill-tops, was positively gorgeous. In each house I visited, whether in city or suburbs, we came to count upon the last hour of each day as the vehicle that should bring a glorious spectacle to the view; a more and more glorious one, it seemed, as the conditions of nature varied with clouds or fog, or that supernal clearness which is seen on that coast at times, and which all but forces a doubt of the existence of any atmosphere whatsoever. At such times Italy can boast no bluer sky, and nature lavishes upon the hills and water an extravagance of color. One would expect San Francisco to develop a considerable artistic element, led by a coterie of great painters. And exceptional water-color work might be expected to go out from there in the travelling effects of most well-to-do visitors, for the dominant tones in nature lend themselves exquisitely to water-color reproduction. In fact, the city is already the home of some notable painters. I saw fine

SEAL ROCKS.

work by half a dozen at least, and the city has just loaned to London a portrait-painter who is making a stir there. But it is to San Francisco's discredit that her artists are not handsomely supported or encouraged. In the reason for this we shall see one phase of the defect that is the most striking and important failing of that people as a community. Those citizens who deal in high-class pictures say that while the very wealthiest men and women of the city have bought very few world-famous paintings, they have none the less expended a large sum in foreign works of art of lesser grades, and almost nothing at all in the products of home talent. There is among San Franciscans, however, a considerable number of cultivated folk, living upon incomes of $5000 a year and upwards, who give the local painters what support they get. One intelligent dealer of wide experience said that these patrons of the local progress turn instinctively to the best work, that they maintain homes as beautifully and elegantly appointed as any persons of their means enjoy in this country, and that they form a very large class in the city and suburbs. This cream of San Francisco society can do little for the public and general adornment of the city except through the moral influence it can exert.

To their presence I ascribe the fine clubs, the really notable retail shops, and the beautiful homes on such streets as Pacific Avenue, and scattered about Saucelito, Alameda, and Oakland. And to their powerlessness must be due the fact that, more than any city of its size I ever saw, San Francisco lacks those evidences of culture and local pride which are exhibited in the forms of statues, monuments, free galleries, fountains, libraries, elegant parks, well-kept streets, and noble boulevards.

The early motive that we call the Puritan spirit, and which showed itself in the foundation of cities over the greater part of our country, took note at the outset of the communal needs. It supplied first a school-house, and next, a church in each settlement. This action was only indicative of a larger public concern, which continued to be exhibited not alone in more and better school-houses and in elegant churches, but in all the other concomitants of civic pride and polish which, for want of another term, we might call communal betterments — the public "plant." In neither her shabby churches nor her flimsy school-houses do we detect that unselfish, affectionate, and almost tender regard for those institutions which most of our other cities exhibit. I can easily invent possible reasons for this — in the Spanish origin of the place, in the climate, in the large admixture of Southerners, with their habit of lavishing every luxury upon their homes, in the long period of speculative temper and unrest among the settlers, in the sequestration of the city, in a score of influences—but let that be; I state only the condition of what I saw. As for the purely public works of San Francisco—which include the school-houses and the streets—it ill becomes a stranger to take part in the local controversy in which one side boasts of an exceedingly small city tax (popularly called the "dollar limit"), and the other side groans because of a lack of money for every public need. Creditable as is the financial standing of San Francisco so far as her debt is concerned, the case reminds me of that of the man who tried to train his dog to live without eating, and who said, "I had almost succeeded when the dog died." Among the public papers that lie on my desk are the pathetic appeal of the chief of the only partially paid fire department for more hydrants and engines, and the reports of other officials complaining of lack of means for their work. As for the streets of the city, they may be said to cry out for themselves.

JEFFERSON SQUARE

Against these the **small** debt of the corporation **makes an impression such as** others may characterize.

But there are **strong** signs that the **city** is undergoing a revolution from **which** it will enter upon a very different career. In **a** short article upon the Golden Gate Park in HARPER's WEEKLY, I spoke of one hint of this new spirit. The rapid development of a stately avenue in Market Street is another **and** a proud sign of this awakening of the west **coast** metropolis. Those **who** planned **this** splendid commercial boulevard **conceived an avenue** of such proportions **as only** the **most progressive** city could be expected to appoint **with** buildings of commensurate height **and dignity, yet already the noble** thoroughfare commands a place among **the** finest streets in Christendom, **and plans** have been filed **for** several structures of a cost **and** size exceeding those of any which now grace the street. Until recently San Francisco stood alone as the great settlement upon that coast. She has no rival now, but other towns are growing apace and sharing the increasing commerce. It is plain that **the metropolis does not** intend that **any** one of **them** shall lessen **the** distance **she has** ever **maintained** between her own proud position and that **of her foremost** follower.

Comparable in width with no streets in our part of the country except Broad Street, in Newark (New **Jersey), and the Bowery, in** New York, this great new thoroughfare **in San** Francisco finds an almost level way for three miles, despite the hills that so strangely distinguish that city. In a short time it is to be doubled in length, and will connect the harbor wharves with the ocean beach. On either side of it rise such huge latter-day structures **as** the Palace Hotel, the new *Chronicle* **building, and several others.** Here the fine retail stores **are** centring, and the street cars, business wagons, and fine private equipages create what our grandfathers would have called a brave showing or "a fine confusion" on the roadway. Here also the people gather in the greatest numbers, and, however it may grieve a New-Yorker to hear it, the scene in parts of the street recalls the crowds upon Broadway. The San-Franciscans have their own etiquette—in nothing, I think, more peculiar to us than their habit of leaving the city in summer *to get warm*—and this leads the very nice ladies to shop in the morning and leave the street to "the crowd" in the afternoon. But knowing this, at one time or other we may see them all. It is while viewing the Market Street parade that we realize that we are looking upon a decidedly cosmopolitan community, and one that is stamped as foreign in a great degree. We have heard that not more than half the people are American, and on Market Street we get ocular confirmation of the news.

Since the best of the street is the shopping part, and most of the shoppers are women, we may pause to look at the fairer moiety of the town. They are almost Parisian in the fulness of their development, the graceful outlines of their forms, and the stylishness of their dress. The crowds are full of pretty women, and there is among them a greater abundance of that great concomitant and source of beauty, good health, than I remember ever to have noticed elsewhere. Very curiously, you see the two extremes, the blond and brunette, side by side, and numerously represented. Of flaxen-haired, blue-eyed women, with complexions of rose-tint on wax, you see scores; of olive-faced, jet-haired, black-orbed daughters of the South, you meet hundreds. There is a Spanish foundation to the population and a Spanish colony in the city; there are many Portuguese, some French, and for the rest, they are of the hodge-podge of

MARKET STREET

races that constitute that which we call the American And ever and again, as we view the daily parade, there patters by a Chinese woman, bareheaded, with plastered hair and almost ghastly face, wearing a long-sleeved coat and glazed trousers. Japanese and darkies, Greeks, Sandwich-Islanders, and Chinamen a-plenty—all are in the crowds.

The spectacle is a particularly gay one, because the women wear more pronounced colors than you see even in Paris. I mean the women of the masses. The goods they wear are not different from those we see on our streets, but bright colors find a readier sale there than here. Whether it is due to the climate, or to the nationalities of so large a part of the populace, I don't know; in all probability it is due to both. But the effect is enlivening and picturesque to a degree, and it has to be taken largely into account in considering the attractions of this noble street. It has pleased many San-Franciscans, there and here, to assert that an Eastern man quickly discovers a freedom of behavior on the part of the women on the streets, a fondness for flirting, such as is witnessable nowhere else. Nevertheless, it is my opinion that there is no more orderly concourse in any city I ever visited than in San Francisco. There, even that form of vice whose control puzzles so many municipalities hides itself in alleys, and no more vaunts itself on the highways than if it did not exist.

It is unnecessary for me to say that the names in the city directory of San Francisco include some of those of the finest families in the Middle and Southern States and (perhaps to a less extent) in New England, or that I enjoyed more or less acquaintance with some of the most lovely homes I ever found anywhere. A heap of cruel and wicked nonsense can be generated in a distance of three thousand miles. I fancy a great many persons, there and here, believe that the revelations of Chinatown are appalling, even to a professional traveller, yet in making the tour of that peculiar region twice, with the ablest guides the local and Federal governments could provide, I failed to see any reason why the Caucasian should lose the palm for wickedness. I did not go to "the Barbary Coast," but unless that purlieu is worse than I was told it is, I shall continue to think San Francisco a particularly well-governed and virtuous city.

The city is scarcely what a strict Sabbatarian would order it. It is said that California is the only State with no Sunday law, and certainly there is little general notice taken of Sunday, so far as the appearance of the city goes, beyond the closing of the wholesale shops, and the hint conveyed in certain street signs which announce, "Boot-blacking, five cents; Sundays and holidays, ten cents." The drinking-places are not shut up, and in the residence portions the shops are nearly all wide open. The day is a happy one, it seemed to me, for the masses, but it is not at all our Sunday.

In Market Street and in the Seal Rocks the San-Franciscans have two grand possessions, the former one giving them the means to ennoble their city to whatsoever degree they please, the latter making it unique in the enjoyment of a most interesting exhibition. They will have a third grand possession when they have pushed their great park to completion, if they finish it as they have finished the first 180 acres. Not even the near presence of Sutro Heights, decked as might become a gigantic factory of plaster casts, can lessen the charms of the entrancing view from the Cliff House over the ocean and down upon the rocky islets, where the accommodating seals are ever present and ever at their gambols. For the edification of the public at large, it needs

UNION SQUARE

to be said that **Mr.** Sutro—who **lent his name to the** famous tunnel—has **laid out** some very **pretty** grounds **upon an** eminence **above the** Cliff House, and philanthropically permits the **public to enjoy** the garden and accompanying **conservatory.** But, in my humble judgment, he more than offsets this **by** literally peppering the entire grounds and walls **and face of** the **hill with** plaster **statues,** statuettes, **heads, busts, and figures.** The effect is—but I leave that **for the** imagination.

Would you know how **San Francisco looks?** It is a strangely foreign-looking **place.** Its site is broken by half **a score of** hills, and **other hills frame it all** around. **They are not** of **the sort** that **our Murray Hill is, but** " sure enough" hills, as Uncle **Remus** would declare, and they reach their height of hundreds of feet by very steep inclines. The business part **of** the city lies at the feet of several of these eminences, on a partly natural, partly artificial plateau along the water's edge. There the stores and houses **are** largely of stone, iron, or brick, and are very **little** different from those **of** any **other such** district in **the East. But** the dwellings of **the city are so** generally of wood **that you may count upon the** fingers of your two hands all **that are of other materials.** Whether **the** great Palace Hotel set the fashion **by giving** every outer **room a** bay-window, or **why** it is, I don't **know,** but seven in ten **of** the residences are **adorned with these** projecting windows **wherever** they **can be put.** This was the fashion of the town until Van Ness Avenue ceased **to be the** finest street, and it grows tiresome **to** the eye; but the last two or three years have seen erected **a great many fine** dwellings, planned by architects of **taste for persons** who exercise individual judgment. And now, **as I write,** the danger from earth**quakes** seems **wholly** discounted, and I saw several fine **brick** houses **and** stones ones going up. It is evident in many such ways that San Francisco is putting her best foot forward; and a very showy, fine foot it will prove to be. But, as it stands, you can scarcely imagine the foreignness of the effect of looking down on the city from one of its hills. Over a very great district the entire hill-studded view is covered with brown-painted wooden houses, mainly very small and low, and built in rows to the tops of many of the hills. As each house is seen with photographic distinctness in that clear air, the whole is as like a great painting of some place in a foreign land as if you viewed it from within the enclosure of a cyclorama.

But now of the joys I speak of having experienced during my stay. They were too many for more than mere mention. In the first place, in thirty days I only saw half a dozen that were foggy; and as for the wind, when I found that San Francisco dresses, as we would say, "for winter" all the year round, I put on my heavy under-clothes, and the cool breezes at once became delightful. Then there were the joys of the cable-cars—a solution of the problem of surmounting hills that is so perfect that I believe no city in the world is better served with means of inter-transit. The cable-cars were invented and first put to use in San Francisco. They usually run as a train, composed of a little open "dummy," or grip-car, and a closed car, like one of our horse-cars. A man who loves fresh air and open-air riding fancies that no king rides more gloriously than a San Franciscan clerk may in a "dummy." He goes flying up the hills and coasting down them as if he were a tobogganer, having all the fun and none of the work. The cables run at seven miles an hour, which is faster than our "elevated," in my opinion, and nearly as fast as our Bridge cars.

Then there are the flowers. They need a chapter as

CLIFF HOUSE

long as this article. They grow with an **abundance** past **belief,** and attain a **size and glory** of color we wot not of. You **may** buy your armful of cut flowers for "two bits," which is to say a quarter. And if the flowers demanded a chapter, the fruits would require a book. Say what any one will, they are quite as **luscious** as ours; not here —because they **pick** them green for shipment, and **only** a Bartlett pear undergoes that **course** with **advantage**— but out there, fresh off the trees. And **they have fruits we** know not of—green **figs, for** instance. **Was there** ever a greater delicacy than **green figs sliced and served in cream?** Apricotes **are more common there** than with us; persimmons are cultivated, **but not** common. Strawberries, finer than any grown west of England, are to be had during half the year, and for half what we are charged when we think them cheap. Peaches, pears, and grapes **are very** plenty, and **I am** told that cherries are so at one season. Limes are plenty, and lemons scarce. Artichokes are a staple, and California **is the** land of **salads.** Those **made** of shrimps and alligator-pears are **two delicacies worth** going to San Francisco to enjoy.

But San Francisco is a gourmet'**s sixth heaven. It** has a wondrous market, with **fishes with** which we are unfamiliar, with no refrigerated factory meats, and with **an eclectic** school of cookery **to w**hich China, Japan, **Spain,** Mexico, and Hawaii **are** contributors. There is **no better** restaurant in America **than** the "Poodle Dog," and business men in New York **know** no better **luncheon** place **than "Ned's." The Palace** Hotel restaurant would rank **high here,** and **out there** they have four or **five** as good.

The trees are **a study** in themselves. The eucalyptus **from** Australia **is** useful in disciplining the sand hills, **but it is a beast of a tree, skimpy** and **ragged. The** pepper-tree is one of the prettiest lawn and street ornaments I ever saw, and the acacia and fig and bay tree and live-oak are all beautiful. The palms are always interesting to strangers to them. The scrub oak of Oakland and the suburbs generally is picturesque far beyond the wolf-willow and the alder that European painters never tire of celebrating. The redwoods are stately and noble fellows. As for the orchard trees, my rides through the fruit plantations near San Francisco were revelations. It was a never-to-be-forgotten experience to see miles of French chestnuts, English walnuts, prune plums, figs, pears, apples, almonds, apricots, and peaches growing as they grow there, often weighing the trees down until the branches had to be tied up and supported on poles.

My opinion of Oakland changed when I discovered that a watering-pot or a hose could turn what looked like Spain into what might have been our Mohawk Valley. And Oakland is crowded with pretty homes where the magic of the hose is understood, and where the lawns and flower plots are as fine as any under the sun. But I like Alameda better than Oakland, and Saucelito better yet. Saucelito is very Swiss, perched upon terraces, one above another, up a steep hill beside the Golden Gate. Every view from it is of the glorious harbor, blue as indigo, with great "square-riggers" riding on it, and gulls and porpoises enlivening the scene, while, better than all, the most comfortable great ferry-boats in America ply to and fro between Oakland and San Francisco, with their fortunate passengers drinking in the wondrous colors of the harbor, while good string bands feast their ears with melody.

CALIFORNIA STREET

XIII

WAYS OF CITY GOVERNMENT OUT WEST

One has a feeling that the young Lochinvar of perfected city government may yet come out of the West. That is where the loves of men for the cities they live in pass the understanding of us Easterners. That is where old traditions count for the least, and enterprise and progress mark most of the affairs of man. There are signs of the advent, though they are small and weak thus far. A study of the subject in Chicago, Minneapolis, and St. Paul is a revelation of a movement like that of a bandmaster's bâton along the sides of a triangle, from mayoral supremacy to diluted control by commissions, and from these to vicarious government by State Legislatures. But the more their cases are pondered, the more the wonder grows that those communities should be governed as well as they are. We shall see that they offer rich ground for the good seed that is to come; that the weeds there are fewer and less vicious than those that beset our own municipal fields.

In the unrest and striving of the Western people is found the hope that the mark will yet be reached by them. When we consider how very sharp the struggle has been to meet the business demands of a rapid national development; when we realize how nearly completely that struggle has monopolized every individual's attention; when we remember the poor and mortgaged beginnings of all the Western districts, and realize that where the debts have disappeared, the recollection of them is yet vivid—then the story of Western experiments in city government will find very lenient and charitable readers.

I see in Chicago two communities, we will say—one composed of twelve hundred thousand persons in the city at large, and one of four thousand men and women in the office building called "the Rookery." One body of persons has its wants attended to by officers they elect for the purpose; the other body relies on a syndicate of speculators to manage the building in which they pay rent, and in which they spend as many hours as they give to their life in their homes. Why should there be any difference in the temper and spirit in which these two communities are managed? Each set of governors has the same duties to perform. Each must provide protection, drainage, cleaning, lighting, and varying conveniences and forms of attendance. We say that there is a difference—that one is a city, and the other is a business. The very devil must have invented the difference, or put the notion of it in our heads, for it has no substance; it does not appear unless we put it there before we go to search for it. The syndicate of business men who manage the Rookery bend every effort to make money. And how? By providing every improvement and attraction which, when economically obtained, will leave a fair and legitimate margin of profit out of receipts that are governed by the charges for like service in other buildings. These receipts are what would be the taxes if the Rookery were a city; the profits would take the form of a surplus in the treasury—at least until they were wisely spent. The analogy never falters, however far we pursue it. The Rookery managers gladden the eye with onyx, marble, and bronze, as the city fathers treat their tenants with parks and lakes and fountains. **The Rookery** managers give to their tenants the **best** elevator service **ever** yet devised **in the** world, batteries of the swiftest cars, some of which **run as** express trains, while others stop at every floor. They control these, **and** see that they are the best, **as** the city fathers should control their street railways, **if** they should **not own them.** The street-cleaning **department of the Rookery** is composed **of** a corps of **orderly,** respectful, hard-working, faithful men, who keep **the** dozen corridors and storiesful of offices **as neat as the** domain **of** a Dutch **housewife. The air** is not **tainted;** the litter and **rubbish are whisked out of sight** with due **regard** for decency; the corridors are never torn **up with** pits and trenches at times when they are in use. Alterations in the building are made at night, when the work will annoy and inconvenience the fewest tenants. The Rookery water supply and that which corresponds to its sewage system are the best that can be provided; in some cities **out West** I found office buildings where the landlords had sunk artesian wells for pure water— because they believed **the water provided for the** people generally was unfit to drink **in one case; because it cost** too much in another. In both **instances the people of** those cities were scandalously **wronged, of** course. **To** return to **the** Rookery, **the building is** policed efficiently without the creation of a uniformed class of bullies. In short, it is a pleasure to visit such a building, where every official and servant constantly exhibits a desire to **do** his duty **and** to give satisfaction.

I instance the Rookery building merely for convenience. I might as **well** have spoken of any of the great office buildings of any **of the** great cities. They are all subject to the same rivalry towards providing the most modern **conveniences and the** most attractive and well-**managed interiors. I have yet to** hear of one in the management of which politics plays the slightest part. The owners do not throw away money to pay salaries to men who do not earn them; they do not make rules to please the German tenants, and then wink at the violation of them to tickle the Irish or any other persons; they do not permit their servants to steal a little of every sum of money that passes through their hands; they do not allow rubbish and filth to collect in the thoroughfares; they do not recruit their forces of servants with the ne'er-do-well or disreputable friends of men who send tenants to their buildings; they do not discharge all their trained help and drill in a new force biennially; in fact, they never discharge a good servant or keep an incompetent one. Since the management of a lot of daytime tenements is a business by itself, and has no connection with the Bering Sea question or the policy of trade relations with Australia, they do not feel obliged to buy Democratic brooms, or Republican coal, or Tammany soap, unless those happen to be the best and most economical wares. In one respect they enjoy an immense advantage over every city government in this country—they are permitted to manage their own businesses. No State Legislatures are continually changing their modes of conducting their affairs.

Chicago does not yet manage its district of homes as the landlords manage their districts of offices, but I do not believe that any good reason can be given why it should not try to do so, or be permitted to try to. Nor do I believe there is an intelligent man who honestly thinks the business plan cannot be adopted with as close an approach to business results as is possible where the selfish and personal incentive to success is lacking. And for that may be substituted the desire for honor and public approbation — powerful forces which have wrought wonders in **the governments of Glasgow, Birmingham, Sheffield, and** other Old World cities.

The city government of Chicago recalls that garment **of** which a humble poet has written,

> "His coat so large dat he couldn't **pay de tailor,**
> And it won't go half-way round."

It is a Josephian coat of many colors, made up of patches of county methods on top of city rule. And the patches are, some of them, far from neatly **joined.** Like the **immortal** Topsy, it has "just growed." It discloses **at once** the worst and the best examples of management, **the one** being so very bad as to seem like a caricature on **the** most vicious systems elsewhere, while the other extreme copies that which is the essence of the good work in the best-governed city in the world. Chicago therefore offers an extremely valuable opportunity for the study and comparison of municipal methods in general.

The worst feature, **that** which seems almost to caricature the worst **products** of partisan politics, is seen in the Mayor's **office.** The Mayor of Chicago has to hide behind a series of locked **doors, and it is** almost as difficult to see him as it **would be to visit** the Prefect **of** Police in Paris. When he leaves his **office he** slips out **of** a side door—the same by which he seeks **his** desk. The **charm** that the door possesses for his eyes **is that** it is at a distance from the public antechamber of his suite of offices. When he goes to luncheon he takes a closed cab, and is driven **to some** place a mile or more away, in order that he may eat in peace.* The reason for this extraordinary **and** undemocratic condition of affairs is that the Mayor of Chicago **is** the worst victim of the spoils system that has yet been created in America. **The** chase

---

* This was the state **of** affairs **in** 1891–92.

for patronage fetches up at his door, and all the avenues employed in it end at his person. He is almost the sole source and dispenser of public place of every grade.

The system was established a great many years ago, and they say in Chicago that it "worked well enough" under Carter Harrison, because after he got his municipal organization complete he was elected and re-elected several times, and had little difficulty in keeping the machinery of government in smooth running order. It was a city of only 400,000 population in those days, but the conditions were the same. The experience of a succeeding and very recent Mayor was needed to demonstrate the possibilities of an office so constituted. He spent the first year at his desk in handling patronage. He could do nothing else because he undertook to do that. He made it his rule that there should be no appointments that were not approved by him. The present Mayor is of the opposite mind. He has found that if he manages the patronage he cannot perform the other duties of his office. He has inaugurated a new departure, and seeks to make the heads of the subordinate departments responsible for their own appointments. This works only partially, because the place-hunters are not to be deceived. They know what his powers are as well as he does, and if they do not get what they want from his deputies, they fall back upon him. He orders them back again to the deputies, and so the game goes on. By setting apart one day in the week for the scramble, and by locking himself up like a watchman in a safe-deposit vault, he manages to serve as Mayor. But he finds the nuisance very great, and says so. When told that it seemed singular to find a Mayor behind bolts and locks, and accessible only to those who "get the combination," as the safe-makers would say, he replied that only by such a plan was he able to do any work. Mr. Washburne, the present Mayor, is a square-headed, strong-jawed, forcible-looking man, who gives his visitors the impression that he will leave as good a record as the system can be forced to afford.

Chicago is a Republican city, but is rapidly becoming Democratic. There are no "bosses" or "machines" there. Western soil does not seem suitable for those growths. The Democrats have been trying to effect an organization like that of Tammany Hall, but they are divided into two factions, and the plan has fallen between the two. The Republicans have recently recovered from a mild attempt at bossism. They are also divided, and only unite under favorable circumstances. The assessment evil is said not to be very great. Candidates or their friends contribute towards the cost of election contests, and public employés are assessed for the same purpose, but these outrageous taxes seem to be laid on lightly. It's your machine that always calls for excessive oiling, and it is noticeable that the chief engineers nearly always grow mysteriously rich.

In the city government there are four charter officers who are elected by the people—the Mayor, the City Treasurer, the City Attorney, and the City Clerk. Each is independent of the other, and the Mayor is not vested with power to remove the others. The City Attorney is in charge of the litigations into which the corporation is drawn; but the more important legal officer is the Corporation Counsel, who acts as adviser to the government, and is appointed by the Mayor. The manner in which this office came to be created is peculiar. It is said that a score or more years ago there was elected to the City Attorney's place a man who knew no law, and proved worse than no attorney at all. A competent adviser was needed, and so the new office was created, and has ever since remained a feature of the government.

We still find justices of the peace in Chicago, and in great force of numbers. They are county officers. They have jurisdiction everywhere, as they please to exercise it, and live upon their fees—a plan that works no better there than elsewhere, that causes rivalry and confusion where there should be only the dignity of law, and that creates courts which are inclined to rule against the defendants, and to extort money from all from whom it can be got. These justices are named by the judges of record of the county, and the list is sent to the Legislature for approval and appointment. From the lot the police magistrates are selected by the Mayor. There are ten police courts and twelve magistrates, and the reason there are two more judges than courts lets in a flood of light upon the situation. There are two very busy courts, and in order to share their business it became the custom for other judges than those appointed by the Mayor to hire apartments next door to these courts, and in them to hold courts of their own. These piratical justices inspired the lawyers and prisoners appearing before the regular courts to demand a change of venue and bring their causes next door, the incentive being a promise of more satisfactory treatment than the regular courts would be likely to vouchsafe — lighter fines, for instance, or other perversions of justice. It became, and it remains to-day, a custom for these motions for a change of venue to be offered in the most commonplace and perfunctory manner, the magistrates administering the oath, and the others solemnly swearing that they ask a change of venue because they are of the opinion that they cannot get justice in the court in question. To break this custom at its strongest points the Mayor has appointed additional magistrates for the principal police courts, and they hold court in rooms adjoining those of their associates, so that those who insist upon a change of venue are taken one door away to **obtain** the same quality of justice which they would have obtained in **the** first court. The justices, who may be called the Mayor's magistrates, are salaried. The busy ones get **$5000 a year, the others less.**

The saloon **license** system is another village development. The regular fee is $500, and there are only **5000** licenses, but any man of what is called "good character" may get a license on his own application, and the license is then issued *to the person*. He may sell his liquors anywhere that he pleases within the city limits. The law declares that the drinking-saloons shall be closed at midnight. It has proved extremely difficult to enforce this ordinance, but the present Mayor has been making a brave battle towards that end. He is of those who believe that all evils which seem either necessary or ineradicable should be regulated, and his idea was to enforce the law for closing the saloons, and to issue licenses to sell liquor in the restaurants which keep open all night, the drinks to be sold only with food. He found, what was no new discovery, that the reform was loudly opposed by the worst element in the business, who **said** that they could and did sell **liquor** in their restaurants, anyway, and that there was **no need** for licenses. **He also found** that the ultra-temperance folk took sides with these defiers of order by opposing the reform on the usual ground that licensing liquor-selling was recognizing and authorizing the evil. As late as the end of last **autumn** the Mayor was manfully holding to his determination to enforce the midnight closing law, and it was said by all with whom I spoke that it was extremely difficult to obtain even a glass of beer after twelve o'clock, and that no saloons displayed lights or open doors after hours.

He was able to enforce his orders and perform this function of his office for a reason that points a moral for every student of the subject to remember. He holds the power to dismiss those who disobey him. He promised to discharge any policeman upon whose post a drink was sold or a saloon was kept open after hours. He could discharge every policeman, from the Chief down, and they all knew it. It will be remembered that almost similar authority is vested in the police-magistrates in the most progressive English cities. The result is wholesome everywhere.

Some past work of the Chicago police has made the force famous. The World's Fair commissioners who went abroad to urge foreign participation in the exposition found their way paved before them by the good opinion of Chicago that had been aroused by her treatment of the anarchists. But the force has deteriorated. It looks as if it had run down at the heels and needed a soldier in command to discipline it and develop among its members an *esprit de corps*. The almost all-powerful Mayor recognizes this, and has appointed Major R. W. McClaughry to the chieftaincy on account of that gentleman's reputation for administrative ability and for disciplinary force. As warden of Joliet (Illinois) Penitentiary, and later of a reformatory at Huntingdon, Pennsylvania, he caused these qualities to attract attention. The Chicago police force had become a hospital for the political toughs of the city, and any man could join it provided only that he had "inflooence." He might be a man just out of State-prison, or only thirty days in America, but if he was the protégé of a politician he was made a policeman. There were regulations as to fitness, both mental, moral, and physical, but they were disregarded. The plan for rehabilitating the force is an adaptation of civil service methods. The men are cross-questioned like school-boys at a quarterly examination. Their moral character is looked into less sharply than their ability **to** comprehend the true nature **of a** policeman's duties and relation to the people. Politics **are** not shown the door. The wards and "heelers" of the politicians are the candidates as before, but after a man is admitted to be examined it is asserted that his political backing ceases to affect his fate. He must obtain a grade of seventy in a possible one hundred, and when twelve candidates have passed the examination, **if** only six are needed, the best six are taken.

But even before this reform began, the Western **habit** of experimenting with new ideas had **led to** the introduction of features of police service which we in **New** York could have copied with advantage, and must copy sooner or later. On that corner of Clark Street where the Grand Pacific Hotel stands, one day towards the middle of last October, I saw a policeman try to arrest a maniacal victim of delirium tremens. It was at six o'clock, and the streets were crowded. Had the case occurred in New York, our public would have witnessed **a brutal and sickening** "clubbing match," for in no other way than by stunning the man could one of our officers have handled him. If the **policeman would** have **preferred** help, he would have beaten the sidewalk with his club and waited, while the maniac fought like a tiger, until another policeman arrived. Ringing a club on a pavement is better than springing a rattle, as **our** police did a century ago—but that **is not** saying much in its favor. However, this was in Chicago.

There **they** have discovered the advantages of a perfected electrical system of communication between the police-stations and the patrolmen on duty. In this case the policeman stepped to one of those patrol boxes that are so numerous as to seem always at hand, and flashed a signal to the nearest station for help. In a jiffy a **wagon-load of** policemen dashed up to the spot, the men leaped out, the rum-crazed offender was bundled into the wagon, and it was driven back to the station. A neater, cleaner, more admirable bit of police work I never saw; but the frequent sight of these wagons flying through the streets assured me that such work, in such cases, is the rule with that force.

It is not the purpose here to describe other than what may be called the peculiarities of these city governments, and of the general plan of Chicago's management there is little more to say. After the Mayor has appointed his heads of departments (and all the 8000 or 9000 "feet," if he chooses), he divides his further powers with the Common Council, which has been but little shorn of its inherited functions. Its committees follow the more important divisions of the government, and one of them, the finance committee, acting like New York's Board of Estimate and Apportionment, determines the cost of each year's undertakings. The Council is a very large body, and contains two members from each of the thirty-four wards of the city, one being elected from each ward every year. They are paid on the *per diem* plan for actual service, and, like almost all the officers of the government, are moderately recompensed. The city has experimented with bureaus headed by commissions and with intrusting the patronage to the Common Council. It has now had for years what is popularly known as "one-man power." It is often said that this is whatever the one man proves himself, but the experience of the present time in Chicago is that if the Mayor was a saint, so long as the spoils system obtains, he would find it difficult to succeed in dispensing the patronage and attending to his duties—at least, during the first year of his two-year term.

But there are other municipal corporations in Chicago with which the Mayor has nothing to do. They are the park boards. It is a strange thing about Chicago **that** those monuments of her public spirit, enterprise, and taste which are at once her glory and her pride are out of the control of her city government. It is to the management of them that I have referred as exemplifying the very best method of the administration of local affairs. They do **not** do this in their origin **because** they are the creatures of either the courts or the State government, whereas to be as they should they must be the products of popular and home rule. But in the methods and work of the boards is seen that which produces the **best** government. There seem to be no "politics" about them. They appear to be doing business on business principles. They have produced one of the notable park systems of the world by methods so wise and economical that the people have witnessed the spectacle of a wondrous and beautiful park development without feeling the tax by which the cost has been met. The park commissioners serve without pay and in the belief that their duties **bring** honor with them. They are inspired to give the public their best service by the consciousness that when the plans for the pleasure-grounds have been executed, it will be worth as much as a monument to any man to have been concerned in the work.

Even in the City Hall and among the politicians students of the city government are referred to the parks as examples of the best public work that has been performed in **Chicago**. And in the City Hall I was told that the reason for this is that the Park Commissioners are unhampered by political obligations.

There are three of these corporations — the South Park, the Lincoln Park, and the West Park commissioners, and they not only are independent of the city government, but they have jurisdiction over all the parkways and boulevards, at least one of which reaches to the very heart of the business quarter in the thick of the town. They enact their own ordinances, and maintain police to enforce them. They build, repair, clean, and police the parks and boulevards in their charge; and have been, by the courts, declared to be quasi-municipal corporations in themselves. Each commission is maintained by a direct tax upon the district or division of the city which it benefits.

It will not be profitable to study all the commissions: one does not differ materially from another. The South Side Commission, headed by President William Best, consists of five members, who are appointed for five-year terms by the judges of the Circuit Court. When the majority of the judges are Democrats, they appoint Democrats; and Republican majorities appoint Republican commissioners; but beyond that point I am assured that politics cut no figure in the case. At present there are three Democrats and two Republicans on the board. One member is a real-estate dealer, one is vice-president of the stock-yards, one is a tobacco merchant, one is a coal-dealer, and one is an editor. All are well-to-do and middle-aged men. One has served fifteen years, another twelve years, and another, ten years. Mr. H. W. Harmon, the secretary, has held that place nineteen years; and Mr. Foster, the Superintendent, has filled that position seventeen years.

This commission performed its functions for three towns originally—South Chicago, Hyde Park, and Lake. They now comprise a part of the city. They are assessed for $300,000 annually, South Chicago paying 80 per cent., and the other towns 10 per cent. each. In addition, a tax of one mill is levied on the taxable valuation of the district, because the fixed sum of $300,000 proved insufficient. The additional tax is to be imposed as long as the commission has any bonds outstanding.

The weight of the total tax upon the community is 2⅜ mills, and is presumably an unfelt burden. For this the commission maintains Michigan Avenue, the boulevard that leads into the heart of the city; Drexel Boulevard, modelled after one of the noblest avenues in Paris; the Grand Boulevard, a splendid thoroughfare; Washington Park, which is one of the most grand and beautiful breathing-spots in the city; Jackson Park, where the Columbian Exposition is to be held; and many other boulevards and park extensions. Lakes, notable floral collections, boats, restaurants, picnic and play grounds, park phaetons, a zoological collection, sprinkling-carts, police, laborers, a nursery for trees, and a score of other sources of expense or attractions are thus provided for. The commission employs a force that is mainly composed of Swedes and Germans. The same men are retained year after year. They are skilled in their several lines of work; they own their little homes, and feel secure in their places; they are not told how to vote, nor are they watched at the polls. The work of the commission embraces several sources of income, but no effort is made to force profits out of the conveniences and playthings provided for the people.

Lincoln Park is the one that all visitors to Chicago are certain to be advised to see. It is only 250 acres in extent, but it lies along the curving shore of Lake Michigan, a fringe of sward and shade beside a sheet of turquoise. We in New York waited until we were 200 years old before we built such parks. Chicago waited only forty years. Already statues, fountains, and a conservatory are ornaments piled on ornament in Lincoln Park. A lake a mile long is being added for aquatic sports, and the noble Lake Shore Drive, which is a part of the park, is to be faced with a paved beach and a seawall, and is to connect with the drive to Fort Sheridan, distant twenty-five miles northward on the lake front. There are five commissioners in charge of this park and the boulevarded streets that approach it. They are appointed by the Governor of Illinois, with the approval of the Senate, and serve five years. Three are Democrats and two are Republicans, but their employés are chosen for fitness as workmen, and the trust is managed practically and economically.

William C. Goudy, the president, was counsel to the commission for fifteen years before he was chosen president. General Joseph Stockton has been a commissioner twenty-two years, and E. S. Taylor has been the secretary since the organization of the board in 1869. The commission bought its land for only $900,000, and in five years will have extinguished that debt. Now it is borrowing half a million to meet the cost of reclaiming from the lake land that will be worth millions as soon as it is made. The tax rate last year was eight mills on the low assessed valuation that prevails in Chicago. During the twenty-two years of existence of the commission there never has been the slightest taint or suspicion of jobbery or impropriety of any sort in its relation to its work, its employés, or the people.

It is true that these park boards are the products of the organization of Cook County, which extends around and beyond Chicago. The absurd justices of the peace are the old village squires of the county system also. Though there are only about 100,000 persons in the county outside the city, the Cook County Board of Commissioners exercises an authority that is perfectly independent of the City Council. The parks are therefore managed by the State, and not the city, and this is cause for offence to all who hold that perfected city government must be complete self-government. The argument is too solid to be broken down by any exception, **and** yet these commissions are singular in presenting the spectacle of State organizations freed from politics in a city where the local organization is poisoned to the core with partisan allegiance and spoils-grabbing. But beyond that is the renewed proof that local government succeeds **best** when administered by non-politicians working in no interest but that of the public.

That is what the Chicago park managers newly demonstrate. Call them county officers, as they are, yet they are of and for Chicago. They are Chicago business men, and they have been induced to give **up what** time they can spare from private business because they feel it a distinction and an honor to be intrusted with the execution of what every man in Chicago thinks is to become the greatest and most beautiful park system in the world. They are anxious to prove that no mistake was made in choosing them as men of business ability. The instant politicians are chosen they begin to pay off their debts to the party with which they have bargained for **a living**. They pay their debts with the valuables that belong to the people. Their constant thoughts and best efforts are put forth to strengthen their party and to please **its managers. The non-politician** in office has no one to please but the public.

In Minneapolis, a city of 164,000 population, the striking feature of the city government is the system of licensing saloons. Of the government in general there is little more to be said than that it appears to be reasonably satisfactory to the people, and business-like in its general plan and results. There are no bosses, "halls," or other organizations among the politicians. Here the Mayor becomes a figure-head, and the Chicago plan is diametrically reversed. A recent Mayor made this public comment on the case: "The Mayor has but little authority; he has hardly more than an advisory power in any department." The government is by the Common Council, and the most important official is the City Engineer. His salary is $4500; the Mayor's is $2000. The Mayor appoints his Chief of Police, and may appoint the policemen. He also appoints his own secretary. The other officials, high and low, are the appointees of the Council. This consists of two Aldermen from each of thirteen wards, who also order all public improvements and repairs and grant all licenses. Politically the present Council consists of sixteen Republicans and ten Democrats, and the membership is principally American, something like twenty of the twenty-six having been born in this country. That important bureau the Board of Tax Levy consists of the City Auditor, the Comptroller, the chairman of the Board of County Commissioners, the president of the Board of Education, and the chairman of the committee of ways and means of the City Council. It fixes the maximum limit of city expenditures; and the Council, in consultation with the various local boards, may determine upon any sum of outlay within but not above the levy. The assessed valuation on which the levy is based is thought to be a liberal one (50 to 66⅔ per cent. of the actual value), and the tax is 21.4 mills, but nine wards pay an added tax of two mills for street extension and improvements, or 23.4 mills in all.

But the noticeable and most admirable single feature of the government is the licensing plan. Dram-selling is kept away from the residence portions of the town, and is confined to the business and manufacturing districts. As we have seen in a previous paper on the cities of the Northwest, Minneapolis is distinctively and peculiarly a city of homes. It spreads itself, with elbow-room for nearly every dwelling, over fifty-three square miles of territory. The entire city area is very park-like in its appearance and surroundings, and up and down its beautiful residence avenues and along its scores of semi-rural streets the home atmosphere and influence are unbroken by the presence of saloons. They are relegated and confined to a comparatively small fraction of the space covered by the town. This is called "the patrol district," and the plan is named, after it, "the patrol limit system." It is not easy to understand why it is so called, since the whole city is patrolled, but a study of the map shows that the territory in which the licenses are granted is mainly in two narrow belts along the river, in the more thickly built, older parts of the two towns that have since become one city. As it is a city of superb area, most of the dwellings are at a distance from the outer edges of the saloon districts. The electric-car lines are numerous, and the cars are swift, but those who feel that peculiar thirst which can only be quenched while the sufferer leans against a bar must make a long journey and pay ten cents car fare to obtain relief.

Minnesota is a high-license State, and the fee for a permit to maintain a saloon or hotel bar in cities of more than 100,000 population is $1000. To obtain a permit in Minneapolis the applicant must be twenty-one years of age, and must not have had a previous license revoked, or been convicted of an offence against the liquor laws or ordinances within a year of the date of his application. The applicant must manage his place himself and for himself. He may not have more than one license. He may not sell liquor in or next door to any theatre, or within 400 feet of a public school, or within 200 feet of a park or parkway. All this he must swear to, and agree that if he has sworn falsely in any particular in his affidavit his license may be revoked. He must, together with his application and affidavit, also file a bond in $4000, with two sureties, who shall not be on any other similar bond.

The license is for a fixed place as well as for a person, and carries further conditions against Sunday selling, gambling, and disorderly conduct on the premises, as well as against selling to minors or to public-school pupils or drunkards. The applicant goes before the City Clerk, pays a fee of one dollar, and registers his application and bond. If it appears that his case comes within the requirements, and his proposed saloon is to be within the patrol district, the application is published once a week for two weeks in the official newspaper of the city. If any citizen then protests against the granting of the license, a hearing is had before the City Council. If the license is granted, it is not assignable to any other person, though the executor or administrator of a deceased licensee may carry on the business under the license. It is not transferable to any other place, though the alteration of the neighborhood around the saloon may make it necessary for the city to grant a permit for removal. In case a license is revoked by the Mayor or City Council "for reasons authorized or required by the laws of the State," then the liquor-seller shall have refunded to him "a sum proportional to one-half the sum paid for such license for the unexpired term thereof." But if the courts order the license revoked, the dealer loses all that he has paid. The courts may order a license revoked on the first conviction for a breach of the law. On a second conviction they must revoke it.

Last year 274 persons took out licenses, and there is a liquor-seller to every 675 inhabitants, as against one to every 177 persons in New York city. But the fee of $1000 makes the liquor-dealers pay into the Minneapolis treasury $274,000, or about $52,000 more than the cost of the police force of the city. This Minneapolis plan speaks for itself. It does not easily lend itself to a city like New York, where the population is squeezed into a narrow space, and there is no broad division of the city into a residence and a business part. But it will be seen that it could be applied to most of the cities of the country, especially when it is noted that even in Minneapolis there are irregularities in the patrol district to meet each eccentricity of the city's growth. The more worldly-wise the reader is, the more likely he will be to ask at once whether the law is enforced, and whether the druggists (who are everywhere the "silent partners" in the liquor trade) are not, as usual, violating it wherever the people have sought to make it prohibitory. The answers to these questions are that the appearances and general testimony go to show that the law is absolutely enforced as to the liquor saloons, but that there is some illicit drinking in many of the apothecary shops. These are popularly known as "blind pigs" in Minneapolis, a term that is not so happily chosen as that adopted by the good citizens of Asbury Park, New Jersey, who call such illicit groggeries their "speak-easies." It is said that it would be impossible for a stranger in Minneapolis to get a drink in a drug store. Even if the authorities do not wage war on such druggists as violate the law, one would think that where such a high fee as $1000 is paid for the right to sell liquor, the licensed traders would take measures against drug-store abuses. The fact that the saloon-keepers are not complaining in Minneapolis seems proof to me that the abuse is not considerable or general.

In an earlier chapter I dwelt on the beauty and original character of the Minneapolis parks, and only need to say further that the city finds within its limits a number of pretty little lakes, incidents in that natural arrangement which renders all the surroundings of

Lake Superior a great sponge-like territory, and which gives to Minnesota alone no less than 7000 lakes. Each little body of water in Minneapolis is made the central feature of a park or the ornament of a parkway. But while there are half a dozen such bodies of water, there are thirty-four parks under the control of the Park Board, and those which are joined by the eighteen miles of boulevards that have been laid out now form a beautiful cordon around two sides of the town. The city's parks comprise 1469 acres, and are valued at $3,918,000, yet so wisely was the land purchased that it cost the city only $80,000 to acquire it. That certainly appears to have been a bit of honest, business-like governmental work.

It was in St. Paul that a leading official confided to me his observation that "the better a municipal commission is, the worse for the tax-payers." He argued that in howsoever great a degree the head of a department evinces a desire to distinguish himself by his work, in just that degree he will increase the cost of his department. That is true; but whether that will prove the worse for the tax-payers depends entirely upon whether the money spent is wisely put out. A very thoughtful friend of mine is in the habit of saying that "the greater the tax is, the less will be the burden." He finds property values and the general comfort so increased by wise public expenditures that the people in progressive communities feel the benefits more than they feel the taxes. It is in the out-of-the-way and backward rural districts, where very inferior roads and schools are the only visible returns, that the people complain aloud against having to pay taxes whose sum totals seem to others ridiculously small. What might seem a great deal of money has been spent in Minneapolis in developing the tracts that have been set aside for parks (something like a million and a half of dollars since 1883). The method of raising the money for new work is to issue bonds for ten years, payable one-tenth annually by assessment on adjacent property. Yet a tax-payer there, in speaking of park improvements that had been made near various plots of his real estate, declared that the increase in values had been so great in each case that he never felt like complaining of the heightened taxes he had been called upon to pay.

The Minneapolis Park Board consists of twelve members, who are elected by the people, and of three *ex officio* members—the Mayor, the chairman of the Council Committee on Roads and Bridges, and the chairman of the Council Committee on Public Grounds and Buildings. It is politically partisan, and much of the lesser patronage changes with changes of political complexion. The board gets authority from the Legislature to issue bonds when it wishes to purchase land, but all such issues are subject to a charter limitation of the bonded indebtedness of the city to 5 per cent. of the assessed valuation of the taxable property. The regular assessment is less than one mill. Under the circumstances the good work of the board must be credited to the enthusiastic and watchful interest the people have taken in the work. In Mr. Charles M. Loring, a wealthy miller and extra public-spirited citizen, they found a practical business man to direct their enterprises. He was able and willing to travel abroad for the purpose of studying the notable park systems elsewhere. It is only fair to say that other excellent men were found to work with him.

In making the short journey to St. Paul we pass to still another experiment in city government. There they enjoy the same very excellent system of liquor-licensing. In confining the saloons to the business and manufacturing precincts, whole wards where the dwellings are found are under the taboo. They issue about 390 licenses a year in St. Paul, at $1000 each, and keep a license-inspector at $1500 a year and the cost of a horse and buggy, to protect the licensees and the city. The officials boasted to me that there is not one unlicensed saloon in St. Paul. As was the case in Minneapolis, they said that strangers could not procure liquor to be drunk on the premises in those drug stores which violate the law. But while, in the main, the same excellent method of liquor-licensing obtains in both towns, I was permitted to gather the notion that in St. Paul there is a looseness about minor details of the superintendence which does not exist in Minneapolis. For instance, it is found impossible to close the saloons at eleven o'clock at night or on Sundays, as the law commands. They keep open until midnight, or even later, and on Sunday follow the New York device of closing the front doors and opening those side or rear doors which for some hidden reason are in New York called "family entrances."

When I was first told that the law could not be enforced, it occurred to me that perhaps the impossibility was like that which defeated the better impulses of a little child of my acquaintance when he ate an apple which he was carrying to his sister. He explained that he "truly could not help eating it; it really would be eaten, and he could not stop it." But I found afterwards that the law was an enactment of the State Legislature and not of the local authorities, and that the city is different from Minneapolis in that it possesses a very much more mixed population of transplanted Europeans. The failure to enforce the law therefore emphasized two well-established points: first, that cities should govern themselves; and second, that laws which reflect the prejudices or peculiar **tenets of a class or** race are extremely difficult **to enforce** in a mixed community. Yet it is always a pity when they **are** loosely administered and disobeyed. Such a condition is a grave misfortune, for nothing but harm can come of permitting any community to witness the contemptuous treatment of any **law.** Would that all officials charged with carrying **out the statutes** were of General Grant's mind, **to** insist upon the enforcement **of** mistaken **as** well as **wise** laws, that the first sort might **the sooner** be repealed! The city of St. Paul **is** said to **contain** fully 65 persons **of** foreign birth in every 100 of **its population. It has one** saloon to every 370 inhabitants.

I found St. Paul undergoing a governmental revolution, owing to a gift of a new charter from the Legislature. Again the Mayor here rose to importance, and divided honors and work with the Common Council—he making half the appointments, and they administering the **more** important trusts. **But** it is a dual Council—**a double-barrelled** board of supervisors—called Aldermen and Assemblymen. Each ward elects one Alderman, and there are eleven in all, while the **nine** Assemblymen are elected at large from all **over the city.** Both **serve** two years and receive $100 **a** year, presumably for car fares. They meet on alternate Tuesdays. The ma**jority of the** members of the two houses are Irish **or Irish** Americans. The city is Democratic. The Mayor appoints the Chief of Police and the policemen under him, and has the power to remove as well as to appoint. He does so with the advice and consent of the Council; but it is said that no conflicts have arisen in the matter of removals, either under this or the former charter. The Mayor's salary has been raised from $1000 to $2500. **The** judges of the municipal court are elected; they receive $4000 **a year, and** have civil jurisdiction where the sum at issue is under $500. A feature that would seem to be the outcome of sage reflection is the Conference Committee. It is composed of the Mayor, president of the Assembly, chairman of the Ways and Means Committee of the Aldermen, the Comptroller, Treasurer, Engineer, and the heads of nearly all the bureaus of the city government. They come together once a month to confer upon the work each has in hand.

I asked a high official of the city government, who is a "practical" Democratic politician, why the new charter had established a return to the old plan of a double legislative body. He said that it was a Republican effort to put a check to Democratic expenditure. When I asked if it would have that effect, he dropped in my ear this astonishing reflection, which I will set down without any further comment than that it appears to possess the quality of frankness in a marked degree.

"Among politicians," said he, "*all legislation is trading.* You know that as well as I do. We all use our opportunities and influence to help those who have been of service to us. That is the main consideration in politics. Every Alderman who is elected is indebted to certain influential men in his ward, and he expects to legislate to pay his debts. It cannot be so easy to do this if the legislation must afterward pass a body of men elected at large, and not indebted to the same persons for their election."

If the goverment of St. Paul has been slow in providing parks, it remains to be said that the lack has been little felt amid environs that offer many of the best advantages of cultivated pleasure-grounds. And the city government has been so far from idle as to have produced by prodigious energy within the past few years public works which have raised its conditions from those of a village to those which entitle it to rank with the most progressive cities of its size in the country. Its streets, sewers, railroad crossings, fire-defence, public buildings, water-supply plant, and half a dozen other important features of the public service have taken on a first-class character, and in some of these developments no city of the first grade surpasses it. A quicker, longer leap from hap-hazard to perfected conditions is not recorded anywhere in the **West**.

The machinery of government by which this was effected has been changed, but we know that there was nothing novel about it, and that the change has brought nothing novel to it. The credit lies with the public-spirited, enterprising people behind the government, and it is a pity that they cannot be left alone to work out their own administrative methods with the same forehandedness they exhibit despite the interference of the State Legislature.

And now, to end this glance at the more stiking features of the management of the public business in this group of cities, I come to a subject which has been taken up with hesitation because I know that it is fashionable and popular to hold but one opinion with regard to it— that is, the public-school management. It seems to me that nothing in the West—not even the strides she is making in population, wealth, and power—is so remarkable as the footing upon which the common schools are maintained.

The last Mayor of Chicago uses these words in his second annual message: "It is gratifying that the public-school system of our city receives that generous support and attention to which its magnitude and importance entitle it. In 1887 the amount appropriated and otherwise available for educational purposes was nearly $2,250,000; in 1888, nearly $2,500,000; in 1889, about the same amount; in 1890, nearly $4,750,000; and the present year, over $5,500,000. Thus it will be seen that over $17,250,000 have been appropriated during the past five years for the construction and maintenance of our schools. About 86 per cent. of this amount is from taxation; the balance, the revenue from school property. ... The total enrolment of pupils for the school year reaches nearly 139,000. ... Night schools cost the city nearly $77,000 during the year; the compulsory feature, about $15,000; deaf-and-dumb tuition, $5000; manual training, $10,000; music, nearly $13,000; drawing, over $17,500; physical culture, about $15,500; foreign languages, over $115,000. It is estimated that the average pupil leaves the public schools about the age of twelve to fourteen years."

The Comptroller of the City of Minneapolis in his last report places the disbursements for schools at $923,619. The secretary of the Board of Education of that city reports the supervision of the studies of 20,000 children. All allusions to the city's school work in the official reports are enthusiastic, and it appears that a high rank has been accorded the Minneapolis schools by those engaged in public educational work throughout the country. The Mayor, in his reference to the schools in a recent message, notes the fact that the manual-training branch of the teaching operates to retain an increased number of pupils in the high schools. This discovery of a means for lessening the disproportion usually noticeable between the number of high-school pupils and the numbers in the lower schools will doubtless be hailed with joy by those who find the system generally and greatly underbalanced all over the country.

The 17,227 pupils in the schools of St. Paul enjoyed the benefits of an expenditure of $1,205,000 last year. (The total cost is as above in the Comptroller's report: the Treasurer places the disbursement at $1,310,000.)

The Superintendent of Schools reports that the city maintains a carefully graded course of tuition, covering *a period of eight years!* It includes tuition in civil government, physics, hygiene, manual training, Greek, Latin, French, German, political economy, common law, zoology, astronomy, chemistry, and English literature.

Here I note the first attempt to curb these expenses. The St. Paul School Board possessed almost complete legislative powers to raise and to spend what money it pleased. The Council was obliged to grant its demands; in addition the Board issued bonds and certificates of indebtedness. "It was like sacrilege to complain," an official told me. Now the new charter subordinates the school inspectors. Their pay-rolls and bills must be approved by the Council, which may reduce salaries. Moreover, another board of city officials buys all the supplies for the schools.

But in no city in the West is there a sign that public education will not remain the most costly branch of government. There are two ways to look at such a condition, but, in my opinion, the two ways are not what they are commonly supposed to be. One way should be to look with envy on the rich, who thus may send their children to school for eight years, while the poor, who must put their little ones to work at tender ages, foot the greater part of the cost. The other way might well be to commiserate the poor who are deceived by sentimental clap-trap into inflating the common-school system in such a manner that at last their share in its benefits becomes microscopic.

Two things that are novel to a visitor attract attention in all the far Western towns and cities. Neither is a branch of government, yet both affect it. The first is the stand-point from which vice is regarded as a factor in public affairs, especially in the smaller cities. It is a trick of the popular mind where I have been (between Chicago and the Pacific coast) to gauge the vitality and prosperity of a town by the showing it makes in what may be called its "night side." It is part of the quality of hospitality, and is born of the desire to entertain all comers as they would wish to be entertained. These cities are far apart, and are the centres of great regions. It is understood that those who visit them come to spend money not only upon necessaries and luxuries, but at drinking and gaming, in concert-halls, dance-houses, and the like. If a large and lively section of a town ministers to these appetites, visitors are taken to see it. If such a quarter languishes, good citizens apologize, and seek to show that the city is not backward in other respects. In discussing this subject, a very pushing Western man of national and honorable reputation said: "There is wisdom and experience behind all that. If I am asked to buy lots or to locate in a city, I would visit the place, and if I didn't see a good lively 'after-dark quarter,' and didn't hear chips rattling and corks popping, there would be no need to tell me about the geographical position of the town or its jobbing trade or banking capital; I would have none of it."

The other novelty in Western town life is the inevitable combination of leading citizens pledged to promote the best interests of their town. Such a body is variously called a Board of Trade, a Chamber of Commerce, or a Commercial Club. It is the burning-glass which focusses the public spirit of the community. Its most competent officer is usually the highly salaried secretary. He does for his town what a railroad passenger agent or a commercial traveller does for his employers, that is to say, he secures business. He invites manufacturers to set up workshops in his city, offering a gift of land, or of land and money, or of exemption from taxation for a term of years. **The merchants, and** perhaps the city officials also, support his promises. In a South Dakota city I have known a fine brick warehouse to be built and given, with the land under it, to a wholesale grocery **firm** for doing business there. In a far Northwestern city there was talk during **the** winter of 1891–92 of sending **a** man East on salary to stay away until he could bring back capital **to** found **a** smelter. **These** boards of trade often organize local companies to **give a** city what **it** needs. They urge the people to subscribe **for stock in** associations that are **to** build electric rail**ways, opera-houses,** hotels, convention halls, water supply, and illuminating companies, often dividing **an** acknowledged financial loss for the sake of a public gain. Thus these boards provide the machinery by which the most ambitious, forward, and enterprising communities in the world expend and utilize their energy.

The student **of the** many experiments in municipal management **in the West** will find Denver's progress interesting. **That city** recently **experienced a** revolution in government. **A ring** had **fastened upon** the offices. The elections **were dishonest. The police** aided in keeping the **ring in** power. **In** the mean **time the city was growing like a** weed, and **was about to make large ex**penditures in needed improvements. In 1889 **a** movement led by **the** Chamber of Commerce resulted in the drafting of charter amendments to create new boards to be appointed **by** the Governor. **The** new rule was instituted, but, for various reasons, the change was not **felt** until after 1891. Then came a political revolution, overturning the ring, and putting the Democrats in charge. It was a non-partisan uprising.

The succeeding Board of Public Works consisted of **three resident** land-owners and tax-payers, appointed by **the Governor, to hold office two years.** Two were Republicans, and all were Denver business men. They had authority to expend three millions of dollars for specified public works, which, in what seems a magically short time, have advanced Denver to a high place among our Western cities. The paving of the principal streets alone transformed the city. All the work was well, promptly, and honestly done. As in Omaha, the Fire and Police departments were put under one board, with absolute control of all the moneys set apart for it by the Common Council, as well as the appointing power over both departments. The Police and Fire Board consists of three resident land-owners and tax-payers appointed by the Governor with the consent of the Senate. One must be of a different political faith from the Governor, who may revoke any appointment for cause. The appointees, who serve two years and go out together, were a real-estate agent, who has been postmaster, the proprietor of an extensive "transfer" system, and a veteran Coloradoan, who was "the father of the bill."

If these were not the best possible appointments, they yet served the people in rescuing the city from the element that had misgoverned it. The fire and police forces have been recruited from both political parties. It was easily possible to reform the Fire Department, which is winning its way to the pride and affection of the citizens. The Chief recommends only those who show fitness for the work, and the board follows his desires. The police force has been fully reformed by the heads of its divisions. It is not yet properly disciplined or instructed, but the worst of the old offenders are out of it.

The "night side" of Denver had been very lively, loud, and far-Western in its character. Even now (1893) there are gambling "hells" that are as busy, crowded, and public as mercantile exchanges, and the quarter inhabited by abandoned women is notorious in the West. Before the local revolution the saloons never closed, and the "games" were open all the time except on Sundays. Most of the shooting affrays and murders which disgraced the city took place after midnight. Now, drinking and gaming cease at midnight, under a new law, which is exceptionally well enforced. Mondays had been "field-days" for the trials of arrested drunkards, but the number decreased remarkably. A similar decrease of the cases of destitution was noticed. About 400 saloons pay $240,000 into the city treasury each year. The city appoints policemen to keep order in the gambling "hells" at the expense of the proprietors. As one official expressed it, "The government has been considering the advisability of raiding the disorderly houses twice a year to obtain the equivalent of a license fee from each one. The reason it has not been done is that the inmates are too poor."

A neglected law set apart the police-court fines to benefit the public library. Now a fixed sum of $500 a month is given to the library. The city gives $12,000 a year to an organization of philanthropic citizens, who raise far more other money, and aim to abolish street mendicancy and to aid the needy. The county commissioners should attend to this, but do not. Former Health Boards had been criminally careless. The new commissioner and his assistants are Republicans. The Chief Inspector, a Democrat, has chosen aides regardless of politics. Mayor Platt Rogers determined to have this board do more than collect vital statistics. On his motion the leading physicians formed a voluntary advisory board, and induced a retired practitioner, Dr. Steele, to be Health Commissioner, with two young expert medical assistants, between whom his salary is divided that they may give their whole time to the public. An earnest Chief Inspector has closed 800 wells, cleaned up the alleys, enforced house to house inspection, investigated the sources of contagious diseases, and instituted the inspection of meat, fruit, and milk. Thus the death rate was brought down from about 25 to 13.30 in October last. During the ten months ending with September 30, 1890, there were 131 deaths from typhoid fever, but for the ten months preceding September 30, 1892, the number was reduced to 39.

Mayor Rogers insists that in national politics he is an "offensive partisan" (Democrat), but he considers municipal affairs "pure matters of business into which the introduction of politics can serve but to impair the efficiency of the government." He has been violently opposed, despite his high standing as a citizen, and the work of the new boards also aroused the opposition of the Common Council, which struggled to retain its powers. Indeed, Denver still feels the shock that accompanied its elevation to a place among the well-governed cities of our land. When the character of the dominant element there is considered, it seems unlikely that those who abused their power will ever force the city back into their control. Denver's progress was not in the line of home-rule. Popular education in self-government has been only slightly furthered. The responsibility was shouldered on the Governor instead. Yet the people dictated the change, and in so far as it is an improvement they are to be congratulated.

THE END

INTERESTING WORKS

OF

TRAVEL AND DESCRIPTION.

On Canada's Frontier.
Sketches of History, Sport, and Adventure; and of the Indians, Missionaries, Fur-traders, and Newer Settlers of Western Canada. By JULIAN RALPH. Illustrated. 8vo, Cloth, Ornamental, $2 50.

Harper's Chicago and the World's Fair.
The Chapters on the Exposition being Collated from Official Sources and Approved by the Department of Publicity and Promotion of the World's Columbian Exposition. By JULIAN RALPH, Author of "On Canada's Frontier," etc. With Seventy-three Full-page Illustrations. 8vo, Cloth, Ornamental, $3 00.

The Danube,
From the Black Forest to the Black Sea. By F. D. MILLET. Illustrated by the Author and ALFRED PARSONS. Crown 8vo, Cloth, Ornamental, Uncut Edges and Gilt Top, $2 50.

London.
By WALTER BESANT, Author of "Fifty Years Ago," etc. Illustrated. 8vo, Cloth, Ornamental, Uncut Edges and Gilt Top, $3 00.

The West from a Car-Window.
By RICHARD HARDING DAVIS, Author of "Van Bibber and Others," etc. Illustrated. Post 8vo, Cloth, Ornamental, $1 25.

The Praise of Paris.
By THEODORE CHILD, Author of "Art and Criticism," etc. Profusely Illustrated. 8vo, Cloth, Ornamental, Uncut Edges and Gilt Top, $2 50.

A Tour Around New York,
And My Summer Acre: Being the Recreations of Mr. Felix Oldboy. By JOHN FLAVEL MINES, LL.D. Illustrated. 8vo, Cloth, Uncut Edges and Gilt Top, $3 00.

Along New England Roads.
By WILLIAM C. PRIME, LL.D., Author of "I Go a-Fishing," etc. 16mo, Cloth, Ornamental, Uncut Edges and Gilt Top, $1 00.

Morocco As It Is,
With an Account of Sir Charles Euan Smith's Recent Mission to Fez. By STEPHEN BONSAL, Jr., Special Correspondent of the London *Central News*. Illustrated. Post 8vo, Cloth, Ornamental, $2 00.

A House-Hunter in Europe.
By WILLIAM HENRY BISHOP, Author of "Old Mexico and Her Lost Provinces," etc. With Plans and Illustration. Post 8vo, Cloth, Ornamental, $1 50.

The Blue-Grass Region.
The Blue-Grass Region of Kentucky, and Other Kentucky Articles. By JAMES LANE ALLEN. Illustrated. 8vo, Cloth, Ornamental, $2 50.

Pharaohs, Fellahs, and Explorers.
By AMELIA B. EDWARDS. Profusely Illustrated. 8vo, Cloth, $4 00.

Hearn's West Indies.
Two Years in the French West Indies. By LAFCADIO HEARN. Illustrated. Post 8vo, Cloth, Ornamental, $2 00.

Jinrikisha Days in Japan.
   By Eliza Ruhamah Scidmore. Illustrated. Post 8vo, Cloth, Ornamental, $2 00.

Spanish-American Republics.
   By Theodore Child. Profusely Illustrated. Square 8vo, Cloth, $3 50.

The Tsar and His People;
   Or, Social Life in Russia. By Theodore Child, and Others. Profusely Illustrated. Square 8vo, Cloth, Uncut Edges and Gilt Top, $3 00.

Summer Holidays.
   Travelling Notes in Europe. By Theodore Child. Post 8vo, Cloth, $1 25.

Our Italy.
   An Exposition of the Climate and Resources of Southern California. By Charles Dudley Warner. Illustrated. 8vo, Cloth, Ornamental, $2 50.

Warner's South and West.
   Studies in the South and West, with Comments on Canada. By Charles Dudley Warner. Post 8vo, Half Leather, $1 75.

The Capitals of Spanish America.
   By William Eleroy Curtis. With a Colored Map and 358 Illustrations. 8vo, Cloth, Extra, $3 50.

Winters in Algeria.
   Written and Illustrated by Frederick Arthur Bridgman. Square 8vo, Cloth, Ornamental, $2 50.

Our Journey to the Hebrides.
   By Joseph Pennell and Elizabeth Robins Pennell. Illustrated. Post 8vo, Cloth, Ornamental, $1 75.

A Flying Trip Around the World.
By ELIZABETH BISLAND. With Portrait. 16mo, Cloth, Ornamental, $1 25.

Boots and Saddles;
Or, Life in Dakota with General Custer. By ELIZABETH B. CUSTER. With Portrait. Post 8vo, Cloth. Ornamental, $1 50.

Following the Guidon.
By ELIZABETH B. CUSTER. Illustrated. Post 8vo, Cloth, Ornamental, $1 50.

Mrs. Wallace's Travel Sketches.
The Storied Sea. By SUSAN E. WALLACE. 18mo, Cloth, $1 00.

Campaigning with Crook,
And Stories of Army Life. By Captain CHARLES KING, U.S.A. Illustrated. Post 8vo, Cloth, $1 25.

A Tramp Trip.
How to See Europe on Fifty Cents a Day. By LEE MERIWETHER. With Portrait. 12mo, Cloth, Ornamental, $1 25.

Nordhoff's California.
Peninsular California. Some Account of the Climate, Soil, Productions, and Present Condition chiefly of the Northern Half of Lower California. By CHARLES NORDHOFF. Maps and Illustrations. Square 8vo. Cloth, $1 00; Paper, 75 cents.

Published by HARPER & BROTHERS, New York.

☞ HARPER & BROTHERS *will send any of the above works by mail, postage prepaid, to any part of the United States, Canada, or Mexico, on receipt of the price.*

www.ingramcontent.com/pod-product-compliance
Lightning Source LLC
Chambersburg PA
CBHW021418300426
44114CB00010B/550